The Harbrace Anthology of Poetry

FIFTH EDITION

The Harbrace Anthology of Poetry

FIFTH EDITION

EDITORS

Jon C. Stott, Emeritus
University of Alberta

Raymond E. Jones, Emeritus
University of Alberta

NELSON / EDUCATION

NELSON / EDUCATION

The Harbrace Anthology of Poetry, Fifth Edition
by Jon C. Stott and Raymond E. Jones

Vice President, Editorial Director:
Evelyn Veitch

Editor-in-Chief, Higher Education:
Anne Williams

Executive Editor:
Laura Macleod

Senior Marketing Manager:
Amanda Henry

Developmental Editor:
Jacquelyn Busby

Permissions Coordinator:
Natalie Russell

Content Production Manager:
Claire Horsnell

Production Service:
Integra

Copy Editor:
Carrie MacGregor

Proofreader:
Rebecca Roby

Indexer:
Edwin Durbin

Senior Production Coordinator:
Ferial Suleman

Design Director:
Ken Phipps

Managing Designer:
Franca Amore

Interior Design:
Katherine Strain

Cover Design:
Sharon Lucas

Cover Image:
Helen Vaughn/Getty Images

Compositor:
Integra

Printer:
RR Donnelley

Library and Archives Canada Cataloguing in Publication Data

Main entry under title:

The Harbrace anthology of poetry / senior editors, Jon C. Stott, Raymond E. Jones.—5th ed.

Includes bibliographical references and index.
ISBN 978-0-17-650275-1

1. English poetry. 2. American poetry. 3. Canadian poetry (English). 4. College readers. I. Stott, Jon C., 1939– II. Jones, Raymond E

PN6101.H37 2010   821.008
C2010-904022-8

ISBN-13: 978-0-17-650275-1
ISBN-10: 0-17-650275-0

CONTENTS

POETRY

Alexander Pope

Thomas Gray

William Blake

William Wordsworth

Samuel Taylor Coleridge

PREFACE

"We imagine ourselves, we create ourselves, we touch ourselves into being with words, words that are important to us," writes Native North American author Gerald Vizenor. One means by which we imagine or create ourselves is through the reading of literature.

The Harbrace Anthology of Poetry uses three approaches to encourage its readers in this activity. First, it presents significant and representative works from the increasingly widening canon of literature in English. Second, it provides strategies to assist readers in their appreciation of works of literature. Third, by introducing readers to the language of literature, both simple and complex, and by suggesting methods for articulating responses, it provides opportunities to explore literature and to respond to language in its rich and varied forms.

Although no anthology can include all of its readers' favourite works, the editors have attempted to make their selections as varied and diverse as possible. Thus, The Harbrace Anthology of Poetry offers many contemporary poems, by men and women alike, from a variety of cultures and backgrounds, in addition to many of those works that have always formed an integral part of the accepted canon of literature in English. It also includes a large sampling of English-Canadian literature in the belief that Canadian students should have the opportunity to experience the major works of their literary tradition both on their own terms and within the larger context of literature written in English.

Individual works in The Harbrace Anthology of Poetry mirror the diversity of backgrounds and interests of Canadian students as well as reflecting an expanded canon. The poems and short stories reveal many of the characteristic themes and artistic techniques of their authors; they also reflect the cultural and social contexts in which they were written. In particular, they embody, as the eighteenth-century poet Alexander Pope observed, "what oft was thought but ne'er so well expressed." Most readers of this anthology will find its works speaking directly to them and addressing their most deeply felt concerns.

The Harbrace Anthology of Poetry is organized by author. Selections within each genre are chronological, according to the birth dates of their authors. Following a selection, its date of publication is printed in parentheses on the right; when it differs significantly and is known, the date of composition appears in parentheses on the left. Such an organizational pattern, based on chronology rather than on pedagogical or theoretical concerns, invites a broad range of responses to a work, unencumbered by artificial or purely technical groupings based on content or theme. It does, of course, implicitly suggest a historical continuity in literature: that works from a specific period often have technical and thematic similarities; and that earlier works and authors can influence later ones.

The General Introduction considers the reading of literature both as a personal, necessary, lifelong activity and as a discipline. It explores how reading poems and short stories allows individuals to understand their own lives and responses to literature in relation to those of other people. It also demonstrates how readers can engage more deeply with a text, experiencing it more fully and relating it more completely to their own lives.

The introduction to each genre focuses directly on the characteristics and conventions of the genre, using examples from the literature presented in *The Harbrace Anthology of Poetry*. Discussions of individual characteristics are intended not to offer explanations or explications, but to indicate ways in which authors have used the various elements of the genre. For the reader, an awareness of these characteristics may assist in engagement with the text and lead to a broader range of responses.

Each group of poems by the same author, is prefaced by a brief headnote establishing a biographical and literary context. The headnote may also touch on technique or theme. Explanatory footnotes identify historical, fictional, and mythological personages; literary and artistic works; real and fictional places; and terms not usually found in standard dictionaries. This material provides resources to assist readers in the personal creation of meaning—not to impose a critical viewpoint or to force interpretation in a specific, narrow direction.

For this poetry anthology, the Glossary has been tailored to offer definitions of key terms, providing for readers both an awareness of essential concepts and a standard vocabulary for use in discussing poetry.

A Note from the Publisher

Thank you for selecting *The Harbrace Anthology of Literature*, Fifth Edition, edited by Jon C. Stott and Raymond E. Jones. The editors and publisher have devoted considerable time and care to the development of this book. We appreciate your recognition of this effort and accomplishment.

A Note to the Reader

We would like to draw your attention to two elements of this text:

1. *Dates at the end of poems:* One or two dates follow each poem in the poetry section. The date on the left is the date of the poem's original composition, and the date on the right is the date of the poem's first publication. Where the date of the poem's creation is unknown or where it is the same as the date of the poem's first publication, the date on the left has been omitted.

2. *Stanza continuation symbol* (→): We have introduced a unique feature in the poetry section of this text. Because stanzas often flow onto a new page, it is sometimes difficult for the reader to establish whether a stanza ends at the bottom of the page or continues on the next page. Stanza breaks often have significant implications for the interpretation of poems. To avoid confusion about where stanzas end or continue, we

have placed the symbol "→" below the last line on a page to indicate that a stanza continues on the next page. We hope this will assist your reading of the poetry.

A Note on the Harbrace Anthologies of Poetry and Short Fiction

The publisher has made available individual anthologies representing two of the genres previously included in *The Harbrace Anthology of Literature*. These are *The Harbrace Anthology of Poetry* and *The Harbrace Anthology of Short Fiction*. These one-genre anthologies offer greater choice to instructors teaching courses in these areas. Each of the one-genre anthologies includes the following elements:

- the general introduction to literature
- the introduction to the specific genre
- a glossary, tailored to the specific genre

GENERAL INTRODUCTION

One of the favorite folktales of the Ashanti people of Ghana recounts how Anansi the Spiderman acquires stories for the people. The Sky-God, who possesses all the stories, agrees to give them to him only if he succeeds in completing four impossible tasks. Ridiculing him as small and insignificant, the Sky-God reminds him that other, apparently more capable, individuals had previously failed to complete the tasks and therefore had not earned the right to the stories. Anansi is not deterred. Armed with only a few very simple props and the talent of knowing how to use words and also when not to use them, he captures a leopard, a python, a swarm of hornets, and a dancing fairy. When he returns with his captives, the Sky-God praises him and gives him stories, which Anansi takes home and shares with others. For the first time, therefore, people have stories. Anansi succeeds because he is a storyteller: he deceives his victims with simple narratives. Skilled with words himself, he receives the gift of words formed into stories.

The popularity of this story among the Ashanti, as well as the popularity of similar tales among many other peoples, indicates how important stories—and, by extension, literature in general—have been for preliterate cultures. In addition to myths, legends, and folktales about such topics as the creation of the world, the seasonal cycles, and the characteristics of the physical world, these cultures created narratives that explained the origins of what some people have called a basic need: literature. Canadian literary critic Northrop Frye, for instance, emphasized the importance of literature, observing that "whenever a society is reduced to the barest primary requirements of food, sex, and shelter, the arts, including poetry, stand out sharply in relief as ranking with those primary requirements."

While some literature may simply entertain or allow escape from everyday lives, the works that ultimately stay with their readers are those that challenge, engage, or make demands. Well-crafted literature invites its readers to laugh, to cry, to wonder, to analyze, to explore, to understand.

Throughout our lives, we seek to understand ourselves, our emotions, our experiences, and our relationships with others. We also attempt to define our connections to larger social and cultural institutions. One way that we can do so is through literature, for works of literature are the records of individual response to the world in which we live.

Because of our own experiences, we are able to understand the self-doubts and uncertainties expressed in T. S. Eliot's "The Love Song of J. Alfred Prufrock," the anguish of Phyllis Webb's "Treblinka Gas Chamber" and the wife's sense of betrayal in "Bliss." The specific experiences may be different from our own, but we recognize similarities in the thoughts and emotions of the characters; examination and reflection may lead to clearer insights into our own lives.

Because works of literature are often demanding, they offer great rewards. Readers come to fuller awareness of themselves and others. They discover both the uniqueness and the universality of human experience; they explore both their own world and worlds they may never otherwise see. Through critical response to literature, readers question a work, examine their relationship to the author, consider the author's role, and develop an appreciation of the work, both on its own terms and as an expression of the author's vision of life. Readers may also explore a work in the context of its times, whether social, historical, or ideological.

Until fairly recently, much of the literature studied in English courses was chosen from a list of works deemed important by a majority of critics and scholars, a list referred to as the canon of English literature. Like most of these critics and scholars, most of the writers were white, male, and British or of British descent. The list usually began with the anonymous creator of the Anglo-Saxon epic "Beowulf " and ended with such early-twentieth-century writers as T. S. Eliot, W. H. Auden, and Dylan Thomas. Because it included very few works by women, members of ethnic minorities, or writers from the British colonies, however, it could not be said to reflect the diversity of writing in English.

The past 50 years have seen a remarkable change in our society as a whole: the recognition of the equal place of all people in it, regardless of gender or ethnic origin. As a consequence, many literary scholars and critics have vigorously sought to expand the canon so that it speaks to everyone. They have demanded the inclusion of the many voices whose stories and poems are worthy of study, both on their own merits and because of the insights they offer into a very large segment of the population of the English-speaking world. Such critics have argued that literature should certainly present universal human concerns but should also help readers understand how gender, cultural background, and social position influence responses to life. The works in this anthology reflect this expanded canon.

Reading and reflecting on works of literature reveal human similarities as well as differences. The poetry of Oodgeroo Noonuccal (Kath Walker) reveals a modern Australian aboriginal woman examining her people's past and its troubled relationships with both government and newcomers. Thomas King's "Borders" captures the sense of alienation many aboriginal Canadians feel in their own land.

Readers who come actively to such works with an open, questioning mind will be able to join with their authors in making explicit the implicit. They will appreciate that an author has used language connotatively, choosing words that, in addition to their dictionary meanings, suggest a range of emotions, ideas, or associations. They will recognize the symbolic nature of actions, characters, and objects. As the German literary critic Wolfgang Iser has commented, literary texts are incomplete; they contain gaps that readers fill in or bridge to create meaning. Readers anticipate, make inferences, draw conclusions; in short, they actively work with the language of a piece of literature to arrive at meaning.

Reading for meaning is a very personal act. It is not simply a matter of paraphrasing or summarizing a story or play, of transforming poetry into prose, or of examining literary technique or metaphorical language. Each reader is unique and will, therefore, respond differently—perhaps slightly, perhaps dramatically—to a work. A Dubliner will no doubt react differently to James Joyce's "Araby" than will a Winnipegger; a woman will react differently to Margaret Atwood's "The Resplendent Quetzal" than will a man. People who have read many works of each of these authors or who have a well-developed knowledge of literature would likely have a different and broader interpretation of these works than someone who seldom reads. Readers draw on personal experience, knowledge, and awareness of both specific literature and literary techniques to appreciate and interpret a literary work.

One way readers can increase their understanding and appreciation of the works with which they engage is to make use of some of the critical and theoretical approaches that specialists have developed for the study of literature. These approaches are many and varied, and they frequently overlap each other. In discussing them, we shall, for convenience, categorize them as either textual (approaches that focus on elements found entirely within the texts, the works of literature themselves) or contextual (approaches that relate the works to elements outside of the texts).

Formalism, the first of three textual approaches that we will briefly consider, holds that a work of literature has a unity that is created through the interrelationship of the parts. Formalist critics, therefore, examine a work analytically, reading a text closely and finding relationships among the elements in it in order to discover its form or pattern. New Criticism, a critical school within formalism, applies this approach to a detailed analysis of such elements as imagery, symbolism, paradox, and irony, particularly in shorter poems, but also in passages of longer poems and works of prose. Structuralism also maintains that literature forms patterns; it maintains, however, that the patterns of significance are not the unique ones found in single works, but the general forms of which specific works are individual embodiments. Structural critics therefore conduct a systematic analysis of many works, seeking the conventions, patterns, and systems that they believe exist in literature.

Whereas formalist and structuralist critics attempt to discover and define objectively recognizable fixed patterns within individual works or within literature in general, deconstructionist critics deny that any patterns found in literature are stable or fixed. That is because language, they argue, is unstable and cannot create fixed, definite meaning. These critics thus look closely at works of literature to show how the meanings they appear to communicate break down. Because meanings do deconstruct, works can have alternate, conflicting, and ambiguous meanings.

Several of the contextual approaches can be termed historical because they consider biographical factors and influences of literary, political, and cultural history on authors and their writings. Biographical criticism studies works in relation to authors' lives. By examining facts about, among other things, authors' education and reading, places of residence and travels, friends and relatives, and recreation and employment, readers may acquire factual information that casts light on details in pieces of literature and that helps them to understand better the work as a whole. They can also discover the process of creation that has led to the completion of a work and can see to what extent the content is autobiographical and, if it is, how the facts of the author's life have been altered.

Historical critics examine a work within the various contexts of its time. Knowledge of social, political, and cultural beliefs and events can increase understanding of both specific details and overall themes of a work. They also discuss how a work reflects and comments on its physical and intellectual context. They thus consider not only physical conditions, but also fashions in literature and in the arts, political trends and events, scientific discoveries, and various ideologies. As well, they study the forces that influence the creation, production, and sale of works of literature, seeking to answer a variety of complex questions: In what ways does popular taste influence or affect writers? Why do publishers decide to print certain books? Why are some books better received by reviewers and more popular with buyers? Why do readers re-discover books that have been virtually unknown for decades or even centuries? Historical scholars also examine attitudes toward various cultural and social groups, including women and minorities, in particular time periods and how these attitudes influence the writing and publishing of books and the way these people are portrayed.

Psychological critics use the tenets of such well-known psychiatrists as Sigmund Freud, Carl Jung, and Jacques Lacan to cast light on authors and their works. Freud advanced the theory that dreams were symbolic manifestations of repressed, unconscious drives and that the interpretation of dreams provided a means for understanding the problems experienced by the dreamers. Similarly, he stated that works of art, although more fixed, were manifestations of the unconscious of their creators. Many critics have applied these principles to the study of literature, using their analysis to better understand the authors. Other critics, following Freud's lead, also use the ideas of psychoanalysis to study the motivations and conflicts of characters in literature, suggesting that, even if the authors didn't know Freud's work, they intuitively understood the psychological elements that he articulated. Students of Jung and Lacan have similarly applied psychological principles to both authors and works.

Gender criticism is closely related to psychological criticism in so far as it examines the nature of males and females. Some critics argue that, by nature, men and women perceive, feel, and think differently from each other and, therefore, that they read and write differently. These critics enumerate the differences that they find in works written by men and women. Such an approach has also been applied to gay and lesbian writers.

Other critics disagree with this kind of approach toward gender, arguing that cultural attitudes and beliefs about gender have much greater influence on how people behave. Accordingly, they study the attitudes toward gender that have prevailed in different times and different cultures in order to understand not only how these have influenced the portrayals of men and women in literature, but also how they have, in part, influenced which works were published and which were well received.

In addition to exploring the way mainstream literature has sought to impose on culture ideas about how women should behave and even how they should feel about themselves, feminist criticism also studies the history of women's writing and the economic and social conditions under which women wrote and published. As a result, these critics have re-discovered many works that had been little read or had been unread for many years and have introduced them to new and generally receptive audiences. Some of them have also suggested feminist reconsiderations of traditional "male" literature.

The above approaches focus on contexts influencing the creation and publication of texts and the texts themselves. Reader response criticism focuses on the way texts are received. Critics taking this contextual approach insist that a work does not possess a fixed meaning; it can have as many meanings as it has readers. Reader response critics argue that people give the words meaning as they read them and as they reflect on them after reading. According to these critics, the process of reading involves readers in developing a series of expectations about a work, modifying these in the process of moving through the text, and coming up with some kind of meaning on completing it. Subsequent readings may result in readers creating new or modified meanings. The contexts readers bring to their encounters with a text influence the meanings they create. Their own personalities and experiences, their factual knowledge, the cultural environment in which they live, and their previous literary experiences, including earlier encounters with the work at hand, influence the nature of their encounters. By being aware of the various elements that they bring to their encounter with a specific work, readers can further enrich their literary experiences.

What are the rewards of becoming active readers and interpreters? An answer can be found by returning to this introduction's opening discussion of essential human needs. Poems and short stories are artistic and articulate responses to life that offer emotional, intellectual, and imaginative nourishment to their readers. Anthologies such as this provide exposure to literature that enhances the readers' knowledge of themselves and the world outside of themselves. Such experiences can lead to self-discovery and a life-long love of reading.

POETRY

INTRODUCTION

DEFINING POETRY

Throughout history, whenever people have wanted to give elevated verbal expression to deeds or ideas, whenever they have wanted to make memorable their thoughts, whenever they have wanted to convey their feelings, they have turned to poetry. Today, however, we are just as likely to hear someone announcing the death of poetry as a meaningful art form, or students who are forced to study it complaining that it is not relevant to their lives, or some group objecting to grants to poets as wastes of money. For all such detractors, poetry seems like a cultural aberration in a technological world, a carryover from previous times that has limited appeal and even more limited meaning to contemporary society. In spite of what these and other detractors may say, poetry has not been taken to the cultural acute care ward, where it lingers on government-sponsored life support while an elite few listen to its rasping final breaths. It is true that poetry is no longer, as it once was, a major source of celebration, entertainment, stories, jokes, descriptions, and reflections. Novels, movies, and television have definitely replaced many of its storytelling functions, but poetry is both alive and healthy.

Poetry is, in fact, everywhere in the contemporary world. Parents continue to recite it to their children, who delight in the rollicking metres of nursery rhymes and the cumulative absurdity of Dr. Seuss's *Green Eggs and Ham*. It thus forms an important role in language acquisition. Teenagers and adults hear it on the radio in the form of rap or the lyrics of popular songs that express and interpret their feelings about experience, particularly with the opposite sex. People also meet poetry in radio, television, and theatre commercials, for advertisers count on poetry's power to linger in the memory when they devise slogans to sell their products. Because it is a significant component of the sacred texts and hymns of many religions, poetry continues to have a prominent role in arousing and expressing religious feelings. Furthermore, although poetry may not be a central element in such important public ceremonies as coronations, inaugurations, and victory celebrations—although some poetry may still be recited during these ceremonies—it still plays a part in private milestones, such as birthdays, weddings, and funerals: people continue to mark such special occasions, that is, by communicating their feelings through greeting-card verse that ranges in mood from the mawkishly sentimental to the humorously bawdy. Of course, numerous magazines—and not just the "little magazines" devoted to the subject—still include some poetry, and book publishers annually announce new poetry collections in their catalogues. Clearly, there is still a market for poetry. What is more, in an age that often demands elaborate spectacles in its public entertainments, poetry readings, in which people simply stand before a crowd and read their compositions, enjoy remarkable popularity. In short, people continue to write, to read, and to hear this most ancient of literary forms, and they continue to find that it gives them enjoyment, consolation, and understanding.

Defining poetry, however, is like wrestling with Proteus: just when we think we have pinned it into submission, it changes shape, like the ancient Greek god, and eludes us. Poetry, that is, is so varied in form and content that comprehensive definitions always seem inadequate. Nevertheless, some of the most accomplished poets have tried to identify the essence of their art. Many have emphasized the emotional and intellectual depth of poetry. William Wordsworth said that "poetry is the spontaneous overflow of powerful feelings" and that "poetry is the breath and finer spirit of all knowledge...." Emily Dickinson emphasized emotional response: "If I read a book and it makes my whole body so cold no fire can ever warm me I know that is poetry. If I feel physically as if the top of my head were taken off, I know that is poetry." Percy Bysshe Shelley defined poetry as "the record of the best and happiest moments of the happiest and best minds." Similarly, Matthew Arnold declared: "Poetry is simply the most beautiful, impressive and wisely effective mode of saying things, and hence its importance." Twentieth-century poets have given their own cast to such ideas. Wallace Stevens stressed the metaphysical: "Poetry is a search for the inexplicable." Adrienne Rich has emphasized poetry's power, its ability to condense and communicate significant meaning: "Poetry is above all a concentration of the *power* of language, which is the power of our ultimate relationship to everything in the universe. It is as if forces we can lay claim to in no other way become present to us in sensuous form." Robert Frost was more colourful: "Poetry is a way of taking life by the throat." The Canadian poet Irving Layton has described it as a way of bridging the gap between mundane reality and the world of imagination, a process that creates a separate world: "Mercifully, all poetry, in the final analysis, is about poetry itself; creating through its myriad forms a world in which the elements of reality are sundered; are, as it were, preserved for a time in suspension."

Instead of defining poetry through its connections to feelings, ideas, and actions, however, some writers have tried to look at the aesthetic and technical elements of the craft. Edgar Allan Poe called poetry "*the Rhythmical Creation of Beauty.*" Samuel Taylor Coleridge avoided both the emphasis on refined feelings or ideas and the insistence on beauty when he stressed verbal craftsmanship in this equation: "poetry = the best words in their best order." Throughout the twentieth century, writers have returned to this concept of craftsmanship in their definitions. Dylan Thomas, for instance, described the task of creating poetry as "constructing a formally watertight compartment of words." Frost defined poetry even more simply as "a performance in words." Wallace Stevens probably went as far as possible in dissociating the poet's task from that described in definitions stressing ethical thought, declaring: "Poetry is poetry, and one's objective as a poet is to achieve poetry precisely as one's objective in music is to achieve music."

The precise nature of the poetic achievement is, as these disparate definitions suggest, very much open to debate. Poetry does not seem to depend upon content: poems may be about beauty or ugliness, refined feelings or base ones, matters of perpetual importance or of transient interest. Neither is any single technical feature, such as rhyme, rhythm, or division into lines with ragged right margins, the determinant: it is possible for a good poem to exhibit none of these features. Probably the best we can do is to describe poetry as a concentrated form of literary expression. Poetry employs evocative, often rhythmical language that describes or comments on ideas and experiences and that evokes feelings about them. In poetry the manner of expression is as important as the matter.

POETRY AND LITERARY READING

Because each word in a poem is charged with meaning and feeling to a degree rarely possible in prose, reading poetry may require patience. One reading is simply not sufficient to allow readers to engage with the text, to sense all of its intellectual, emotional, and aesthetic resources. Literary reading demands re-reading, and no single reading procedure is adequate in all circumstances. In fact, theorists do not agree on how poems work and how they should be read. Competing theories emphasize different elements of the relationships among poet, reader, and poem. Nevertheless, readers who are aware of the various biographical, historical, and theoretical contexts may find their reading of a poem more meaningful and, therefore, more enjoyable.

Understanding biographical and cultural contexts may at first seem to be a separate area of study, but these contexts can be vital in constructing meaning. Many critics and theorists, that is, insist that poems do not exist in isolation from the poets who wrote them or apart from the societies in which the poets lived. Personal feelings and experiences shape what poets write and how they write. In turn, their feelings and experiences, if not directly shaped by cultural situations, have often been influenced by the social and moral assumptions, that is, the ideology, of their societies. No one argues that readers must know everything about a poet's life to enjoy a poem. Many critics do suggest, however, that an understanding of a poet's life and artistic ideas may provide information that will help readers to understand the mind and verbal habits of the poet and thus better to construct meaning when reading poetry. The poet's gender and attitudes to gender, for example, may be crucial. The American poet Adrienne Rich says, "I had been taught that poetry should be 'universal,' which meant, of course, nonfemale." In her own poems, therefore, she seeks to express her feelings as a female whose views and experiences may be distinct from those previously celebrated as universal.

Similarly, some critics claim that an understanding of cultural history is sometimes essential. First, literary conventions and habits of expression change from generation to generation; understanding these may help in the understanding of works written during an earlier period. Second, what people of any age write reflects their connection to the dominant culture of their time. Literature may thus openly express attitudes officially sanctioned by a given society. This is the belief of Thomas Carlyle, who saw poetry as a mirror of the spirit of an age: "The history of a nation's poetry is the essence of its history, political, scientific, religious." Of course, as Marxist and other theorists concerned with class and economic factors note, poetry may also seek, often covertly, to subvert the dominant culture.

In developing meaning, the contemporary reader may thus require an understanding of the sometimes latent assumptions within a poem. Many contemporary theorists insist that readers can acquire this understanding only through an examination of cultural history that looks at more than the major battles, legislative acts, scientific discoveries, and social movements of the poet's time. This understanding may require a knowledge of what we may call historical sociology: the child-rearing practices, family living arrangements, health policies, sexual mores, religious affiliations, racial attitudes, class assumptions, labour laws, attitudes toward literacy and artistic expression, and many other factors that shape a living culture. These factors, and more, are part of any culture's ideology, the usually unexamined assumptions by which that culture maintains and regulates itself. Knowledge of such cultural facts and the ways in which given cultures perceived or even denied these facts can help a reader to assess a poem's cultural function, its particular contribution to supporting or undermining ideology.

Readers may also have to know something about the reception of the poem. Understanding how readers from various classes, genders, or political positions responded to the poem can aid contemporary readers in assessing the cultural function of the poem, that is, what effect it had on both literary and non-literary communities. Such an analysis ultimately leads to questions about why any given literary work has enjoyed canonical status as a significant cultural product or has been relegated to the role of a minor work. In turn, this analysis leads to questions of literary authority: who determines that a literary work is great, and why do they make such judgments? Finally, all of these questions lead back again to the biographical ones: how did such issues affect the poet, and how did the poet feel about them?

Many other theorists downplay the significance of such biographical and cultural contexts. For some of these, poetry is an artifact, like a Greek vase, that exists separate from the reader and must be understood on its own terms. For others, poetry is more of a tool kit or an Erector set that the reader plays with, constructing and reconstructing meaning. One group argues for the realization of a final meaning inherent in the work; the other argues that no single meaning can be inherent in the work and, instead, stresses the process of reading rather than the results. The more traditional theorists point out that the word *poetry* comes from a Greek root meaning "thing made" and that a poet is a "maker." They see poems as carefully constructed, unified artifacts, and they argue that the reader needs to note the contribution of all of the parts of a work to discover its inherent meaning. For example, some of these theorists argue that a poem's basic structure is a set of binary oppositions, such as life and death or virtue and sin, and that meaning comes when the poem "privileges," or gives approval to, one set of these oppositions. They believe that the reader's task in understanding a poem is to locate the structure of binary oppositions. Those who look at poetry more as the tool kit that the reader uses take differing approaches. Some have extended this notion of binary oppositions, arguing that every literary work actually contains not only oppositions but also contradictions and that, therefore, no poem can have a determinate meaning. They contend that a work "deconstructs" itself, saying two contradictory things at once. Finally, another group of theorists concentrates on the reader's involvement with poems, arguing that the work itself contains no meaning: a poem is simply a series of squiggles on the page until the reader engages with the text and actively creates meaning from it. The reader not only "decodes" individual words—deciding, for example, that the letters d-o-g refer to a particular kind of animal—but also, because of previous personal and literary experiences, associates particular ideas and attitudes with each word decoded: when faced with the word dog, some readers will envisage a slavering attack beast, whereas others will envisage a friendly lapdog. Although many poems use what Wolfgang Iser calls "response-inviting structures," devices that encourage readers to read in particular ways, these devices cannot possibly limit readers to one single response. Because each person's experiences and associations are different, each will read a given poem differently.

Although the competition between rival theories may suggest to some readers that a poem means anything a given reader thinks it means, all theories imply that literary understanding begins with close attention to words. Many theories stress that poetry is a playful use of language, even in poems about serious matters, and that a playful attitude in reading, an attitude that brings all of a person's associations and experiences to bear on each word, makes it easier to discover or construct meaning.

In truth, few readers are concerned about competing theories when first reading a poem; instead, most readers ordinarily want to construct at least a provisional meaning as soon as possible. Such readers may find some guidelines useful as the basis for beginning a significant reading of a work.

Because poetry is an art that depends upon achieving the maximum effect from each word, readers need to understand both the **denotations**, or dictionary meanings, of words and the **connotations**, or implications, of these words. Some words, that is, carry extra meaning: they have negative or positive associations that may influence interpretation. We may think positively about an adult who is childlike, but negatively about one who is childish. We may also have different attitudes about speakers who use colloquial language and speakers who consistently use elaborate, formal language. Sensitivity to words and their nuances is an important step in meaningful reading.

Traditionally, readers have also found useful a number of basic questions about the content and form of a poem. The first questions focus on the speaker in the poem: Who is the speaker? To whom is he or she speaking? What are the circumstances? These questions may not be very important in a poem like Tennyson's "The Eagle," but they are crucial considerations in dramatic monologues such as Browning's "The Bishop Orders

His Tomb at Saint Praxed's Church," in which an understanding of the speaker's character and the context in which he or she is speaking is necessary to make the poem meaningful. Another question concerns the arrangement of content: How is the poem organized to develop its ideas? The order in which details are presented can influence our attitudes toward them and our understanding of the development of major ideas within the poem. In Browning's "My Last Duchess," the duke's description of the fate of his last wife precedes his discussion of arrangements for a new bride, making him seem especially arrogant, cynical, and brutal. In Sonnet 73, Shakespeare emphasizes both the narrator's age and the brevity of time by arranging images that imply death: he creates a sequence that moves from larger to smaller measures of time, from a season, to a day, to the moment when a fire is dying out.

Readers may also find it useful to ask questions about the technical elements of a poem: How do techniques or elements such as rhythm, sound devices, images, and diction influence our understanding? The purpose of examining techniques is not to catalogue them but to understand their role in shaping our ideas and feelings within the poem as a whole. For example, readers who notice the difference in rhythm in the first and final sections of Marvell's "To His Coy Mistress" can determine how it influences their understanding of the narrator's attitudes toward traditional ideals of courtship and his own growing sense of urgency. Finally, readers often find it useful to consider literary contexts: How does this poem compare to other poems, especially those with similar forms, those from the same period, and those about similar subjects? An understanding of conventions of form or subject matter and of literary "schools" or literary periods enables readers to place the work in a literary and historical context that can be helpful in understanding the poem. Shakespeare's Sonnet 130, "My mistress' eyes are nothing like the sun," for instance, is far more meaningful to readers who understand something of the Petrarchan tradition of love sonnets and have read some English love sonnets by such poets as Wyatt, Surrey, Sidney, and Constable.

FIGURATIVE LANGUAGE (1): IMAGERY, SIMILE, METAPHOR, CONCEIT

Poetry, A. E. Housman said, is "more physical than intellectual." Poetry, that is, is a sensual medium. Sound, discussed later, and imagery, the subject of this section, appeal to the senses, stimulating an imaginative body of impressions, feelings, and ideas. These may be new, or they may be familiar, but the sensory appeals of poetry give them an immediacy that directly involves readers.

At its most basic level, **imagery** is language that creates images, or pictures, in the imagination. Some poems, like "The Red Wheelbarrow," by William Carlos Williams, rely almost exclusively on verbal pictures. Most poems, however, use imagery to develop statements about feelings and ideas. The opening section of Wordsworth's "Lines Composed a Few Miles above

Tintern Abbey" creates a picture of the scene, describing such things as "These hedge-rows, hardly hedge-rows, little lines / Of sportive wood run wild...." In this way, the narrator impresses on readers the power that the setting holds over him as a scene of "beauteous forms."

Although the roots of the word suggest a visual element, imagery is not exclusively visual; it frequently makes appeals to touch, taste, and sound. In the final stanza of "To Autumn," for example, Keats describes the "music" of autumn, with such sound images as "Then in a wailful choir the small gnats mourn / Among the river sallows...." In "Dover Beach," Arnold uses sound imagery to convey "The eternal note of sadness": he describes "the grating roar / Of pebbles" flung back and forth by the waves.

Images, like all appeals to the senses, can evoke emotional reactions. Because they can give concrete form to ideas by forcing readers to understand one idea in terms of another, they also can be a medium of intellectual discourse. This linking of objects or ideas is the basis of most figurative language, language that goes beyond the literal denotation of the words by imaginatively extending their meanings.

The most common figures of speech are similes and metaphors. Both tend to give concrete form to abstract ideas or to make the unfamiliar clearer and more forceful by linking it to something familiar. Simile expresses similarity between things and always uses such linking terms as *like*, *as*, *than*, or *as if*. Keats, in "On First Looking into Chapman's Homer," conveys the magnitude of his feelings of discovery with a simile that connects his reactions upon reading a book to a rarer but more public experience: "Then felt I like some watcher of the skies / When a new planet swims into his ken." In the opening simile of T. S. Eliot's "The Love Song of J. Alfred Prufrock," the narrator provides a clue to his own emotional numbness by saying that "the evening is spread out against the sky / Like a patient etherised upon a table." **Metaphor** compares by equating things. In Shakespeare's Sonnet 73, the metaphor in which the boughs become "Bare ruin'd choirs" creates a sense of collapse and destruction because it implicitly equates the trees in late autumn and abandoned, ruined churches. In "The Flea," John Donne's narrator uses metaphor as part of his strategy of seduction, aggrandizing the flea: "This flea is you and I, and this / Our marriage bed, and marriage temple is."

Not every comparison is as brief as those just discussed. More elaborate and extended comparisons, whether similes or metaphors, are called **conceits**. The **Petrarchan conceit**, developed by those who followed the example of the Italian Petrarch, the poet who popularized the sonnet form, uses rather conventional extended comparisons, as in Wyatt's "My galley...," which compares the lover to a ship at sea, or Surrey's "Love that doth reign...," which personifies love as a military leader. More original and startling comparisons are called **metaphysical conceits** because they were developed by the so-called **metaphysical poets** of the seventeenth century, who linked physical with metaphysical or spiritual elements in their images. John Donne's "A Valediction: Forbidding Mourning" contains the most famous of these, his comparison of separated lovers to "stiff twin compasses."

FIGURATIVE LANGUAGE (2): PERSONIFICATION, APOSTROPHE, METONYMY, SYNECDOCHE, SYMBOL, MOTIF

Other figurative devices also link ideas. **Personification** gives human qualities to abstractions or to things that do not possess them. Thus, William Wordsworth, in "The world is too much with us," suggests the sensuousness of nature through personification: "This Sea that bares her bosom to the moon." In one of his odes, John Keats personifies an object, an ancient Greek urn, as a "Sylvan historian," suggesting that it can tell much about life. Personification often develops through **apostrophe**, a direct address to a thing or abstraction, as in Shelley's "O wild West Wind, thou breath of Autumn's being" or Donne's "Death be not proud." Apostrophe is not always part of personification because the device also includes direct addresses to an absent or dead person, as in Wordsworth's "Milton! thou shouldst be living at this hour." In either case, it gives immediacy and concreteness to people, events, and ideas.

Two other linking devices are frequently used to condense complex experiences into images. **Metonymy**, or "substitute naming," uses an associated idea to name something. In "London, 1802," for example, Wordsworth talks of "altar, sword, and pen," instead of the clergy, soldiers, and authors, in order to suggest concretely both the people and the function of those people. A related device is **synecdoche**, in which a part stands for the whole, or the whole stands for the part. It is most evident in such expressions as "All hands on deck!" in which *hands* stands for *sailors*, and in the prayer for "daily bread," in which *bread* stands for all food. In Eliot's "Prufrock," synecdoche, which is evident in the naming of a part instead of the whole crab or lobster, suggests the narrator's lack of a fully developed identity: "I should have been a pair of ragged claws / Scuttling across the floors of silent seas." Synecdoche is most shockingly apparent, however, in the vision of death in Marvell's "To His Coy Mistress," which reduces the woman's morality to sexual organs: " ... then worms shall try / That long preserved virginity, / And your quaint honour turn to dust."

The linking device that many readers find most difficult to grasp is symbolism. *Symbol* comes from the Greek "to throw together." A symbol throws together objects, people, or actions and a meaning that is not necessarily inherent in them. Symbols fall into two major categories, conventional symbols and contextual symbols. **Conventional symbols** are those that traditionally carry a particular meaning. Sometimes, the symbol is conventional only within a given culture. A cross, for example, means something quite different to Christians in North America than to Buddhists in China. The rose, to cite another example, traditionally suggests love or beauty in Western culture. Such conventional symbols may be the basis of relatively simple ideas: "Gather ye rose-buds while ye may," the opening line of Herrick's "To the Virgins, To Make Much of Time," develops the *carpe diem* ("seize the day") idea of living for the moment because, like the rose, youth and beauty fade. They may also develop more complex and even ambiguous ideas, as in William Blake's "The Sick Rose," in which the rose suggests ideas of love but leaves open to speculation the exact nature of that love and of the worm that destroys it. Not all conventional symbols are limited to a specific culture. Some seem to be universal, having appeared so frequently and for such a long time in the literatures of various cultures that their meanings seem to be natural. These are known as **archetypes**. One such archetype is the description of the sun's movement from sunrise to sunset to symbolize aging in human beings. This archetype appears in such different works as Herrick's "To the Virgins, To Make Much of Time," where it reinforces the idea that youth must live for the moment, and Earle Birney's "Bushed," where it suggests the rapidly approaching death of the trapper.

Readers acquire understanding of conventional symbols by familiarity with a large number of works using them. In Frost's "Stopping by Woods on a Snowy Evening," for example, repetition of the last line, "And miles to go before I sleep," puts such additional stress on both *miles* and *sleep* that these words imply more than they literally say. Readers familiar with other poems that use either a journey or sleep as a symbol can see this poem as using the conventional archetypal symbol of a journey toward death, an additional implication that coexists with its surface meaning of a journey on a winter's night.

Contextual symbols, however, become symbolic only within the context of a given work; they may not have the same symbolic meaning, or even any symbolic meaning, in a different work. For example, the tiger symbolizes, among other things, fierceness and destructiveness in Blake's "The Tyger," but it symbolizes the repressed dreams of a conventional woman in Adrienne Rich's "Aunt Jennifer's Tigers." Sometimes the accumulation of details creates a contextual symbol, as it does in Shelley's "Ozymandias," in which the ruined statue of the pharaoh gradually becomes a general symbol of mutability and the vanity of human desires. Such contextual symbols are not always obvious: during an initial reading, they may seem to be simply a part of the concrete description or narrative movement of the poem. Re-reading is therefore important. With each re-reading, a poem becomes more familiar, and its details, patterns, and emphases—the elements that create contextual symbols—become more apparent.

Furthermore, with each re-reading, the links to other poems, in addition to the connecting links within the poem itself, become more apparent. Any poem using an archetype, for example, is using an element that occurs in many works. Understanding the archetype in one poem thus helps in understanding others. Archetypes and symbols are not the only recurring elements, of course. Images, characters, objects, settings, situations, or themes may recur in many works; these recurring elements are called **motifs**. The *carpe diem* theme, for example, is a thematic motif, whether or not it is expressed by the archetype of the setting sun. Elements can also be repeated to link the parts of an individual work. For example, Margaret Atwood's "Progressive Insanities of a Pioneer" contains several references to water and to terms associated with measurement and enclosure. Such recurring elements within an individual work, whether recurring words, phrases, images, situations, or themes, are also sometimes called motifs, although they are more generally called **leitmotifs**. Readers who note such recurring devices will be able to respond more completely to the poem, to link together its various parts, to connect the poem to other works and to situations outside the poem itself, and to construct more meaning.

IRONY, PARADOX, OXYMORON, ZEUGMA

Simile, metaphor, symbol, and other devices of figurative language discussed above link images to feelings and ideas, but they do not always forge their links in the way that we may at first expect. Sometimes another device, irony, twists the connections. **Irony** is a discrepancy between appearance and reality, expectation and result, or surface meaning and implied meaning. Traditionally, critics have described three major kinds of irony: dramatic irony, situational irony, and verbal irony. Dramatic irony, a device found more frequently in drama and fiction than in poetry, is the discrepancy between what a character says or does and what the reader knows to be the truth of the situation. Situational irony, which is also inherent in dramatic irony, presents a situation in which the result is the reverse of what a character or speaker expected. Verbal irony reverses the denotation of words so that a given statement actually means the opposite of what it says literally, as when we call "graceful" someone who has just tripped.

Whatever its form, irony is a device that is often integral to the **theme**, the central idea developed by a poem. In "Ozymandias," for example, both verbal irony, the boast that Ozymandias makes about his greatness, and situational irony, the image of a shattered statue upon whose base the boastful words are carved, reverse the pharaoh's intention: instead of celebrating glorious, lasting achievements, both the words and the statue make a moving statement about mutability and the impermanence of human achievement. Similarly, in Margaret Atwood's "Progressive Insanities of a Pioneer," the language of measurement and geometry, normally a sign of logic and control, reverses itself to reveal the mad egocentricity of the pioneer. Unable to recognize nature for what it is, he tries to impose his vision on it and stands "a point / on a sheet of green paper / proclaiming himself the centre." His failure of vision eventually leads to his defeat by the very forces he sought to dominate. Irony can also be a powerful device for political comment and protest. Wilfred Owen deliberately uses the juxtaposition of the title phrase in "*Dulce et Decorum Est*" and the scene of a soldier dying in a gas attack to reverse the wartime propaganda that called it glorious for the young to die for their country.

Two other devices found frequently in poetry depend upon an unusual link of expression and idea. **Paradox** is a statement that seems contradictory on the surface but contains a truth on deeper examination. Among the most famous of paradoxes is Wordsworth's statement that "The Child is father of the Man," a claim that is biologically absurd but psychologically profound: the statement concisely expresses the idea that the experiences of childhood shape adult lives. Paradox often serves to convey complex spiritual and psychological truths, as in Donne's Holy Sonnet XIV ("Batter my heart"), which concludes with a notable and shocking set of paradoxes about the narrator's relationship with God:

> Take me to you, imprison me, for I
> Except you enthral me, never shall be free,
> Nor ever chaste, except you ravish me.

A related device is **oxymoron**, a word whose Greek roots imply "sharp stupidity" or "wise foolishness." Oxymoron contains a contradiction: it links opposites in the surface expression in order to defamiliarize or make unusual the connections we expect. Thus, Milton describes hell as having "darkness visible."

Although found less frequently than paradox and oxymoron, another notable device also twists connections for comical or critical effect. **Zeugma** grammatically links a term to two words, but the linkage is logically appropriate in a different way for each word. One of the most famous examples is in Pope's *The Rape of the Lock*: "Or stain her Honour, or her new Brocade." With its first object, "Honour," the verb "stain" indicates the ruin of a woman's virtue; with its second, "Brocade," it merely points to the soiling of a gown. By linking these two incompatible meanings in one sentence, Pope succinctly and wittily implies that women in high society do not discriminate between realms of morality and fashion, that both are equally trivial, or equally important, to them. Zeugma does not, however, have to be a comic device. In "The Devil's Language," for example, Marilyn Dumont speaks of the mother who "fed you bannock and tea / and syllables." By linking food and language, zeugma here stresses that language is part of nurture and that it thus has both cultural and emotional significance.

LINE, LENGTH, METRE, AND RHYTHM

Two things immediately distinguish poetry from prose: the look upon the page and the sound when read aloud. The distinctive look of most poetry comes from its organization into lines. In most English poems written before the twentieth century, the line lengths were dependent upon **metre**. English, with its stressed syllables (indicated by ´) and unstressed syllables (indicated by ˘), naturally creates rhythm, the flow of rising and falling sounds, but poetry organizes rhythm, as prose and common speech do not. Metre, a word derived from the Greek "to measure," measures the organization of repeated stressed and unstressed syllables, giving names to the rhythmic patterns within a poem.

At various times and in various places, different systems of measurement have been used. French poetry, for example, counts only syllables. The same is true of the Japanese haiku, a form sometimes adopted by writers in English: it contains three lines of five, seven, and five syllables, respectively. Anglo-Saxon, or Old English, poetry, on the other hand, is accentual: it measures only the stresses in a given line and does not count the unstressed syllables. Furthermore, it organizes the stresses by placing two in each half, or hemistich, of a line, by having three stresses share an **alliterative** sound, and by separating each half with a **caesura**, or pause. A few poets have tried to use this form with modern English. In "Anglosaxon Street," for example, Earle Birney graphically indicates the hemistiches by using a wide space for each caesura:

> Dáwndrízzle ended   dámpness stéams from
> blótching brick and   blánk plásterwaste

The most common system for measuring poetry in modern English, however, considers both the **accents** and the number of syllables in a line. The base of the system is the **foot**, a unit consisting of one or more syllables, usually with one stressed. Repetition of the pattern of stressed and unstressed syllables found within a given foot creates a regular **rhythm**, and each of the various regular rhythms has a name based on the pattern within the foot and the number of feet composing the line. Table 1 lists the names and shows the patterns of the metrical feet. The dominant rhythm in a poem will probably be one of the first four patterns: the others are normally variations within a regular rhythm. Table 2 names the various line lengths according to the number of feet in each. A process called **scansion** indicates graphically the metre of a poem. This process requires the marking of all stressed and unstressed syllables and the clear division of feet from each other by means of a vertical line. Scansion graphically shows, for example, that the opening line of Shakespeare's Sonnet 73 is iambic pentameter, a pattern formed from five iambic feet:

Thăt tíme ǀ ŏf yéar ǀ thŏu máyst ǀ ĭn mé ǀ bĕhóld

Table 1   The Metrical Feet

Noun	Adjective	Pattern	Example
iamb	iambic	‿ ´	remote
trochee	trochaic	´ ‿	joker
anapest	anapestic	‿ ‿ ´	interrupt
dactyl	dactylic	´ ‿ ‿	heavenly
spondee	spondaic	´ ´	heartbreak
pyrrhic	pyrrhic	‿ ‿	in the
amphibrach	amphibrachic	‿ ´ ‿	soprano
amphimacer (or cretic)	amphimacric	´ ‿ ´	first and last

Table 2   Line Lengths

Number of Feet in Line	Name of Line Length
1	monometer
2	dimeter
3	trimeter
4	tetrameter
5	pentameter
6	hexameter
7	heptameter
8	octameter

Rhythmic Variation

Poets do not always write according to strict metre. They frequently introduce variations within their lines not only to avoid the potential monotony of a regular metre but also to emphasize particular words or ideas. Consider, for example, the opening lines of John Donne's Holy Sonnet XIV:

Báttĕr | mў héart, | thŕee-pér | sŏn'd God; | fŏr ўou

Aͮs yét | bŭt knóck, | breáth, shíne, | ănd seék | tŏ ménd;

Thăt Í | măy ŕise, | ănd stánd, | ó'erthrów | me, ănd bénd

Yoŭr fóŕce | tŏ bréak | blóẃ, búrn, | ănd máke | mĕ néẃ

Sonnets conventionally employ iambic pentameter, ten-syllable lines consisting of five feet, each with an unstressed syllable followed by a stressed one. Although the iamb certainly dominates in this poem, Donne immediately disrupts expectations and emphasizes the violence that he believes is essential to remaking him by beginning with a trochee, a stressed syllable followed by an unstressed one. More importantly, he inserts a spondee, that is, a foot consisting of two stressed syllables, into each of the first four lines. He thereby produces in each of these lines three stressed syllables in a row. Generally, a sequence of unaccented syllables quickens the flow, or pace, of a line, whereas a sequence of stressed syllables slows it. Especially in the second and fourth lines, where the three consecutive stresses fall on action verbs, the pace slows to emphasize the action that Donne's narrator is beseeching. The effect is something like that of hammer blows. (Even more subtly, these three heavy stresses may, as some critics have suggested, emphasize that each of the accented actions is that of one person of the Christian Trinity.) Incidentally, readers may also note that Donne uses eleven, not ten, syllables in the third line, introducing a further variation of the iambic pentameter rhythm that one expects in sonnets.

While it is common to vary rhythm within lines by using metrical feet that deviate from the dominant pattern and by adding extra feet or extra syllables to a line, poets can affect the flow of their lines in other ways. One is by judicious use of the caesura, or pause (indicated in scansion by two vertical lines). Because the most emphatic positions in any unit of expression (line, phrase, sentence, paragraph) are first, at the end, and second, at the beginning, the caesura creates emphasis by increasing the number of these positions. In Tennyson's "Ulysses," for example, the caesura effectively halts the flow of the lines to emphasize tedium:

Hŏw dúll | iĭ ́ iś | tŏ páuse, || tŏ máke | ăn énd.

Tŏ rúst | uͮnbúrn | ĭsh'd, || ńot | tŏ shíne | iͮn uͮse!

In the first line, "pause" immediately precedes a pause, and "end" comes at the end of the line, the meaning of both words thus being effectively reinforced by their position. In the second line, the caesura comes in the middle of a foot, disrupting the regular flow and creating an oral counterpoint to it. Strictly speaking, that is, metre expresses the division into feet according to the stresses of syllables, and this line is a perfectly regular iambic line. Dramatic reading of it, however, provides a different sense of how the line flows. If we consider the caesura as creating a pause that divides this line into two units, we would scan this line for reading by marking it as consisting of an iamb, amphibrach, amphimacer, and iamb:

> Tŏ rust | un̆búrnĭsh'd, || nŏt tŏ shíne | ĭn úse!

The dramatic, interpretive rhythm exists simultaneously with the regular metre. The interpretive rhythm insists on a pause, accentuating the contrast between the sedentary state and the active one that follows; the conventional metre pulls the reader forward in expectation of completing the iambic pattern. Interpretive rhythm could also make the contrast between the two parts of the line even more emphatic: when "not to shine" is read as an anapest, the two unaccented syllables quicken the pace, indicating joy, and place an even more meaningful and emphatic stress on shine.

In the lines just quoted, Tennyson uses **end-stopped lines**, lines that terminate with a natural pause. Such lines are usually indicated by punctuation, which reinforces this pause. Poets often vary the flow of their lines by using run-on lines, or **enjambment** (from the French for "striding over"). Tennyson uses enjambment throughout "Ulysses":

> Ĭ ćan | Ĭ nŏt rest | from tŕav | ĕl; || Í | Ĭ will drink
> Lífe tŏ | t h̆e lées.

Because of the caesura in the middle of a foot in the first line and the shift to trochee in the first foot of the second line, the key words I, *drink*, *Life*, and *lees* are all accented and are all visually, grammatically, or by strict measure in positions of emphasis, at the beginning or end of a unit. The enjambment, however, creates a variation in the rhythmic flow, linking the last part of the first line to the first part of the second line: although the iambic pentameter pattern is completed with *drink*, the reader cannot pause at the end of the line because the idea is incomplete; instead, the reader must continue until the completion of the idea in the middle of the second line.

Beyond Scansion: Free Verse and Shaped Verse

Not every poem displays a dominant rhythm that can be scanned like those in the preceding examples. Some poems are written in **free verse** or **vers libre**, terms popularized by Ezra Pound, among others. Pound compared the conventional patterns of regularly repeated metrical feet to the monotonous beat of a metronome. He argued that the lines of a poem should be free from the conventional system, that, instead, lines should follow the more natural patterns evident in spoken language and music. (Incidentally, free verse should not be confused with **blank verse**, a form popular in Elizabethan England, which usually means an unrhymed line of iambic pentameter.) Other writers, however, may organize lines by meaning. In "The Country

North of Belleville," for example, Al Purdy intensifies the irony of defeat by placing each stage of the farmer's recognition of futility in a separate line:

> without grandeur or self deception in
> noble struggle
> of being a fool—

Margaret Atwood is even subtler in her description of the man standing in a field in "Progressive Insanities of a Pioneer":

> with no walls, no borders
> anywhere; the sky no height
> above him, totally un-
> enclosed

She divides the lines to place words suggesting measurement and logical calculation in emphatic positions. Furthermore, she breaks up the word "unenclosed" to emphasize the ironic discrepancy between the pioneer's perception that he is "enclosed," which leads him to shout insanely that he wants out, and the reader's understanding that nothing actually encloses him.

Line length may also graphically reflect meaning. George Herbert's "The Altar" arranges lines to form a picture that represents the central idea of the poem. Lines in such shaped verse convey meaning, but they must be seen on the page to be fully appreciated. Much the same is true of concrete poetry, a form popular in the 1960s and early 1970s. In some concrete poems, however, the lines forming the picture may be letters or other typographical elements that can have no meaning on their own. Meaning exists entirely in the picture as a whole.

RHYME AND STANZA FORM

Many poems, especially those written before the twentieth century, link lines by more than subject matter and rhythm: they use **rhyme**, the repetition of accented vowels and all syllables following the accented vowel. **Single rhymes**, or **masculine rhymes**, repeat only the last syllable of words: *know, go; delight, fight*. **Double rhymes**, also called **feminine rhymes** or **trochaic rhymes**, repeat identical sounds in both an accented syllable and the following unaccented syllable: *kissing, missing; seasons, reasons*. **Triple rhymes**, or **dactylic rhymes**, also occur: *tenderly, slenderly; scornfully, mournfully*. Rhymes most frequently occur as **end rhymes,** in which the rhyming words are at the end of lines. **Internal rhymes** operate within lines, as in this example from "The Rime of the Ancient Mariner": "And every *day*, for food or *play*."

All the examples so far have been **exact rhymes** or **true rhymes**. In some cases, poets use **near rhyme** (also known as **slant, off, imperfect**, or **oblique rhyme**), a rhyme that approximates rather than exactly repeats a sound: *bridge, hedge; still, wheel; tucker, supper*. Slant rhyme usually depends on similarity of the final consonant, but it can include such imperfect rhymes as *flew* and *boot*, which rhyme the vowel but not the consonant. Another form is **eye** rhyme, or **sight rhyme**, in which words spelled similarly but pronounced differently are treated as rhymes. In some cases, as with Shakespeare's rhyming of *proved* and *loved*, the words may have been pronounced similarly at the time the poem was written. In other cases, such as Coleridge's rhyming of *prow* and *blow* in "The Rime of the Ancient Mariner," the rhymes are purely visual.

Rhyme can be a mnemonic device, something that helps poets, listeners, and readers to remember a work; it is also an important structural device that helps to group lines into meaningful sections. The normal grouping of lines is called the **stanza**. Table 3 provides the general names for stanzas according to the number of lines they contain. Stanzas are infinitely variable, but a number of poetic forms specify the precise number of lines the stanza can contain and the pattern of rhymes, known as the rhyme scheme, that those lines must follow.

Table 3   Names of Stanzas and Line Groupings

Number of Lines	Name
2	couplet
3	tercet (triplet when all three lines rhyme together)
4	quatrain
5	quintet
6	sestet
7	septet
8	octave

Table 4 names and describes the most notable of these fixed forms. We describe rhyme schemes by using a separate letter for each end rhyme. Thus, we indicate a stanza in which the first and fourth lines and the second and third lines rhyme by the formula *a b b a*. Sometimes, however, we must resort to a more complex description because line lengths vary. In these cases, we describe a stanza by indicating its predominant rhythm and by noting with each letter of the rhyme scheme the number of feet in that line. Consider the opening stanza of "Sir Patrick Spens," which we could describe as predominantly iambic with a rhyme scheme of 4*a*, 3*b*, 4*c*, 3*b*:

Thĕ Kíng ǀ sĭts ĭñ ǀ Dŭmfér ǀ lĭñg toúne,	*a* (4 feet)
Drĭnkĭñg ǀ thĕ blúde- ǀ reĭd wíne:	*b* (3 feet)
"Ŏ whár ǀ wĭll Ĭ gét ǀ gŭĭd ǀ sáilŏr,	*c* (4 feet)
Tŏ sáil ǀ thĭs schíp ǀ ŏf míne?"	*b* (3 feet)

This pattern is known as ballad measure; many other patterns also have names, and knowing these can simplify the description.

Stanzas depend upon a few basic patterns in their rhymes. **Couplets** are pairs of rhyming lines: *a a b b*. Heroic couplets are in iambic pentameter. If the idea expressed by the couplet is completed within the compass of the two lines, the couplet is a **closed couplet**. **Triplets** or **tercets** consist of three lines, rhymed or unrhymed. A **quatrain** is any group of four lines, rhymed or unrhymed; it is the most common form in English poetry. A **sestet** is a unit of six lines, whereas an **octave** is one of eight lines.

These last three—the quatrain, the sestet, and the octave—are important terms in describing one of the most pervasive and highly controlled of poetic forms, the sonnet. The **Italian** or **Petrarchan sonnet** is a fourteen-line iambic pentameter form usually rhyming *abba abba cdecde* (but the last six lines have many variations in rhyme scheme). The Italian sonnet develops an idea in the octave, and then uses a **volta,** or turn (often signalled by such words as "yet" or "but"), before concluding that idea in the sestet. The **English** or **Shakespearean sonnet** is an iambic pentameter poem rhyming *abab cdcd efef gg*. It consists of three quatrains and a heroic couplet. Its turn of thought occurs in the couplet and must be more compressed and concentrated than that in an Italian sonnet. A Spenserian sonnet is similar, except that it rhymes *abab bcbc cdcd ee*. A fourth variation is the **Miltonic sonnet**. It follows the Italian form, but it does not pause after the octave.

Table 4   Notable Fixed and Complex Forms

Number of Lines in Poem or Stanza	Name and Description
3	TERZA RIMA: tercets of iambic pentameter with linked rhymes (*aba bcb cdc ...*)
4	COMMON MEASURE: a quatrain in iambic metre, with the first and third lines having four iambic feet and the second and fourth having three iambic feet (*abcb*)
	BALLAD STANZA: similar to common measure but the four lines can be in any metre, with four metrical feet in the first and third and three in the second and fourth lines (*abcb*)
6	ITALIAN SESTET: six lines of iambic pentameter (*abcabc*)
	SICILIAN SESTET: six lines of iambic pentameter (*ababab*)
	HEROIC SESTET: six lines of iambic pentameter (*ababcc*)
7	RIME ROYAL: seven lines of iambic pentameter (*ababbcc*)
8	OTTAVA RIMA: eight lines of iambic pentameter (*abababcc*)
	ITALIAN OCTAVE: eight lines of iambic pentameter (*abbaabba*)
	SICILIAN OCTAVE: eight lines of iambic pentameter (*abababab*)
9	SPENSERIAN STANZA: nine lines rhyming *ababbcbcc* with the first eight in iambic pentameter and the last in iambic hexameter (which is called an Alexandrine)

(continued)

Table 4   Notable Fixed and Complex Forms (continued)

Number of Lines in Poem or Stanza	Name and Description
10	ENGLISH (KEATSIAN) ODE: three ten-line iambic pentameter stanzas, each with the same rhyme scheme (*ababcdecde*)
14	SONNET: fourteen iambic pentameter lines
	ENGLISH (SHAKESPEAREAN) SONNET (*abab cdcd efef gg*)
	SPENSERIAN SONNET (*abab bcbc cdcd ee*)
	PETRARCHAN (ITALIAN) SONNET (*abba abba cde cde* or *abba abba cdcdcd*)
19	VILLANELLE: nineteen lines of any length, divided into five tercets and one quatrain; built on two rhymes and two refrains (shown by superscripts $R1$ and $R2$), both of which end with the *a* rhyme ($a^{R1}ba^{R2}aba^{R1}aba^{R2}aba^{R1}aba^{R2}aba^{R1}a^{R2}$)

Some stanzaic forms can be very complicated, requiring the poet to possess exceptional skill in order both to meet the technical requirements of the form and to produce a work that is moving or interesting. For example, Dylan Thomas's "Do Not Go Gentle into That Good Night" is built on a medieval French form called the **villanelle**: this nineteen-line form requires five tercets and one quatrain, contains only two rhymes, and uses two refrains that must appear in a specified order.

Line length, rhythm, rhyme, and stanzaic form contribute to the development of thought and feeling. Whether the work is in free verse or follows a restrictive form like that of the villanelle, these elements emphasize certain words and create links between words and groups of lines. Readers who note these emphases are not only better able to appreciate the craft of the poet, but they are better able to understand the textures of a poem's ideas and to feel its emotional shadings.

SOUND AND SOUND DEVICES

The rhythmic flow of a line of poetry is not entirely a matter of rhythm patterns, caesurae, and run-on lines; the choice of words, their very sounds, can make a line flow more swiftly or slowly. In "An Essay on Criticism," a work not included in this anthology, Alexander Pope argued that "the sound must seem an echo to the sense," and illustrated how word choice and placement can make a strict iambic rhythm seem ponderously slow or light and quick:

When Ajax strives some rock's vast weight to throw,
The line too labors, and the words move slow;
Not so, when swift Camilla scours the plain,
Flies o'er th' unbending corn and skims along the main.

In the first of these lines, Pope slows the reading of the line by using a number of monosyllabic words and cacophony, harsh or unpleasant-sounding language, produced here by a sequence of consonants that are relatively difficult to pronounce together. In the third and fourth lines, he quickens the pace with a careful placement of polysyllabic words and the use of euphony, or pleasant-sounding language with pleasing combinations of vowels and consonants.

Several other sound devices affect a poem's pace and meaning; sometimes these are instrumental in conveying the tone, which is the speaker's attitude toward the subject and the audience (both the audience implied by the context, as in a dramatic monologue, and the audience actually reading or listening to the poem). One of the most notable of these is **alliteration**, the repetition of initial consonants. In Donne's Holy Sonnet XIV, for example, the *b* sound is repeated when the speaker pleads that God "bend / Your force, to break, blow, burn, and make me new." Alliteration tends to emphasize words, giving them extra force and linking them as a unit. Here, the *b* sound emphasizes the violence of the action Donne requests of God and suggests that it will require all of God's force to save the speaker. Alliteration, therefore, suggests both the difficulty of the task and the intensity of the speaker's desire for renewal. It can, of course, be used for gentler effects, as in Christina Rossetti's "Song": "When I am dead, my dearest, / Sing no sad songs for me." In this case, the heaviness of the *d* sounds in the first line suggests the sadness normally associated with death, but the softness of the *s* sounds in the second line lightens the mood to indicate the speaker's contrary feeling. Furthermore, the alliteration surrounds the word *no*, a word that in scansion receives an accent, or heavy beat, creating a contrast that emphasizes the word and its idea even more.

Repetition of sound is also central to assonance and consonance. **Assonance** is the repetition of vowel sounds, as in the *i* sound of "swift Camilla" and "skims" in Pope's lines quoted above. **Consonance** is the repetition of consonant sounds within or at the end of words, as with the repeated *l* sounds in the last line of Archibald Lampman's "Winter Evening": "Glittering and still shall come the awful night."

One other important device is **onomatopoeia**, or imitative harmony, in which a word imitates or echoes a sound, as in "clip clop" to suggest the movement of horses, or as in the word *break* in Donne's alliterative "break, blow, bend" quoted above, or as in this famous example from a long poem that does not appear in this anthology, Tennyson's *The Princess* (1847): "The moan of doves in immemorial elms, / And murmuring of innumerable bees." Here *moan* and *murmur* imitate natural sounds, and alliteration of the *m* heightens and extends the effect throughout both lines.

Although it has been necessary to examine them separately, sound devices most frequently work together. In the final line of Shakespeare's Sonnet 73, "To love that well which thou must leave ere long," alliteration links *love*, *leave*, and *long*, emphasizing these three important words. Moreover, the two major terms, *love* and *leave*, are further linked and intensified by internal slant rhyme. Finally, consonance links *love* and *well*, uniting these words into a single concept. Readers who notice such uses of sound gain a greater appreciation of the resources and technical demands of the craft of poetry, but they also gain something personally enriching. Sensitivity to sound enables readers to respond more fully to the nuances of language and, thus, to be more open to both emotional stimulation and intellectual meaning in their reading.

POETRY AND PLEASURE

The preceding sections have explored only the major technical elements that make poetry such a complex literary form. Poems can use these techniques in inexhaustible combinations. Poems, however, are much more than compilations of techniques, and reading poetry is more than cataloguing techniques. Poems express the deepest feelings, the most moving thoughts, the heartiest laughter, the most scathing denunciations that people throughout the ages have felt. Poems are expressions of unique personalities and bear the marks of originating in particular social, cultural, and historical contexts, but poems are open to all readers who take the time to open themselves to them, who listen to the rhythms and the sounds, who imaginatively perceive the imagery. The more readers discover about a poem, its context, and literature and poetry in general, the more they can extend their appreciation and enjoyment of poetry. The key to such appreciation and enjoyment, however, is to forget that a poem is a work of "serious literature" that must be studied. Readers need to approach the poem in the same way they approach music, plays, short stories, and novels; they should, that is, be willing to be entertained, be open to new sensations and ideas, be ready to be teased and puzzled, be eager to enter into the imaginative life of the poem. This willingness allows readers to experience an array of emotions and ideas they may not otherwise have. Reading poetry in this way can thus become an act of self-revelation that makes readers more deeply aware of their own humanity. Such reading does not, however, lock us into ourselves. Because poetry originates in another's mind and voice and because it touches on nearly universal experiences and feelings, such reading can connect us to other human beings. It can also make the moments of reading moments of pleasure. That, in itself, is a worthwhile reason for reading poetry.

Anonymous Medieval Lyrics and Ballads

Medieval lyrics and ballads may be remnants of the popular entertainment of the twelfth to fifteenth centuries. In the case of the lyrics, it is unlikely that the polished poems recorded in manuscripts are unaltered compositions of the common people. Their history is not clear, but lyrics probably began among the common people as songs. The conventions of this folk poetry probably influenced the art of the minstrels and educated poets, whose compositions have been preserved. In any case, from its beginnings as oral poetry to its later manifestation as written compositions, the medieval lyric remained relatively unaltered in form and content. Its very conventionality in constantly returning to such themes as the joy of spring, the sorrow of lost love, the inevitability of death, and the sacrifice of Christ suggests that these lyrics represent direct expression of ideas that the medieval world considered to be of compelling universal importance.

Many ballads also originated in the medieval period, but they were not recorded until the eighteenth century, being preserved for centuries almost entirely through oral performances. Unlike the lyrics, which express feelings, these anonymous songs concentrate on events. Ballads are not, however, fully developed narratives. Usually, that is, they focus on a climactic episode, often involving murder, tragic death, or supernatural phenomena. Events leading to the climax typically function as a series of condensed scenes, and the events that link them are omitted or swiftly passed over. The narrator seldom offers interpretations or judgements, allowing the story to advance through a spare recitation of events and a heavy reliance on dialogue. Because they are set to music, ballads have a simple stanzaic structure and rhythm: they usually consist of quatrains in which each line has four stresses or in which lines of four stresses and three stresses alternate. They also commonly employ refrains, or repeated phrases, some of which contain nonsense phrases. As a kind of common man's romance, ballads offer evidence of the intense passions, the fears, and the heroism that have entertained and inspired people for hundreds of years and that continue to do so in some contemporary songs.

Anonymous Lyrics

Western Wind

Western wind, when will thou blow,
    The small rain down can rain?
Christ, if my love were in my arms
    And I in my bed again!

Sumer is icumen in (The Cuckoo Song)

Sumer is icumen in,
    Lhude[1] sing cuccu;
Groweth sed and bloweth[2] med[3]
    And springth the wode[4] nu.[5]
5   Sing cuccu!
Awe[6] bleteth after lamb,
    Lhouth[7] after calve cu[8]
Bulluc sterteth,[9] bucke verteth[10]
    Murie[11] sing cuccu.
10   Cuccu, Cuccu,
    Wel singes thu, cuccu,
    Ne swik[12] thu[13] never nu.

Sing cuccu nu! Sing cuccu!
Sing cuccu! Sing cuccu nu!

I sing of a maiden

I sing of a maiden
    That is makeles,[1]
King of all kinges
    To[2] her sone sche ches.[3]
5 He cam also stille[4]
    There[5] his moder was
As dew in Aprille
    That falleth on the grass.
He cam also stille
10   To his moderes bour,[6]
As dew in Aprille
    That falleth on the flour.
He cam also stille
    There his moder lay,
15 As dew in Aprille
    That falleth on the spray.
Moder and maiden
    Was never non but sche

→

[1]loud. [2]blows, or blooms, into flower. [3]meadow. [4]wood. [5]now. [6]ewe. [7]loweth. [8]cow. [9]the bullock starts, or leaps. [10]farteth; eating fresh green grass causes flatulence. [11]merry, merrily. [12]nor cease. [13]thou. [1]both matchless (incomparable) and mateless. [2]as, for. [3]chose. [4]as quietly or gently. [5]where. [6]bower; boudoir.

Well may swich a lady
20   Godes[7] moder be.

Adam Lay Y-bounden

Adam lay y-bounden,
        Bounden in a bond;
Four thousand winter
        Thought he not to[1] long;
5   And al was for an appel,
        An appel that he took,
As clerkės[2] finden writen
        In herė[3] book.
Ne hedde the appel takė been,[4]
10   The appel takė been,
Ne heddė never our Lady
        A been hevene-queen.[5]
Blessėd be the time
        That appel takė was!
15   Therefore we moun singen
        'Deo Gracias!'[6]

Anonymous Popular Ballads

Sir Patrick Spens

The king sits in Dumferling toune,[1]
        Drinking the blude-reid wine:[2]
"O whar will I get guid sailor,
        To sail this schip of mine?"

5   Up and spak an eldern knicht,
        Sat at the kings richt kne:
"Sir Patrick Spens is the best sailor
        That sails upon the se."

[7]God's. [1]too. [2]scholars, learned men. [3]their. [4]had not the apple been taken. [5]our Lady would never have been heaven's queen. [6]Thanks be to God. [1]Dunfermline, in eastern Scotland, was a favourite residence of Scottish king. [2]blood-red.

The king has written a braid[3] letter,
 And signed it wi' his hand,
And sent it to Sir Patrick Spens,
 Was walking on the sand.

The first line that Sir Patrick red,
 A loud lauch[4] lauched he;
The next line that Sir Patrick red,
 The teir blinded his ee.[5]

"O wha is this has don this deid,
 This ill deid don to me,
To send me out this time o'the yeir,
 To sail upon the se?"

"Mak haste, mak haste, my mirry men all,
 Our guid schip sails the morne."
"O say na sae,[6] my master deir,
 For I feir a deadlie storme."

"Late late yestreen I saw the new moone
 Wi' the auld moone in her arme;
And I feir, I feir, my deir master,
 That we will come to harme."

O our Scots nobles were richt laith[7]
 To weet[8] their cork-heild schoone;[9]
Bot lang owre[10] a' the play were played,
 Their hats they swam aboone.[11]

O lang, lang may their ladies sit
 Wi' their fans into their hand,
Or eir they see Sir Patrick Spens
 Come sailing to the land.

O lang, lang may the ladies stand
 Wi' their gold kerns[12] in their hair,
Waiting for their ain[13] deir lords,
 For they'll see thame na mair.[14]

Haf owre, haf owre[15] to Aberdour,[16]
 It's fiftie fadom[17] deip:
And there lies guid Sir Patrick Spens
 Wi' the Scots lords at his feit.

---

[3]broad. [4]laugh. [5]eye. [6]not so. [7]loath. [8]wet. [9]cork-heeled shoes. [10]ere; before. [11]above. [12]combs. [13]own. [14]no more. [15]half(way) over. [16]Aberdeen. [17]fathoms.

Bonny Barbara Allan

It was in and about the Martinmas time,[1]
 When the green leaves were a falling,
That Sir John Graeme, in the West Country,
 Fell in love with Barbara Allan.

5 He sent his men down through the town
 To the place where she was dwelling:
"O haste and come to my master dear,
 Gin ye be Barbara Allan."

O hooly,[2] hooly rose she up,
10 To the place where he was lying,
And when she drew the curtain by,
 "Young man, I think you're dying."

"O it's I'm sick, and very, very sick,
 And't is a' for Barbara Allan."
15 "O the better for me ye's[3] never be,
 Tho your heart's blood were a spilling."

"O dinna, ye mind, young man," said she,
 "When ye was in the tavern a drinking,
That ye made the healths gae round and round,
20 And slighted Barbara Allan?"

He turned his face unto the wall,
 And death was with him dealing:
"Adieu, adieu, my dear friends all,
 And be kind to Barbara Allan."

25 And slowly, slowly raise she up,
 And slowly, slowly left him,
And sighing said, she could not stay,
 Since death of life had reft[4] him.

She had not gane a mile but twa,
30 When she heard the dead-bell ringing,
And every jow[5] that the dead-bell geid,[6]
 It cried, Woe to Barbara Allan!

"O mother, mother, make my bed!

➜

[1]November 11, the feast day if Saint Martin of Tours. [2]cautiously, slowly. [3]ye shall. [4]torn from; robbed. [5]ring or toll. [6]gave or made.

O make it saft and narrow!
Since my love died for me to-day,
I'll die for him to-morrow."

35

The Renaissance Sonnet

The sonnet originated in thirteenth-century Italy, but the sonnet sequences of Dante (1265–1321) and Petrarch (1304–1374) made the form popular throughout Europe during the fifteenth and sixteenth centuries. In every country, the topics and attitudes of the sonnet were quite conventional. The Platonic love themes developed by the Italian masters created a pattern of contemplation, love, and rejection: the Lover begs acceptance of the Lady through various metaphors of agony, disenchantment, and bliss; she, with studied disregard, rebuffs or ignores his advances; such rejection only intensifies his next attempt. Even when it did not speak of unrequited love, however, the sonnet was frequently artificial in its expression. This artificiality is evident in Henry Constable's "My lady's presence makes the roses red," a conventional celebration of the beloved, and in the biting satire of common formulaic comparisons in Sonnet 130 ("My mistress' eyes are nothing like the sun"), which is among the sonnets included in the author entry for William Shakespeare. The seven poems in this section represent various approaches to the love sonnet that dominated the Renaissance. For a sonnet that presents Petrarchan conventions from a woman's viewpoint, see the author entry for Lady Mary Wroth. For Renaissance sonnets on other topics, see the author entries for John Donne and John Milton.

Although the sonnet is rigid in length, it can be remarkably varied in structure and rhyme. Sir Thomas Wyatt, who introduced the sonnet to England through free English translations of Petrarch, preserved the rhyming of the Italian octave (*abba abba*), but he concluded the sestet with the couplet, a device that became characteristic of the English sonnet. His contemporary, Henry Howard, Earl of Surrey, established the division into three quatrains and a couplet (*abab cdcd efef gg*). This structural change altered the Italian conception of the sonnet as a poem divided into two parts: an eight-line exposition of the problem or an observation and a six-line statement of conclusion or resolution. The English sonnet allows greater repetition and development of the problem while forcing a concentrated resolution in the epigrammatic couplet. Furthermore, because English is harder to rhyme than Italian, this structure gave greater freedom by permitting seven instead of the conventional five rhymes. Note, however, that variations in the three-quatrain scheme are possible: Surrey's "Love that doth reign," for example, contains only six rhymes. Edmund Spenser made a further adaptation, linking quatrains through the couplet created when one quatrain begins with the rhyme with which the previous one ends (*abab bcbc cdcd ee*). Sir Philip Sidney, although he usually followed Wyatt in using the Italian pattern in his octaves and a closing couplet in his sestet, also experimented with alternating rhyme in "Loving in truth" (*abab abab cdcd ee*). The last great poet of the Renaissance, John Milton, followed the true

Italian pattern *(abba abba cdecde)*, but he intensified the unity of his sonnets by having the octave run into the sestet. After Milton's death, the sonnet lost favour, but it was revived as a powerful lyrical force by the Romantics, notably Wordsworth and Keats (see their author entries). See also the author entries for Charles G. D. Roberts, e. e. cummings, Edna St. Vincent Millay, and George Elliott Clarke.

Sir Thomas Wyatt   (1503–1542)

My galley charged with forgetfulness

The lover compareth his state to a ship in perilous storm tossed on the sea.

My galley charged with forgetfulness,
Through sharp seas, in winter nights, doth pass
'Tween rock and rock; and eke[1] my foe, alas,
That is my lord,[2] steereth with cruelness:
5 And every hour, a thought in readiness,
As though that death were light in such a case.
An endless wind doth tear the sail apace
Of forced sighs and trusty fearfulness;
A rain of tears, a cloud of dark disdain,
10 Have done the wearied cords great hinderance:
Wreathed with error, and with ignorance;
The stars[3] be hid that lead me to this pain;
        Drown'd is reason that should be my comfort,
        And I remain, despairing of the port.

(1520–30?)   (1557)

Henry Howard, Earl of Surrey   (1517–1547)

Love that doth reign

Love that doth reign and live within my thought,
And built his seat within my captive breast,

→

[1] also. [2] i.e., Cupid. [3] i.e., the lady's eyes.

Clad in the arms wherein with me he fought,
Oft in my face he doth his banner rest.
5 But she that taught me love and suffer pain,
My doubtful hope and eke[1] my hot desire
With shamefast[2] look to shadow and refrain,
Her smiling grace converteth straight to ire.
And coward love then to the heart apace
10 Taketh his flight, where he doth lurk and plain[3]
His purpose lost, and dare not show his face.
For my lord's guilt thus faultless bide I pain;
Yet from my lord shall not my foot remove.
Sweet is the death that taketh end by love.

(1542?)   (1557)

Edmund Spenser (1552–1599)

One day I wrote her name upon the strand

One day I wrote her name upon the strand;[1]
But came the waves, and washed it away:
Agayne, I wrote it with a second hand;
But came the tyde, and made my paynes his pray.
5 Vayne man, sayd she, that doest in vaine assay
A mortall thing so to immortalize;
For I my selve shall lyke to this decay,
And eke[2] my name bee wyped out lykewize.
Not so, quod I; let baser things devize
10 To dy in dust, but you shall live by fame:
My verse your vertues rare shall eternize,
And in the hevens wryte your glorious name.
    Where, when as death shall all the world subdew,
    Our love shall live, and later life renew.

(1595)

[1]also. [2]shamefaced. [3]complain. [1]beach. [2]also.

Sir Philip Sidney   (1554–1586)

Who will in fairest book of nature know

Who will in fairest book of nature know,
How virtue may best lodged in beauty be,
Let him but learn of love to read in thee
Stella, those fair lines which true Beauty show.
5 There shall he find all vices' overthrow;
Not by rude force, but sweetest sovereignty
Of reason, from whose light, the night birds fly;
That inward sun in thine eyes shineth so.
And not content to be perfection's heir
10 Thyself, dust strive all minds that way to move,
Who mark in thee what is in thee most fair.
So while thy beauty drives my heart to love,
As fast thy virtue bends that love to good:
"But ah," desire still cries, "give me some food."

(1581–83?)   (1591)

Henry Constable   (1562–1613)

My lady's presence makes the roses red

My lady's presence makes the roses red
Because to see her lips they blush for shame.
The lilies' leaves for envy pale became,
And her white hands in them this envy bred.
5 The marigold the leaves abroad doth spread
Because the sun's and her power is the same:
The violet of purple colour came,
Dyed in the blood she made my heart to shed.
In brief, all flowers from her their virtue take;
10 From her sweet breath their sweet smell do proceed;
The living heat which her eyebeams doth make
Warmeth the ground and quickeneth the seed.

The rain wherewith she watereth the flowers
Falls from mine eyes which she dissolves in showers.

(1594)

Michael Drayton   (1563–1631)

Since there's no help, come let us kiss and part

Since there's no help, come let us kiss and part,
Nay, I have done: you get no more of me,
And I am glad, yea glad with all my heart,
That thus so cleanly I myself can free;
5 Shake hands forever, cancel all our vows,
And when we meet at any time again,
Be it not seen in either of our brows
That we one jot of former love retain.
Now at the last gasp of love's latest breath,
10 When his pulse failing, passion speechless lies,
When faith is kneeling by his bed of death,

And innocence is closing up his eyes,
    Now if thou would'st, when all have given him over,
    From death to life, thou might'st him yet recover.

(1619)

Thomas Carew   (c. 1595–c. 1640)

Mediocrity in Love Rejected

Give me more love, or more disdain;
    The torrid or the frozen zone
Bring equal ease unto my pain,
    The temperate affords me none:
5 Either extreme, of love or hate,
Is sweeter than a calm estate.

Give me a storm: it if he love,
    Like Danæ in that golden shower,[1]
I swim in pleasure; if it prove
10   Disdain, that torrent will devour
My vulture hopes; and he's possessed
Of heaven, that's but from hell released.
    Then crown my joys, or cure my pain:
    Give me more love, or more disdain.

(1640)

Sir Walter Ralegh   (c. 1552–1618)

Ralegh is perhaps best known for his colonization of Virginia and for popularizing the use of tobacco in England. He was also friend and patron to Edmund Spenser. Notoriously proud, ambitious, and ostentatious, he commanded extremes of loyalty and hatred through the power of his public personality. Though he was a favourite of Queen Elizabeth in the 1580s, Ralegh spent most of the final fifteen years of his life imprisoned in the Tower by James I. While in the Tower, Ralegh wrote the bulk of his voluminous *History of the World.* But he was a poet as well as a man of action and confirmed sceptic. His is a hard-minded poetic vision that rejects easy idealizations. Released from prison in 1616 to lead the ill-fated Guiana expedition in search of gold for the English treasury, Ralegh was tried on charges of reopening hostilities with Spain and beheaded.

The Nymph's Reply[1]

If all the world and love were young,
And truth in every shepherd's tongue,

[1]Danae, whom her father had imprisoned in a bronze house, gave birth to the hero Perseus after her union with Zeus, who appeared to her in a shower of gold. [1]reply to Christopher Marlowe's "The Passionate Shepherd to His Love" (see page 35)

These pretty pleasures might me move
To live with thee and be thy love.

5 But time drives flocks from field to fold,
When rivers rage and rocks grow cold;
And Philomel[2] becometh dumb;
The rest complains of cares to come.

The flowers do fade, and wanton fields
10 To wayward winter reckoning yields:
A honey tongue, a heart of gall,
Is fancy's spring, but sorrow's fall.

Thy gowns, thy shoes, thy beds of roses,
Thy cap, thy kirtle, and thy posies,
15 Soon break, soon wither, soon forgotten,—
In folly ripe, in reason rotten.

Thy belt of straw and ivy buds,
Thy coral clasps and amber studs,—
All those in me no means can move
20 To come to thee and be thy love.

But could youth last, and love still breed;
Had joys no date, nor age no need;
Then those delights my mind might move
To live with thee and be thy love.

(1600)

Christopher Marlowe   (1564–1593)

The son of a Canterbury shoemaker, Christopher Marlowe received the M.A. degree from Cambridge in 1587. He gained prominence that same year with *Tamburlaine*, which introduced his "mighty line," the blank verse metre that became the poetic medium of Shakespearean and Renaissance drama. Although he was best known as a dramatic poet, Marlowe demonstrated technical virtuosity in his translation of such classics as Ovid's *Amores* and the first book of Lucan's *Pharsalia*. His unfinished erotic narrative, *Hero and Leander*, demonstrates an ability to produce irony in smooth-flowing couplets. Although his short poem "The Passionate Shepherd to His Love" is not entirely representative of his poetry, it has long been celebrated as an example of pastoral verse, and it has been permanently linked to Sir Walter Ralegh's sceptical "answer."

[2]nightingale (mythological).

The Passionate Shepherd to His Love

Come live with me, and be my love;
And we will all the pleasures prove[1]
That hills and valleys, dales and fields,
Woods, or steepy mountain yields.

5 And we will sit upon the rocks,
Seeing the shepherds feed their flocks
By shallow rivers, to whose falls
Melodious birds sing madrigals.

And I will make thee beds of roses,
10 And a thousand fragrant posies;
A cap of flowers, and a kirtle[2]
Embroidered all with leaves of myrtle;

A gown made of the finest wool
Which from our pretty lambs we pull;
15 Fair-lined slippers for the cold,
With buckles of the purest gold;

A belt of straw and ivy-buds,
With coral clasps and amber-studs:
And if these pleasures may thee move,
20 Come live with me, and be my love.

The shepherd-swains shall dance and sing
For thy delight each May-morning;
If these delights thy mind may move,
Then live with me, and be my love.

(1599)

William Shakespeare (1564–1616)

Shakespeare was born in Stratford-upon-Avon, probably a day or two previous to his christening on April 26, 1564. It is traditional that his birthday be celebrated on April 23, which is the feast day of St. George, England's patron saint. Much of Shakespeare's adult life was spent in London as an actor and playwright with the Globe Theatre.

[1]try. [2]a skirt or loose gown.

Although celebrated as the foremost dramatist in the language, Shakespeare is also a sonneteer. His 154 sonnets were published in 1609 but were noted previously by Francis Meres, who in 1598 made mention of Shakespeare's "sugared sonnets among his private friends." The sonnets, however, are far from sugary. They are profound moral and aesthetic contemplations that adapt metaphors from the theatrical world and from the world of human emotions. Investigators have been fascinated by the biographical possibilities of Shakespeare's sonnets, but they are primarily metaphorical contemplations that probe the complexities of love, death, fame, and mutability.

Sonnets

18

Shall I compare thee to a summer's day?
Thou art more lovely and more temperate:
Rough winds do shake the darling buds of May,
And summer's lease hath all too short a date:
5 Sometime too hot the eye of heaven shines,
And often is his gold complexion dimm'd;
And every fair from fair sometime declines
By chance or nature's changing course untrimm'd;
But thy eternal summer shall not fade
10 Nor lose possession of that fair thou ow'st;[1]
Nor shall Death brag thou wander'st in his shade,
When in eternal lines to time thou grow'st:
    So long as men can breathe or eyes can see,
    So long lives this and this gives life to thee.

(1609)

55

Not marble, nor the gilded monuments
Of princes, shall outlive this powerful rime;
But you shall shine more bright in these contents
Than unswept stone besmear'd with sluttish time.
5 When wasteful war shall statues overturn,
And broils root out the work of masonry,
Nor Mars his sword nor war's quick fire shall burn
The living record of your memory.
'Gainst death and all-oblivious enmity

➡

[1]ownest.

10 Shall you pace forth: your praise shall still find room
Even in the eyes of all posterity
That wear this world out to the ending doom.
  So, till the judgement that yourself arise,[1]
  You live in this, and dwell in lovers' eyes.

(1609)

73

That time of year thou mays in me behold
When yellow leaves, or none, or few, do hang
Upon those boughs which shake agains the cold,
Bare ruin'd choirs where late the sweet birds sang,
5 In me thou see'st the twilght of such day
As after sunset fadeth in the west;
Which by and by black night doth take away,
Death's second self, that seals up all in rest.
In me thou see'st the glowing of such fire
10 That on the ashes of his youth doth lie,
As the death-bed whereon it must expire,
Consumed with that it was nourish'd by.
  This thou perceiv'st, which makes thy love more strong,
  To love that well which thou must leave ere long.

(1609)

116

Let me not to the marriage of true minds
Admit impediments. Love is not love
Which alters when it alteration finds,
Or bends with the remover to remove:
5 O, no! it is an ever-fixed mark,
That looks on tempests and is never shaken;
It is the star to every wandering bark,[1]
Whose worth's unknown, although his height be taken.
Love's not Time's fool,[2] though rosy lips and cheeks
10 Within his bending sickle's compass come;
Love alters not with his brief hours and weeks,
But bears it out even to the edge of doom.
  If this be error and upon me proved,
  I never writ, nor no man ever loved.

(1609)

[1]i.e., "So until you arise from the dead on Judgment Day." [1]sailing ship. [2]i.e., victim.

130

My mistress' eyes are nothing like the sun;
Coral is far more red than her lips' red:
If snow be white, why then her breasts are dun;
If hairs be wires, black wires grow on her head.
5 I have seen roses damask'd,[1] red and white,
But no such roses see I in her cheeks;
And in some perfumes is there more delight
Than in the breath that from my mistress reeks.
I love to hear her speak, yet well I know
10 That music hath a far more pleasing sound:
I grant I never saw a goddess go;
My mistress, when she walks, treads on the ground:
    And yet, by heaven, I think my love as rare
    As any she belied[2] with false compare.

(1609)

Thomas Campion   (1567–1620)

Born in London, Thomas Campion studied law at both Peterhouse College, Cambridge, and Gray's Inn, London, although he never took a degree or received a call to the bar. In 1602, he went to France and enrolled at the University of Caen, graduating with a medical degree in 1605. While maintaining his career as a doctor in London, Campion also wrote masques for the court of James I. He is best known, though, for his lyric poetry. An accomplished lutenist, he was unusual among poets of his day in his ability to compose his own musical settings for his words. He published the first of his songs in *A Book of Airs to be Sung to the Lute, Orpherian and Bass Viol* (1601). Campion also published an important work of music theory, *New Way of Making Four Parts in Counter-point* (c. 1617), and a controversial *Observations on the Art of English Poesy* (1602), in which he advocated the use of Latin quantitative metres and attacked the custom of using rhyme in poetry. (In practice, Campion himself used rhyme.) Because he crafted his words to musical rhythms, rather than to spoken ones, his lyrics are best appreciated in performance as songs. Nevertheless, even without the accompaniment of music, they stand out as among the most elegant, polished, and metrically varied of Renaissance lyrics.

[1]mingled, variegated. [2]misrepresented.

My Sweetest Lesbia[1]

My sweetest Lesbia, let us live and love,
And though the sager sort our deeds reprove,
Let us not weigh them; heaven's great lamps do dive
Into their west, and straight again revive,
5   But soon as once set is our little light,
Then must we sleep one ever-during night.

If all would lead their lives in love like me,
Then bloody swords and armour should not be;
No drum nor trumpet peaceful sleeps should move,
10   Unless alarm came from the camp of love;
But fools do live, and waste their little light,
And seek with pain their ever-during night.

When timely death my life and fortune ends,
Let not my hearse be vext with mourning friends,
15   But let all lovers, rich in triumph, come
And with sweet pastimes grace my happy tomb;
And, Lesbia, close up thou my little light,
And crown with love my ever-during night.

(1601)

John Donne   (1572–1631)

John Donne was a talented young man hopeful of worldly advancement. Appointed private secretary to Sir Thomas Egerton in 1598, Donne ruined hope of further preferment in that household when his secret marriage to Sir Thomas's seventeen-year-old niece became public. But Donne's gifts of learning, intelligence, and social grace would not let him fade away from the public eye. On the encouragement of King James himself, Donne took holy orders and was appointed Dean of St. Paul's Cathedral, London, in 1621.

Next to nothing of Donne's literary output was published during his own lifetime. (The first edition of his collected poems appeared in 1633.) His brilliance as a "metaphysical" poet is a virtual rediscovery by twentieth-century criticism, and he is now recognized as one of the greatest English love poets. Donne's forceful exposition and bold metaphorical style also made him one of the greatest preachers of the seventeenth century, as well as a significant religious poet. He seemed singularly adept at uniting passion and intellect. The two periods of "Jack Donne," lyrical poet, and "Doctor Donne," learned divine, into which Donne himself separated his life might not seem all that irreconcilable in light of the powerful rhetoric and deep meditational technique common to both.

[1]a partial translation and imitation of a lyric by the Roman poet Catullus (c. 84 B.C.–c. 54 B.C.).

Song

Go, and catch a falling star,
　　Get with child a mandrake root,
Tell me where all past years are,
　　Or who cleft the Devil's foot,
5　Teach me to hear Mermaids singing,
Or to keep off envy's stinging,
　　　　And find
　　　　What wind
Serves to advance an honest mind.

10　If thou be'st born to strange sights,
　　Things invisible to see,
Ride ten thousand days and nights,
　　Till age snow white hairs on thee,
Thou, when thou return'st, wilt tell me
15　All strange wonders that befell thee,
　　　　And swear
　　　　No where
Lives a woman true, and fair.

If thou find'st one, let me know,
20　　Such a Pilgrimage were sweet;
Yet do not, I would not go,
　　Though at next door we might meet,
Though she were true, when you met her,
And last, till you write your letter,
25　　　　Yet she
　　　　Will be
False, ere I come, to two, or three.

(1633)

A Valediction: Forbidding Mourning

As virtuous men pass mildly away,
　　And whisper to their souls, to go,
Whilst some of their sad friends do say,
　　The breath goes now, and some say, no:

5　So let us melt, and make no noise,
　　No tear-floods, nor sigh-tempests move,

→

'Twere profanation of our joys
    To tell the laity our love.

Moving of th' earth brings harms and fears,
10   Men reckon what it did and meant,
But trepidation of the spheres,[1]
    Though greater far, is innocent.

Dull sublunary lovers' love
    (Whose soul is sense) cannot admit
15 Absence, because it doth remove
    Those things which elemented it.

But we by a love, so much refin'd,
    That ourselves know not what it is,
Inter-assured of the mind,
20   Care less eyes, lips, and hands to miss.

Our two souls therefore, which are one,
    Though I must go, endure not yet
A breach, but an expansion,
    Like gold to aery thinness beat.

25 If they be two, they are two so
    As stiff twin compasses are two,
Thy soul the fixed foot, makes no show
    To move, but doth, if th' other do.

And though it in the centre sit,
30   Yet when the other far doth roam,
It leans, and hearkens after it,
    And grows erect, as that comes home.

Such wilt thou be to me, who must
    Like th' other foot, obliquely run;
35 Thy firmness draws my circle just,
    And makes me end, where I begun.

                      (1633)

The Canonization

For God's sake hold your tongue, and let me love;
    Or chide my palsy, or my gout,

[1] in pre-Copernican cosmology, the shaking of the nine concentric spheres around the earth.

My five grey hairs, or ruin'd fortune flout;
     With wealth your state, your mind with arts improve,
          Take you a course, get you a place,
          Observe his Honour, or his Grace,
Or the King's real, or his stamped face
     Contemplate; what you will, approve,
     So you will let me love.

Alas, alas, who's injur'd by my love?
     What merchant's ships have my sighs drown'd?
Who says my tears have overflow'd his ground?
     When did my colds a forward spring remove?
          When did the heats which my veins fill
          Add one more to the plaguy bill?[1]
Soldiers find wars, and lawyers find out still
     Litigious men, which quarrels move,
     Though she and I do love.

Call us what you will, we are made such by love;
     Call her one, me another fly,
We're tapers too, and at our own cost die,
     And we in us find the Eagle and the Dove.
          The Phœnix riddle hath more wit
          By us; we two being one, are it.
So to one neutral thing both sexes fit,
     We die and rise the same, and prove
     Mysterious by this love.

We can die by it, if not live by love,
     And if unfit for tombs and hearse
Our legend be, it will be fit for verse;
     And if no piece of Chronicle we prove,
          We'll build in sonnets pretty rooms;
          As well a well-wrought urn becomes
The greatest ashes, as half-acre tombs,
     And by these hymns, all shall approve
     Us canonized for Love:

And thus invoke us; You whom reverend love
     Made one another's hermitage;
You, to whom love was peace, that now is rage;

---

[1] i.e., add one more name to the weekly list (bill) of plague victims.

40   Who did the whole world's soul contract, and drove
                Into the glasses of your eyes
                (So made such mirrors, and such spies,
        That they did all to you epitomize,)
                Countries, Towns, Courts: beg from above
45   A pattern of your love!

(1633)

The Flea

Mark but this flea, and mark in this,
How little that which thou deny'st me is;
It suck'd me first, and now sucks thee,
And in this flea, our two bloods mingled be;
5   Thou know'st that this cannot be said
A sin, nor shame, nor loss of maidenhead,
        Yet this enjoys before it woo,
        And pamper'd swells with one blood made of two,
        And this, alas, is more than we would do.

10   Oh stay, three lives in one flea spare,
Where we almost, yea more than married are.
This flea is you and I, and this
Our marriage bed, and marriage temple is;
Though parents grudge, and you, we're met,
15   And cloistered in these living walls of jet.
        Though use make you apt to kill me,
        Let not to that, self murder added be,
        And sacrilege, three sins in killing three.

Cruel and sudden, hast thou since
20   Purpled thy nail, in blood of innocence?
Wherein could this flea guilty be,
Except in that drop which it suck'd from thee?
Yet thou triumph'st, and say'st that thou
Find'st not thyself, nor me, the weaker now;
25   'Tis true, then learn how false, fears be;
        Just so much honour, when thou yield'st to me,
        Will waste, as this flea's death took life from thee.

(1633)

Holy Sonnet X

Death be not proud, though some have called thee
Mighty and dreadful, for, thou art not so,
For, those, whom thou think'st, thou dost overthrow,
Die not, poor death, nor yet canst thou kill me.
From rest and sleep, which but thy pictures be,
Much pleasure, then from thee, much more must flow,
And soonest our best men with thee do go,
Rest of their bones, and soul's delivery.
Thou art slave to Fate, Chance, kings, and desperate men,
And dost with poison, war, and sickness dwell,
And poppy, or charms can make us sleep as well,
And better than thy stroke; why swell'st thou then?
One short sleep past, we wake eternally,
And death shall be no more; death, thou shalt die.

(1633)

Holy Sonnet XIV

Batter my heart, three-person'd God; for you
As yet but knock, breathe, shine, and seek to mend;
That I may rise, and stand, o'erthrow me, and bend
Your force, to break, blow, burn, and make me new.
I, like an usurp'd town, to another due,
Labour to admit you, but Oh, to no end,
Reason your viceroy in me, me should defend,
But is captiv'd, and proves weak or untrue.
Yet dearly I love you, and would be loved fain,
But am betroth'd unto your enemy:
Divorce me, untie, or break that knot again,
Take me to you, imprison me, for I
Except you enthral me, never shall be free,
Nor ever chaste, except you ravish me.

(1633)

Elegy XIX To His Mistress Going to Bed

Come, Madam, come, all rest my powers defy,
Until I labour, I in labour lie.

→

The foe oft-times having the foe in sight,
Is tired with standing though he never fight.
5   Off with that girdle, like heaven's Zone glistering,
But a far fairer world encompassing.
Unpin that spangled breastplate which you wear,
That th' eyes of busy fools may be stopt there.
Unlace yourself, for that harmonious chime
10   Tells me from you, that now it is bed time.
Off with that happy busk, which I envy,
That still can be, and still can stand so nigh.
Your gown going off, such beauteous state reveals,
As when from flowry meads th' hill's shadow steals.
15   Off with that wiry Coronet and show
The hairy Diadem which on you doth grow:
Now off with those shoes, and then safely tread
In this love's hallow'd temple, this soft bed.
In such white robes, heaven's Angels used to be
20   Receiv'd by men; thou Angel bring'st with thee
A heaven like Mahomet's Paradise;[1] and though
Ill spirits walk in white, we easily know,
By this these Angels from an evil sprite,
Those set our hairs, but these our flesh upright.
25   Licence my roving hands, and let them go,
Before, behind, between, above, below.
O my America! my new-found-land,
My kingdom, safeliest when with one man mann'd,
My Mine of precious stones, My Empery,
30   How blest am I in this discovering thee!
To enter in these bonds, is to be free;
Then where my hand is set, my seal shall be.
        Full nakedness! All joys are due to thee,
As souls unbodied, bodies uncloth'd must be,
35   To taste whole joys. Gems which you women use
Are like Atalanta's balls,[2] cast in men's views,
That when a fool's eye lighteth on a Gem,
His earthly soul may covet theirs, not them.

[1] i.e., the paradise of the Prophet Muhammad, where *houris*, beautiful women, attend faithful Muslim men. [2] Donne here reverses the story of Atalanta, who agreed to marry Hippomenes if he could defeat her in a foot race. During the race, whenever Hippomenes saw Atalanta closing the distance between them, he threw down a golden apple. Distracted, Atalanta repeatedly stopped to pick up the apples and lost the race.

Like pictures, or like books' gay coverings made
40 For lay-men, are all women thus array'd;
Themselves are mystic books, which only we
(Whom their imputed grace will dignify)
Must see reveal'd. Then, since that I may know,
As liberally, as to a Midwife, show
45 Thyself: cast all, yea, this white linen hence,
There is no penance due to innocence.
　　　To teach thee, I am naked first; why then
What needst thou have more covering than a man?

(1669)

Ben Jonson　(1572–1637)

Scholar, poet, playwright, classicist, and controversialist—Jonson's career consolidates the emergence of professional letters in the English Renaissance. He was the first English poet to publish his own works, in 1616, and his first play, *Every Man in His Humour* (1598), included actor William Shakespeare in the cast. Master of the English plain style, Jonson, whose output was voluminous and various, held pride of place at the Mermaid Tavern, where he presided over a club of aspiring poets known as the "sons of Ben."

　　　Jonson was also a man of action who, while a soldier in Flanders, killed an enemy champion in hand-to-hand combat—a biographical fact that he gloried in relating to his host, William Drummond of Hawthornden. Argumentative, satirical, and pugnacious, Jonson was a professional writer who took his business seriously enough to insist on its critical appreciation in both the public playhouse and the private masquing house where he also triumphed as author. With stage architect Inigo Jones (a detested rival), Jonson prepared many lavish ceremonial masques for the court of James I, and he was still a significant cultural spokesperson in the reign of Charles I.

Song: To Celia

Drink to me only with thine eyes,
　　And I will pledge with mine;
Or leave a kiss within the cup,
　　And I'll not look for wine.
5 The thirst that from the soul doth rise,
　　Doth ask a drink divine;

→

But might I of Jove's nectar sup,
    I would not change for thine.

I sent thee late a rosy wreath,
10   Not so much honouring thee,
As giving it a hope that there
    It could not withered be.
But thou thereon didst only breathe,
    And sent'st it back to me;
15 Since when it grows, and smells, I swear,
    Not of itself, but thee.

                                      (1616)

On My First Son

Farewell, thou child of my right hand, and joy;
My sin was too much hope of thee, lov'd boy:
Seven years thou wert lent to me, and I thee pay,
Exacted by thy fate, on the just day.
5 O, could I lose all father,[1] now! for why,
Will man lament the state he should envy?
To have so soon scaped world's, and flesh's rage,
And, if no other misery, yet age!
Rest in soft peace, and ask'd, say here doth lie
10 BEN JONSON his hest piece of poetry:
For whose sake henceforth all his vows be such,
As what he loves may never like too much.

(1603?)   (1616)

Lady Mary Wroth (1587–1653?)

Lady Mary Wroth was the first woman in England to publish a Petrarchan sonnet sequence, *Pamphilia to Amphilanthus*, which was included at the end of her prose romance, *The Countess of Montgomery's Urania* (1621), the earliest original prose work in English credited to a woman. The daughter of Sir Robert Sidney, a courtier and poet, she counted among her relatives Sir Philip Sidney, the Elizabethan soldier and poet, and Mary Sidney, Countess of Pembroke, a celebrated patron and writer. After her arranged marriage in 1604, she became part of the court in London.

[1]i.e., give up all gentle, fatherly thoughts.

Widowed in 1614, she began an affair with her cousin William Herbert, by whom she gave birth to two children. She apparently also began her career as a writer at this point. Her poetry attracted the notice of other writers, notably Ben Jonson, who said that reading her poems had made him "a better lover, and much better Poet." She dropped out of favour, however, because powerful courtiers denounced her *Urania* for fictionalizing their private lives, and because the birth of her illegitimate children eventually created a scandal. Her work subsequently faded into obscurity until it was republished near the end of the twentieth century. Mary Wroth did not follow Jacobean literary trends; she was a traditionalist who echoed the work of Elizabethan writers, especially Sir Philip Sidney. Nevertheless, she did offer an alternative view of love from that presented in the traditional Petrarchan sonnet. By giving voice to the female lover, whom male Petrarchanists characterized as cold and indifferent, she dramatized women as being torn by desire, pain, and confusion.

Song (Love, a child, is ever crying)

Love, a child, is ever crying,
Please him, and he straight is flying;
Give him, he the more is craving,
Never satisfied with having.

5 His desires have no measure,
Endless folly is his treasure;
What he promiseth he breaketh;
Trust not one word that he speaketh.

He vows nothing hut false matter,
10 And to cozen you he'll flatter;
Let him gain the hand,[1] he'll leave you,
And still glory to deceive you.

He will triumph in your wailing,
And yet cause be of your failing:
15 These his virtues are, and slighter
Are his gifts, his favours lighter.

Feathers are as firm in staying,
Wolves no fiercer in their preying.
As a child then leave him crying,
20 Nor seek him, so giv'n to flying.

(1621)

---

[1]gain the upper hand, or control.

In this strange labyrinth how shall I turn?[1]

In this strange labyrinth how shall I turn?
    Ways[2] are on all sides, while the way I miss:
    If to the right hand, there in love I burn;
    Let me go forward, therein danger is;

5   If to the left, suspicion hinders bliss;
    Let me turn back, shame cries I ought return,
    Nor faint,[3] though crosses[4] with my fortunes kiss;
    Stand still is harder, although sure to mourn.

Thus let me take the right, or left-hand way,
10   Go forward, or stand still, or back retire;
    I must these doubts endure without allay
    Or help, but travail[5] find for my best hire.[6]

Yet that which mast my troubled sense doth move
Is to leave all, and take the thread of love.[7]

(1621)

Robert Herrick   (1591–1674)

Herrick was a clergyman from London who found himself at the age of 38 posted to the tiny vicarage of Dean Prior, Devonshire. There he performed the social and religious rituals for a largely illiterate population, all the while recording his own witty poetic observations on his flock. But his observations are never condescending. His rural themes are consistently simple, often playful, but seldom trivial: beauty, love, art, natural splendour, religious devotion. And his speaking voice or persona—somewhat risqué for a bachelor country parson—no doubt occasioned the final couplet in the first part of his collection: "To his book's end this last line he'd have placed: / Jocund his Muse was, but his life was chaste."

[1]the opening poem in a sequence of fourteen called "A Crown of Sonnets Dedicated to Love," included in *Pamphilia to Amphilanthus* (1621). The crown, or *corona* as it is called in Italian, is a formal sequence in which the last line of each poem becomes the first line of the following poem, and the last poem concludes with the first line of the initial poem. [2]paths. [3]lose spirit or courage. [4]troubles, with a possible pun meaning intersections in the labyrinth. [5]effort, toil, or suffering, with a pun on *travel*, the word that replaced the manuscript's *travail* in the 1621 printing. [6]wages or reward. [7]an allusion to the Greek tale of Theseus, to whom Ariadne gave a thread that he could unwind as he entered the labyrinth at Crete; after slaying the Minotaur in the centre of the labyrinth, Theseus was able to find the path out by following this thread.

Expelled from his vicarage in 1647 as a Royalist sympathizer, Herrick went back to London, where he published his verses in a single volume, *Hesperides* (1648), comprising over fourteen hundred sacred and secular lyrics. After the Puritan interregnum, Herrick was reinstated under Charles II and lived out the end of his long life in Dean Prior.

To the Virgins, To Make Much of Time

Gather ye rose-buds while ye may,
    Old time is still a flying,
And this same flower that smiles to-day,
    To-morrow will be dying.

5 The glorious lamp of Heaven, the sun,
    The higher he's a getting,
The sooner will his race be run,
    And neerer he's to setting.

That age is best which is the first,
10   When youth and blood are warmer;
But being spent, the worse, and worst
    Times still succeed the former.

Then be not coy, but use your time,
    And while ye may, go marry;
15 For having lost but once your prime,
    You may for ever tarry.

(1648)

Upon Julia's Clothes

Whenas in silks my Julia goes,
Then, then, me thinks, how sweetly flows
That liquefaction of her clothes.

Next, when I cast mine eyes and see
5 That brave vibration, each way free,
O how that glittering taketh me!

(1648)

George Herbert   (1593–1633)

George Herbert was born into an ancient and respected Welsh family. His brother Edward was the philosopher-statesman Lord Herbert of Cherbury, and another brother, Sir Henry, was Master of the Revels in England, whose job it was to censor and approve public entertainment during the Stuart reign. George was more private, if (it seems) no less ambitious. A scholar and ecclesiastic, he attained the position of Public Orator at Cambridge University but never received the place at court that he must surely have coveted. Instead, in 1629 he accepted a minor church living at Bemerton near Salisbury, where he lived out the rest of his short life in good works, holy contemplation, and poetic composition.

Herbert's poetry is sharply expressed, richly imaginative, and concrete. Here, a poem's shape expresses meaning, souls have voices, love speaks. Consistently devotional, his verse has an artistic originality and cleverness that mark it as among the most exalted of the "metaphysical" mode.

The Altar

A broken ALTAR, Lord, thy servant rears,
Made of a heart, and cemented with tears:
Whose parts are as thy hand did frame;
No workman's tool hath touch'd the same.
A HEART alone
Is such a stone,
As nothing but
Thy power doth cut.
Wherefore each part
Of my hard heart
Meets in this frame,
To praise thy name:
That, if I chance to hold my peace,
These stones to praise thee may not cease.
O let thy blessed Sacrifice be mine,
And sanctify this Altar to be thine.

5
10
15

(1633)

Easter Wings

Lord, who createdst man in wealth and store,[1]
Though foolishly he lost the same,
Decaying more and more,
Till he became
Most poor:

With Thee
O let me rise
As larks, harmoniously,
And sing this day Thy victories:
Then shall the fall further the flight in me.

My tender age in sorrow did begin:
And still with sicknesses and shame
Thou didst so punish sin,
That I became
Most thin.

With Thee
Let me combine,
And feel this day Thy victory,
For, if I imp[2] my wing on Thine,
Affliction shall advance the flight in me.

(1633)

John Milton   (1608–1674)

Milton was born into a middle-class London family. Prodigiously intellectual, he received a thorough education at St. Paul's School, London, and in Christ's College, Cambridge. Later, he travelled on the Continent, where he met the aged and broken Galileo. Milton, too, would later survey the heavens, but as a blind poet with a self-proclaimed mandate to "justify the ways of God to men" (*Paradise Lost* I.26).

Milton was also a public figure who held the position of Latin Secretary to Oliver Cromwell during the Puritan interregnum. His journalism on topical matters such as divorce, church government, and censorship, in addition to diplomatic and political matters, was prolific. He lived out his final days after the restoration of Charles II in humble circumstances. But it was during this time that Milton gained his immortal reputation as a poet. His poetry is celebrated for its profound

---

[1]abundance. [2]to graft a feather on a falcon's wing or tail, either to repair a deficiency or to improve its power of flight.

spiritual and metaphorical sense of inquiry. Considered by many as the highest achievement in English non-dramatic verse, his epic *Paradise Lost* stands as testament to his genius.

Lycidas[1]

In this Monody the Author bewails a learned Friend,[2] unfortunately drowned in his passage from Chester on the Irish Sea, 1637; and, by occasion, foretells the ruin of our corrupted Clergy, then in their height.

Yet once more, O ye laurels, and once more,
Ye myrtles brown, with ivy never sere,[3]
I come to pluck your berries harsh and crude,
And with forced fingers rude
5 Shatter your leaves before the mellowing year.
Bitter constraint and sad occasion dear
Compels me to disturb your season due;
For Lycidas is dead, dead ere his prime,
Young Lycidas, and hath not left his peer.
10 Who would not sing for Lycidas? he knew
Himself to sing, and build the lofty rhyme.
He must not float upon his watery bier
Unwept, and welter to the parching wind,
Without the meed[4] of some melodious tear.
15 Begin, then, Sisters of the sacred well[5]
That from beneath the seat of Jove doth spring;
Begin, and somewhat loudly sweep the string.
Hence with denial vain and coy excuse:
So may some gentle Muse
20 With lucky words favour my destined urn,
And as he passes turn,
And bid fair peace to be my sable shroud!
For we were nursed upon the self-same hill,
Fed the same flock, by fountain, shade, and rill;
25 Together both, ere the high lawns appeared
Under the opening eyelids of the morn,
We drove a-field, and both together heard
What time the grey-fly winds her sultry horn,
Battening our flocks with the fresh dews of night,
30 Oft till the star that rose at evening bright

---

[1]traditional pastoral name for a shepherd. [2]Edward King, a fellow student of Milton's acquaintance at Cambridge. [3]laurels, myrtles, ivy: evergreens associated with poetic inspiration and honour. [4]reward. [5]i.e., the nine sister Muses responsible for the flow of poetic inspiration.

Toward heaven's descent had sloped his westering wheel.
Meanwhile the rural ditties were not mute;
Tempered to the oaten flute,
Rough Satyrs danced, and Fauns with cloven heel
35 From the glad sound would not be absent long;
And old Damœtas[6] loved to hear our song.

But O! the heavy change, now thou art gone,
Now thou art gone and never must return!
Thee, Shepherd, thee the woods and desert caves,
40 With wild thyme and the gadding vine o'ergrown,
And all their echoes, mourn.
The willows, and the hazel copses green,
Shall now no more be seen
Fanning their joyous leaves to thy soft lays.
45 As killing as the canker to the rose,
Or taint-worm to the weanling herds that graze,
Or frost to flowers, that their gay wardrobe wear,
When first the white-thorn blows;
Such, Lycidas, thy loss to shepherd's ear.
50 Where were ye, Nymphs,[7] when the remorseless deep
Closed o'er the head of your loved Lycidas?
For neither were ye playing on the steep
Where your old bards, the famous Druids,[8] lie,
Nor on the shaggy top of Mona high,
55 Nor yet where Deva spreads her wizard stream.[9]
Ay me! I fondly dream
"Had ye been there,"—for what could that have done?
What could the Muse herself that Orpheus[10] bore,
The Muse herself, for her enchanting son,
60 Whom universal nature did lament,
When, by the rout that made the hideous roar,
His gory visage down the stream was sent,
Down the swift Hebrus to the Lesbian shore?[11]

Alas! what boats[12] it with uncessant care
65 To tend the homely, slighted, shepherd's trade,
And strictly meditate the thankless Muse?
Were it not better done, as others use,

[6]traditional pastoral name which perhaps refers to a specific Cambridge don known to both Milton and King. [7]female nature spirits. [8]priestly class in ancient Britain. [9]Mona: isle of Anglesey; Deva: the river Dee in Cheshire that empties into the Irish Sea. [10]archetypal poet born of the muse Calliope. [11]decapitated by angered and overzealous celebrants, Orpheus's head floated down the river Hebrus to the isle of Lesbos. [12]profits.

To sport with Amaryllis in the shade,
Or with the tangles of Neæra's hair?[13]
70 Fame is the spur that the clear spirit doth raise
(That last infirmity of noble mind)
To scorn delights and live laborious days;
But the fair guerdon[14] when we hope to find,
And think to burst out into sudden blaze,
75 Comes the blind Fury with the abhorred shears,[15]
And slits the thin-spun life. "But not the praise,"
Phœbus[16] replied, and touched my trembling ears:
    "Fame is no plant that grows on mortal soil,
Nor in the glistering foil
80 Set off to the world, nor in broad rumour lies
But lives and spreads aloft by those pure eyes
And perfect witness of all-judging Jove;
As he pronounces lastly on each deed,
Of so much fame in heaven expect thy meed."
85   O fountain Arethuse, and thou honoured flood,
Smooth-sliding Mincius, crowned with vocal reeds,[17]
That strain I heard was of a higher mood.
But now my oat[18] proceeds,
And listens to the Herald of the Sea,[19]
90 That came in Neptune's plea.
He asked the waves, and asked the felon winds,
What hard mishap hath doomed this gentle swain?
And questioned every gust of rugged wings
That blows from off each beaked promontory.
95 They knew not of his story;
And sage Hippotades[20] their answer brings,
That not a blast was from his dungeon strayed:
The air was calm, and on the level brine
Sleek Panope[21] with all her sisters played.
100 It was that fatal and perfidious bark,
Built in the eclipse, and rigged with curses dark,
That sunk so low that sacred head of thine.
    Next, Camus,[22] reverend sire, went footing slow,
His mantle hairy, and his bonnet sedge,

➡️

[13]Amaryllis, Neæra: pastoral names for pretty shepherdesses. [14]reward. [15]i.e., Atropos, the Fate who finally cuts off the thread of life. [16]i.e., Phoebus Apollo, god of poetry. [17]Arethuse, a spring; Mincius, a river: Italian locations associated respectively with the great pastoral poets Theocritus and Virgil. [18]i.e., "oaten flute" (line 33). [19]Triton is Neptune's "herald of the sea." [20]god of winds. [21]sea nymph: one of 50 sisters who were daughters of Nereus. [22]god of the river Cam, upon which Cambridge University is situated.

105 Inwrought with figures dim, and on the edge
Like to that sanguine flower inscribed with woe.
    "Ah! who hath reft," quoth he, "my dearest pledge?"
Last came, and last did go,
The Pilot of the Galilean Lake;[23]
110 Two massy keys he bore of metals twain
(The golden opes, the iron shuts amain).
He shook his mitred locks, and stern bespake:—
"How well could I have spared for thee, young swain,
Enow of such as, for their bellies' sake,
115 Creep, and intrude, and climb into the fold!
Of other care they little reckoning make
Than how to scramble at the shearers' feast,
And shove away the worthy bidden guest.
Blind mouths! that scarce themselves know how to hold
120 A sheep-hook, or have learnt aught else the least
That to the faithful herdman's art belongs!
What recks it them? What need they? They are sped;
And, when they list, their lean and flashy songs
Grate on their scrannel[24] pipes of wretched straw;
125 The hungry sheep look up, and are not fed,
But, swoln with wind and the rank mist they draw,
Rot inwardly, and foul contagion spread;
Besides what the grim wolf with privy paw
Daily devours apace, and nothing said.
130 But that two-handed engine at the door
Stands ready to smite once, and smite no more."
    Return, Alpheus;[25] the dread voice is past
That shrunk thy streams; return Sicilian Muse,
And call the vales, and bid them hither cast
135 Their bells and flowerets of a thousand hues.
Ye valleys low, where the mild whispers use
Of shades, and wanton winds, and gushing brooks,
On whose fresh lap the swan star[26] sparely looks,
Throw hither all your quaint enamelled eyes,
140 That on the green turf suck the honeyed showers,
And purple all the ground with vernal flowers.
Bring the rathe[27] primrose that forsaken dies,

---

[23]i.e., St. Peter. [24]thin, meagre. [25]Arcadian river, symbol for gentle pastoral verse. [26]Sirius, the Dog Star of late summer. [27]early.

The tufted crow-toe, and pale jessamine,
The white pink, and the pansy freaked[28] with jet,
145 The glowing violet,
The musk-rose, and the well-attired woodbine,
With cowslips wan that hang the pensive head,
And every flower that sad embroidery wears;
Bid amaranthus[29] all his beauty shed,
150 And daffadillies fill their cups with tears,
To strew the laureate hearse where Lycid lies.
For so, to interpose a little ease,
Let our frail thoughts dally with false surmise,
Ay me! whilst thee the shores and sounding seas
155 Wash far away, where'er thy bones are hurled;
Whether beyond the stormy Hebrides,[30]
Where thou perhaps under the whelming tide
Visit'st the bottom of the monstrous world;
Or whether thou, to our moist vows denied,
160 Sleep'st by the fable of Bellerus[31] old,
Where the great Vision of the guarded mount
Looks toward Namancos and Bayona's hold.[32]
Look homeward, Angel, now, and melt with ruth:
And, O ye dolphins, waft the hapless youth.
165 Weep no more, woeful shepherds, weep no more,
For Lycidas, your sorrow, is not dead,
Sunk though he be beneath the watery floor.
So sinks the day-star[33] in the ocean bed,
And yet anon repairs his drooping head,
170 And tricks his beams, and with new-spangled ore
Flames in the forehead of the morning sky:
So Lycidas sunk low, but mounted high,
Through the dear might of Him that walked the waves,
Where, other groves and other streams along,
175 With nectar pure his oozy locks he laves,
And hears the unexpressive nuptial song,
In the blest kingdoms meek of joy and love.
There entertain him all the Saints above,
In solemn troops, and sweet societies,

---

[28]freckled. [29]imaginary flower that is always in bloom. [30]islands off the coast of Scotland that mark the northern boundary of the Irish Sea. [31]imaginary giant supposed to be buried at Land's End, Cornwall. [32]Namancos, Bayona: locations on the coast of Spain, imagined as visible from St. Michaels Mount, Cornwall. [33]i.e., the sun.

180 That sing, and singing in their glory move,
And wipe the tears for ever from his eyes.
Now, Lycidas, the shepherds weep no more;
Henceforth thou art the Genius[34] of the shore,
In thy large recompense, and shalt be good
185 To all that wander in that perilous flood.

      Thus sang the uncouth swain to the oaks and rills,
While the still morn went out with sandals grey:
He touched the tender stops of various quills,
With eager thought warbling his Doric lay:[35]
190 And now the sun had stretched out all the hills,
And now was dropt into the western bay.
At last he rose, and twitched his mantle blue:
To-morrow to fresh woods, and pastures new.

                                                (1638)

When I consider how my light is spent

When I consider how my light is spent
    Ere half my days in this dark world and wide,
    And that one talent which is death to hide
    Lodged with me useless, though my soul more bent
5 To serve therewith my Maker, and present
    My true account, lest He returning chide,
    "Doth God exact day-labour, light denied?"
    I fondly ask. But Patience, to prevent
That murmur, soon replies, "God doth not need
10   Either man's work or his own gifts. Who best
    Bear his mild yoke, they serve him best. His state
Is kingly: thousands at his bidding speed,
    And post o'er land and ocean without rest;
    They also serve who only stand and wait."

(1652?)   (1673)

On the Late Massacre in Piedmont[1]

Avenge, O Lord, thy slaughtered saints, whose bones
    Lie scattered on the Alpine mountains cold;

---

[34]i.e., protective local deity. [35]i.e., simple song. [1]the Piedmont region of northwestern Italy, bounded by France and Switzerland. On April 24, 1655, Italian troops massacred the Protestant Piedmontese for their dissenting views.

Even them who kept thy truth so pure of old,
When all our fathers worshiped stocks and stones,
5   Forget not: in thy hook record their groans
Who were thy sheep, and in their ancient fold
Slain by the bloody Piemontese, that rolled
Mother with infant down the rocks. Their moans
The vales redoubled to the hills, and they
10   To heaven. Their martyred blood and ashes sow
O'er all the Italian fields, where still doth sway
The triple Tyrant;[2] that from these may grow
A hundredfold, who, having learnt thy way,
Early may fly the Babylonian woe.[3]

(1655)   (1673)

Anne Bradstreet   (c. 1612–1672)

Born in Northampton, England, Anne Bradstreet, unlike most young women of her day, read widely in classical and English poetry. When she was eighteen years old, she came to Massachusetts with her family and husband. While taking care of the family's frequent moves and raising eight children, she wrote a great deal of poetry and later gained recognition as one of the first important American poets. Although she wrote many long, complex works on theological subjects, she is best remembered for those poems that sensitively communicate her feelings and observations about her home and family.

To my Dear and loving Husband

If ever two were one, then surely we.
If ever man were lov'd by wife, then thee;
If ever wife was happy in a man,
Compare with me ye women if you can.
5   I prize thy love more than whole Mines of gold,
Or all the riches that the East doth hold.
My love is such that Rivers cannot quench,
Nor ought but love from thee, give recompence.
Thy love is such I can no way repay,

[2]i.e., the pope, identified by his triple crown.   [3]apocalyptic destruction; see Revelation 18.

NEL

10 The heavens reward thee manifold I pray.
Then while we live, in love lets so persever,[1]
That when we live no more, we may live ever.

(1678)

Upon the burning of our house, July 10, 1666

In silent night when rest I took,
For sorrow neer I did not look,
I waken'd was with thundring nois
And Piteous shreiks of dreadfull voice.
5 That fearfull sound of fire and fire,
Let no man know is my Desire.

I, starting up, the light did spye,
And to my God my heart did cry
To strengthen me in my Distresse
10 And not to leave me succourlesse.[1]
Then coming out beheld a space,
The flame consume my dwelling place.

And, when I could no longer look,
I blest his Name that gave and took,
15 That layd my goods now in the dust:
Yea so it was, and so 'twas just.
It was his own: it was not mine;
Far be it that I should repine.

He might of All justly bereft,
20 But yet sufficient for us left.
When by the Ruines oft I past,
My sorrowing eyes aside did cast,
And here and there the places spye
Where oft I sate, and long did lye.

25 Here stood that Trunk, and there that chest;
There lay that store I counted best:
My pleasant things in ashes lye,
And them behold no more shall I.
Under thy roof no guest shall sitt,
30 Nor at thy Table eat a bitt.

[1]persevere. [1]without help.

No pleasant tale shall e'er be told,
Nor things recounted done of old.
No Candle e'er shall shine in Thee,
Nor bridegroom's voice e'er heard shall bee.
35 In silence ever shall thou lye;
Adeiu, Adeiu; All's vanity.

Then streight I gin my heart to chide,
And did thy wealth on earth abide?
Didst fix thy hope on mouldring dust,
40 The arm of flesh didst make thy trust?
Raise up thy thoughts above the skye
That dunghill mists away may flie.

Thou hast an house on high erect
Fram'd by that mighty Architect,
45 With glory richly furnished,
Stands permanent tho' this bee fled.
It's purchasèd, and paid for too
By him who hath enough to doe.

A Prise so vast as is unknown,
50 Yet, by his Gift, is made thine own.
Ther's wealth enough, I need no more;
Farewell my Pelf,[2] farewell my Store.
The world no longer let me Love,
My hope and Treasure lyes Above.

(1678)

Andrew Marvell   (1621–1678)

The son of a Yorkshire clergyman, Andrew Marvell obtained his B.A. at Trinity College, Cambridge, and proceeded to travel widely on the Continent. Adept at learning, he absorbed French, Italian, Dutch, and Spanish—languages important for an Englishman bent on a career in public service and diplomacy. He was appointed assistant to Cromwell's Latin Secretary, John Milton, in 1658, and was later elected M.P. for Hull. Marvell apparently brought some influence to bear upon securing the release and safety of Milton at the Restoration. Throughout his career in public life, Marvell was prudent, honest, and committedly faithful to Puritan politics during and after the time of Cromwell's administration.

[2]property, earthly possessions.

He was, however, also a poet. His verses, none of which were published in his lifetime, are smooth and urbane, with a quality of irony that reinvests conventional images with freshness. Although overshadowed in reputation by Milton, Marvell is a major metaphysical poet who created lucid images of nature and time with wit and precision.

To His Coy Mistress

Had we but world enough, and time,
This coyness, lady, were no crime.
We would sit down, and think which way
To walk, and pass our long love's day.
5 Thou by the Indian Ganges' side
Should'st rubies find: I by the tide
Of Humber[1] would complain. I would
Love you ten years before the flood,
And you should, if you please, refuse
10 Till the conversion of the Jews;[2]
My vegetable[3] love should grow
Vaster than empires, and more slow;
An hundred years should go to praise
Thine eyes, and on thy forehead gaze;
15 Two hundred to adore each breast,
But thirty thousand to the rest;
An age at least to every part,
And the last age should show your heart.
For, lady, you deserve this state,
20 Nor would I love at lower rate.
      But at my back I always hear
Time's winged chariot hurrying near,
And yonder all before us lie
Deserts of vast eternity.
25 Thy beauty shall no more be found,
Nor, in thy marble vault, shall sound
My echoing song: then worms shall try
That long preserved virginity,
And your quaint[4] honour turn to dust,
30 And into ashes all my lust:

→

---

[1] a river flowing through Hull, Marvell's home town. [2] an event expected at the end of time. [3] following Aristotle, Renaissance scientists saw humans as possessing three qualities: the rational, the sensitive, and the vegetative; the vegetative provided only life and growth. [4] fastidious, prim, with a vulgar pun on the female sexual organ.

The grave's a fine and private place,
But none, I think, do there embrace.
  Now therefore, while the youthful hue
Sits on thy skin like morning dew,
35 And while thy willing soul transpires
At every pore with instant fires,
Now let us sport us while we may,
And now, like amorous birds of prey
Rather at once our time devour,
40 Than languish in his slow-chapped[5] power.
Let us roll all our strength and all
Our sweetness up into one ball,
And tear our pleasures with rough strife,
Thorough[6] the iron gates of life;
45 Thus, though we cannot make our sun
Stand still, yet we will make him run.

(1650–58?)   (1681)

The Garden

How vainly men themselves amaze,[1]
To win the palm, the oak, or bays,[2]
And their incessant labours see
Crowned from some single herb, or tree,
5 Whose short and narrow-verged shade
Does prudently their toils upbraid,
While all the flowers, and trees, do close
To weave the garlands of repose!

  Fair Quiet, have I found thee here,
10 And Innocence, thy sister dear?
Mistaken long, I sought you then
In busy companies of men.
Your sacred plants, if here below,
Only among the plants will grow;
15 Society is all but rude
To this delicious solitude.

  No white nor red was ever seen
So amorous as this lovely green.
Fond lovers, cruel as their flame,

→

---

[5]i.e., slow-jawed, slow-chewing, [6]through. [1]bewilder, perplex. [2]classical trophies for military, civic, or poetic achievement.

20 Cut in these trees their mistress' name:
Little, alas! they know or heed,
How far these beauties her exceed!
Fair trees! where'er your barks I wound,
No name shall but your own be found.

25 　　When we have run our passion's heat,
Love hither makes his best retreat.
The gods, who mortal beauty chase,
Still in a tree did end their race;
Apollo hunted Daphne so,
30 Only that she might laurel grow;
And Pan did after Syrinx speed,
Not as a nymph, but for a reed.[3]

　　What wond'rous life is this I lead!
Ripe apples drop about my head;
35 The luscious clusters of the vine
Upon my mouth do crush their wine;
The nectarine, and curious peach,
Into my hands themselves do reach;
Stumbling on melons, as I pass,
40 Insnared with flowers, I fall on grass.

　　Meanwhile the mind, from pleasure less,
Withdraws into its happiness;—
The mind, that ocean where each kind
Does straight its own resemblance find;[4]—
45 Yet it creates, transcending these,
Far other worlds, and other seas,
Annihilating all that's made
To a green thought in a green shade.

　　Here at the fountain's sliding foot,
50 Or at some fruit-tree's mossy root,
Casting the body's vest aside,
My soul into the boughs does glide:
There, like a bird, it sits and sings,
Then whets and combs its silver wings,
55 And, till prepared for longer flight,

➡️

[3]Marvell here alters the motivation of the gods in Ovid's *Metamorphoses*, in which the nymphs Daphne and Syrinx elude pursuit by the lustful gods Apollo and Pan by turning themselves into a laurel tree and a reed, respectively. [4]the sea was supposed to contain creatures corresponding to all those on land.

Waves in its plumes the various light.

    Such was that happy garden-state,
While man there walked without a mate:
After a place so pure and sweet,
60   What other help could yet he meet!
But 'twas beyond a mortal's share
To wander solitary there:
Two paradises 'twere in one,
To live in paradise alone.

65   How well the skilful gardener drew
Of flowers, and herbs, this dial[5] new,
Where, from above, the milder sun
Does through a fragrant zodiac run,
And, as it works, the industrious bee
70   Computes its time as well as we!
How could such sweet and wholesome hours
Be reckoned but with herbs and flowers?

(1650–58?)   (1681)

Katherine Philips   (1631–1664)

Celebrated as "The Matchless Orinda" and "The English Sappho," Katherine Philips became widely known for her poetry celebrating the friendship of women. The daughter of John Fowler, a prosperous Presbyterian merchant, she began organizing groups of friends when she was sent to boarding school. When she was just sixteen, Katherine married fifty-four-year-old James Philips, the son of her mother's second husband. They had two children, a boy, who died in infancy, and a girl. James Philips was a member of Parliament during the Interregnum, but she had decidedly Royalist leanings, and after the Restoration, she became popular at court. She cultivated friends through her Society of Friendship, a group composed mainly of women, all of whom adopted classical pseudonyms. Adopting for herself the name Orinda, she dedicated more than half of her poems to Anne Owen, known as Lucasia. Although the relationship between these women was regarded as a model of platonic love, some modern scholars see Philips, whether or not she physically consummated this or her other intense relationships with women, as a pioneer in expressing lesbian feelings. Her poems, which had circulated in manuscript, first received publication in a pirated edition in 1664, the same year that she died of smallpox during a visit to London. An authorized edition was published posthumously in 1667. Although she was highly praised in the years following her death and she inspired the next generation of women

[5]sundial.

poets, her reputation faded within fifty years. Now, however, critics are again looking at a poet who, although sometimes imitating Donne's love poems or expressing, as in "Against Love," common Cavalier themes, gave intense expression to female emotions and passions.

To My Excellent Lucasia, on Our Friendship, 17th July 1651

I did not live until this time
    Crowned my felicity,
When I could say without a crime,
    I am not thine, but thee.

5   This carcass breathed, and walked, and slept,
    So that the world believed
There was a soul the motions kept;
    But they were all deceived.

For as a watch by art is wound
10   To motion, such was mine:
But never had Orinda found
    A soul till she found thine;

Which now inspires, cures and supplies,
    And guides my darkened breast:
15   For thou art all that I can prize,
    My joy, my life, my rest.

Nor bridegroom's nor crowned conqueror's mirth
    To mine compared can be:
They have but pieces of this earth,
20   I've all the world in thee.

Then let our flame still light and shine,
    (And no bold[1] fear control)
As innocent as our design,
    Immortal as our soul.

(1664)

Against Love

Hence, Cupid! with your cheating toys,
Your real griefs, and painted joys,

➡

[1] all seventeenth-century printed texts employ the word "false" here; but "bold" appears in a copy book version in Philips's own handwriting.

Your pleasure which itself destroys.
　　　Lovers like men in fevers burn and rave,
5　　　　And only what will injure them do crave.
Men's weakness makes love so severe,
They give him power by their fear,
And make the shackles which they wear.
　　　Who to another does his heart submit
10　　　Makes his own idol, and then worships it.
Him whose heart is all his own,
Peace and liberty does crown;
He apprehends no killing frown.
　　　He feels no raptures, which are joys diseased,
15　　　And is not much transported, but still pleased.

(1667)

Alexander Pope　(1688–1744)

Pope dominated English poetry during the first half of the eighteenth century. His greatest poems were satires, public statements that had the power to change the course of public events. Like most poets of his own and the previous age, Pope wrote primarily in heroic couplets (i.e., closed iambic pentameter couplets); unlike others, however, Pope lived on his earnings as a poet. He had to, since he faced two devastating handicaps. He was born into a Roman Catholic family, which meant that he was forbidden by law from attending university, holding public office, or even living in London. Even worse, when he was a boy he contracted tuberculosis of the spine, which stunted his growth (he was never more than about four-foot-eight in height), made his body crooked, and gave him almost constant pain during his adult life. Fortunately, however, he had kindly and well-to-do parents, who raised him just outside London and saw that he had a thorough education in classical literature. Pope's poetic career falls into three distinct phases. His early poems, up to about 1713, were witty and playful satires; *The Rape of the Lock,* first published in 1712, is the gem of these early poems and still his best-known work. During a middle period, from roughly 1713 to 1726, he devoted himself to translating Homer's two great epics, the *Iliad* (completed in 1720) and the *Odyssey* (completed in 1726), and to producing an edition of Shakespeare's plays (1725). These projects gave him financial security, and from 1727 onward Pope again wrote his own poetry, but now of a much more sober nature: satires, including the autobiographical *Epistle to Dr. Arbuthnot* (1735) and *The Dunciad* (1728–43), a mock-epic celebrating the triumph of duncedom in contemporary Britain; moral essays in verse upon such topics as the proper use of riches; and his philosophical poem *An Essay on Man,* published anonymously in 1733–34.

The Rape of the Lock;
An Heroi-Comical Poem[1]

Nolueram, Belinda, tuos violare capillos,
Sed juvat hoc precibus me tribuisse tuis.

—Martial[2]

TO

Mrs.[3] *ARABELLA FERMOR.*

Madam,

It will be in vain to deny that I have some Regard for this Piece, since I Dedicate it to You. Yet You may bear me Witness, it was intended only to divert a few young Ladies, who have good Sense and good Humour enough, to laugh not only at their Sex's little unguarded Follies, but at their own. But as it was communicated with the Air of a Secret, it soon found its Way into the World. An imperfect Copy having been offer'd to a Bookseller, You had the Good-Nature for my Sake to consent to the Publication of one more correct: This I was forc'd to before I had executed half my Design, for the *Machinery* was entirely wanting to compleat it.[4]

The *Machinery*, Madam, is a Term invented by the Criticks, to signify that Part which the Deities, Angels, or Dæmons, are made to act in a Poem: For the ancient Poets are in one respect like many modern Ladies; Let an Action be never so trivial in it self, they always make it appear of the utmost Importance. These Machines I determin'd to raise on a very new and odd Foundation, the *Rosicrucian*[5] Doctrine of Spirits.

I know how disagreeable it is to make use of hard Words before a Lady; but 'tis so much the Concern of a Poet to have his Works understood, and particularly by your Sex, that You must give me leave to explain two or three difficult Terms.

The *Rosicrucians* are a People I must bring You acquainted with. The best Account I know of them is in a French Book call'd *Le Comte de Gabalis*, which both in its Title and Size is so like a *Novel*, that many of the Fair Sex

---

[1]Pope's title alludes to the poem's origin. A quarrel had developed between two prominent Roman Catholic families when Robert, Lord Petre, cut off a lock from the head of Arabella Fermor, a celebrated beauty known as "Belle." John Caryll, Pope's friend, urged Pope to write a poem that would restore good feelings. Pope's subtitle alludes to the poem's genre: it is a mock-epic, and the well-known features of epic poems are comically transformed. The combat of heroic warriors becomes the drawing-room war between the sexes; the rape of Helen becomes that of a lock of hair; the arming of the hero for combat becomes the heroine's dressing and beautification for a social engagement, and so on. [2]Pope's epigraph is slightly altered from the Roman satirist Martial: "I did not wish, Belinda, to profane your locks, but it pleases me to have granted this to your prayers." [3]"Mrs." was used for ladies, whether married or single. [4]in its original (1712) form, the poem consisted of two cantos of 334 lines; as Pope explains, he expanded the poem to five cantos in 1714 by adding the "machinery" (the supernatural agents found in epic poems). [5]eccentric occult religion that originated in Germany early in the seventeenth century.

have read it for one by Mistake.[6] According to these Gentlemen, the four Elements[7] are inhabited by Spirits, which they call *Sylphs, Gnomes, Nymphs,* and *Salamanders.* The *Gnomes,* or Dæmons of Earth, delight in Mischief; but the *Sylphs,* whose Habitation is in the Air, are the best-condition'd Creatures imaginable. For they say, any Mortals may enjoy the most intimate Familiarities with these gentle Spirits, upon a Condition very easie to all true *Adepts,* an inviolate Preservation of Chastity.

As to the following Canto's, all the Passages of them are as Fabulous, as the Vision at the Beginning, or the Transformation at the End; (except the Lass of your Hair, which I always mention with Reverence.) The Human Persons are as Fictitious as the Airy ones; and the Character of *Belinda,* as it is now manag'd, resembles You in nothing but in Beauty.

If this Poem had as many Graces as there are in Your Person, or in Your Mind, yet I could never hope it should pass thro' the World half so Uncensured as You have done. But let its Fortune be what it will, mine is happy enough, to have given me this Occasion of assuring You that I am, with the truest Esteem,

Madam,

Your Most *Obedient*

Humble Servant.

A. *Pope*

CANTO I.

What dire Offence from am'rous Causes springs,
What mighty Contests rise from trivial Things,[8]
I sing—This Verse to *Caryll,* Muse! is due;
This, ev'n *Belinda* may vouchsafe to view:
5   Slight is the Subject, but not so the Praise,
If She inspire, and He approve my Lays.
    Say what strange Motive, Goddess! cou'd compel
A well-bred *Lord* t'assault a gentle *Belle?*[9]
Oh say what stranger Cause, yet unexplor'd,
10   Cou'd make a gentle *Belle* reject a *Lord?*
In Tasks so bold, can Little Men engage,
And in soft Bosoms dwells such mighty Rage?
    Sol thro' white Curtains shot a tim'rous Ray,
And Op'd those Eyes that must eclipse the Day;

➡

[6]in fact, *Le Comte de Gabalis* (1670), written by the Abbé de Montfaucon de Villars, is a facetious and largely fictitious summary of Rosicrucianism that had been published as a novel when translated into English in 1680. [7]air, earth, water, and fire, according to traditional science. [8]like Homer, Virgil, and Milton, Pope begins his poem with a concise statement of its theme, immediately followed by an invocation of the Muse. [9]again, like Virgil and Milton, before plunging into the action of his poem Pope asks questions about the causes of all that will follow.

15 Now Lapdogs give themselves the rowzing Shake,
And sleepless Lovers, just at Twelve, awake:
Thrice rung the Bell, the Slipper knock'd the Ground,[10]
And the press'd Watch return'd a silver Sound.[11]
Belinda still her downy Pillow prest,
20 Her Guardian *Sylph* prolong'd the balmy Rest.
'Twas he had summon'd to her silent Bed
The Morning-Dream that hover'd o'er her Head.[12]
A Youth more glitt'ring than a *Birth-night Beau*,[13]
(That ev'n in Slumber caus'd her Cheek to glow)
25 Seem'd to her Ear his winning Lips to lay,
And thus in Whispers said, or seem'd to say.
     Fairest of Mortals, thou distinguish'd Care
Of thousand bright Inhabitants of Air!
If e'er one Vision touch'd thy infant Thought,
30 Of all the Nurse and all the Priest have taught,[14]
Of airy Elves by Moonlight Shadows seen,
The silver Token,[15] and the circled Green,[16]
Or Virgins visited by Angel-Pow'rs,[17]
With Golden Crowns and Wreaths of heav'nly Flow'rs,
35 Hear and believe! thy own Importance know,
Nor bound thy narrow Views to Things below.
Some secret Truths from Learned Pride conceal'd,
To Maids alone and Children are reveal'd:
What tho' no Credit doubting Wits may give?
40 The Fair and Innocent shall still believe.
Know then, unnumber'd Spirits round thee fly,
The light *Militia* of the lower Sky;
These, tho' unseen, are ever on the Wing,
Hang o'er the *Box*,[18] and hover round the *Ring*.[19]
45 Think what an Equipage[20] thou hast in Air,

[10]ladies summoned their maids by ringing a hand-bell or by knocking on the floor with a high-heeled shoe. [11]England was famous for its "repeater" watches; when the stem was pressed, the watch chimed the most recent hour and quarter-hour. [12]epic heroes often receive warnings about coming events from the gods in dreams; cf. Eve's dream in *Paradise Lost* V.28–93. [13]courtier splendidly dressed for the royal birthday. [14]the traditional promulgators of superstitions. [15]fairies were believed to skim off the cream from jugs of milk left standing overnight, leaving a coin as payment. [16]"fairy rings" (withered circles in grass) were thought to be caused by fairies dancing. [17]many saints were virgins to whom angels appeared in mystic visions (St. Theresa of Avila, for instance). [18]the theatre box, where the elite among playgoers sat. [19]a fashionable circular drive in Hyde Park. [20]carriage with horses and footmen.

And view with scorn *Two Pages* and a *Chair*.[21]
As now your own, our Beings were of old,
And once inclos'd in Woman's beauteous Mold;
Thence, by a soft Transition, we repair
50 From earthly Vehicles[22] to these of Air.
Think not, when Woman's transient Breath is fled,
That all her Vanities at once are dead:
Succeeding Vanities she still regards,
And tho' she plays no more, o'erlooks the Cards.
55 Her Joy in gilded Chariots, when alive,
And Love of *Ombre*,[23] after Death survive.
For when the Fair in all their Pride expire,
To their first Elements[24] their Souls retire:
The Sprights[25] of fiery Termagants[26] in Flame
60 Mount up, and take a *Salamander's*[27] Name.
Soft yielding Minds to Water glide away,
And sip with *Nymphs*, their Elemental Tea.
The graver Prude sinks downward to a *Gnome*,
In search of Mischief still on Earth to roam.
65 The light Coquettes in *Sylphs* aloft repair,
And sport and flutter in the Fields of Air.
        Know farther yet; Whoever fair and chaste
Rejects Mankind, is by some *Sylph* embrac'd:
For Spirits, freed from mortal Laws, with ease
70 Assume what Sexes and what Shapes they please.[28]
What guards the Purity of melting Maids,
In Courtly Balls, and Midnight Masquerades,[29]
Safe from the treach'rous Friend, the daring Spark,[30]
The Glance by Day, the Whisper in the Dark;
75 When kind Occasion prompts their warm Desires,
When Musick softens, and when Dancing fires?
'Tis but their *Sylph*, the wise Celestials know,
Tho' *Honour* is the Word with Men below.
        Some Nymphs there are, too conscious of their Face,

---

[21]sedan-chair, in which passengers were carried. [22]meaning both carriages and bodies (the body is the vehicle of the soul). [23]popular card game (see note 73). [24]traditionally, the four elements of all matter (earth, air, fire, water) had their counterparts in the four "humours" or fluids of the human body (black bile, yellow bile, blood, phlegm); one of these humours was supposed to dominate each person, determining his or her temperament. [25]spirits. [26]shrews. [27]salamanders were believed able to live in fire. [28]as Milton had explained in *Paradise Lost* I.423–31. [29]masked balls. [30]fop or beau.

80 For Life predestin'd to the *Gnomes'* Embrace.
These swell their Prospects and exalt their Pride,
When Offers are disdain'd, and Love deny'd.
Then gay Ideas crowd the vacant Brain;
While Peers and Dukes, and all their sweeping Train,
85 And Garters, Stars, and Coronets[31] appear,
And in soft Sounds, *Your Grace*[32] salutes their Ear.
'Tis these that early taint the Female Soul,
Instruct the Eyes of young *Coquettes* to roll,
Teach Infant-Cheeks a bidden Blush to know,
90 And little Hearts to flutter at a *Beau.*
     Oft when the World imagine Women stray,
The *Sylphs* thro' mystick Mazes guide their Way,
Thro' all the giddy Circle they pursue,
And old Impertinence expel by new.
95 What tender Maid but must a Victim fall
To one Man's Treat,[33] but for another's Ball?
When *Florio* speaks, what Virgin could withstand,
If gentle *Damon* did not squeeze her Hand?
With varying Vanities, from ev'ry Part,
100 They shift the moving Toyshop of their Heart;
Where Wigs with Wigs, with Sword-knots[34] Sword-knots strive,
Beaus banish Beaus, and Coaches Coaches drive.
This erring Mortals Levity may call,
Oh blind to Truth! the *Sylphs* contrive it all.
105   Of these am I, who thy Protection claim,
A watchful Sprite, and *Ariel* is my Name.
Late, as I rang'd the Crystal Wilds of Air,
In the clear Mirror of thy ruling *Star*
I saw, alas! some dread Event impend,
110 Ere to the Main this Morning Sun descend.
But Heav'n reveals not what, or how, or where:
Warn'd by thy *Sylph*, oh Pious Maid beware!
This to disclose is all thy Guardian can.
Beware of all, but most beware of Man!
115   He said; when *Shock*,[35] who thought she slept too long,
Leapt up, and wak'd his Mistress with his Tongue.
'Twas then *Belinda*! if Report say true,

→

---

[31]garters, stars, and coronets are all insignia of noble rank. [32]the courtesy title used to address a duke or duchess. [33]feast, entertainment. [34]ribbons tied to the hilt of a sword. [35]Belinda's lap dog.

Thy Eyes first open'd on a *Billet-doux;*[36]
Wounds, *Charms*, and *Ardors*, were no sooner read,
120   But all the Vision vanish'd from thy Head.
     And now, unveil'd, the *Toilet*[37] stands display'd,
Each Silver Vase in mystic Order laid.
First, rob'd in White, the Nymph intent adores
With Head uncover'd, the *Cosmetic* Pow'rs.
125   A heavn'ly Image in the Glass appears,
To that she bends, to that her Eyes she rears;
Th'inferior Priestess,[38] at her Altar's side,
Trembling, begins the sacred Rites of Pride.
Unnumber'd Treasures ope at once, and here
130   The various Off'rings of the World appear;
From each she nicely[39] culls with curious[40] Toil,
And decks the Goddess with the glitt'ring Spoil.
This Casket *India's* glowing Gems unlocks,
And all *Arabia* breathes from yonder Box.
135   The Tortoise here and Elephant unite,
Transform'd to *Combs*, the speckled and the white.
Here Files of Pins extend their shining Rows,
Puffs, Powders, Patches, Bibles, Billet-doux.
Now awful[41] Beauty puts on all its Arms;
140   The Fair each moment rises in her Charms,
Repairs her Smiles, awakens ev'ry Grace,
And calls forth all the Wonders of her Face;
Sees by Degrees a purer Blush arise,
And keener Lightnings quicken in her Eyes.
145   The busy *Sylphs* surround their darling Care;
These set the Head, and those divide the Hair,
Some fold the Sleeve, whilst others plait the Gown;
And *Betty's* prais'd for Labours not her own.

CANTO II.

Not with more Glories, in th' Etherial Plain,
The Sun first rises o'er the purpled Main,
Than issuing forth, the Rival of his Beams
Lanch'd on the Bosom of the Silver *Thames*.[42]

---

[36]love letter. [37]dressing table. [38]Belinda's maid Betty. [39]fastidiously. [40]careful.
[41]awe-inspiring. [42]Belinda travels by boat up the Thames from London to Hampton Court
Palace, the royal palace some ten kilometres upstream.

Fair Nymphs, and well-drest Youths around her shone,
But ev'ry Eye was fix'd on her alone.
On her white Breast a sparkling *Cross* she wore,
Which *Jews* might kiss, and Infidels adore.[43]
Her lively Looks a sprightly Mind disclose,
Quick as her Eyes, and as unfix'd as those:
Favours to none, to all she Smiles extends,
Oft she rejects, but never once offends.
Bright as the Sun, her Eyes the Gazers strike,
And, like the Sun, they shine on all alike.
Yet graceful Ease, and Sweetness void of Pride,
Might hide her Faults, if *Belles* had Faults to hide:
If to her share some Female Errors fall,
Look on her Face, and you'll forget 'em all.
    This Nymph, to the Destruction of Mankind,
Nourish'd two Locks, which graceful hung behind
In equal Curls, and well conspir'd to deck
With shining Ringlets the smooth Iv'ry Neck.
Love in these Labyrinths his Slaves detains,
And mighty Hearts are held in slender Chains.
With hairy Sprindges[44] we the Birds betray,
Slight Lines of Hair surprize the Finny Prey,
Fair Tresses Man's Imperial Race insnare,
And Beauty draws us with a single Hair.
    Th' Adventrous *Baron* the bright Locks admir'd,
He saw, he wish'd, and to the Prize aspir'd:
Resolv'd to win, he meditates the way,
By Force to ravish, or by Fraud betray;
For when Success a Lover's Toil attends,
Few ask, if Fraud or Force attain'd his Ends.
    For this, ere *Phœbus*[45] rose, he had implor'd
Propitious Heav'n, and ev'ry Pow'r ador'd,
But chiefly *Love*—to *Love* an Altar built,
Of twelve vast *French* Romances,[46] neatly gilt.
There lay three Garters, half a Pair of Gloves;
And all the Trophies of his former Loves.

---

[43]kissing or adoration of the cross marked conversion to Christianity. [44]snares, traps; pronounced *sprin-jez*. [45]the sun. [46]notoriously long and idealized love stories, written by seventeenth-century French aristocrats and set in ancient Greece and Rome.

With tender *Billet-doux* he lights the Pyre,
And breathes three am'rous Sighs to raise the Fire.
Then prostrate falls, and begs with ardent Eyes
Soon to obtain, and long possess the Prize:
45 The Pow'rs gave Ear, and granted half his Pray'r,
The rest, the Winds dispers'd in empty Air.[47]
        But now secure[48] the painted Vessel glides,
The Sun-beams trembling on the floating Tydes,
While melting Musick steals upon the Sky,
50 And soften'd Sounds along the Waters die.
Smooth flow the Waves, the Zephyrs[49] gently play,
Belinda smil'd, and all the World was gay.
All but the *Sylph*—With careful Thoughts opprest,
Th'impending Woe sate heavy on his Breast.
55 He summons strait his Denizens of Air;
The lucid Squadrons round the Sails repair:[50]
Soft o'er the Shrouds[51] Aerial Whispers breathe,
That seem'd but *Zephyrs* to the Train beneath.
Some to the Sun their Insect-Wings unfold,
60 Waft on the Breeze, or sink in Clouds of Gold.
Transparent Forms, too fine for mortal Sight,
Their fluid Bodies half dissolv'd in Light.
Loose to the Wind their airy Garments flew,
Thin glitt'ring Textures of the filmy Dew;
65 Dipt in the richest Tincture of the Skies,
Where Light disports in ever-mingling Dies,
While ev'ry Beam new transient Colours flings,
Colours that change whene'er they wave their Wings.
Amid the Circle, on the gilded Mast,
70 Superior by the Head,[52] was *Ariel* plac'd;
His Purple Pinions opening to the Sun,
He rais'd his Azure Wand, and thus begun.
        Ye *Sylphs* and *Sylphids*,[53] to your Chief give Ear,
Fays, Fairies, Genii, Elves, and *Dæmons* hear![54]
75 Ye know the Spheres and various Tasks assign'd,
By Laws Eternal, to th' Aerial Kind.

---

[47]in epics, the gods frequently grant only half of a character's prayer, with the other half being abandoned to the winds. [48]free from care. [49]gentle breezes. [50]gather. [51]ropes. [52]epic heroes are usually taller than their followers. [53]female sylphs. [54]the epic hero normally rallies his forces for action by a stirring speech that begins by addressing each of the ranks present in turn.

Some in the Fields of purest *aether*[55] play,
And bask and whiten in the Blaze of Day.
Some guide the Course of wandring Orbs on high,
Or roll the Planets thro' the boundless Sky.
Some less refin'd, beneath the Moon's pale Light
Pursue the Stars that shoot athwart the Night,
Or suck the Mists in grosser Air below,
Or dip their Pinions in the painted Bow,
Or brew fierce Tempests on the wintry Main,
Or o'er the Glebe[56] distill the kindly Rain.
Others on Earth o'er human Race preside,
Watch all their Ways, and all their Actions guide:
Of these the Chief the Care of Nations own,
And guard with Arms Divine the *British Throne*.
　　　Our humbler Province is to tend the Fair,
Not a less pleasing, tho' less glorious Care.
To save the Powder from too rude a Gale,
Nor let th' imprison'd Essences[57] exhale,
To draw fresh Colours from the vernal[58] Flow'rs,
To steal from Rainbows ere they drop in Show'rs
A brighter Wash;[59] to curl their waving Hairs,
Assist their Blushes, and inspire their Airs;
Nay oft, in Dreams, Invention we bestow,
To change a *Flounce*, or add a *Furbelo*.[60]
　　　This Day, black Omens threat the brightest Fair
That e'er deserv'd a watchful Spirit's Care;
Some dire Disaster, or by Force, or Slight,[61]
But what, or where, the Fates have wrapt in Night.
Whether the Nymph shall break *Diana's*[62] Law,
Or some frail *China* Jar receive a Flaw,
Or stain her Honour, or her new Brocade,
Forget her Pray'rs, or miss a Masquerade,
Or lose her Heart, or Necklace, at a Ball;
Or whether Heav'n has doom'd that *Shock* must fall.
Haste then ye Spirits! to your Charge repair;
The flutt'ring Fan be *Zephyretta's* Care;
The Drops[63] to thee, *Brillante*, we consign;
And, *Momentilla*, let the Watch be thine;

→

80

85

90

95

100

105

110

---

[55]the air above the moon was considered pure and was known as the aether. [56]farmland. [57]perfumes. [58]spring. [59]lotion, rinse. [60]ruffle. [61]sleight, trick. [62]Diana was the Roman goddess of the hunt and the protector of chastity. [63]diamond earrings.

115 Do thou, *Crispissa*, tend her fav'rite Lock;
   Ariel himself shall be the Guard of *Shock*.
       To Fifty chosen *Sylphs*, of special Note,
   We trust th'important Charge, the *Petticoat:*
   Oft have we known that sev'nfold Fence to fail,
120 Tho' stiff with Hoops, and arm'd with Ribs of Whale.
   Form a strong Line about the Silver Bound,
   And guard the wide Circumference around.
       Whatever Spirit, careless of his Charge,
   His Post neglects, or leaves the Fair at large,
125 Shall feel sharp Vengeance soon o'ertake his Sins,
   Be stopt in *Vials*, or transfixt with *Pins*;
   Or plung'd in Lakes of bitter *Washes* lie,
   Or wedg'd whole Ages in a *Bodkin's*[64] Eye:
   Gums and *Pomatums*[65] shall his Flight restrain,
130 While clog'd he beats his silken Wings in vain;
   Or Alom-*Stypticks*[66] with contracting Power
   Shrink his thin Essence like a rivell'd[67] Flower.
   Or as *Ixion*[68] fix'd, the Wretch shall feel
   The giddy Motion of the whirling Mill,[69]
135 In Fumes of burning Chocolate shall glow,
   And tremble at the Sea that froaths below!
       He spoke; the Spirits from the Sails descend;
   Some, Orb in Orb, around the Nymph extend,
   Some thrid the mazy Ringlets of her Hair,
140 Some hang upon the Pendants of her Ear;
   With beating Hearts the dire Event they wait,
   Anxious, and trembling for the Birth of Fate.

CANTO III.

   Close by those Meads for ever crown'd with Flow'rs,
   Where *Thames* with Pride surveys his rising Tow'rs,
   There stands a Structure of Majestick Frame,[70]
   Which from the neighb'ring *Hampton* takes it Name.
5 Here *Britain's* Statesmen oft the Fall foredoom
   Of Foreign Tyrants, and of Nymphs at home;

[64]needle's. [65]ointments. [66]astringents to stop bleeding. [67]shrivelled, wrinkled. [68]in Greek mythology, Ixion was a king whose punishment for his attempt to seduce the goddess Hera was to be bound in hell to a perpetually turning wheel. [69]for beating chocolate. [70]Hampton Court Palace, largest of the royal palaces.

Here Thou, Great *Anna!*[71] whom three Realms obey,
Dost sometimes Counsel take—and sometimes *Tea*.
    Hither the Heroes and the Nymphs resort,
10 To taste awhile the Pleasures of a Court;
In various Talk th' instructive hours they past,
Who gave the *Ball*, or paid the *Visit* last:
One speaks the Glory of the *British Queen*,
And one describes a charming *Indian Screen*;
15 A third interprets Motions, Looks, and Eyes;
At ev'ry Word a Reputation dies.
Snuff, or the *Fan*, supply each Pause of Chat,
With singing, laughing, ogling, and all that.
    Mean while declining from the Noon of Day,
20 The Sun obliquely shoots his burning Ray;
The hungry Judges soon the Sentence sign,
And Wretches hang that Jury-men may Dine;
The Merchant from th' *Exchange*[72] returns in Peace,
And the long Labours of the *Toilette* cease—
25 *Belinda* now, whom Thirst of Fame invites,
Burns to encounter two adventrous Knights,
At *Ombre*[73] singly to decide their Doom;
And swells her Breast with Conquests yet to come.
Strait the three Bands prepare in Arms to join,
30 Each Band the number of the Sacred Nine.
Soon as she spreads her Hand, th' Aerial Guard
Descend, and sit on each important Card:
First *Ariel* perch'd upon a *Matadore*,[74]
Then each, according to the Rank they bore;
35 For *Sylphs*, yet mindful of their ancient Race,
Are, as when Women, wondrous fond of Place.[75]
    Behold, four *Kings* in Majesty rever'd,
With hoary Whiskers and a forky Beard;

→

[71]Queen Anne, ruler of England, Scotland, and Ireland. [72]the Royal Exchange in London's financial district, where merchants, bankers, and stockbrokers met to do business. [73]Belinda's card game mimics the epic games at which warriors relax and at the same time celebrate their heroic code; see Homer's *Iliad*, Book XXIII. Ombre (pronounced *om-ber*, from the Spanish *hombre*, meaning man) is played by three persons with 40 cards, the eights, nines, and tens being removed from the deck. Nine cards are dealt to each player, and nine tricks are played, with the highest card winning each. One player, called the "Ombre," undertakes to win more tricks than either of the other two and chooses which suit will be trumps. [74]one of the three cards of highest value; they are, in order, the ace of spades, the two of the trump suit (when, as here, a black suit is trumps), the ace of clubs. [75]rank.

And four fair *Queens* whose hands sustain a Flow'r,
40 Th' expressive Emblem of their softer Pow'r;
Four *Knaves* in Garbs succinct,[76] a trusty Band,
Caps on their heads, and Halberds[77] in their hand;
And Particolour'd Troops, a shining Train,
Draw forth to Combat on the Velvet Plain.
45   The skilful Nymph reviews her Force with Care;
Let Spades be Trumps! she said, and Trumps they were.[78]
       Now move to War her Sable *Matadores*,
In Show like Leaders of the swarthy *Moors*.
Spadillio[79] first, unconquerable Lord!
50 Led off two captive Trumps, and swept the Board.
As many more *Manillio*[80] forc'd to yield,
And march'd a Victor from the verdant Field.
Him *Basto*[81] follow'd, but his Fate more hard
Gain'd but one Trump and one *Plebeian* Card.
55 With his broad Sabre next, a Chief in Years,
The hoary Majesty of *Spades* appears;
Puts forth one manly Leg, to sight reveal'd;
The rest of his many-colour'd Robe conceal'd.
The Rebel-*Knave*, who dares his Prince engage,
60 Proves the just Victim of his Royal Rage.
Ev'n mighty *Pam*[82] that Kings and Queens o'erthrew,
And mow'd down Armies in the Fights of *Lu*,
Sad Chance of War! now, destitute of Aid,
Falls undistinguish'd by the Victor *Spade*!
65   Thus far both Armies to *Belinda* yield;
Now to the *Baron* Fate inclines the Field.
His warlike *Amazon*[83] her Host invades,
Th' Imperial Consort of the Crown of *Spades*.
The *Club's* black Tyrant first her Victim dy'd,
70 Spite of his haughty Mien, and barb'rous Pride:
What boots the Regal Circle on his Head,
His Giant Limbs in State unwieldy spread?
That long behind he trails his pompous Robe,
And of all Monarchs only grasps the Globe?

[76] girded up. [77]battle-axes attached to long spears. [78]cf. Genesis 1:3: "And God said, Let there be light; and there was light." [79]the ace of spades. [80]the two of spades. [81]the ace of clubs. [82]the knave of clubs, highest card in the game of Loo, or Lu. [83]the queen of spades.

75   The *Baron* now his *Diamonds* pours apace;
Th' embroider'd *King* who shows but half his Face,
And his refulgent[84] *Queen*, with Pow'rs combin'd,
Of broken Troops an easie Conquest find.
Clubs, Diamonds, Hearts, in wild Disorder seen,
80 With Throngs promiscuous strow the level Green.
Thus when dispers'd a routed Army runs,
Of *Asia's* Troops, and *Africk's* Sable Sons,
With like Confusion different Nations fly,
Of various Habit and of various Dye,
85 The pierc'd Battalions dis-united fall,
In Heaps on Heaps; one Fate o'erwhelms them all.
    The *Knave of Diamonds* tries his wily Arts,
And wins (oh shameful Chance!) the *Queen of Hearts*.
At this, the Blood the Virgin's Cheek forsook,
90 A livid Paleness spreads o'er all her Look;
She sees, and trembles at th' approaching Ill,
Just in the Jaws of Ruin, and *Codille*.[85]
And now, (as oft in some distemper'd State)
On one nice[86] *Trick* depends the gen'ral Fate.
95 An *Ace* of Hearts steps forth: The *King* unseen
Lurk'd in her Hand, and mourn'd his captive *Queen*.
He springs to Vengeance with an eager pace,
And falls like Thunder on the prostrate *Ace*.[87]
The Nymph exulting fills with Shouts the Sky,
100 The Walls, the Woods, and long Canals reply.
    Oh thoughtless Mortals! ever blind to Fate,
Too soon dejected, and too soon elate!
Sudden these Honours shall be snatch'd away,
And curs'd for ever this Victorious Day.
105   For lo! the Board with Cups and Spoons is crown'd,
The Berries crackle, and the Mill[88] turns round.
On shining Altars of *Japan*[89] they raise
The silver Lamp; the fiery Spirits[90] blaze.
From silver Spouts the grateful[91] Liquors glide,
110 While *China's* Earth[92] receives the smoking Tyde.
At once they gratify their Scent and Taste,

[84]shining, glorious. [85]if the Ombre failed to win more tricks than one of the other players, he or she was said to be given "codille" (from the Spanish for elbow). [86]precise. [87]when a black suit is trumps, the king, queen, and knave of a red suit outrank the ace; Belinda thus wins the trick and the game. [88]the coffee mill, which grinds coffee beans (the "Berries"). [89]japanned or lacquered tables. [90]in spirit-lamps. [91]pleasing. [92]cups of china, i.e., fine earthenware.

And frequent Cups prolong the rich Repast.
Strait hover round the Fair her Airy Band;
Some, as she sip'd the fuming Liquor fann'd,
115   Some, o'er her Lap their careful Plumes display'd,
Trembling, and conscious of the rich Brocade.
Coffee, (which makes the Politician wise,
And see thro' all things with his half-shut Eyes)
Sent up in Vapours to the *Baron's* Brain
120   New Stratagems, the radiant Lock to gain.
Ah cease rash Youth! desist ere 'tis too late,
Fear the just Gods, and think of *Scylla's*[93] Fate!
Chang'd to a Bird, and sent to flit in Air,
She dearly pays for *Nisus*' injur'd Hair!
125   But when to Mischief Mortals bend their Will,
How soon they find fit Instruments of Ill!
Just then, *Clarissa* drew with tempting Grace
A two-edg'd Weapon from her shining Case;
So Ladies in Romance assist their Knight,
130   Present the Spear, and arm him for the Fight.
He takes the Gift with rev'rence, and extends
The little Engine on his Fingers' Ends,
This just behind *Belinda's* Neck he spread,
As o'er the fragrant Steams she bends her Head:
135   Swift to the Lock a thousand Sprights repair,
A thousand Wings, by turns, blow back the Hair.
And thrice they twitch'd the Diamond in her Ear,
Thrice she look'd back, and thrice the Foe drew near.
Just in that instant, anxious *Ariel* sought
140   The close Recesses of the Virgin's Thought;
As on the Nosegay[94] in her Breast reclin'd,
He watch'd th' Ideas rising in her Mind,
Sudden he view'd, in spite of all her Art,
An Earthly Lover lurking at her Heart.
145   Amaz'd, confus'd, he found his Pow'r expir'd,
Resign'd to Fate, and with a Sigh retir'd.
        The Peer now spreads the glitt'ring *Forfex*[95] wide,
T'inclose the Lock; now joins it, to divide.
Ev'n then, before the fatal Engine clos'd,

[93]according to legend, Scylla was the daughter of King Nisus, whose life and kingdom depended on a purple hair growing on his head. Scylla fell in love with King Minos, who was besieging her father's kingdom, and plucked out the hair and took it to Minos; he rejected it with horror, and she was turned into a sea bird. [94]corsage of flowers. [95]the Latin word for scissors.

150 A wretched *Sylph* too fondly interpos'd;
Fate urg'd the Sheers, and cut the *Sylph* in twain,
(But Airy Substance soon unites again)[96]
The meeting Points the sacred Hair dissever
From the fair Head, for ever and for ever!
155   Then flash'd the living Lightning from her Eyes,
And Screams of Horror rend th' affrighted Skies.
Not louder Shrieks to pitying Heav'n are cast,
When Husbands or when Lap-dogs breathe their last,
Or when rich *China* Vessels, fal'n from high,
160 In glittring Dust and painted Fragments lie!
    Let Wreaths of Triumph now my Temples twine,
(The Victor cry'd) the glorious Prize is mine!
While Fish in Streams, or Birds delight in Air,
Or in a Coach and Six the *British* Fair,
165 As long as *Atalantis*[97] shall be read,
Or the small Pillow grace a Lady's Bed,
While *Visits* shall be paid on solemn Days,
When numerous Wax-lights in bright Order blaze,
While Nymphs take Treats, or Assignations give,
170 So long my Honour, Name, and Praise shall live!
    What Time wou'd spare, from Steel receives its date,
And Monuments, like Men, submit to Fate!
Steel cou'd the Labour of the Gods[98] destroy,
And strike to Dust th' Imperial Tow'rs of *Troy*;
175 Steel cou'd the Works of mortal Pride confound,
And hew Triumphal Arches to the Ground.
What Wonder then, fair Nymph! thy Hairs shou'd feel
The conqu'ring Force of unresisted Steel?

CANTO IV.

But anxious Cares the pensive Nymph opprest,
And secret Passions labour'd in her Breast.
Not youthful Kings in Battel seiz'd alive,
Not scornful Virgins who their Charms survive,
5 Not ardent Lovers robb'd of all their Bliss,

---

[96]just as Milton's Satan does when pierced by Michael's sword (*Paradise Lost* VI.330–31).
[97]*The New Atalantis* (1709), by Delarivier Manley, a popular novel consisting largely of thinly veiled accounts of scandals in high life. [98]Troy was believed to have been built by two gods, Apollo and Poseidon.

Not ancient Ladies when refus'd a Kiss,
Not Tyrants fierce that unrepenting die,
Not *Cynthia* when her *Manteau's*[99] pinn'd awry,
E'er felt such Rage, Resentment and Despair,
10 As Thou, sad Virgin! for thy ravish'd Hair.
     For, that sad moment, when the *Sylphs* withdrew,
And *Ariel* weeping from *Belinda* flew,
Umbriel,[100] a dusky melancholy Spright,
As ever sully'd the fair face of Light,
15 Down to the Central Earth, his proper Scene,[101]
Repair'd to search the gloomy Cave of *Spleen*.[102]
     Swift on his sooty Pinions flitts the *Gnome*,
And in a Vapour[103] reach'd the dismal Dome.
No cheerful Breeze this sullen Region knows,
20 The dreadful *East*[104] is all the Wind that blows.
Here, in a Grotto, sheltred close from Air,
And screen'd in Shades from Day's detested Glare,
She sighs for ever on her pensive Bed,
Pain at her Side, and *Megrim*[105] at her Head.
25 Two Handmaids wait the Throne: Alike in Place,
But diff'ring far in Figure and in Face.
Here stood *Ill-nature* like an *ancient* Maid,
Her wrinked Form in *Black* and *White* array'd;
With store of Pray'rs, for Mornings, Nights, and Noons,
30 Her Hand is fill'd; her Bosom with Lampoons.
     There *Affectation* with a sickly Mien
Shows in her Cheek the Roses of Eighteen,
Practis'd to Lisp, and hang the Head aside,
Faints into Airs, and languishes with Pride;
35 On the rich Quilt sinks with becoming Woe,
Wrapt in a Gown, for Sickness, and for Show.[106]
The Fair-ones feel such Maladies as these,
When each new Night-Dress gives a new Disease.

[99]loose robe or cloak. [100]a Gnome (see I.63–64); his name is from the Latin word *umbra*, meaning shadow. [101]Umbriel's journey to the cave of Spleen imitates the epic hero's visit to the underworld in search of knowledge unavailable on earth; see Homer's *Odyssey*, Book XI, and Virgil's *Aeneid*, Book VI. [102]the spleen, thought to be the seat of the emotions in traditional medicine, became the name of a fashionable psychosomatic ailment of the rich and leisured; it consisted of ill temper, depression, and hypochondria. [103]suitably, since the disease known as "the spleen" was also called "the vapours" (see lines 39 and 59 of this canto). [104]the east wind was considered unhealthy; it was thought to provoke the spleen. [105]migraine headache. [106]ladies often received formal visits in bed

A constant *Vapour* o'er the Palace flies;
40 Strange Phantoms rising as the Mists arise;
Dreadful, as Hermit's Dreams in haunted Shades,
Or bright as Visions of expiring Maids.
Now glaring Fiends, and Snakes on rolling Spires,[107]
Pale Spectres, gaping Tombs and Purple Fires:
45 Now Lakes of liquid Gold, *Elysian*[108] Scenes,
And Crystal Domes, and Angels in Machines.[109]
Unnumber'd Throngs on ev'ry side are seen
Of Bodies chang'd to various Forms by *Spleen*.[110]
Here living *Teapots* stand, one Arm held out,
50 One bent; the Handle this, and that the Spout:
A Pipkin[111] there like *Homer's Tripod*[112] walks;
Here sighs a Jar, and there a Goose-pye talks;
Men prove with Child, as powr'ful Fancy works,
And Maids turn'd Bottels, call aloud for Corks.
55 Safe past the *Gnome* thro' this fantastick Band,
A Branch of healing *Spleenwort*[113] in his hand.
Then thus addrest the Pow'r—Hail wayward Queen!
Who rule the Sex to Fifty from Fifteen,
Parents of Vapours and of Female Wit,
60 Who give th' *Hysteric* or *Poetic* Fit,
On various Tempers act by various ways,
Make some take Physick,[114] others scribble Plays;
Who cause the Proud their Visits to delay,
And send the Godly in a Pett, to pray.
65 A Nymph there is, that all thy Pow'r disdains,
And thousands more in equal Mirth maintains.
But oh! if e'er thy *Gnome* could spoil a Grace,
Or raise a Pimple on a beauteous Face,
Like Citron-Waters[115] Matrons' Cheeks inflame,
70 Or change Complexions at a losing Game;
If e'er with airy Horns[116] I planted Heads,
Or rumpled Petticoats, or tumbled Beds,

[107]spirals. [108]Elysium in Greek mythology was the abode of the blessed after death, and so a place of ideal happiness. [109]stage machinery. [110]one symptom of the spleen was suffering from hallucinations. [111]small earthen pot. [112]in the *Iliad* (XVIII.439 ff.), Homer tells how Hephaistos made walking tripods (three-legged stools). [113]just as Aeneas carries a golden bough to guarantee safe passage through the underworld in the *Aeneid*, Umbriel carries a branch of spleenwort, a fern believed to protect one against the spleen. [114]medicine. [115]brandy flavoured with lemon peel. [116]the traditional emblem of the cuckold.

Or caus'd Suspicion when no Soul was rude,
Or discompos'd the Head-dress of a Prude,
75   Or e'er to costive[117] Lap-Dog gave Disease,
Which not the Tears of brightest Eyes could ease:
Hear me, and touch *Belinda* with Chagrin;
That single Act gives half the World the Spleen.
    The Goddess with a discontented Air
80   Seems to reject him, tho' she grants his Pray'r.
A wondrous Bag with both her Hands she binds,
Like that where once *Ulysses* held the Winds;[118]
There she collects the Force of Female Lungs,
Sighs, Sobs, and Passions, and the War of Tongues.
85   A Vial next she fills with fainting Fears,
Soft Sorrows, melting Griefs, and flowing Tears.
The *Gnome* rejoicing bears her Gifts away,
Spreads his black Wings, and slowly mounts to Day.
    Sunk in *Thalestris*'[119] Arms the Nymph he found,
90   Her Eyes dejected and her Hair unbound.
Full o'er their Heads the swelling Bag he rent,
And all the Furies issued at the Vent.
Belinda burns with more than mortal Ire,
And fierce *Thalestris* fans the rising Fire.
95   O wretched Maid! she spread her Hands, and cry'd,
(While *Hampton's* Ecchos, wretched Maid! reply'd)
Was it for this you took such constant Care
The *Bodkin*,[120] *Comb*, and *Essence* to prepare;
For this your Locks in Paper-Durance[121] bound,
100   For this with tort'ring Irons wreath'd around?
For this with Fillets[122] strain'd your tender Head,
And bravely bore the double Loads of Lead?[123]
Gods! shall the Ravisher display your Hair,
While the Fops envy, and the Ladies Stare!
105   *Honour* forbid! at whose unrival'd Shrine
Ease, Pleasure, Virtue, All, our Sex resign.

[117]constipated. [118]Aeolus, god of winds, gave Odysseus, or Ulysses, a bag containing all the winds that could prevent him from returning home; Odysseus's men opened the bag when he was asleep and the ensuing storms drove them far away (*Odyssey* X.19 ff.). [119]the name of a legendary warrior-queen of the Amazons. [120]needle used as a hairpin. [121]inflated epic diction for curling papers, the papers that were wrapped around curling irons (the "tort'ring" of line 100) to prepare the elaborate coiffures worn by women. [122]headbands. [123]the elaborate upright coiffures of ladies were arranged upon a wooden frame; strips of pliant lead attached to the frame kept the curls in place.

Methinks already I your Tears survey,
Already hear the horrid things they say,
Already see you a degraded Toast,[124]
110 And all your Honour in a Whisper lost!
How shall I, then, your helpless Fame defend?
'Twill then be Infamy to seem your Friend!
And shall this Prize, th' inestimable Prize,
Expos'd thro' Crystal to the gazing Eyes,
115 And heighten'd by the Diamond's circling Rays,
On that Rapacious Hand for ever blaze?
Sooner shall Grass in *Hide*-Park *Circus*[125] grow,
And Wits take Lodgings in the Sound of *Bow*;[126]
Sooner let Earth, Air, Sea, to *Chaos* fall,
120 Men, Monkies, Lap-dogs, Parrots, perish all!
      She said; then raging to *Sir Plume*[127] repairs,
And bids her *Beau* demand the precious Hairs:
(*Sir Plume*, of *Amber Snuff-box* justly vain,
And the nice Conduct of a *clouded*[128] *Cane*)
125 With earnest Eyes, and round unthinking Face,
He first the Snuff-box open'd, then the Case,
And thus broke out—"My Lord, why, what the Devil?
"Z—ds![129] damn the Lock! 'fore Gad, you must be civil!
"Plague on't! 'tis past a Jest—nay prithee, Pox!
130 "Give her the Hair"—he spoke, and rapp'd his Box.
      It grieves me much (reply'd the Peer again)
Who speaks so well shou'd ever speak in vain.
But by this Lock, this sacred Lock I swear,
135 (Which never more shall join its parted Hair,
Which never more its Honours[130] shall renew,
Clipt from the lovely Head where late it grew)
That while my Nostrils draw the vital Air,
This Hand, which won it, shall for ever wear.
He spoke, and speaking, in proud Triumph spread
140 The long-contended Honours of her Head.
      But *Umbriel*, hateful *Gnome*! forbears not so;
He breaks the Vial whence the Sorrows flow.
Then see! the *Nymph* in beauteous Grief appears,

[124]woman whose health is often drunk by men. [125]the Ring (see I.44), where carriages kept the grass from growing. [126]within the sound of St. Mary-le-Bow in Cheapside, the unfashionable commercial quarter of London. [127]Sir George Browne, Arabella's kinsman, who chiefly fomented the quarrel. [128]mottled. [129]Zounds, a corrupted version of "God's wounds"—an oath expressing indignation. [130]beauties, graces (as well as honours); see also line 140 of this canto.

Her Eyes half-languishing, half-drown'd in Tears;
145 On her heav'd Bosom hung her drooping Head,
Which, with a Sigh, she rais'd; and thus she said.
　　　For ever curs'd be this detested Day,[131]
Which snatch'd my best, my fav'rite Curl away!
Happy! ah ten times happy, had I been,
150 If *Hampton-Court* these Eyes had never seen!
Yet am not I the first mistaken Maid,
By Love of *Courts* to num'rous Ills betray'd.
Oh had I rather un-admir'd remain'd
In some lone Isle, or distant *Northern* Land;
155 Where the gilt *Chariot* never marks the Way,
Where none learn *Ombre*, none e'er taste *Bohea*![132]
There kept my Charms conceal'd from mortal Eye,
Like Roses that in Desarts bloom and die.
What mov'd my Mind with youthful Lords to rome?
160 O had I stay'd, and said my Pray'rs at home!
'Twas this, the Morning *Omens* seem'd to tell;
Thrice from my trembling hand the *Patch-box* fell;
The tott'ring *China* shook without a Wind,
Nay, *Poll* sate mute, and *Shock* was most Unkind!
165 A *Sylph* too warn'd me of the Threats of Fate,
In mystic Visions, now believ'd too late!
See the poor Remnants of these slighted Hairs!
My hands shall rend what ev'n thy Rapine spares:
These, in two sable Ringlets taught to break,
170 Once gave new Beauties to the snowie Neck.
The Sister-Lock now sits uncouth, alone,
And in its Fellow's Fate foresees its own;
Uncurl'd it hangs, the fatal Sheers demands;
And tempts once more thy sacrilegious Hands.
175 Oh hadst thou, Cruel! been content to seize
Hairs less in sight, or any Hairs but these!

CANTO V.

She said: the pitying Audience melt in Tears,
But *Fate* and *Jove* had stopp'd the *Baron's* Ears.
In Vain *Thalestris* with Reproach assails,
For who can move when fair *Belinda* fails?

---

[131]imitation of Achilles's lament for Patroclus in the *Iliad* (XVIII.107 ff.). [132]costly kind of tea.

5 Not half so fixt the *Trojan* cou'd remain,
While *Anna* begg'd and *Dido* rag'd in vain.[133]
Then grave *Clarissa* graceful wav'd her Fan;
Silence ensu'd, and thus the Nymph began.[134]
    Say, why are Beauties prais'd and honour'd most,
10 The wise Man's Passion, and the vain Man's Toast?
Why deck'd with all that Land and Sea afford,
Why Angels call'd, and Angel-like ador'd?
Why round our Coaches crowd the white-glov'd Beaus,
Why bows the Side-box[135] from its inmost Rows?
15 How vain are all these Glories, all our Pains,
Unless good Sense preserve what Beauty gains:
That Men may say, when we the Front-box grace,
Behold the first in Virtue, as in Face!
Oh! if to dance all Night, and dress all Day,
20 Charm'd the Small-pox,[136] or chas'd old Age away;
Who would not scorn what Huswife's Cares produce,
Or who would learn one earthly Thing of Use?
To patch, nay ogle, might become a Saint,
Nor could it sure be such a Sin to paint.
25 But since, alas! frail Beauty must decay,
Curl'd or uncurl'd, since Locks will turn to grey,
Since painted, or not painted, all shall fade,
And she who scorns a Man, must die a Maid;
What then remains, but well our Pow'r to use,
30 And keep good Humour still whate'er we lose?
And trust me, Dear! good Humour can prevail,
When Airs, and Flights, and Screams, and Scolding fail.
Beauties in vain their pretty Eyes may roll;
Charms strike the Sight, but Merit wins the Soul.
35   So spoke the Dame, but no Applause ensu'd;
Belinda frown'd, *Thalestris* call'd her Prude.
To Arms, to Arms! the fierce Virago[137] cries,
And swift as Lightning to the Combate flies.

[133]Aeneas, burdened with his divine mission of founding a new Troy, left Carthage and Queen Dido, despite her furious reproaches and the prayers of her sister Anna (*Aeneid* IV.296–449).
[134]when Pope published his collected early poetry in 1717, he added Clarissa's speech to the five-canto Rape of 1714 in order, as he explained, "to open the moral of the poem, in a parody of the speech of Sarpedon to Glaucus in Homer"; Sarpedon's speech is an appeal to his comrade to earn in battle the honour they both enjoy as leaders (*Iliad* XII.371–96). [135]gentlemen preferred the side boxes at the theatre, ladies the front boxes facing the stage (see line 17 of this canto). [136]before vaccination, smallpox was common and deadly; the Lord Petre of this poem died of smallpox in 1713. [137]man-like woman, female warrior.

All side in Parties, and begin th' Attack;
40 Fans clap, Silks russle, and tough Whalebones crack;
Heroes' and Heroins' Shouts confus'dly rise,
And base, and treble Voices strike the Skies.
No common Weapons in their Hands are found,
Like Gods they fight, nor dread a mortal Wound.
45   So when bold *Homer* makes the Gods engage,[138]
And heavn'ly Breasts with human Passions rage;
'Gainst *Pallas*,[139] *Mars*; *Latona*,[140] *Hermes* arms;
And all *Olympus* rings with loud Alarms.
Jove's Thunder roars, Heav'n trembles all around;
50 Blue *Neptune* storms, the bellowing Deeps resound;
Earth shakes her nodding Tow'rs, the Ground gives way;
And the pale Ghosts start at the Flash of Day!
        Triumphant *Umbriel* on a Sconce's[141] Height
Clapt his glad Wings, and sate to view the Fight:
55 Propt on their Bodkin Spears, the Sprights survey
The growing Combat, or assist the Fray.
        While thro' the Press enrag'd *Thalestris* flies,
And scatters Deaths around from both her Eyes,
A *Beau* and *Witling*[142] perish'd in the Throng,
60 One dy'd in *Metaphor*, and one in *Song*.
O cruel Nymph! a living Death I bear,
Cry'd *Dapperwit*,[143] and sunk beside his Chair.
A mournful Glance Sir *Fopling* upwards cast,
Those Eyes are made so killing—was his last:
65 Thus on *Meander's*[144] flow'ry Margin lies
Th' expiring Swan, and as he sings he dies.[145]
        When bold Sir *Plume* had drawn *Clarissa* down,
Chloe stept in, and kill'd him with a Frown;
She smil'd to see the doughty Hero slain,
70 But at her Smile, the Beau reviv'd again.
        Now *Jove* suspends his golden Scales in Air,[146]
Weighs the Men's Wits against the Lady's Hair;
The doubtful Beam long nods from side to side;

[138]see the *Iliad* XX.91 ff. [139]Pallas Athena, the Greek goddess of war (also the goddess of wisdom). [140]the mother of the Greek deities Apollo and Artemis. [141]candlestick attached to the wall. [142]tiny wit. [143]like "Sir Fopling" in the next line, a type-name for a fop and would-be wit in Restoration comic plays. [144]celebrated winding river in Asia Minor. [145]swans were believed to sing beautifully only as they died. [146]epic convention when a decisive battle is about to take place; see the *Iliad* VIII.87 ff. and the *Aeneid* XIII.725 ff.

At length the Wits mount up, the Hairs subside.

75   See fierce *Belinda* on the *Baron* flies,
With more than usual Lightning in her Eyes;
Nor fear'd the Chief th'unequal Fight to try,
Who sought no more than on his Foe to die.
But this bold Lord, with manly Strength indu'd,
80 She with one Finger and a Thumb subdu'd:
Just where the Breath of Life his Nostrils drew,
A Charge of *Snuff the* wily Virgin threw;
The *Gnomes* direct, to ev'ry Atome just,
The pungent Grains of titillating Dust.
85 Sudden, with starting Tears each Eye o'erflows,
And the high Dome re-ecchoes to his Nose.

     Now meet thy Fate, incens'd *Belinda* cry'd,
And drew a deadly *Bodkin* from her Side.
(The same,[147] his ancient Personage to deck,
90 Her great great Grandsire wore about his Neck
In three *Seal-Rings*; which after, melted down,
Form'd a vast *Buckle* for his Widow's Gown:
Her infant Grandame's *Whistle* next it grew,
The *Bells* she gingled,[148] and the *Whistle* blew;
95 Then in a *Bodkin* grac'd her Mother's Hairs,
Which long she wore, and now *Belinda* wears.)

     Boast not my Fall (he cry'd) insulting Foe!
Thou by some other shalt be laid as low.
Nor think, to die dejects my lofty Mind;
100 All that I dread, is leaving you behind!
Rather than so, ah let me still survive,
And burn in *Cupid's* Flames,—but burn alive.

     Restore the Lock! she cries; and all around
Restore the Lock! the vaulted Roofs rebound.
105 Not fierce *Othello* in so loud a Strain
Roar'd for the Handkerchief that caus'd his Pain.
But see how oft Ambitious Aims are cross'd,
And Chiefs contend 'till all the Prize is lost!
The Lock, obtain'd with Guilt, and kept with Pain,
110 In ev'ry place is sought, but sought in vain:
With such a Prize no Mortal must be blest,

[147]what follows is a parody of epic descriptions of a hero's armour and its descent through the generations in his family. [148]jingled.

So Heav'n decrees! with Heav'n who can contest?
    Some thought it mounted to the Lunar Sphere,
Since all things lost on Earth, are treasur'd there.[149]
There Heroes' Wits are kept in pondrous Vases,
And Beaus' in *Snuff-boxes* and *Tweezer-Cases.*
There broken Vows, and Death-bed Alms are found,
And Lovers' Hearts with Ends of Riband[150] bound;
The Courtier's Promises, and Sick Man's Pray'rs,
The Smiles of Harlots, and the Tears of Heirs,
Cages for Gnats, and Chains to Yoak a Flea;
Dry'd Butterflies, and Tomes of Casuistry.[151]
    But trust the Muse—she saw it upward rise,
Tho' mark'd by none but quick Poetic Eyes:
(So *Rome's* great Founder to the Heav'ns withdrew,
To *Proculus* alone confess'd in view.)[152]
A sudden Star, it shot thro' liquid[153] Air,
And drew behind a radiant *Trail of Hair.*
Not *Berenice's*[154] Locks first rose so bright,
The Heav'ns bespangling with dishevel'd Light.
The *Sylphs* behold it kindling as it flies,
And pleas'd pursue its Progress thro' the Skies.
This the *Beau-monde*[155] shall from the *Mall*[156] survey,
And hail with Musick its propitious Ray.
    This, the blest Lover shall for *Venus* take,
And send up Vows from *Rosamonda's* Lake.[157]
This *Partridge*[158] soon shall view in cloudless Skies,
When next he looks thro' *Galileo's* Eyes;[159]
And hence th' Egregious Wizard shall foredoom

115
120
125
130
135

---

[149]in a striking episode in *Orlando Furioso* (1532), the chivalric epic by the Italian poet Ariosto, the hero's lost wits are found on the moon, where all things that are lost on earth maybe found. [150]ribbon. [151]casuistry, the branch of theology that studies the application of general ethical rules to particular cases, had become a synonym for hair-splitting rationalization. [152]Romulus, the founder and first king of Rome, disappeared from earth in the midst of a storm; the senator Proculus affirmed that Romulus had ascended to the heavens. [153]clear, transparent. [154]Berenice, wife of King Ptolemy III of ancient Egypt, vowed to sacrifice her hair to the gods if her husband returned safe from battle; upon his return, she placed her hair in the temple of Aphrodite, but the next day it had disappeared and was believed to have become a constellation. [155]fashionable world. [156]Pall Mall, a walk laid out by Charles II in St. James's Park. [157]pond in St. James's Park considered to be the haunt of unhappy lovers; it was named after Rosamund Clifford (died 1177), known as "Fair Rosamond," mistress of Henry II, who was, according to legend, made to drink poison by his queen. [158]quack astrologer of the time, who predicted every year that the pope and King Louis XIV of France would fall from power that year (see line 140). [159]i.e., telescope; Galileo constructed the first telescope in 1609.

140 The Fate of *Louis*, and the Fall of *Rome*.
   Then cease, bright Nymph! to mourn thy ravish'd Hair
Which adds new Glory to the shining Sphere!
Not all the Tresses that fair Head can boast
Shall draw such Envy as the Lock you lost.
145 For, after all the Murders of your Eye,
When, after Millions slain, your self shall die;
When those fair Suns shall sett, as sett they must,
And all those Tresses shall be laid in Dust;
This Lock, the Muse shall consecrate to Fame,
150 And mid'st the Stars inscribe *Belinda's* Name!

               (1714)

Thomas Gray   (1716–1771)

Thomas Gray, a shy scholar, wrote very few poems, but among them is one of the best-known and most-loved poems in the language, *Elegy Written in a Country Church-Yard* (or, as it is usually called, Gray's *Elegy*). Gray spent his entire adult life as a scholar at Cambridge University; known as one of the most learned men in Europe, he helped to create scholarly interest in Welsh, Old Norse, and medieval English poetry. Gray published his *Elegy* in 1751. His shyness led him to turn down the position of Poet Laureate when he was offered it in 1757; although named Professor of Modern History at Cambridge, he was unable to deliver a single lecture. Nevertheless, as soon as his *Elegy* was published, he became recognized as the greatest lyric poet of the age. His contemporary Samuel Johnson memorably sums up the poem's appeal: "The *Church-Yard* abounds with images which find a mirror in every mind, and with sentiments to which every bosom returns an echo."

Elegy Written in a Country Church-Yard

The Curfew tolls the knell of parting day,
The lowing herd wind slowly o'er the lea,[1]
The plowman homeward plods his weary way,
And leaves the world to darkness and to me.

5 Now fades the glimmering landscape on the sight,
And all the air a solemn stillness holds,
Save where the beetle wheels his droning flight,
And drowsy tinklings lull the distant folds;

---

[1] open field, grassland.

Save that from yonder ivy-mantled tow'r
10   The mopeing owl does to the moon complain
Of such, as wand'ring near her secret bow'r,
Molest her ancient solitary reign.

Beneath those rugged elms, that yew-tree's shade,
Where heaves the turf in many a mould'ring heap,
15   Each in his narrow cell for ever laid,
The rude[2] Forefathers of the hamlet sleep.

The breezy call of incense-breathing Morn,
The swallow twitt'ring from the straw-built shed,
The cock's shrill clarion, or the echoing horn,
20   No more shall rouse them from their lowly bed.

For them no more the blazing hearth shall burn,
Or busy houswife ply her evening care:
No children run to lisp their sire's return,
Or climb his knees the envied kiss to share.

25   Oft did the harvest to their sickle yield,
Their furrow oft the stubborn glebe[3] has broke;
How jocund did they drive their team afield!
How bow'd the woods beneath their sturdy stroke!

Let not Ambition mock their useful toil,
30   Their homely joys, and destiny obscure;
Nor Grandeur hear with a disdainful smile,
The short and simple annals of the poor.

The boast of heraldry, the pomp of pow'r,
And all that beauty, all that wealth e'er gave,
35   Awaits alike th' inevitable hour.
The paths of glory lead but to the grave.

Nor you, ye Proud, impute to These the fault,
If Mem'ry o'er their Tomb no Trophies raise,
Where thro' the long-drawn isle[4] and fretted vault
40   The pealing anthem swells the note of praise.

Can storied urn or animated bust
Back to its mansion call the fleeting breath?
Can Honour's voice provoke the silent dust,
Or Flatt'ry sooth the dull cold ear of Death?

[2]uneducated. [3]soil. [4]aisle.

45 Perhaps in this neglected spot is laid
Some heart once pregnant with celestial fire,
Hands, that the rod of empire might have sway'd,
Or wak'd to extasy the living lyre.

But Knowledge to their eyes her ample page
50 Rich with the spoils of time did ne'er unroll;
Chill Penury repress'd their noble rage,[5]
And froze the genial[6] current of the soul.

Full many a gem of purest ray serene,
The dark unfathom'd caves of ocean bear:
55 Full many a flower is born to blush unseen,
And waste its sweetness on the desert air.

Some village-Hampden,[7] that with dauntless breast
The little Tyrant of his fields withstood;
Some mute inglorious Milton here may rest,
60 Some Cromwell guiltless of his country's blood.

Th' applause of list'ning senates to command,
The threats of pain and ruin to despise,
To scatter plenty o'er a smiling land,
And read their hist'ry in a nation's eyes

65 Their lot forbad: nor circumscrib'd alone
Their growing virtues, but their crimes confin'd;
Forbad to wade through slaughter to a throne,
And shut the gates of mercy on mankind,

The struggling pangs of conscious truth to hide,
70 To quench the blushes of ingenuous shame,
Or heap the shrine of Luxury and Pride
With incense kindled at the Muse's flame.

Far from the madding[8] crowd's ignoble strife,
Their sober wishes never learn'd to stray;
75 Along the cool sequester'd vale of life
They kept the noiseless tenor of their way.

Yet ev'n these bones from insult to protect
Some frail memorial still erected nigh,
With uncouth rhimes and shapeless sculpture deck'd,
80 Implores the passing tribute of a sigh.

---

[5]rapture, ardour. [6]creative. [7]John Hampden (1594–1643), member of Parliament who defended the rights of the people against Charles I and became a leader of the Puritan cause in the Civil War. [8]frenzied, maddened.

Their name, their years, spelt by th' unletter'd muse,
The place of fame and elegy supply:
And many a holy text around she strews,
That teach the rustic moralist to die.

85 For who to dumb Forgetfulness a prey,
This pleasing anxious being e'er resign'd,
Left the warm precincts of the chearful day,
Nor cast one longing ling'ring look behind?

On some fond breast the parting soul relies,
90 Some pious drops the closing eye requires;
Ev'n from the tomb the voice of Nature cries,
Ev'n in our Ashes live their wonted Fires.

For thee, who mindful of th' unhonour'd Dead
Dost in these lines their artless tale relate;
95 If chance,[9] by lonely contemplation led,
Some kindred Spirit shall inquire thy fate,

Haply some hoary-headed Swain[10] may say,
"Oft have we seen him at the peep of dawn
Brushing with hasty steps the dews away
100 To meet the sun upon the upland lawn.

"There at the foot of yonder nodding beech
That wreathes its old fantastic roots so high,
His listless length at noontide wou'd he stretch,
And pore upon the brook that babbles by.

105 "Hard by yon wood, now smiling as in scorn,
Mutt'ring his wayward fancies he wou'd rove,
Now drooping, woeful wan, like one forlorn,
Or craz'd with care, or cross'd in hopeless love.

"One morn I miss'd him on the custom'd hill,
110 Along the heath and near his fav'rite tree;
Another came; nor yet beside the rill,
Nor up the lawn, nor at the wood was he;

"The next with dirges due in sad array
Slow thro' the church-way path we saw him borne.
115 Approach and read (for thou can'st read) the lay,
Grav'd on the stone beneath yon aged thorn."

[9]by chance. [10]shepherd.

NEL

The Epitaph

HERE *rests his head upon the lap of Earth*
A Youth to Fortune and to Fame unknown,
Fair Science[11] frown'd not on his humble birth,
120   *And Melancholy mark'd him for her own.*

Large was his bounty, and his soul sincere,
Heav'n did a recompence as largely send:
He gave to Mis'ry all he had, a tear,
He gain'd from Heav'n ('twas all he wish'd) a friend.

125   *No farther seek his merits to disclose,*
Or draw his frailties from their dread abode,
(There they alike in trembling hope repose)
The bosom of his Father and his God.

(1751)

William Blake   (1757–1827)

Born in London, William Blake studied art at the Royal Academy as a boy before serving an apprenticeship to an engraver. His first collection of poems, *Poetic Sketches* (1783), indicated his departure from the neoclassical conventions that had dominated the eighteenth century. However, *Songs of Innocence and Experience* (1794), illustrated by his own hand-painted engravings, marked the first flowering of his genius. Lyrics revealing the influence of Elizabethan and seventeenth-century English poetry, they present "two contrasting states of the human mind." Many are companion poems, using the lives and views of children to symbolize innocence and experience. During the 1790s, Blake was influenced by radical political, religious, and philosophical currents prevalent in England and wrote in his poems about tyranny and oppression, the power of "God & his Priest & King," as they affected the lives of common people, especially children. He celebrated the visionary powers of the imagination in a series of "Prophetic Books" written after the publication of the *Songs*. Complex and often obscure, they develop a philosophy in which human life is seen as progressing from the initial innocence of childhood, to the complexity and pain of experience, and finally to a higher, more fulfilled innocence. Relatively ignored during his lifetime and in the 50 years after his death, Blake's works began to be studied seriously during the twentieth century, and he is now recognized as one of the greatest Romantic poets.

[11]learning.

The Lamb

      Little Lamb who made thee
      Dost thou know who made thee
Gave thee life & bid thee feed,
By the stream & o'er the mead;[1]
5   Gave thee clothing of delight,
Softest clothing wooly bright;
Gave thee such a tender voice,
Making all the vales rejoice!
      Little Lamb who made thee
10   Dost thou know who made thee

      Little Lamb I'll tell thee,
      Little Lamb I'll tell thee!
He is called by thy name,
For he calls himself a Lamb:
15   He is meek & he is mild,
He became a little child:
I a child & thou a lamb,
We are called by his name.
      Little Lamb God bless thee.
20   Little Lamb God bless thee.

(1789)

The Little Black Boy

My mother bore me in the southern wild,
And I am black, but O! my soul is white;
White as an angel is the English child:
But I am black as if bereav'd[1] of light.

5   My mother taught me underneath a tree
And sitting down before the heat of day,
She took me on her lap and kissed me,
And pointing to the east began to say.

Look the rising sun: there God does live
10 And gives his light, and gives his heat away.
And flowers and trees and beasts and men receive
Comfort in morning joy in the noon day.

[1]meadow [1]deprived.

And we are put on earth a little space,
That we may learn to bear the beams of love,
And these black bodies and this sun-burnt face
Is but a cloud, and like a shady grove.

For when our souls have learn'd the heat to bear
The cloud will vanish we shall hear his voice.
Saying: come out from the grove my love & care,
And round my golden tent like lambs rejoice.

Thus did my mother say and kissed me,
And thus I say to little English boy.
When I from black and he from white cloud free,
And round the tent of God like lambs we joy:

I'll shade him from the heat till he can bear,
To lean in joy upon our fathers knee.
And then I'll stand and stroke his silver hair,
And be like him and he will then love me.

(1789)

The Chimney Sweeper

When my mother died I was very young,
And my father sold me while yet my tongue,
Could scarcely cry weep weep weep weep.
So your chimneys I sweep & in soot I sleep.

There's little Tom Dacre, who cried when his head
That curl'd like a lambs back, was shav'd, so I said.
Hush Tom never mind it, for when your head's bare,
You know that the soot cannot spoil your white hair.

And so he was quiet, & that very night,
As Tom was a sleeping he had such a sight,
That thousands of sweepers, Dick, Joe, Ned & Jack,
Were all of them lock'd up in coffins of black,

And by came an Angel who had a bright key,
And he open'd the coffins & set them all free.
Then down a green plain leaping laughing they run
And wash in a river and shine in the Sun.

Then naked & white, all their bags left behind,
They rise upon clouds, and sport in the wind.
And the Angel told Tom if he'd be a good boy,
He'd have God for his father & never want joy.

And so Tom awoke and we rose in the dark
And got with our bags & our brushes to work.
Tho' the morning was cold, Tom was happy & warm,
So if all do their duty, they need not fear harm.

(1789)

Holy Thursday[1]

Twas on a Holy Thursday their innocent faces clean
The children walking two & two in red & blue & green
Grey headed beadles walkd before with wands as white as snow
Till into the high dome of Pauls[2] they like Thames waters flow

5   O what a multitude they seemd these flowers of London town
Seated in companies they sit with radiance all their own
The hum of multitudes was there but multitudes of lambs
Thousands of little boys & girls raising their innocent hands

Now like a mighty wind they raise to heaven the voice of song
10 Or like harmonious thunderings the seats of heaven among
Beneath them sit the aged men wise guardians of the poor
Then cherish pity, lest you drive an angel from your door

(1789)

Nurse's[1] Song

When the voices of children are heard on the green
And laughing is heard on the hill,
My heart is at rest within my breast
And every thing else is still

5   Then come home my children, the sun is gone down
And the dews of night arise
Come come leave off play, and let us away
Till the morning appears in the skies

No no let us play, for it is yet day
10 And we cannot go to sleep
Besides in the sky, the little birds fly
And the hills are all covered with sheep

---

[1]in the Anglican tradition, the Thursday 40 days after Easter, when Christ is said to have ascended to heaven. [2]St. Paul's Cathedral, London. [1]woman hired to care for a young child.

Well well go & play till the light fades away
And then go home to bed
15   The little ones leaped & shouted & laugh'd
And all the hills ecchoed

(c.1784)   (1789)

The Tyger

Tyger Tyger, burning bright,
In the forests of the night;
What immortal hand or eye,
Could frame thy fearful symmetry?

5   In what distant deeps or skies!
Burnt the fire of thine eyes?
On what wings dare he aspire?
What the hand, dare seize the fire?

And what shoulder, & what art,
10   Could twist the sinews of thy heart?
And when thy heart began to beat,
What dread hand? & what dread feet?

What the hammer? what the chain?
In what furnace was thy brain?
15   What the anvil? what dread grasp,
Dare its deadly terrors clasp?

When the stars threw down their spears
And water'd heaven with their tears;
Did he smile his work to see?
20   Did he who made the Lamb make thee?

Tyger Tyger, burning bright,
In the forests of the night;
What immortal hand or eye,
Dare frame thy fearful symmetry?

(1790–92)   (1794)

The Chimney Sweeper

A little black thing among the snow:
Crying weep, weep, in notes of woe!
Where are thy father & mother? say?
They are both gone up to the church to pray.

5   Because I was happy upon the heath,[1]
    And smil'd among the winters snow:
    They clothed me in the clothes of death,
    And taught me to sing the notes of woe.

    And because i am happy, & dance & sing,
10   They think they have done me no injury:
    And are gone to praise God & his Priest & King
    Who make up a heaven of our misery.

    (1790–92)   (1794)

Holy Thursday

    Is this a holy thing to see,
    In a rich and fruitful land,
    Babes reducd to misery,
    Fed with cold and usurous hand?

5   Is that trembling cry a song?
    Can it be a song of joy?
    And so many children poor?
    It is a land of poverty!

    And their sun does never shine.
10   And their fields are bleak & bare.
    And their ways are fill'd with thorns.
    It is eternal winter there.

    For where-e'er the sun does shine,
    And where-e'er the rain does fall:
15   Babe can never hunger there,
    Nor poverty the mind appall.

                                                      (1794)

Nurse's Song

    When the voices of children are heard on the green
    And whisprings are in the dale:
    The days of my youth rise fresh in my mind,
    My face turns green and pale.

[1]open countryside containing scrubby vegetation.

5   Then come home my children, the sun is gone down
And the dews of night arise
Your spring & your day are wasted in play
And your winter and night in disguise.

(1794)

The Sick Rose

O Rose thou art sick.
The invisible worm,
That flies in the night
In the howling storm:

5   Has found out thy bed
Of crimson joy:
And his dark secret love
Does thy life destroy.

(1794)

London

I wander thro' each charter'd[1] street,
Near where the charter'd Thames does flow.
And mark in every face I meet
Marks of weakness, marks or woe.

5   In every cry of every Man,
In every Infants cry of fear,
In every voice; in every ban,
The mind-forg'd manacles I hear

How the Chimney-sweepers cry
10   Every blackning Church appalls,
And the hapless Soldiers sigh
Runs in blood down Palace walls

But most thro' midnight streets I hear
How the youthful Harlots curse
15   Blasts the new-born Infants tear
And blights with plagues the Marriage hearse.

(1794)

[1]protected as private property.

William Wordsworth (1770–1850)

Born in Cockermouth, near the English Lake District, William Wordsworth attended Cambridge University and then travelled widely in Europe, spending a year in France during the Revolution. There he fathered an illegitimate child, Caroline, referred to indirectly in his sonnet "It is a beauteous evening." In 1798, with his friend Samuel Taylor Coleridge, he published *Lyrical Ballads*, a collection in which, as Coleridge stated, Wordsworth gave "the charm of novelty to things of everyday." In the Preface to the 1800 edition, written in response to criticism of the first edition, Wordsworth explained the theory underlying his poems. Reacting in part against the dominant poetic tastes and conventions of the eighteenth century, he stated that the poems were created from "emotion recollected in tranquillity," an idea illustrated in "Lines Composed a Few Miles above Tintern Abbey," and later in "I wandered lonely as a cloud." He chose as his subjects "incidents and situations of common life," presented in "language really used by men." In 1802, influenced in part by his reading of John Milton, who is addressed in "London, 1802," Wordsworth wrote a number of sonnets considered by many critics to be the finest to have appeared since the seventeenth century. Wordsworth's reputation increased steadily during his lifetime, and, in 1843, he was appointed Poet Laureate. He is now recognized not only as one of the greatest of the Romantics and a major English poet, but as one who, in his portrayal of common people and nature, radically altered the course of English poetry in the nineteenth century.

Lines

COMPOSED A FEW MILES ABOVE TINTERN ABBEY,[1] ON REVIS-
ITING THE BANKS OF THE WYE DURING A TOUR. JULY 13, 1798

Five years have past; five summers, with the length
Of five long winters! and again I hear
These waters, rolling from their mountain-springs
With a soft inland murmur.—Once again
5   Do I behold these steep and lofty cliffs,
That on a wild secluded scene impress
Thoughts of more deep seclusion; and connect
The landscape with the quiet of the sky.
The day is come when I again repose
10   Here, under this dark sycamore, and view
These plots of cottage-ground, these orchard-tufts,
Which at this season, with their unripe fruits,
Are clad in one green hue, and lose themselves

➡

[1]ruined Cistercian abbey located on the Wye River, Wales.

'Mid groves and copses. Once again I see
These hedge-rows, hardly hedge-rows, little lines
Of sportive wood run wild: these pastoral farms,
Green to the very door; and wreaths of smoke
Sent up, in silence, from among the trees!
With some uncertain notice, as might seem
Of vagrant dwellers in the houseless woods,
Or of some Hermit's cave, where by his fire
The Hermit sits alone.
                              These beauteous forms,
Through a long absence, have not been to me
As is a landscape to a blind man's eye:
But oft, in lonely rooms, and 'mid the din
Of towns and cities, I have owed to them
In hours of weariness, sensations sweet,
Felt in the blood, and felt along the heart;
And passing even into my purer mind,
With tranquil restoration:—feelings too
Of unremembered pleasure: such, perhaps,
As have no slight or trivial influence
On that best portion of a good man's life,
His little, nameless, unremembered, acts
Of kindness and of love. Nor less, I trust,
To them I may have owed another gift,
Of aspect more sublime; that blessed mood,
In which the burthen of the mystery,
In which the heavy and the weary weight
Of all this unintelligible world,
Is lightened:—that serene and blessed mood,
In which the affections gently lead us on,—
Until the breath of this corporeal frame
And even the motion of our human blood
Almost suspended, we are laid asleep
In body, and become a living soul:
While with an eye made quiet by the power
Of harmony, and the deep power of joy,
We see into the life of things.
                              If this
Be but a vain belief, yet, oh! how oft—
In darkness and amid the many shapes
Of joyless daylight; when the fretful stir

→

Unprofitable, and the fever of the world,
Have hung upon the beatings of my heart—
55 How oft, in spirit, have I turned to thee,
O sylvan Wye! thou wanderer thro' the woods,
How often has my spirit turned to thee!
        And now, with gleams of half-extinguished thought,
With many recognitions dim and faint,
60 And somewhat of a sad perplexity,
The picture of the mind revives again:
While here I stand, not only with the sense
Of present pleasure, but with pleasing thoughts
That in this moment there is life and food
65 For future years. And so I dare to hope,
Though changed, no doubt, from what I was when first
I came among these hills; when like a roe
I bounded o'er the mountains, by the sides
Of the deep rivers, and the lonely streams,
70 Wherever nature led: more like a man
Flying from something that he dreads than one
Who sought the thing he loved. For nature then
(The coarser pleasures of my boyish days,
And their glad animal movements all gone by)
75 To me was all in all.—I cannot paint
What then I was. The sounding cataract
Haunted me like a passion: the tall rock,
The mountain, and the deep and gloomy wood,
Their colours and their forms, were then to me
80 An appetite; a feeling and a love,
That had no need of a remoter charm,
By thought supplied, nor any interest
Unborrowed from the eye.—That time is past,
And all its aching joys are now no more,
85 And all its dizzy raptures. Not for this
Faint I, nor mourn nor murmur; other gifts
Have followed; for such loss, I would believe,
Abundant recompense. For I have learned
To look on nature, not as in the hour
90 Of thoughtless youth; but hearing oftentimes
The still, sad music of humanity,
Nor harsh nor grating, though of ample power
To chasten and subdue. And I have felt

A presence that disturbs me with the joy
95 Of elevated thoughts; a sense sublime
Of something far more deeply interfused,
Whose dwelling is the light of setting suns,
And the round ocean and the living air,
And the blue sky, and in the mind of man:
100 A motion and a spirit, that impels
All thinking things, all objects of all thought,
And rolls through all things. Therefore am I still
A lover of the meadows and the woods,
And mountains; and of all that we behold
105 From this green earth; of all the mighty world
Of eye, and ear,—both what they half create,
And what perceive; well pleased to recognise
In nature and the language of the sense
The anchor of my purest thoughts, the nurse,
110 The guide, the guardian of my heart, and soul
Of all my moral being.
                              Nor perchance,
If I were not thus taught, should I the more
Suffer my genial spirits to decay:
For thou art with me here upon the banks
115 Of this fair river; thou my dearest Friend,[2]
My dear, dear Friend; and in thy voice I catch
The language of my former heart, and read
My former pleasures in the shooting lights
Of thy wild eyes. Oh! yet a little while
120 May I behold in thee what I was once,
My dear, dear Sister! and this prayer I make,
Knowing that Nature never did betray
The heart that loved her; 'tis her privilege,
Through all the years of this our life, to lead
125 From joy to joy: for she can so inform
The mind that is within us, so impress
With quietness and beauty, and so feed
With lofty thoughts, that neither evil tongues,
Rash judgments, nor the sneers of selfish men,
130 Nor greetings where no kindness is, nor all
The dreary intercourse of daily life,
Shall e'er prevail against us, or disturb

→

[2]Wordsworth's sister, Dorothy.

Our cheerful faith, that all which we behold
Is full of blessings. Therefore let the moon
135   Shine on thee in thy solitary walk;
And let the misty mountain-winds be free
To blow against thee: and, in after years,
When these wild ecstasies shall be matured
Into a sober pleasure; when thy mind
140   Shall be a mansion for all lovely forms,
Thy memory be as a dwelling-place
For all sweet sounds and harmonies; oh! then,
If solitude, or fear, or pain, or grief,
Should be thy portion, with what healing thoughts
145   Of tender joy wilt thou remember me,
And these my exhortations! Nor, perchance—
If I should be where I no more can hear
Thy voice, nor catch from thy wild eyes these gleams
Of past existence—wilt thou then forget
150   That on the banks of this delightful stream
We stood together; and that I, so long
A worshipper of Nature, hither came
Unwearied in that service: rather say
With warmer love—oh! with far deeper zeal
155   Of holier love. Nor wilt thou then forget
That after many wanderings, many years
Of absence, these steep woods and lofty cliffs,
And this green pastoral landscape, were to me
More dear, both for themselves and for thy sake!

(1798)

She dwelt among the untrodden ways

She dwelt among the untrodden ways
    Beside the springs or Dove,[1]
A Maid whom there were none to praise
    And very few to love:

5   A violet by a mossy stone
    Half hidden from the eye!
—Fair as a star, when only one
    Is shining in the sky.

[1] one of several rivers and streams named Dove is in Wordworth's Lake District, in the north-west of England.

She lived unknown, and few could know
    When Lucy ceased to be;
But she is in her grave, and, oh,
    The difference to me!

(1799)   (1800)

It is a beauteous evening, calm and free

It is a beauteous evening, calm and free,
The holy time is quiet as a Nun
Breathless with adoration; the broad sun
Is sinking down in its tranquillity;
The gentleness of heaven broods o'er the Sea:
Listen! the mighty Being is awake,
And doth with his eternal motion make
A sound like thunder—everlastingly.
Dear Child![1] dear Girl! that walkest with me here,
If thou appear untouched by solemn thought,
Thy nature is not therefore less divine:
Thou liest in Abraham's bosom[2] all the year;
And worshipp'st at the Temple's inner shrine,
God being with thee when we know it not.

(1802)   (1807)

London, 1802

Milton! thou shouldst be living at this hour:
England hath need of thee: she is a fen
Of stagnant waters: altar, sword, and pen,
Fireside, the heroic wealth of hall and bower,
Have forfeited their ancient English dower
Of inward happiness. We are selfish men;
Oh! raise us up, return to us again;
And give us manners, virtue, freedom, power.
Thy soul was like a Star, and dwelt apart;
Thou hadst a voice whose sound was like the sea:
Pure as the naked heavens, majestic, free,
So didst thou travel on life's common way,

---

[1]Wordsworth's illegitimate daughter, Caroline.   [2]heavenly rest, peace. Cf. Luke 16:22–23.

In cheerful godliness; and yet thy heart
The lowliest duties on herself did lay.

(1802)   (1807)

The world is too much with us

The world is too much with us; late and soon,
Getting and spending, we lay waste our powers:
Little we see in Nature that is ours;
We have given our hearts away, a sordid boon!
5   This Sea that bares her bosom to the moon;
The winds that will be howling at all hours,
And are up-gathered now like sleeping flowers;
For this, for everything, we are out of tune;
It moves us not.—Great God! I'd rather be
10 A Pagan suckled in a creed outworn;
So might I, standing on this pleasant lea,
Have glimpses that would make me less forlorn;
Have sight of Proteus[1] rising from the sea;
Or hear old Triton[2] blow his wreathèd horn.

(c. 1802)   (1807)

I wandered lonely as a cloud

I wandered lonely as a cloud
That floats on high o'er vales and hills,
When all at once I saw a crowd,
A host, of golden daffodils;
5   Beside the lake, beneath the trees,
Fluttering and dancing in the breeze.

Continuous as the stars that shine
And twinkle on the milky way,
They stretched in never-ending line
10 Along the margin of a bay:
Ten thousand saw I at a glance,
Tossing their heads in sprightly dance.

---

[1]Greek sea deity who had the power of prophecy.   [2]Greek sea deity who was half man and
half fish and who had the power to calm the ocean.

The waves beside them danced; but they
Out-did the sparkling waves in glee:
15 A poet could not but be gay,
In such a jocund company:
I gazed—and gazed—but little thought
What wealth the show to me had brought:

For oft, when on my couch I lie
20 In vacant or in pensive mood,
They flash upon that inward eye
Which is the bliss of solitude;
And then my heart with pleasure fills,
And dances with the daffodils.

(1804)   (1807)

Samuel Taylor Coleridge   (1772–1834)

Born in the small town of Ottery St. Mary, Devonshire, Samuel Taylor Coleridge grew up in London, an intelligent, but very lonely, unhappy child. He studied at Cambridge, spent a year in the army, and interested himself in radical politics. In 1797, he met William Wordsworth, and a year later the two published *Lyrical Ballads*. Coleridge's contributions were poems written on supernatural or romantic subjects, designed to create in the reader what he called "that willing suspension of disbelief for the moment, which constitutes poetic faith." Of these poems, the best known is "The Rime of the Ancient Mariner." Adapting the traditional ballad stanza, which had become popular during the last half of the eighteenth century, he drew on his voluminous reading in folklore and science to create the account of the title figure's symbolic journey of sin, guilt, repentance, and redemption, and the effect its retelling has on the somewhat self-satisfied wedding guest. Also written during this period was "Kubla Khan," which Coleridge said was based on an opium-induced dream. "Frost at Midnight" expresses his intense longing as well as his hope that nature would provide his son with the opportunities and satisfactions that he himself had been denied. Although Coleridge continued to write poetry throughout his life, his most noted later work is *Biographia Literaria* (1817), a combination of autobiography, philosophy, and literary criticism.

Kubla Khan[1]

In Xanadu[2] did Kubla Khan
A stately pleasure-dome decree:
Where Alph, the sacred river, ran
Through caverns measureless to man

---

[1]thirteenth-century emperor of China. He was the grandson of Genghis Khan and a patron of the arts.   [2]Shang-tu, a city founded by Kubla Khan, on the site of modern Beijing.

5   Down to a sunless sea.
So twice five miles of fertile ground
With walls and towers were girdled round:
And there were gardens bright with sinuous rills,
Where blossomed many an incense-bearing tree;
10   And here were forests ancient as the hills,
Enfolding sunny spots of greenery.
But oh! that deep romantic chasm which slanted
Down the green hill athwart a cedarn cover![3]
A savage place! as holy and enchanted
15   As e'er beneath a waning moon was haunted
By woman wailing for her demon-lover!
And from this chasm, with ceaseless turmoil seething,
As if this earth in fast thick pants were breathing,
A mighty fountain momently was forced:
20   Amid whose swift half-intermitted burst
Huge fragments vaulted like rebounding hail,
Or chaffy grain beneath the thresher's flail:
And 'mid these dancing rocks at once and ever
It flung up momently the sacred river.
25   Five miles meandering with a mazy motion
Through wood and dale the sacred river ran,
Then reached the caverns measureless to man,
And sank in tumult to a lifeless ocean:
And 'mid this tumult Kubla heard from far
30   Ancestral voices prophesying war!
        The shadow of the dome of pleasure
        Floated midway on the waves
        Where was heard the mingled measure
        From the fountain and the caves.
35   It was a miracle of rare device,
A sunny pleasure-dome with caves of ice!

        A damsel with a dulcimer
        In a vision once I saw:
        It was an Abyssinian maid,
40   And on her dulcimer she played,
        Singing of Mount Abora.[4]
        Could I revive within me

[3]covered by cedar trees.   [4]possibly Mt. Amara, in Abyssinia, now Ethiopia.

Her symphony and song,
   To such a deep delight 'twould win me,
45   That with music loud and long,
I would build that dome in air,
That sunny dome! those caves of ice!
And all who heard should see them there,
And all should cry, Beware! Beware!
50   His flashing eyes, his floating hair!
Weave a circle round him thrice,
And close your eyes with holy dread,
For he on honey-dew hath fed,
And drunk the milk of Paradise.

(1797)   (1816)

The Rime of the Ancient Mariner

PART I

It is an ancient Mariner,
And he stoppeth one of three.
"By thy long grey beard and glittering eye,
Now wherefore stopp'st thou me

5   The Bridegroom's doors are opened wide,
And I am next of kin;
The guests are met, the feast is set:
May'st hear the merry din."

He holds him with his skinny hand,
10   "There was a ship," quoth he.
"Hold off! unhand me, grey-beard loon!"
Eftsoons[1] his hand dropt he.

He holds him with his glittering eye—
The Wedding-Guest stood still,
15   And listens like a three years' child:
The Mariner hath his will.

The Wedding-Guest sat on a stone:
He cannot choose but hear;

*An ancient Mariner
meeteth three Gallants
bidden to a wedding feast,
and detaineth one.*

*The Wedding-Guest is
spellbound by the eye of the
old seafaring man, and
constrained to hear his tale.*

→

[1]immediately.

And thus spake on that ancient man,
20 The bright-eyed Mariner.

"The ship was cheered, the harbour cleared,
Merrily did we drop
Below the kirk,[2] below the hill,
Below the lighthouse top.

25 The Sun came up upon the left,
Out of the sea came he!
And he shone bright, and on the right
Went down into the sea.

The Mariner tells how the ship sailed southward with a good wind and fair weather, till it reached the Line.

Higher and higher every day,
30 Till over the mast at noon —"
The Wedding-Guest here beat his breast,
For he heard the loud bassoon.

The bride hath paced into the hall,
Red as a rose is she;
35 Nodding their heads before her goes
The merry minstrelsy.[3]

The Wedding-Guest heareth the bridal music; but the Mariner continueth his tale.

The Wedding-Guest he beat his breast,
Yet he cannot choose but hear;
And thus spake on that ancient man,
40 The bright-eyed Mariner.

"And now the STORM-BLAST came, and he
Was tyrannous and strong:
He struck with his o'ertaking wings,
And chased us south along.

The ship driven by a storm toward the South Pole.

45 With sloping masts and dipping prow,
As who pursued with yell and blow
Still treads the shadow of his foe,
And forward bends his head,
The ship drove fast, loud roared the blast,
50 And southward aye we fled.

And now there came both mist and snow,
And it grew wondrous cold:
And ice, mast-high, came floating by,
As green as emerald.

[2]church. [3]group of minstrels.

55 And through the drifts the snowy clifts
Did send a dismal sheen:
Nor shapes of men nor beasts we ken—[4]
The ice was all between.

The land of ice, and of fearful sounds where no living thing was to be seen.

The ice was here, the ice was there,
60 The ice was all around:
It cracked and growled, and roared and howled,
Like noises in a swound![5]

At length did cross an Albatross,
Thorough the fog it came;
65 As if it had been a Christian soul,
We hailed it in God's name.

Till a great sea-bird, called the Albatross, came through the snow-fog, and was received with great joy and hospitality.

It ate the food it ne'er had eat,
And round and round it flew.
The ice did split with a thunder-fit;
70 The helmsman[6] steered us through!

And a good south wind sprung up behind;
The Albatross did follow,
And every day, for food or play,
Came to the mariners' hollo!

And lo! the Albatross proveth a bird of good omen, and followeth the ship as it returned northward through fog and floating ice.

75 In mist or cloud, on mast or shroud,
It perched for vespers[7] nine;
Whiles all the night, through fog-smoke white,
Glimmered the white Moon-shine."

"God save thee, ancient Mariner!
80 From the fiends, that plague thee thus!—
Why look'st thou so?"—"With my cross-bow
I shot the ALBATROSS.

The ancient Mariner inhospitably killeth the pious bird of good omen.

Part II

The Sun now rose upon the right:
Out of the sea came he,
85 Still hid in mist, and on the left
Went down into the sea.

And the good south wind still blew behind,
But no sweet bird did follow,

[4]know. [5]swoon. [6]person who steers the ship. [7]evening worship; i.e., the bird remained for nine evenings.

Nor any day for food or play
90 Came to the mariners' hollo!

And I had done a hellish thing,
And it would work 'em woe:
For all averred, I had killed the bird
That made the breeze to blow.
95 Ah wretch! said they, the bird to slay,
That made the breeze to blow!

His shipmates cry out against the ancient Mariner, for killing the bird of good luck.

Nor dim nor red, like God's own head,
The glorious Sun uprist:
Then all averred, I had killed the bird
100 That brought the fog and mist.
'Twas right, said they, such birds to slay,
That bring the fog and mist.

But when the fog cleared off, they justify the same, and thus make themselves accomplices in the crime.

The fair breeze blew, the white foam flew,
The furrow followed free;
105 We were the first that ever burst
Into that silent sea.

The fair breeze continues; the ship enters the Pacific Ocean, and sails northward, even till it reaches the Line.

Down dropt the breeze, the sails dropt down,
'Twas sad as sad could be;
And we did speak only to break
110 The silence of the sea!

The ship hath been suddenly becalmed.

All in a hot and copper sky,
The bloody Sun, at noon,
Right up above the mast did stand,
No bigger than the Moon.

115 Day after day, day after day,
We stuck, nor breath nor motion;
As idle as a painted ship
Upon a painted ocean.

Water, water, every where,
120 And all the boards did shrink;
Water, water, every where,
Nor any drop to drink.

And the Albatross begins to be avenged.

The very deep did rot: O Christ!
That ever this should be!
125 Yea, slimy things did crawl with legs
Upon the slimy sea.

About, about, in reel and rout
The death-fires danced at night;
The water, like a witch's oils,
130   Burnt green, and blue and white.

And some in dreams assurèd were
Of the Spirit that plagued us so;
Nine fathom deep he had followed us
From the land of mist and snow.

135   And every tongue, through utter drought,
Was withered at the root;
We could not speak, no more than if
We had been choked with soot.

Ah! well a-day! what evil looks
140   Had I from old and young!
Instead of the cross, the Albatross
About my neck was hung

A Spirit had followed them; one of the invisible inhabitants of this planet, neither departed souls nor angels; concerning whom the learned Jew, Josephus, and the Platonic Constantinopolitan, Michael Psellus, may be consulted. They are very numerous, and there is no climate or element without one or more.

The shipmates, in their sore distress, would fain throw the whole guilt on the ancient Mariner: in sign whereof they hang the dead sea-bird round his neck.

Part III

There passed a weary time. Each throat
Was parched, and glazed each eye.
145   A weary time! a weary time!
How glazed each weary eye,
When looking westward, I beheld
A something in the sky.

The ancient Mariner beholdeth a sign in the element afar off.

At first it seemed a little speck,
150   And then it seemed a mist;
It moved and moved, and took at last
A certain shape, I wist.

A speck, a mist, a shape, I wist!
And still it neared and neared:
155   As if it dodged a water-sprite,[8]
It plunged and tacked and veered.

With throats unslaked, with black lips baked,
We could nor laugh nor wail:
Through utter drought all dumb we stood!
160   I bit my arm, I sucked the blood,
And cried, A sail! a sail!

At its nearer approach, it seemeth him to be a ship; and at a dear ransom he freeth his speech from the bonds of thirst.

[8]spirit living in water.

With throats unslaked, with black lips baked,
Agape they heard me call:
Gramercy![9] they for joy did grin,

A flash of joy;

165 And all at once their breath drew in,
As they were drinking all.

See! see! (I cried) she tacks no more!   *And horror follows. For can*
Hither to work us weal;   *it be a ship that comes*
Without a breeze, without a tide,   *onward without wind or tide?*
170 She steadies with upright keel!

The western wave was all a-flame.
The day was well nigh done!
Almost upon the western wave
Rested the broad bright Sun;
175 When that strange shape drove suddenly
Betwixt us and the Sun.

And straight the Sun was flecked with bars,   *It seemeth him but the*
(Heaven's Mother send us grace!)   *skeleton of a ship.*
As if through a dungeon-grate he peered
180 With broad and burning face.

Alas! (thought I, and my heart beat loud)
How fast she nears and nears!
Are those *her* sails that glance in the Sun,
Like restless gossameres?[10]

185 Are those *her* ribs through which the Sun   *And the ribs are seen as bars*
Did peer, as through a grate?   *on the face of the setting Sun.*
And is that Woman all her crew?   *The Spectre-Woman and her*
Is that a DEATH? and are there two?   *Death-mate, and no other on*
Is DEATH that woman's mate?   *board the skeleton ship.*

190 *Her* lips were red, *her* looks were free,   *Like vessel, like crew!*
Her locks were yellow as gold:
Her skin was as white as leprosy,
The Night-mare LIFE-IN-DEATH was she,   *Death and Life-in-Death*
Who thicks man's blood with cold.   *have diced for the ship's*
                                                  crew, and she (the latter)
                                                  winneth the ancient Mariner.
195 The naked hulk alongside came,
And the twain were casting dice;
'The game is done! I've won! I've won!'
Quoth she, and whistles thrice.

[9]expression of surprise or gratitude, literally, "Great thanks." [10]cobwebs.

The Sun's rim dips; the stars rush out:
200 At one stride comes the dark;
With far-heard whisper, o'er the sea,
Off shot the spectre-bark.[11]

No twilight within the courts of the Sun.

We listened and looked sideways up!
Fear at my heart, as at a cup,
205 My life-blood seemed to sip!
The stars were dim, and thick the night,
The steersman's face by his lamp gleamed white;
From the sails the dew did drip—
Till clomb above the eastern bar
210 The hornèd Moon,[12] with one bright star
Within the nether tip.

At the rising of the Moon,

One after one, by the star-dogged[13] Moon,
Too quick for groan or sigh,
Each turned his face with a ghastly pang,
215 And cursed me with his eye.

One after another,

Four times fifty living men,
(And I heard nor sigh nor groan)
With heavy thump, a lifeless lump,
They dropped down one by one.

His shipmates drop down dead.

220 The souls did from their bodies fly,—
They fled to bliss or woe!
And every soul, it passed me by,
Like the whizz of my cross-bow!"

But Life-in-Death begins her work on the ancient Mariner.

Part IV

"I fear thee, ancient Mariner!
225 I fear thy skinny hand!
And thou art long, and lank, and brown,
As is the ribbed sea-sand.

The Wedding-Guest feareth that a Spirit is talking to him;

I fear thee and thy glittering eye,
And thy skinny hand, so brown."—
230 "Fear not, fear not, thou Wedding-Guest!
This body dropt not down.

But the ancient Mariner assureth him of his bodily life, and proceedeth to relate his horrible penance.

Alone, alone, all, all alone,
Alone on a wide wide sea!

➡

[11]phantom ship. [12]crescent moon. [13]followed by a star.

And never a saint took pity on
235 My soul in agony.

The many men, so beautiful!

He despiseth the creatures of
the calm,

And they all dead did lie:
And a thousand thousand slimy things
Lived on; and so did I.

240 I looked upon the rotting sea,

And envieth that they should
live, and so many lie dead.

And drew my eyes away;
I looked upon the rotting deck,
And there the dead men lay.

I looked to heaven, and tried to pray;
245 But or ever a prayer had gusht,
A wicked whisper came, and made
My heart as dry as dust.

I closed my lids, and kept them close,
And the balls like pulses beat;
250 For the sky and the sea, and the sea and the sky
Lay like a load on my weary eye,
And the dead were at my feet.

The cold sweat melted from their limbs,
Nor rot nor reek did they:

But the curse liveth for him
in the eye of the dead men.

255 The look with which they looked on me
Had never passed away.

An orphan's curse would drag to hell
A spirit from on high;
But oh! more horrible than that
260 Is the curse in a dead man's eye!
Seven days, seven nights, I saw that curse,
And yet I could not die.

The moving Moon went up the sky,
And no where did abide:

In his loneliness and fixed-
ness he yearneth towards the
journeying Moon, and the
stars that still sojourn, yet

265 Softly she was going up,
And a star or two beside—

still move onward; and every
where the blue sky belongs to
them, and is their appointed
rest, and their native country
and their own natural
homes, which they enter
unannounced, as lords that
are certainty expected and
yet there is a silent joy at
their arrival.

Her beams bemocked the sultry main,[14]
Like April hoar-frost spread;
But where the ship's huge shadow lay,

→

[14]sea.

270 The charmèd water burnt alway
A still and awful red.

Beyond the shadow of the ship,
I watched the water-snakes:
They moved in tracks of shining white,
275 And when they reared, the elfish light
Fell off in hoary flakes.

By the light of the Moon he beholdeth God's creatures of the great calm.

Within the shadow of the ship
I watched their rich attire:
Blue, glossy green, and velvet black,
280 They coiled and swam; and every track
Was a flash of golden fire.

O happy living things! no tongue
Their beauty might declare:
A spring of love gushed from my heart,
285 And I blessed them unaware:
Sure my kind saint took pity on me,
And I blessed them unaware.

Their beauty and their happiness.

He blesseth them in his heart.

The self-same moment I could pray;
And from my neck so free
290 The Albatross fell off, and sank
Like lead into the sea.

The spell begins to break.

Part V

Oh sleep! it is a gentle thing,
Beloved from pole to pole!
To Mary Queen[15] the praise be given!
295 She sent the gentle sleep from Heaven,
That slid into my soul.
The silly buckets on the deck,
That had so long remained,
I dreamt that they were filled with dew;
300 And when I awoke, it rained.

By grace of the holy Mother, the ancient Mariner is refreshed with rain.

My lips were wet, my throat was cold,
My garments all were dank;
Sure I had drunken in my dreams,
And still my body drank.

[15]the Virgin Mary, queen of Heaven.

305   I moved, and could not feel my limbs:
  I was so light—almost
  I thought that I had died in sleep,
  And was a blessèd ghost.

  And soon I heard a roaring wind:
310   It did not come anear;
  But with its sound it shook the sails,
  That were so thin and sere.

He heareth sound and seeth strange sights and commotions in the sky and the element.

  The upper air burst into life!
  And a hundred fire-flags sheen,[16]
315   To and fro they were hurried about!
  And to and fro, and in and out,
  The wan stars danced between.

  And the coming wind did roar more loud,
  And the sails did sigh like sedge;
320   And the rain poured down from one black cloud;
  The Moon was at its edge.

  The thick black cloud was cleft, and still
  The Moon was at its side:
  Like waters shot from some high crag,
325   The lightning fell with never a jag,
  A river steep and wide.

  The loud wind never reached the ship,
  Yet now the ship moved on!
  Beneath the lightning and the Moon
330   The dead men gave a groan.

The bodies of the ship's crew are inspired and the ship waves on;

  They groaned, they stirred, they all uprose,
  Nor spake, nor moved their eyes;
  It had been strange, even in a dream,
  To have seen those dead men rise.

335   The helmsman steered, the ship moved on;
  Yet never a breeze up-blew;
  The mariners all 'gan work the ropes,
  Where they were wont to do;
  They raised their limbs like lifeless tools—
340   We were a ghastly crew.

[16]meteors shone.

The body of my brother's son
Stood by me, knee to knee:
The body and I pulled at one rope,
But he said nought to me."

345 "I fear thee, ancient Mariner!"
"Be calm, thou Wedding-Guest!
'Twas not those souls that fled in pain,
Which to their corses[17] came again,
But a troop of spirits blest:

But not by the souls of the men, nor by demons of earth or middle air, but by a blessed troop of angelic spirits, sent down by the invocation of the guardian saint.

350 For when it dawned—they dropped their arms,
And clustered round the mast;
Sweet sounds rose slowly through their mouths,
And from their bodies passed.

Around, around, flew each sweet sound,
355 Then darted to the Sun;
Slowly the sounds came back again,
Now mixed, now one by one.

Sometimes a-dropping from the sky
I heard the sky-lark sing;
360 Sometimes all little birds that are,
How they seemed to fill the sea and air
With their sweet jargoning!

And now 'twas like all instruments,
Now like a lonely flute;
365 And now it is an angel's song,
That makes the heavens be mute.

It ceased; yet still the sails made on
A pleasant noise till noon,
A noise like of a hidden brook
370 In the leafy month of June,
That to the sleeping woods all night
Singeth a quiet tune.

Till noon we quietly sailed on,
Yet never a breeze did breathe:

→

[17]corpses.

375 Slowly and smoothly went the ship,
Moved onward from beneath.

Under the keel nine fathom deep,
From the land of mist and snow,
The spirit slid: and it was he
380 That made the ship to go.
The sails at noon left off their tune,
And the ship stood still also.

The lonesome Spirit from the
South Pole carries on the ship
as far as the Line, in
obedience to the angelic
troop, but still requireth
vengeance.

The Sun, right up above the mast,
Had fixed her to the ocean:
385 But in a minute she 'gan stir,
With a short uneasy motion—
Backwards and forwards half her length
With a short uneasy motion.

Then like a pawing horse let go,
390 She made a sudden bound:
It flung the blood into my head,
And I fell down in a swound.

How long in that same fit I lay,
I have not to declare;
395 But ere my living life returned,
I heard and in my soul discerned
Two voices in the air.

The Polar Spirit's fellow-
demons, the invisible inhabi-
tants of the element, take
part in his wrong; and two of
them relate, one to the other,
that penance long and heavy
for the ancient Mariner hath
been accorded to the Polar
Spirit, who returneth
southward.

'Is it he?' quoth one, 'Is this the man?
By him who died on cross,[18]
400 With his cruel bow he laid full low
The harmless Albatross.

The spirit who bideth by himself
In the land of mist and snow,
He loved the bird that loved the man
405 Who shot him with his bow.'

The other was a softer voice,
As soft as honey-dew:
Quoth he, 'The man hath penance done,
And penance more will do.'

[18]Christ, who was crucified on a cross.

Part VI

FIRST VOICE

410 'But tell me, tell me! speak again,
Thy soft response renewing—
What makes that ship drive on so fast?
What is the ocean doing?'

SECOND VOICE

'Still as a slave before his lord,
415 The ocean hath no blast;
His great bright eye most silently
Up to the Moon is cast—

If he may know which way to go;
For she guides him smooth or grim.
420 See, brother, see! how graciously
She looketh down on him.'

FIRST VOICE

'But why drives on that ship so fast,
Without or wave or wind?'

SECOND VOICE

'The air is cut away before,
425 And closes from behind.

The Mariner hath been cast into a trance; for the angelic power causeth the vessel to drive northward faster than human life could endure.

Fly, brother, fly! more high, more high!
Or we shall be belated:
For slow and slow that ship will go,
When the Mariner's trance is abated.'

430 I woke, and we were sailing on
As in a gentle weather:
'Twas night, calm night, the moon was high;
The dead men stood together.

The supernatural motion is retarded; the Mariner awakes, and his penance begins anew.

All stood together on the deck,
435 For a charnel-dungeon[19] fitter:
All fixed on me their stony eyes,
That in the Moon did glitter.

The pang, the curse, with which they died,
Had never passed away:
440 I could not draw my eyes from theirs,
Nor turn them up to pray.

[19]burial house, or prison in which people are left to die.

And now this spell was snapt: once more
I viewed the ocean green,
And looked far forth, yet little saw
445   Of what had else been seen—

       The curse is finally expiated.

Like one that on a lonesome road
Doth walk in fear and dread,
And having once turned round walks on,
And turns no more his head;
450   Because he knows, a frightful fiend
Doth close behind him tread.

But soon there breathed a wind on me,
Nor sound nor motion made:
Its path was not upon the sea,
455   In ripple or in shade.

It raised my hair, it fanned my cheek
Like a meadow-gale of spring—
It mingled strangely with my fears,
Yet it felt like a welcoming.

460   Swiftly, swiftly flew the ship,
Yet she sailed softly too:
Sweetly, sweetly blew the breeze—
On me alone it blew.

Oh! dream of joy! is this indeed
465   The light-house top I see?
Is this the hill? is this the kirk?
Is this mine own countree?

       And the ancient Mariner
       beholdeth his native country.

We drifted o'er the harbour-bar,[20]
And I with sobs did pray—
470   O let me be awake, my God!
Or let me sleep alway.

The harbour-bay was clear as glass,
So smoothly it was strewn!
And on the bay the moonlight lay,
475   And the shadow of the Moon.

The rock shone bright, the kirk no less,
That stands above the rock:

→

[20]breakwater or sandbar protecting a harbour.

The moonlight steeped in silentness
The steady weathercock.

480   And the bay was white with silent light,
Till rising from the same,
Full many shapes, that shadows were,
In crimson colours came.

The angelic spirits leave dead bodies,

A little distance from the prow
485   Those crimson shadows were:
I turned my eyes upon the deck—
Oh, Christ! what saw I there!

And appear in their own forms of light.

Each corse lay flat, lifeless and flat,
And, by the holy rood![21]
490   A man all light, a seraph-man,[22]
On every corse there stood.

This seraph-band, each waved his hand:
It was a heavenly sight!
They stood as signals to the land,
495   Each one a lovely light;

This seraph-band, each waved his hand,
No voice did they impart—
No voice; but oh! the silence sank
Like music on my heart.

500   But soon I heard the dash of oars,
I heard the Pilot's[23] cheer;
My head was turned perforce away,
And I saw a boat appear.

The Pilot and the Pilot's boy,
505   I heard them coming fast:
Dear Lord in Heaven! it was a joy
The dead men could not blast.

I saw a third—I heard his voice:
It is the Hermit good!
510   He singeth loud his godly hymns
That he makes in the wood.
He'll shrieve[24] my soul, he'll wash away
The Albatross's Mood.

---

[21]the cross on which Christ was crucified.   [22]fiery angel.   [23]person who steers ships into harbour.   [24]administer spiritual absolution.

Part VII

This Hermit good lives in that wood
515   Which slopes down to the sea.
How loudly his sweet voice he rears!
He loves to talk with marineres
That come from a far countree.

The Hermit of the Wood,

He kneels at morn, and noon, and eve—
520   He hath a cushion plump:
It is the moss that wholly hides
The rotted old oak-stump.

The skiff-boat neared: I heard them talk,
'Why, this is strange, I trow!
525   Where are those lights so many and fair,
That signal made but now?'

'Strange, by my faith!' the Hermit said—
'And they answered not our cheer!
The planks looked warped! and see those sails,
530   How thin they are and sere!
I never saw aught like to them,
Unless perchance it were

Approacheth the ship with wonder.

Brown skeletons of leaves that lag
My forest-brook along;
535   When the ivy-tod is heavy with snow,
And the owlet whoops to the wolf below,
That eats the she-wolf's young.'

'Dear Lord! it hath a fiendish look—
(The Pilot made reply)
540   I am a-feared'—'Push on, push on!'
Said the Hermit cheerily.
The boat came closer to the ship,
But I nor spake nor stirred;
The boat came close beneath the ship,
545   And straight a sound was heard.

Under the water it rumbled on,
Still louder and more dread:
It reached the ship, it split the bay;
The ship went down like lead.

The ship suddenly sinketh.

550   Stunned by that loud and dreadful sound,
Which sky and ocean smote,

The ancient Mariner is saved in the Pilot's boat.

➡

Like one that hath been seven days drowned
My body lay afloat;
But swift as dreams, myself I found
555   Within the Pilot's boat.

Upon the whirl, where sank the ship,
The boat spun round and round;
And all was still, save that the hill
Was telling of the sound.

560   I moved my lips—the Pilot shrieked
And fell down in a fit;
The holy Hermit raised his eyes,
And prayed where he did sit.

I took the oars: the Pilot's boy,
565   Who now doth crazy go,
Laughed loud and long, and all the while
His eyes went to and fro.
'Ha! ha!' quoth he, 'full plain I see,
The Devil knows how to row.'

570   And now, all in my own countree,
I stood on the firm land!
The Hermit stepped forth from the boat,
And scarcely he could stand.

'O shrieve me, shrieve me, holy man!'   *The ancient Mariner*
575   The Hermit crossed his brow.   *earnestly entreateth the*
'Say quick,' quoth he, 'I bid thee say—   *Hermit to shrieve him; and*
What manner of man art thou?'   *the penance of life falls on*
                                                                        him.

Forthwith this frame of mine was wrenched
With a woful agony,
580   Which forced me to begin my tale;
And then it left me free.

Since then, at an uncertain hour,   *And ever and anon*
That agony returns: *throughout his future life an*
And till my ghastly tale is told,   *agony constraineth him to*
585   This heart within me burns.   *travel from land to land;*

I pass, like night, from land to land;
I have strange power of speech;
That moment that his face I see,
I know the man that must hear me:
590   To him my tale I teach.

What loud uproar bursts from that door!
The wedding-guests are there:
But in the garden-bower the bride
And bride-maids singing are:
595   And hark the little vesper bell,[25]
Which biddeth me to prayer!

O Wedding-Guest! this soul hath been
Alone on a wide wide sea:
So lonely 'twas, that God himself
600   Scarce seemèd there to be.

O sweeter than the marriage-feast,
'Tis sweeter far to me,
To walk together to the kirk
With a goodly company!—

605   To walk together to the kirk,
And all together pray,
While each to his great Father bends,
Old men, and babes, and loving friends
And youths and maidens gay!

610   Farewell, farewell! but this I tell
To thee, thou Wedding-Guest!
He prayeth well, who loveth well
Both man and bird and beast.

And to teach, by his own example, love and reverence to all things that God made and loveth.

He prayeth best, who loveth best
615   All things both great and small;
For the dear God who loveth us,
He made and loveth all."

The Mariner, whose eye is bright,
Whose beard with age is hoar,[26]
620   Is gone: and now the Wedding-Guest
Turned from the bridegroom's door.

He went like one that hath been stunned,
And is of sense forlorn:
A sadder and a wiser man,
625   He rose the morrow morn.

(1798)

[25]bell calling people to evening worship.   [26]greyish-white.

Frost at Midnight

The Frost performs its secret ministry,
Unhelped by any wind. The owlet's cry
Came loud—and hark, again! loud as before.
The inmates of my cottage, all at rest,
5   Have left me to that solitude, which suits
Abstruser musings: save that at my side
My cradled infant[1] slumbers peacefully.
'Tis calm indeed! so calm, that it disturbs
And vexes meditation with its strange
10 And extreme silentness. Sea, hill, and wood,
This populous village! Sea, and hill, and wood,
With all the numberless goings-on of life,
Inaudible as dreams! the thin blue flame
Lies on my low-burnt fire, and quivers not;
15 Only that film,[2] which fluttered on the grate,
Still flutters there, the sole unquiet thing.
Methinks, its motion in this hush of nature
Gives it dim sympathies with me who live,
Making it a companionable form,
20 Whose puny flaps and freaks the idling Spirit
By its own moods interprets, everywhere
Echo or mirror seeking of itself,
And makes a toy of Thought.

                       But O! how oft,
25 How oft, at school,[3] with most believing mind,
Presageful, have I gazed upon the bars,
To watch that fluttering *stranger*! and as oft
With unclosed lids, already had I dreamt
Of my sweet birth-place,[4] and the old church-tower,
30 Whose bells, the poor man's only music, rang
From morn to evening, all the hot Fair-day,
So sweetly, that they stirred and haunted me
With a wild pleasure, falling on mine ear
Most like articulate sounds of things to come!
35 So gazed I, till the soothing things I dreamt,

[1]his son Hartley. [2]flake of soot or ash; in his note to the poem, Coleridge wrote, "In all parts of the kingdom these films are called *strangers* and supposed to portend the arrival of some absent friend." [3]the grammar school, Christ's Hospital, London. [4]Ottery St. Mary, Devonshire.

Lulled me to sleep, and sleep prolonged my dreams!
And so I brooded all the following morn,
Awed by the stern preceptor's[5] face, mine eye
Fixed with mock study on my swimming book:
40   Save if the door half opened, and I snatched
A hasty glance, and still my heart leaped up,
For still I hoped to see the *stranger's* face,
Townsman, or aunt, or sister more beloved,
My playmate when we both were clothed alike![6]

45   Dear Babe, that sleepest cradled by my side,
Whose gentle breathings, heard in this deep calm,
Fill up the interspersed vacancies
And momentary pauses of the thought!
My babe so beautiful! it thrills my heart
50   With tender gladness, thus to look at thee,
And think that thou shalt learn far other lore
And in far other scenes! For I was reared
In the great city, pent 'mid cloisters dim,
And saw nought lovely but the sky and stars.
55   But *thou*, my babe! shalt wander like a breeze
By lakes and sandy shores, beneath the crags
Of ancient mountain, and beneath the clouds,
Which image in their bulk both lakes and shores
And mountain crags: so shalt thou see and hear
60   The lovely shapes and sounds intelligible
Of that eternal language, which thy God
Utters, who from eternity doth teach
Himself in all, and all things in himself.
Great universal Teacher! he shall mould
65   Thy spirit, and by giving make it ask.

          Therefore all seasons shall be sweet to thee,
Whether the summer clothe the general earth
With greenness, or the redbreast sit and sing
Betwixt the tufts of snow on the bare branch
70   Of mossy apple-tree, while the nigh thatch
Smokes in the sun-thaw; whether the eave-drops fall
Heard only in the trances of the blast,
Or if the secret ministry of frost

➡️

[5]Rev. James Boyer, whom Coleridge describes in the first chapter of his *Biographia Literaria* (1817). [6]until they reached a certain age, Coleridge and his sister Ann would have been dressed in infant clothing, which was the same for males and females.

Shall hang them up in silent icicles,
75   Quietly shining to the quiet Moon.

(1798)

George Gordon, Lord Byron   (1788–1824)

Raised in Aberdeen, Scotland, George Gordon became Lord Byron at age ten, after the death of his uncle. While a student at Cambridge, he became notorious for his flamboyant life. His first major work, *Childe Harold*, cantos I and II (1812), was based in part on his own European travels. An advocate of liberal causes as a member of the House of Lords, he died in Greece while training soldiers for that country's fight for independence. During his life and after, he was regarded as an almost legendary figure: handsome, athletic, proud, talented, but often filled with guilt and remorse. An accomplished craftsman, his works range from the beautiful lyric "She Walks in Beauty," to the long, satirical, and humorous *Don Juan* (1819–24). In "On This Day I Complete My Thirty-Sixth Year," written shortly before his death, Byron portrays himself as a world-weary individual seeking to find meaning in his life through involvement in the political and military struggles of Greece.

She Walks in Beauty

I.

She walks in beauty, like the night
    Of cloudless climes and starry skies;
And all that's best of dark and bright
    Meet in her aspect and her eyes:
5   Thus mellow'd to that tender light
    Which heaven to gaudy day denies.

II.

One shade the more, one ray the less,
    Had half impair'd the nameless grace
Which waves in every raven tress,
10   Or softly lightens o'er her face;
Where thoughts serenely sweet express
    How pure, how dear their dwelling-place.

III.

And on that cheek, and o'er that brow,
    So soft, so calm, yet eloquent,
15 The smiles that win, the tints that glow,
    But tell of days in goodness spent,

→

A mind at peace with all below,
   A heart whose love is innocent!

(1814)   (1815)

On This Day I Complete My Thirty-Sixth Year

Missolonghi, Jan. 22, 1824.

'Tis time this heart should be unmoved,
   Since others it hath ceased to move:
Yet, though I cannot be beloved,
   Still let me love!

5   My days are in the yellow leaf;
   The flowers and fruits of love are gone;
The worm, the canker, and the grief
   Are mine alone!

The fire that on my bosom preys
10   Is lone as some volcanic isle;
No torch is kindled at its blaze—
   A funeral pile.

The hope, the fear, the jealous care,
   The exalted portion of the pain
15 And power of love, I cannot share,
   But wear the chain.

But 'tis not *thus*—and 'tis not *here*—
   Such thoughts should shake my soul, nor *now*,
Where glory decks the hero's bier,
20   Or binds his brow.

The sword, the banner, and the field,
   Glory and Greece, around me see!
The Spartan, borne upon his shield,
   Was not more free.

25 Awake! (not Greece—she *is* awake!)
   Awake, my spirit! Think through *whom*
Thy life-blood tracks its parent lake,
   And then strike home!

Tread those reviving passions down,
30   Unworthy manhood!—unto thee
Indifferent should the smile or frown
   Of beauty be.

If thou regrett'st thy youth, *why live?*
    The land of honourable death
35 Is here:—up to the field, and give
    Away thy breath!

Seek out—less often sought than found—
    A soldier's grave, for thee the best;
Then look around, and choose thy ground,
40   And take thy rest.

(1824)

Percy Bysshe Shelley   (1792–1822)

Born in Field Place, Sussex, Shelley lived a stormy life. Expelled from Oxford for writing a pamphlet on atheism, he eloped with sixteen-year-old Harriet Westbrook, whom he later abandoned for Mary Godwin, the daughter of the political radical William Godwin and author of the novel *Frankenstein*. In 1818, he moved permanently to Italy, but never settled in one place. He drowned after his sailboat was swamped in a squall. Condemned during his life for his unconventional moral, political, and anti-religious beliefs, Shelley is now acknowledged as one of the greatest of Romantic poets. A conscientious craftsman, he employed a variety of poetic forms, ranging from the sonnet "Ozymandias," which satirizes vainglorious tyrants, to the "Ode to the West Wind," which expresses his revolutionary idealism. In all of his poetry, he was able to combine passion and intellectuality, developing symbols, usually from nature, that embody both complex philosophic positions and his attitudes towards them.

Ozymandias[1]

I met a traveller from an antique land
Who said: Two vast and trunkless legs of stone
Stand in the desert ... Near them, on the sand,
Half sunk, a shattered visage lies, whose frown,
5 And wrinkled lip, and sneer of cold command,
Tell that its sculptor well those passions read
Which yet survive, stamped on these lifeless things,
The hand that mocked them, and the heart that fed:
And on the pedestal these words appear:
10 "My name is Ozymandias, king of kings:

[1]Greek variant of the name of the thirteenth-century B.C. Egyptian pharaoh, Ramses II.

Look on my works, ye Mighty, and despair!"
Nothing beside remains. Round the decay
Of that colossal wreck, boundless and bare
The lone and level sands stretch far away.

(1817)   (1818)

Ode to the West Wind

I

O wild West Wind, thou breath of Autumn's being,
Thou, from whose unseen presence the leaves dead
Are driven, like ghosts from an enchanter fleeing,

Yellow, and black, and pale, and hectic red,
5   Pestilence-stricken multitudes: O thou,
Who chariotest to their dark wintry bed

The wingèd seeds, where they lie cold and low,
Each like a corpse within its grave, until
Thine azure sister of the Spring shall blow

10   Her clarion o'er the dreaming earth, and fill
(Driving sweet buds like flocks to feed in air)
With living hues and odours plain and hill:

Wild Spirit, which art moving everywhere;
Destroyer and preserver; hear, Oh hear!

II

15   Thou on whose stream, 'mid the steep sky's commotion,
Loose clouds like earth's decaying leaves are shed,
Shook from the tangled boughs of Heaven and Ocean,

Angels of rain and lightning: there are spread
On the blue surface of thine airy surge,
20   Like the bright hair uplifted from the head

Of some fierce Mænad,[1] even from the dim verge
Of the horizon to the zenith's height
The locks of the approaching storm. Thou dirge[2]

---

[1]female worshippers of Dionysus, the Greek god of wine. [2]song of mourning.

Of the dying year, to which this closing night
25   Will be the dome of a vast sepulchre,
Vaulted with all thy congregated might

Of vapours, from whose solid atmosphere
Black rain, and fire, and hail will burst: Oh hear!

III

Thou who didst waken from his summer dreams
30   The blue Mediterranean, where he lay,
Lulled by the coil of his crystàlline streams,

Beside a pumice isle in Baiæ's bay,[3]
And saw in sleep old palaces and towers
Quivering within the wave's intenser day,

35   All overgrown with azure moss and flowers
So sweet, the sense faints picturing them! Thou
For whose path the Atlantic's level powers

Cleave themselves into chasms, while far below
The sea-blooms and the oozy woods which wear
40   The sapless foliage of the ocean, know

Thy voice, and suddenly grow gray with fear,
And tremble and despoil themselves: Oh hear!

IV

If I were a dead leaf thou mightest bear;
If I were a swift cloud to fly with thee;
45   A wave to pant beneath thy power, and share

The impulse of thy strength, only less free
Than thou, O uncontrollable! If even
I were as in my boyhood, and could be

The comrade of thy wanderings over Heaven,
50   As then, when to outstrip thy skiey speed
Scarce seemed a vision; I would ne'er have striven

As thus with thee in prayer in my sore need.
Oh, lift me as a wave, a leaf, a cloud!
I fall upon the thorns of life! I bleed!

55   A heavy weight of hours has chained and bowed
One too like thee: tameless, and swift, and proud.

---

[3]city in south-western Italy.

V

Make me thy lyre, even as the forest is:
What if my leaves are falling like its own!
The tumult of thy mighty harmonies

60   Will take from both a deep, autumnal tone,
Sweet though in sadness. Be thou, Spirit fierce,
My spirit! be thou me, impetuous one!

Drive my dead thoughts over the universe
Like withered leaves to quicken a new birth!

65   And, by the incantation of this verse,

Scatter, as from an unextinguished hearth
Ashes and sparks, my words among mankind!
Be through my lips to unawakened earth

The trumpet of a prophecy! O, Wind,

70   If Winter comes, can Spring be far behind?

(1819)   (1820)

To a Skylark

Hail to thee, blithe spirit!
    Bird thou never wert,
That from heaven, or near it,
    Pourest thy full heart

5   In profuse strains of unpremeditated art.

Higher still and higher
    From the earth thou springest
Like a cloud of fire;
    The blue deep thou wingest,

10   And singing still dost soar, and soaring ever singest.

In the golden lightning
    Of the sunken sun,
O'er which clouds are brightning,
    Thou dost float and run;

15   Like an unbodied joy whose race is just begun.

The pale purple even
    Melts around thy flight;
Like a star of heaven,

➡

In the broad daylight
20   Thou art unseen, but yet I hear thy shrill delight,

Keen as are the arrows
Of that silver sphere,
Whose intense lamp narrows
In the white dawn clear,
25   Until we hardly see, we feel that it is there.

All the earth and air
With thy voice is loud,
As, when night is bare,
From one lonely cloud
30   The moon rains out her beams, and heaven is overflowed.

What thou art we know not;
What is most like thee?
From rainbow clouds there flow not
Drops so bright to see,
35   As from thy presence showers a rain of melody.

Like a poet hidden
In the light of thought,
Singing hymns unhidden,
Till the world is wrought
40   To sympathy with hopes and fears it heeded not:

Like a high-born maiden
In a palace-tower,
Soothing her love-laden
Soul in secret hour
45   With music sweet as love, which overflows her bower:

Like a glow-worm golden
In a dell of dew,
Scattering unbeholden
Its aërial hue
50   Among the flowers and grass, which screen it from the view:

Like a rose embowered
In its own green leaves,
By warm winds deflowered,
Till the scent it gives
55   Makes faint with too much sweet these heavy-wingèd thieves:

Sound of vernal showers
On the twinkling grass,

→

Rain-awakened flowers,
　　All that ever was
60 Joyous, and clear, and fresh, thy music doth surpass:

Teach us, sprite or bird,
　　What sweet thoughts are thine:
I have never heard
　　Praise of love or wine
65 That panted forth a flood of rapture so divine.

Chorus Hymeneal,[1]
　　Or triumphal chaunt,
Matched with thine would be all
　　But an empty vaunt,
70 A thing wherein we feel there is some hidden want.

What objects are the fountains
　　Of thy happy strain?
What fields, or waves, or mountains?
　　What shapes of sky or plain?
75 What love of thine own kind? what ignorance of pain?

With thy clear keen joyance
　　Languor cannot be:
Shadow of annoyance
　　Never came near thee:
80 Thou lovest; but ne'er knew love's sad satiety.

Waking or asleep,
　　Thou of death must deem
Things more true and deep
　　Than we mortals dream,
85 Or how could thy notes flow in such a crystal stream?

We look before and after,
　　And pine for what is not:
Our sincerest laughter
　　With some pain is fraught;
90 Our sweetest songs are those that tell of saddest thought.

Yet if we could scorn
　　Hate, and pride, and fear;
If we were things born
　　Not to shed a tear,

→

[1]marriage hymn.

95 I know not how thy joy we ever should come near.

> Better than all measures
>> Of delightful sound,
> Better than all treasures
>> That in books are found,
100 Thy skill to poet were, thou scorner of the ground!

> Teach me half the gladness
>> That thy brain must know,
> Such harmonious madness
>> From my lips would flow,
105 The world should listen then, as I am listening now.

(1820)   (1824)

To————(Music, when soft voices die)

Music, when soft voices die,
Vibrates in the memory—
Odors, when sweet violets sicken,
Live within the sense they quicken.

5 Rose leaves, when the rose is dead,
Are heapt for the belovèd's bed;
And so thy thoughts, when thou art gone
Love itself shall slumber on.

(1821)   (1824)

John Keats   (1795–1821)

Born in London, John Keats was orphaned at age fourteen. Although he trained as an apothecary-surgeon, he chose to devote his life to the writing of poetry. His talents matured rapidly, and in 1819, at the age of twenty-four, he wrote his greatest works, "La Belle Dame sans Merci," his six famous odes, and several sonnets that, along with those of William Wordsworth, are considered the finest of the Romantic era. Knowing that his mother and brother had died of tuberculosis and that he was beginning to show signs of the disease, Keats understandably was drawn to themes about death and destruction. He thus meditates on these subjects in "When I have fears" and employs the form and imagery of medieval ballads to dramatize them in "La Belle Dame sans Merci." In "Ode to a Nightingale," "Ode on a Grecian Urn," and "To Autumn," three of his best-known poems, Keats constructs symbols to explore ideas about art, life and death, and permanence and transience. His tightly unified stanzas, evocative imagery, and skilful portrayal of shifting emotions demonstrate that Keats was a craftsman, a philosopher, and an artist of great emotional depth. Although he died before his pen had gleaned his "teeming brain," the quality of the works Keats did write marks him as one of the great English poets.

On First Looking into Chapman's Homer

Much have I travell'd in the realms of gold,
    And many goodly states and kingdoms seen;
    Round many western islands have I been
Which bards in fealty to Apollo[1] hold.
Oft of one wide expanse had I been told
    That deep-brow'd Homer[2] ruled as his demesne;
    Yet did I never breathe its pure serene
Till I heard Chapman[3] speak out loud and bold:
Then felt I like some watcher of the skies
    When a new planet swims into his ken;
Or like stout Cortez[4] when with eagle eyes
    He star'd at the Pacific—and all his men
Look'd at each other with a wild surmise—
    Silent, upon a peak in Darien.[5]

(1816)

When I have fears

When I have fears that I may cease to be
    Before my pen has glean'd my teeming brain,
Before high-piled books, in charact'ry,[1]
    Hold like rich garners the full-ripen'd grain;
When I behold, upon the night's starr'd face,
    Huge cloudy symbols of a high romance,

[1]Greek god of music and poetry; also the sun. [2]ninth-century B.C. Greek poet, author of the *Iliad* and the *Odyssey*. [3]George Chapman, late-sixteenth-century English translator of Homer. [4]sixteenth-century Spanish conquerer of Mexico whom Keats confused with Balboa, the first European to see the Pacific Ocean. [5]former name of the Isthmus of Panama. [1]printed letters.

And think that I may never live to trace
    Their shadows, with the magic hand of chance;
And when I feel, fair creature of an hour!
10   That I shall never look upon thee more,
Never have relish in the faery power
    Of unreflecting love!—then on the shore
Of the wide world I stand alone, and think
    Till love and fame to nothingness do sink.

(1818)   (1848)

Ode to a Nightingale

1

My heart aches, and a drowsy numbness pains
    My sense, as though of hemlock[1] I had drunk,
Or emptied some dull opiate to the drains
    One minute past, and Lethe-wards[2] had sunk:
5 'Tis not through envy of thy happy lot,
    But being too happy in thine happiness,—
        That thou, light-winged Dryad[3] of the trees,
            In some melodious plot
Of beechen green, and shadows numberless,
10   Singest of summer in full-throated ease.

2

O, for a draught of vintage! that hath been
    Cool'd a long age in the deep-delved earth,
Tasting of Flora[4] and the country green,
    Dance, and Provençal song,[5] and sunburnt mirth!
15 O for a beaker full of the warm South,
    Full of the true, the blushful Hippocrene,[6]
        With beaded bubbles winking at the brim,
            And purple-stained mouth;
That I might drink, and leave the world unseen,
20   And with thee fade away into the forest dim:

---

[1]poison derived from a parsnip-like root, not the common hemlock. [2]toward Lethe, in Greek mythology, a river in Hades. Drinking its water caused one to forget the past. [3]tree nymph. [4]Roman goddess of flowers. [5]in the Middle Ages, Provence, in southern France, was famous for its poets and singers. [6]in Greek mythology, the sacred fountain of the muses of poetry.

3

Fade far away, dissolve, and quite forget
    What thou among the leaves hast never known,
The weariness, the fever, and the fret
    Here, where men sit and hear each other groan;
25   Where palsy shakes a few, sad, last gray hairs,
        Where youth grows pale, and spectre-thin, and dies;
           Where but to think is to be full of sorrow
             And leaden-eyed despairs,
        Where Beauty cannot keep her lustrous eyes,
30   Or new Love pine at them beyond to-morrow.

4

Away! away! for I will fly to thee,
    Not charioted by Bacchus[7] and his pards,
But on the viewless wings of Poesy,
    Though the dull brain perplexes and retards:
35   Already with thee! tender is the night,
        And haply the Queen-Moon is on her throne,
           Cluster'd around by all her starry Fays;[8]
             But here there is no light,
        Save what from heaven is with the breezes blown
40   Through verdurous glooms and winding mossy ways.

5

I cannot see what flowers are at my feet,
    Nor what soft incense hangs upon the boughs,
But, in embalmed darkness, guess each sweet
    Wherewith the seasonable month endows
45   The grass, the thicket, and the fruit-tree wild;
        White hawthorn, and the pastoral eglantine;
           Fast fading violets cover'd up in leaves;
             And mid-May's eldest child,
        The coming musk-rose, full of dewy wine,
50   The murmurous haunt of flies on summer eves.

6

Darkling[9] I listen; and, for many a time
    I have been half in love with easeful Death,

---

[7]Roman god of wine, whose chariot was pulled by leopards (pards). [8]fairies. [9]in the dark.

Call'd him soft names in many a mused rhyme,
   To take into the air my quiet breath;
55 Now more than ever seems it rich to die,
   To cease upon the midnight with no pain,
     While thou art pouring forth thy soul abroad
      In such an ecstasy!
   Still wouldst thou sing, and I have ears in vain—
60   To thy high requiem[10] become a sod.

7

Thou wast not born for death, immortal Bird!
   No hungry generations tread thee down;
The voice I hear this passing night was heard
   In ancient days by emperor and clown:
65 Perhaps the self-same song that found a path
   Through the sad heart of Ruth,[11] when, sick for home,
     She stood in tears amid the alien corn;
      The same that oft-times hath
   Charm'd magic casements, opening on the foam
70   Of perilous seas, in faery lands forlorn.

8

Forlorn! the very word is like a bell
   To toll me back from thee to my sole self!
Adieu! the fancy cannot cheat so well
   As she is fam'd to do, deceiving elf.
75 Adieu! adieu! thy plaintive anthem fades
   Past the near meadows, over the still stream,
     Up the hill-side; and now 'tis buried deep
      In the next valley-glades:
   Was it a vision, or a waking dream?
80   Fled is that music:—Do I wake or sleep?

(1819)   (1820)

[10]mass performed for the souls of the dead. [11]in the Old Testament, Ruth was a foreigner who gleaned corn in the fields of ancient Israel; see Ruth 2:3.

Ode on a Grecian Urn

1

Thou still unravish'd bride of quietness,
 Thou foster-child of silence and slow time,
Sylvan[1] historian, who canst thus express
 A flowery tale more sweetly than our rhyme:
5 What leaf-fring'd legend haunts about thy shape
  Of deities or mortals, or of both,
   In Tempe[2] or the dales of Arcady?[3]
What men or gods are these? What maidens loth?
  What mad pursuit? What struggle to escape?
10   What pipes and timbrels?[4] What wild ecstasy?

2

Heard melodies are sweet, but those unheard
 Are sweeter; therefore, ye soft pipes, play on;
Not to the sensual ear, but, more endear'd,
 Pipe to the spirit ditties of no tone:
15 Fair youth, beneath the trees, thou canst not leave
  Thy song, nor ever can those trees be bare;
   Bold Lover, never, never canst thou kiss,
Though winning near the goal—yet, do not grieve;
  She cannot fade, though thou hast not thy bliss,
20   For ever wilt thou love, and she be fair!

3

Ah, happy, happy boughs! that cannot shed
 Your leaves, nor ever bid the Spring adieu;
And, happy melodist, unwearied,
 For ever piping songs for ever new;
25 More happy love! more happy, happy love!
  For ever warm and still to be enjoy'd,
   For ever panting, and for ever young;
All breathing human passion far above,
  That leaves a heart high-sorrowful and cloy'd,
30   A burning forehead, and a parching tongue.

[1]belonging to the woods or forests. [2]quiet valley in Greece, noted for its beauty. [3]mountainous area in Greece, symbol of an ideal rural area. [4]tambourine-like musical instrument.

4

Who are these coming to the sacrifice?
　　To what green altar, O mysterious priest,
Lead'st thou that heifer lowing at the skies,
　　And all her silken flanks with garlands drest?
35 What little town by river or sea shore,
　　Or mountain-built with peaceful citadel,
　　　Is emptied of this folk, this pious morn?
And, little town, thy streets for evermore
　　Will silent be; and not a soul to tell
40 　　　Why thou art desolate, can e'er return.

5

O Attic⁵ shape! Fair attitude! with brede⁶
　　Of marble men and maidens overwrought,
With forest branches and the trodden weed;
　　Thou, silent form, dost tease us out of thought
45 As doth eternity: Cold Pastoral!
　　When old age shall this generation waste,
　　　Thou shalt remain, in midst of other woe
Than ours, a friend to man, to whom thou say'st,
　　"Beauty is truth, truth beauty,"—that is all
50 　　　Ye know on earth, and all ye need to know.

(1819)   (1820)

To Autumn

1

Season of mists and mellow fruitfulness,
　　Close bosom-friend of the maturing sun;
Conspiring with him how to load and bless
　　With fruit the vines that round the thatch-eves run;
5 To bend with apples the moss'd cottage-trees,
　　And fill all fruit with ripeness to the core;
　　　To swell the gourd, and plump the hazel shells
With a sweet kernel; to set budding more,
　　And still more, later flowers for the bees,
10 　　Until they think warm days will never cease,
　　　For Summer has o'er-brimm'd their clammy cells.

⁵belonging to or relating to Attica, whose capital was Athens. ⁶pattern of interwoven designs.

2

Who hath not seen thee oft amid thy store?
　　Sometimes whoever seeks abroad may find
Thee sitting careless on a granary floor,
15　　　Thy hair soft-lifted by the winnowing wind;
Or on a half-reap'd furrow sound asleep,
　　Drows'd with the fume of poppies, while thy hook
　　　　Spares the next swath and all its twined flowers:
And sometimes like a gleaner thou dost keep
20　　　Steady thy laden head across a brook;
　　Or by a cyder-press, with patient look,
　　　　Thou watchest the last oozings hours by hours.

3

Where are the songs of Spring? Ay, where are they?
　　Think not of them, thou hast thy music too,—
25　While barred clouds bloom the soft-dying day,
　　And touch the stubble-plains with rosy hue;
Then in a wailful choir the small gnats mourn
　　Among the river sallows, borne aloft
　　　　Or sinking as the light wind lives or dies;
30　And full-grown lambs loud bleat from hilly bourn;
　　Hedge-crickets sing; and now with treble soft
　　The red-breast whistles from a garden-croft;
　　　　And gathering swallows twitter in the skies.

(1819)　　　　　　　　　　　　　　　　　　　　(1820)

La Belle Dame sans Merci[1]

A BALLAD

I

O what can ail thee, knight-at-arms,
　　Alone and palely loitering?
The sedge has wither'd from the lake,
　　And no birds sing.

[1]the beautiful lady without pity.

II

O what can ail thee, knight-at-arms!
    So haggard and so woe-begone?
The squirrel's granary is full,
    And the harvest's done.

III

I see a lilly on thy brow,
    With anguish moist and fever dew,
And on thy cheeks a fading rose
    Fast withereth too.

IV

I met a lady in the meads,[2]
    Full beautiful—a faery's child,
Her hair was long, her foot was light,
    And her eyes were wild.

V

I made a garland for her head,
    And bracelets too, and fragrant zone;[3]
She look'd at me as she did love,
    And made sweet moan.

VI

I set her on my pacing steed,
    And nothing else saw all day long,
For sidelong would she bend, and sing
    A faery's song.

VII

She found me roots of relish sweet,
    And honey wild, and manna dew,[4]
And sure in language strange she said—
    "I love thee true."

VIII

She took me to her elfin grot,[5]
    And there she wept, and sigh'd full sore,
And there I shut her wild wild eyes
    With kisses four.

---

[2]meadows. [3]belt. [4]food that miraculously fell from heaven. [5]grotto: a cave or cavern.

IX

And there she lulled me asleep,
    And there I dream'd—Ah! woe betide!
35 The latest dream I ever dream'd
    On the cold hill side.

X

I saw pale kings and princes too,
    Pale warriors, death-pale were they all;
They cried—'La Belle Dame sans Merci
40   Hath thee in thrall!'[6]

XI

I saw their starved lips in the gloam,[7]
    With horrid warning gaped wide,
And I awoke and found me here,
    On the cold hill's side.

XII

45 And this is why I sojourn here,
    Alone and palely loitering,
Though the sedge has wither'd from the lake,
    And no birds sing.

(1819)   (1820)

Elizabeth Barrett Browning   (1806–1861)

Barrett Browning, a self-educated classical scholar and poet, was an invalid for much of her life. At the age of forty she left her notoriously tyrannical father and her home in Wimpole Street, London, and eloped with Robert Browning to Italy, where she lived for the remaining fifteen years of her life. The story of this courtship and her gradual growth toward a belief in and an acceptance of love, transformed into poetry, resulted in the sequence of love poems called the *Sonnets from the Portuguese*, the work for which she is still most popularly known, and which, in its adaptation of the sonnet for the female voice, is still considered one of her most notable achievements. Critical interest now, however, focuses more on *Aurora Leigh* (1857), her verse novel exploring the problems faced by Victorian women generally and the Victorian woman poet in particular. Barrett Browning's extensive body of work reveals a

[6]in bondage or slavery. [7]twilight.

wide thematic range and an innovative use of genre. "Hiram Powers's Greek Slave" contains one of her many protests against injustice with an attack on slavery, whereas "A Musical Instrument" explores the nature of poetic creativity. In such works as these, Barrett Browning expands upon the territory traditionally allocated to women poets, replacing the emphasis on love and sensibility with an uncompromising exploration of social and political power.

from Sonnets from the Portuguese[1]

XLIII

How do I love thee? Let me count the ways.
I love thee to the depth and breadth and height
My soul can reach, when feeling out of sight
For the ends of Being and ideal Grace.
5 I love thee to the level of everyday's
Most quiet need, by sun and candle-light.
I love thee freely, as men strive for Right;
I love thee purely, as they turn from Praise.
I love thee with the passion put to use
10 In my old griefs, and with my childhood's faith.
I love thee with a love I seemed to lose
With my lost saints,—I love thee with the breath,
Smiles, tears, of all my life!—and, if God choose,
I shall but love thee better after death.

(1850)

Hiram Powers's Greek Slave[1]

They say Ideal Beauty cannot enter
The house of anguish. On the threshold stands
An alien Image with the shackled hands,
Called the Greek Slave: as if the artist meant her,
5 (That passionless perfection which he lent her,
Shadowed, not darkened, where the sill expands)
To, so, confront man's crimes in different lands,

---

[1]the title was an attempt to disguise the personal nature of the sonnets by suggesting that they were translations. [1]the American sculptor Hiram Powers (1805–1873) first exhibited "The Greek Slave" at the Great Exhibition in London in 1851; it represents a Greek Christian woman captured by the Turks in the Greek war of independence (1821–26).

With man's ideal sense. Pierce to the centre,
Art's fiery finger!—and break up ere long
10 The serfdom of this world! Appeal, fair stone,
From God's pure heights of beauty, against man's wrong!
Catch up in thy divine face, not alone
East griefs but west,—and strike and shame the strong,
By thunders of white silence, overthrown.

(1850)

A Musical Instrument

What was he doing, the great god Pan,[1]
     Down in the reeds by the river?
Spreading ruin and scattering ban,
Splashing and paddling with hoofs of a goat,
5 And breaking the golden lilies afloat
     With the dragon-fly on the river.

He tore out a reed, the great god Pan,
     From the deep cool bed of the river:
The limpid water turbidly ran,
10 And the broken lilies a-dying lay,
And the dragon-fly had fled away,
     Ere he brought it out of the river.

High on the shore sat the great god Pan,
     While turbidly flowed the river;
15 And hacked and hewed as a great god can,
With his hard bleak steel at the patient reed,
Till there was not a sign of a leaf indeed
     To prove it fresh from the river.

He cut it short, did the great god Pan,
20   (How tall it stood in the river!)
Then drew the pith, like the heart of a man,
Steadily from the outside ring,
And notched the poor dry empty thing
     In holes, as he sat by the river.

[1]half animal and half god, Pan combines the creative and destructive forces. In Ovid's
Metamorphoses, he chases the nymph Syrinx, who prays for help and is transformed into reeds.
Pan takes these reeds and produces pipes from them.

25 "This is the way," laughed the great god Pan,
      (Laughed while he sat by the river,)
"The only way, since gods began
To make sweet music, they could succeed."
Then, dropping his mouth to a hole in the reed,
30   He blew in power by the river.

Sweet, sweet, sweet, O Pan!
      Piercing sweet by the river!
Blinding sweet, O great god Pan!
The sun on the hill forgot to die,
35 And the lilies revived, and the dragon-fly
      Came back to dream on the river.

Yet half a beast is the great god Pan,
      To laugh as he sits by the river,
Making a poet out of a man:
40 The true gods sigh for the cost and pain—
For the reed which grows nevermore again
      As a reed with the reeds in the river.

(1860)

Alfred, Lord Tennyson   (1809–1892)

Tennyson, the son of a clergyman, was born in Lincolnshire and educated at Cambridge. Here he joined a group of young intellectuals called the Apostles and formed the friendship with Arthur Hallam that had such an influence upon his work. In May of 1850 Tennyson published *In Memoriam*—the elegy prompted by Hallam's death in 1833—which comprised a cycle of 131 linked poems and which established his reputation. In June of the same year Tennyson married Emily Sellwood, and in November he succeeded Wordsworth as Poet Laureate. His other major works include *The Princess* (1847), an extended narrative, interspersed with lyric, on the question of women's proper sphere, and the *Idylls of the King* (1859–74), a reworking of the Arthurian legends. The languorous, flowing rhythms, which led W. H. Auden to conclude that Tennyson possessed the "finest ear, perhaps, of any English poet," are frequently undercut by sharp dramatic irony. Tennyson, like Browning, used the dramatic monologue, as in "Ulysses," to portray varying psychological states. He was also interested, however, in dramatizing competing social and philosophical positions, especially the tension between the desire to withdraw from social duties to pursue individual or aesthetic goals, and the need for a responsible commitment to society. For many critics, "The Lady of Shalott" and "Ulysses" rank among his finest achievements in symbolically representing this tension.

The Eagle. Fragment

He clasps the crag with crooked hands;
Close to the sun in lonely lands,
Ring'd with the azure world, he stands.

The wrinkled sea beneath him crawls;
He watches from his mountain walls,
And like a thunderbolt he falls.

(1851)

The Lady of Shalott

PART I

On either side the river lie
Long fields of barley and of rye,
That clothe the wold and meet the sky;
And thro' the field the road runs by
        To many-tower'd Camelot;[1]
And up and down the people go,
Gazing where the lilies blow
Round an island there below,
        The island of Shalott.

Willows whiten,[2] aspens quiver,
Little breezes dusk and shiver
Thro' the wave that runs for ever
By the island in the river
        Flowing down to Camelot.
Four gray walls, and four gray towers,
Overlook a space of flowers,
And the silent isle imbowers
        The Lady of Shalott.

By the margin, willow-veil'd,
Slide the heavy barges trail'd
By slow horses; and unhail'd
The shallop flitteth silken-sail'd

---

[1]legendary seat of King Arthur's court. [2]the wind reveals the white underside of the leaves.

Skimming down to Camelot:
But who hath seen her wave her hand?
25 Or at the casement seen her stand?
Or is she known in all the land,
        The Lady of Shalott?

Only reapers, reaping early
In among the bearded barley,
30 Hear a song that echoes cheerly
From the river winding clearly,
        Down to tower'd Camelot:
And by moon the reaper weary,
Piling sheaves in uplands airy,
35 Listening, whispers, "'Tis the fairy
        Lady of Shalott."

PART II

There she weaves by night and day
A magic web with colours gay.
She has heard a whisper say,
40 A curse is on her if she stay
        To look down to Camelot.
She knows not what the curse may be,
And so she weaveth steadily,
And little other care hath she,
45 The Lady of Shalott.

And moving thro' a mirror clear
That hangs before her all the year,
Shadows of the world appear.
There she sees the highway near
50 Winding down to Camelot:
There the river eddy whirls,
And there the surly village-churls,
And the red cloaks of market girls,
        Pass onward from Shalott.

55 Sometimes a troop of damsels glad,
An abbot on an ambling pad,
Sometimes a curly shepherd-lad,
Or long-hair'd page in crimson clad,
        Goes by to tower'd Camelot;

60 And sometimes thro' the mirror blue
The knights come riding two and two:
She hath no loyal knight and true,
    The Lady of Shalott.

But in her web she still delights
65 To weave the mirror's magic sights,
For often thro' the silent nights
A funeral, with plumes and lights
    And music, went to Camelot:
Or when the moon was overhead,
70 Came two young lovers lately wed;
"I am half sick of shadows," said
    The Lady of Shalott.

Part III

A bow-shot from her bower-eaves,
He rode between the barley-sheaves,
75 The sun came dazzling thro' the leaves,
And flamed upon the brazen greaves
    Of bold Sir Lancelot.
A red-cross knight[3] for ever kneel'd
To a lady in his shield,
80 That sparkled on the yellow field,
    Beside remote Shalott.

The gemmy bridle glitter'd free,
Like to some branch of stars we see
Hung in the golden Galaxy.[4]
85 The bridle bells rang merrily
    As he rode down to Camelot:
And from his blazon'd baldric[5] slung
A mighty silver bugle hung,
And as he rode his armour rung,
90   Beside remote Shalott.

All in the blue unclouded weather
Thick-jewell'd shone the saddle-leather,
The helmet and the helmet-feather

→

[3]an allusion to the hero in the first book of Spenser's *The Faerie Queene*, who shows his
Christian devotion by wearing on his chest a red cross. [4]Milky Way. [5]a decorated belt worn
over the shoulder and across the chest.

Burn'd like one burning flame together,
95   As he rode down to Camelot.
As often thro' the purple night,
Below the starry clusters bright,
Some bearded meteor, trailing light,
      Moves over still Shalott.

100   His broad clear brow in sunlight glow'd;
On burnished hooves his war-horse trode;
From underneath his helmet flow'd
His coal-black curls as on he rode,
      As he rode down to Camelot.
105   From the bank and from the river
He flash'd into the crystal mirror,
"Tirra lirra," by the river
      Sang Sir Lancelot.

She left the web, she left the loom,
110   She made three paces thro' the room,
She saw the water-lily bloom,
She saw the helmet and the plume,
      She look'd down to Camelot.
Out flew the web and floated wide;
115   The mirror crack'd from side to side;
"The curse is come upon me," cried
      The Lady of Shalott.

Part IV

In the stormy east-wind straining,
The pale yellow woods were waning,
120   The broad stream in his banks complaining,
Heavily the low sky raining
      Over tower'd Camelot;
Down she came and found a boat
Beneath a willow left afloat,
125   And round about the prow she wrote
      The Lady of Shalott.

And down the river's dim expanse
Like some bold seër in a trance,
Seeing all his own mischance—

¹³⁰ With a glassy countenance
     Did she look to Camelot.
And at the closing of the day
She loosed the chain, and down she lay;
The broad stream bore her far away,
¹³⁵   The Lady of Shalott.

Lying, robed in snowy white
That loosely flew to left and right—
The leaves upon her falling light—
Thro' the noises of the night
¹⁴⁰   She floated down to Camelot:
And as the boat-head wound along
The willowy hills and fields among,
They heard her singing her last song,
     The Lady of Shalott.

¹⁴⁵ Heard a carol, mournful, holy,
Chanted loudly, chanted lowly,
Till her blood was frozen slowly,
And her eyes were darken'd wholly,
     Turn'd to tower'd Camelot.
¹⁵⁰ For ere she reach'd upon the tide
The first house by the water-side,
Singing in her song she died,
     The Lady of Shalott.

Under tower and balcony,
¹⁵⁵ By garden-wall and gallery,
A gleaming shape she floated by,
Dead-pale between the houses high,
     Silent into Camelot.
Out upon the wharfs they came,
¹⁶⁰ Knight and burgher, lord and dame,
And round the prow they read her name,
     The Lady of Shalott.

Who is this? and what is here?
And in the lighted palace near
¹⁶⁵ Died the sound of royal cheer;
And they cross'd themselves for fear,
     All the knights at Camelot:
But Lancelot mused a little space;
He said, "She has a lovely face;

➡

170   God in his mercy lend her grace,
      The Lady of Shalott."

(1833)   (1842)

Ulysses[1]

It little profits that an idle king,
By this still hearth, among these barren crags,
Match'd with an aged wife, I mete and dole
Unequal laws unto a savage race,
5   That hoard, and sleep, and feed, and know not me.
I cannot rest from travel; I will drink
Life to the lees. All times I have enjoy'd
Greatly, have suffer'd greatly, both with those
That loved me, and alone; on shore, and when
10   Thro' scudding drifts the rainy Hyades[2]
Vext the dim sea. I am become a name;
For always roaming with a hungry heart
Much have I seen and known,—cities of men
And manners, climates, councils, governments,
15   Myself not least, but honor'd of them all,—
And drunk delight of battle with my peers,
Far on the ringing plains of windy Troy.
I am a part of all that I have met;
Yet all experience is an arch wherethro'
20   Gleams that untravell'd world whose margin fades
For ever and for ever when I move.
How dull it is to pause, to make an end.
To rust unburnish'd, not to shine in use!
As tho' to breathe were life! Life piled on life
25   Were all too little, and of one to me
Little remains; but every hour is saved
From that eternal silence, something more,
A bringer of new things; and vile it were
For some three suns to store and hoard myself,
30   And this gray spirit yearning in desire
To follow knowledge like a sinking star,
Beyond the utmost bound of human thought.

---

[1]Ulysses (Greek Odysseus) wandered for ten years following the fall of Troy before returning to his island kingdom of Ithaca and to his wife, Penelope, and son, Telemachus. For Tennyson's sources, see particularly Homer's *Odyssey* XI. 100–37 and Dante's *Inferno* XXVI.
[2]cluster of stars in the constellation Taurus that are associated with the rainy season.

This is my son, mine own Telemachus,
To whom I leave the sceptre and the isle,—
35   Well-loved of me, discerning to fulfil
This labor, by slow prudence to make mild
A rugged people, and thro' soft degrees
Subdue them to the useful and the good.
Most blameless is he, centred in the sphere
40   Of common duties, decent not to fail
In offices of tenderness, and pay
Meet adoration to my household gods,
When I am gone. He works his work, I mine.
There lies the port; the vessel puffs her sail;
45   There gloom the dark, broad seas. My mariners,
Souls that have toil'd, and wrought, and thought with me,—
That ever with a frolic welcome took
The thunder and the sunshine, and opposed
Free hearts, free foreheads,—you and I are old;
50   Old age hath yet his honor and his toil.
Death closes all; but something ere the end,
Some work of noble note, may yet he done,
Not unbecoming men that strove with Gods.
The lights begin to twinkle from the rocks;
55   The long day wanes; the slow moon climbs; the deep
Moans round with many voices. Come, my friends.
'Tis not too late to seek a newer world.
Push off, and sitting well in order smite
The sounding furrows; for my purpose holds
60   To sail beyond the sunset, and the baths
Of all the western stars, until I die.
It may be that the gulfs will wash us down;
It may be we shall touch the Happy Isles,[3]
And see the great Achilles,[4] whom we knew.
65   Tho' much is taken, much abides; and tho'
We are not now that strength which in old days
Moved earth and heaven, that which we are, we are,—
One equal temper of heroic hearts,
Made weak by time and fate, but strong in will
70   To strive, to seek, to find, and not to yield.

(1833)   (1842)

---

[3]the abode of dead heroes, also known as Elysium.   [4]Greek hero who fought at Troy. Homer's
Iliad revolves around the wrath of Achilles.

Robert Browning   (1812–1889)

Born in London and educated mostly at home, Browning eloped with Elizabeth Barrett to Italy in 1846 and did not return to live in England until after her death. When his first significant work, *Pauline* (1833), prompted the philosopher and critic J. S. Mill to remark on his "intense and morbid self-consciousness," Browning turned to the objective dramatic mode. He is best known for his development of the dramatic monologue, a form that focuses on a single character whose personality is exposed—often indirectly and ironically—through his or her speech. The culmination of Browning's experiments with this form is *The Ring and the Book* (1869), ten long monologues focusing on a single event, in which he suggests that the only way of knowing "truth" may be through art. His attempt to give this "truth broken into prismatic hues" is represented here by such ironic works as "The Bishop Orders His Tomb at Saint Praxed's Church" (1845) and by the surrealistic psychological study "'Childe Roland to the Dark Tower Came.'" His dramatic monologues, along with his notably "unpo- etic" language and his interests in psychology, philosophy, and arcane learning, had a great influence on modern poetic movements and particularly upon the poetry of Ezra Pound and T. S. Eliot.

My Last Duchess

Ferrara[1]

That's my last Duchess painted on the wall,
Looking as if she were alive. I call
That piece a wonder, now: Frà Pandolf's[2] hands
Worked busily a day, and there she stands.
5   Will't please you sit and look at her? I said
"Frà Pandolf" by design, for never read
Strangers like you that pictured countenance,
The depth and passion of its earnest glance,
But to myself they turned (since none puts by
10   The curtain I have drawn for you, but I)
And seemed as they would ask me, if they durst,
How such a glance came there; so, not the first
Are you to turn and ask thus. Sir, 'twas not
Her husband's presence only, called that spot
15   Of joy into the Duchess' cheek: perhaps
Frà Pandolf chanced to say 'Her mantle laps

➡

---

[1]an Italian town. The Duke of Ferrara's first wife died under suspicious circumstances in 1561. Soon after, he began to negotiate for the hand of the niece of the Count of Tyrol. [2]Brother Pandolf, an imaginary painter.

Over my lady's wrist too much,' or 'Paint
Must never hope to reproduce the faint
Half-flush that dies along her throat': such stuff
20 Was courtesy, she thought, and cause enough
For calling up that spot of joy. She had
A heart—how shall I say?—too soon made glad,
Too easily impressed; she liked whate'er
She looked on, and her looks went everywhere.
25 Sir, 'twas all one! My favour at her breast,
The dropping of the daylight in the West,
The bough of cherries some officious fool
Broke in the orchard for her, the white mule
She rode with round the terrace—all and each
30 Would draw from her alike the approving speech,
Or blush, at least. She thanked men,—good! but thanked
Somehow—I know not how—as if she ranked
My gift of a nine-hundred-years-old name
With anybody's gift. Who'd stoop to blame
35 This sort of trifling? Even had you skill
In speech—(which I have not)—to make your will
Quite clear to such an one, and say, "Just this
Or that in you disgusts me; here you miss,
Or there exceed the mark"—and if she let
40 Herself be lessoned so, nor plainly set
Her wits to yours, forsooth, and made excuse,
—E'en then would be some stooping; and I choose
Never to stoop. Oh sir, she smiled, no doubt,
Whene'er I passed her; but who passed without
45 Much the same smile? This grew; I gave commands;
Then all smiles stopped together. There she stands
As if alive. Will't please you rise? We'll meet
The company below, then. I repeat,
The Count your master's known munificence
50 Is ample warrant that no just pretence
Of mine for dowry will be disallowed;
Though his fair daughter's self, as I avowed
At starting, is my object. Nay, we'll go
Together down, sir. Notice Neptune, though,
55 Taming a sea-horse, thought a rarity,
Which Claus of Innsbruck[3] cast in bronze for me!

(1842)

[3]imaginary sculptor.

The Bishop Orders His Tomb at Saint Praxed's Church[1]

Rome, 15—

Vanity, saith the preacher, vanity![2]
Draw round my bed: is Anselm keeping back?
Nephews[3] of mine ... ah God, I know not! Well—
She, men would have to be your mother once,
5 Old Gandolf envied me, so fair she was!
What's done is done, and she is dead beside,
Dead long ago, and I am Bishop since,
And as she died so must we die ourselves,
And thence ye may perceive the world's a dream.
10 Life, how and what is it? As here I lie
In this state-chamber, dying by degrees,
Hours and long hours in the dead night, I ask
"Do I live, am I dead?" Peace, peace seems all.
Saint Praxed's ever was the church for peace;
15 And so, about this tomb of mine. I fought
With tooth and nail to save my niche, ye know:
—Old Gandolf cozened me, despite my care;
Shrewd was that snatch from out the corner South
He graced his carrion with, God curse the same!
20 Yet still my niche is not so cramped but thence
One sees the pulpit o' the epistle-side,[4]
And somewhat of the choir, those silent seats,
And up into the airy dome where live
The angels, and a sunbeam's sure to lurk:
25 And I shall fill my slab of basalt there,
And 'neath my tabernacle[5] take my rest,
With those nine columns round me, two and two,
The odd one at my feet where Anselm stands:
Peach-blossom marble all, the rare, the ripe
30 As fresh-poured red wine of a mighty pulse.
—Old Gandolf with his paltry onion-stone,[6]
Put me where I may look at him! True peach,
Rosy and flawless: how I earned the prize!
Draw close: that conflagration of my church

[1]Church of Santa Prassede, in Rome. [2]Ecclesiastes 1:2. "Vanity of vanities, saith the Preacher, vanity of vanities; all is vanity." [3]conventional euphemism for illegitimate sons. [4]the right-hand side as one faces the altar. [5]canopy over his tomb. [6]inferior grade of marble.

35 —What then? So much was saved if aught were missed!
My sons, ye would not be my death? Go dig
The white-grape vineyard where the oil-press stood,
Drop water gently till the surface sink,
And if ye find ... Ah God, I know not, I! ...
40 Bedded in store of rotten fig-leaves soft,
And corded up in a tight olive-frail,[7]
Some lump, ah God, of *lapis lazuli*,
Big as a Jew's head cut off at the nape,
Blue as a vein o'er the Madonna's breast ...
45 Sons, all have I bequeathed you, villas, all,
That brave Frascati[8] villa with its bath,
So, let the blue lump poise between my knees,
Like God the Father's globe on both his hands
Ye worship in the Jesu Church[9] so gay,
50 For Gandolf shall not choose but see and burst!
Swift as a weaver's shuttle fleet our years:
Man goeth to the grave, and where is he?
Did I say basalt for my slab, sons? Black—
'Twas ever antique-black I meant! How else
55 Shall ye contrast my frieze to come beneath?
The bas-relief in bronze ye promised me,
Those Pans and Nymphs ye wot of, and perchance
Some tripod, thyrsus,[10] with a vase or so,
The Saviour at his sermon on the mount,
60 Saint Praxed in a glory,[11] and one Pan
Ready to twitch the Nymph's last garment off,
And Moses with the tables ... but I know
Ye mark me not! What do they whisper thee,
Child of my bowels, Anselm? Ah, ye hope
65 To revel down my villas while I gasp
Bricked o'er with beggar's mouldy travertine[12]
Which Gandolf from his tomb-top chuckles at!
Nay, boys, ye love me—all of jasper, then!
'Tis jasper ye stand pledged to, lest I grieve
70 My bath must needs be left behind, alas!
One block, pure green as a pistachio-nut,

→

[7]olive basket. [8]fashionable resort town in the mountains. [9]Church of Il Gesu in Rome.
[10]classical and pagan ornamentation. The tripod is associated with the priestess of Apollo at
Delphi; the thyrsus is the staff carried by Dionysus. [11]with a halo. [12]ordinary limestone.

There's plenty jasper somewhere in the world—
And have I not Saint Praxed's ear to pray
Horses for ye, and brown Greek manuscripts,
75 And mistresses with great smooth marbly limbs?
—That's if ye carve my epitaph aright,
Choice Latin, picked phrase, Tully's[13] every word,
No gaudy ware like Gandolf's second line—
Tully, my masters? Ulpian[14] serves his need!
80 And then how I shall lie through centuries,
And hear the blessed mutter of the mass,
And see God made and eaten all day long,[15]
And feel the steady candle-flame, and taste
Good strong thick stupefying incense-smoke!
85 For as I lie here, hours of the dead night,
Dying in state and by such slow degrees,
I fold my arms as if they clasped a crook,
And stretch my feet forth straight as stone can point,
And let the bedclothes, for a mortcloth,[16] drop
90 Into great laps and folds of sculptor's-work:
And as yon tapers dwindle, and strange thoughts
Grow, with a certain humming in my ears,
About the life before I lived this life,
And this life too, popes, cardinals and priests,
95 Saint Praxed at his sermon on the mount,[17]
Your tall pale mother with her talking eyes,
And new-found agate urns as fresh as day,
And marble's language, Latin pure, discreet,
—Aha, ELUCESCEBAT[18] quoth our friend?
100 No Tully, said I, Ulpian at the best!
Evil and brief hath been my pilgrimage.
All *lapis*, all, sons! Else I give the Pope
My villas! Will ye ever eat my heart?
Ever your eyes were as a lizard's quick,
105 They glitter like your mother's for my soul,
Or ye would heighten my impoverished frieze,
Piece out its starved design, and fill my vase

[13]Cicero. [14]the decadent Latin of Ulpianus was far interior to that of Cicero. [15]reference to doctrine of transubstantiation, the conversion of bread and wine into the body and blood of Christ which is thought to occur during mass. [16]funeral pall. [17]the Bishop is confusing Praxed with Christ. [18]"He was illustrious." Phrase in Ulpianus's Latin, which is part of the inscription on Gandolf's tomb. The Ciceronian form would be *elucebat*.

With grapes, and add a vizor and a Term,[19]
And to the tripod ye would tie a lynx
110 That in his struggle throws the thyrsus down,
To comfort me on my entablature
Whereon I am to lie till I must ask
"Do I live, am I dead?" There, leave me, there!
For ye have stabbed me with ingratitude
115 To death—ye wish it—God, ye wish it! Stone—
Gritstone,[20] a-crumble! Clammy squares which sweat
As if the corpse they keep were oozing through—
And no more *lapis* to delight the world!
Well go! I bless ye. Fewer tapers there,
120 But in a row: and, going, turn your backs
—Ay, like departing altar-ministrants,
And leave me in my church, the church for peace,
That I may watch at leisure if he leers—
Old Gandolf, at me, from his onion-stone,
125 As still he envied me, so fair she was!

(1845)

"Childe Roland to the Dark Tower Came"[1]

I

My first thought was, he lied in every word,
    That hoary cripple, with malicious eye
    Askance to watch the working of his lie
On mine, and mouth scarce able to afford
5 Suppression of the glee, that pursed and scored
    Its edge, at one more victim gained thereby.

II

What else should he be set for, with his staff?
    What, save to waylay with his lies, ensnare
    All travellers who might find him posted there,
10 And ask the road? I guessed what skull-like laugh

---

[19]a visor is the eye covering of a helmet; *Term* is an abbreviation of *Terminus*, the Roman god of boundaries, and thus, a common symbol of mortality. A term was also the tapered pedestal on which a bust, such as that of Terminus, would be placed. [20]sandstone. [1]see Edgar's mad song in Shakespeare's *King Lear* 3.4:171–73. "Child Rowland to the dark tower came, / His word was still—Fie, foh, and fum! / I smell the blood of a British man." A childe is a young knight who has not yet proved himself.

Would break, what crutch 'gin write my epitaph
　　For pastime in the dusty thoroughfare,

III

If at his counsel I should turn aside
　　Into that ominous tract which, all agree,
　　Hides the Dark Tower. Yet acquiescingly
I did turn as he pointed: neither pride
Nor hope rekindling at the end descried,
　　So much as gladness that some end might be.

IV

For, what with my whole world-wide wandering,
　　What with my search drawn out through years, my hope
　　Dwindled into a ghost not fit to cope
With that obstreperous joy success would bring,—
I hardly tried now to rebuke the spring
　　My heart made, finding failure in its scope.

V

As when a sick man very near to death
　　Seems dead indeed, and feels begin and end
　　The tears and takes the farewell of each friend,
And hears one bid the other go, draw breath
Freelier outside, ("since all is o'er," he saith,
　　"And the blow fallen no grieving can amend";)

VI

While some discuss if near the other graves
　　Be room enough for this, and when a day
　　Suits best for carrying the corpse away,
With care about the banners, scarves and staves:
And still the man hears all, and only craves
　　He may not shame such tender love and stay.

VII

Thus, I had so long suffered in this quest,
　　Heard failure prophesied so oft, been writ
　　So many times among "The Band"—to wit,
The knights who to the Dark Tower's search addressed
Their steps—that just to fail as they, seemed best,
　　And all the doubt was now—should I be fit?

VIII

So, quiet as despair, I turned from him,
    That hateful cripple, out of his highway
45   Into the path he pointed. All the day
Had been a dreary one at best, and dim
Was settling to its close, yet shot one grim
    Red leer to see the plain catch its estray.[2]

IX

For mark! no sooner was I fairly found
50   Pledged to the plain, after a pace or two,
    Than, pausing to throw backward a last view
O'er the safe road, 'twas gone; grey plain all around:
Nothing but plain to the horizon's bound.
    I might go on; naught else remained to do.

X

55 So, on I went. I think I never saw
    Such starved ignoble nature; nothing throve:
    For flowers—as well expect a cedar grove!
But cockle, spurge,[3] according to their law
Might propagate their kind, with none to awe,
60   You'd think; a burr had been a treasure-trove.

XI

No! penury, inertness and grimace,
    In some strange sort, were the land's portion. "See
    Or shut your eyes," said Nature peevishly,
"It nothing skills: I cannot help my case:
65 'Tis the Last Judgement's fire must cure this place,
    Calcine[4] its clods and set my prisoners free."

XII

If there pushed any ragged thistle-stalk
    Above its mates, the head was chopped; the bents
    Were jealous else. What made those holes and rents
70 In the dock's harsh swarth leaves, bruised as to balk
All hope of greenness? 'tis a brute must walk
    Pashing their life out, with a brute's intents.

---

[2]someone who has strayed. [3]cockle is any of several weeds that grow in wheat fields; some of the varieties belong to the spurge family and have an acrid milky juice with purgative properties. [4]pulverize by heat.

XIII

As for the grass, it grew as scant as hair
    In leprosy; thin dry blades pricked the mud
75   Which underneath looked kneaded up with blood.
One stiff blind horse, his every bone a-stare,
Stood stupefied, however he came there:
    Thrust out past service from the devil's stud!

XIV

Alive? he might be dead for aught I know,
80   With that red gaunt and colloped⁵ neck a-strain,
    And shut eyes underneath the rusty mane;
Seldom went such grotesqueness with such woe;
I never saw a brute I hated so;
    He must be wicked to deserve such pain.

XV

85 I shut my eyes and turned them on my heart.
    As a man calls for wine before he fights,
    I asked one draught of earlier, happier sights,
Ere fitly I could hope to play my part.
Think first, fight afterwards—the soldier's art:
90   One taste of the old time sets all to rights.

XVI

Not it! I fancied Cuthbert's reddening face
    Beneath its garniture of curly gold,
        Dear fellow, till I almost felt him fold
    An arm in mine to fix me to the place,
95 That way he used. Alas, one night's disgrace!
    Out went my heart's new fire and left it cold.

XVII

Giles then, the soul of honour—there he stands
    Frank as ten years ago when knighted first.
    What honest man should dare (he said) he durst.
100 Good—but the scene shifts—faugh! what hangman-hands
Pin to his breast a parchment? His own bands
    Read it. Poor traitor, spit upon and curst!

⁵in folds or ridges.

XVIII

Better this present than a past like that;
    Back therefore to my darkening path again!
105   No sound, no sight as far as eye could strain.
Will the night send a howler[6] or a bat?
I asked: when something on the dismal flat
    Came to arrest my thoughts and change their train.

XIX

A sudden little river crossed my path
110   As unexpected as a serpent comes.
    No sluggish tide congenial to the glooms;
This, as it frothed by, might have been a bath
For the fiend's glowing hoof—to see the wrath
    Of its black eddy bespate with flakes and spumes.

XX

115 So petty yet so spiteful! All along,
    Low scrubby alders kneeled down over it;
    Drenched willows flung them headlong in a fit
Of mute despair, a suicidal throng:
The river which had done them all the wrong,
120   Whate'er that was, rolled by, deterred no whit.

XXI

Which, while I forded,—good saints, how I feared
    To set my foot upon a dead man's cheek,
    Each step, or feel the spear I thrust to seek
For hollows, tangled in his hair or beard!
125 —It may have been a water-rat I speared,
    But, ugh! it sounded like a baby's shriek.

XXII

Glad was I when I reached the other bank.
    Now for a better country. Vain presage!
    Who were the strugglers; what war did they wage,
130 Whose savage trample thus could pad the dank
Soil to a plash? Toads in a poisoned tank,
    Or wild cats in a red-hot iron cage—

[6]owl.

XXIII

The fight must so have seemed in that fell cirque.
    What penned them there, with all the plain to choose?
135   No foot-print leading to that horrid mews,
None out of it. Mad brewage set to work
Their brains, no doubt, like galley-slaves the Turk
    Pits for his pastime, Christians against Jews.

XXIV

And more than that—a furlong on—why, there!
140   What bad use was that engine for, that wheel,
    Or brake,[7] not wheel—that harrow fit to reel
Men's bodies out like silk? with all the air
Of Tophet's tool,[8] on earth left unaware,
    Or brought to sharpen its rusty teeth of steel.

XXV

145 Then came a bit of stubbed ground, once a wood,
    Next a marsh, it would seem, and now mere earth
    Desperate and done with; (so a fool finds mirth,
Makes a thing and then mars it, till his mood
Changes and off he goes!) within a rood[9]—
150   Bog, clay and rubble, sand and stark black dearth.

XXVI

Now blotches rankling, coloured gay and grim,
    Now patches where some leanness of the soil's
    Broke into moss or substances like boils;
Then came some palsied oak, a cleft in him
155 Like a distorted mouth that splits its rim
    Gaping at death, and dies while it recoils.

XXVII

And just as far as ever from the end!
    Naught in the distance but the evening, naught
    To point my footsteps further! At the thought,
160 A great black bird, Apollyon's bosom-friend,[10]
Sailed past, nor beat his wide wing dragon-penned[11]
    That brushed my cap—perchance the guide I sought.

---

[7]a machine with teeth used for breaking up flax or hemp to separate the fibre; here used as a device of torture. [8]hell's tool. [9]approximately a quarter of an acre. [10]in Revelations 9:11, the devil is called Apollyon, the destroyer. [11]with pinions like a dragon.

XXVIII

For, looking up, aware I somehow grew,
    'Spite of the dusk, the plain had given place
165   All round to mountains—with such name to grace
Mere ugly heights and heaps now stolen in view.
How thus they had surprised me,—solve it, you!
    How to get from them was no clearer case.

XXIX

Yet half I seemed to recognize some trick
170   Of mischief happened to me, God knows when—
    In a bad dream perhaps. Here ended, then,
Progress this way. When, in the very nick
Of giving up, one time more, came a click
    As when a trap shuts—you're inside the den!

XXX

175   Burningly it came on me all at once,
    This was the place! those two hills on the right,
    Crouched like two bulls locked horn in horn in fight;
While to the left, a tall scalped mountain ... Dunce,
Dotard, a-dozing at the very nonce,
180   After a life spent training for the sight!

XXXI

What in the midst lay but the Tower itself?
    The round squat turret, blind as the fool's heart,
    Built of brown stone, without a counterpart
In the whole world. The tempest's mocking elf
185   Points to the shipman thus the unseen shelf
    He strikes on, only when the timbers start.

XXXII

Not see? because of night perhaps?—why, day
    Came back again for that! before it left,
    The dying sunset kindled through a cleft:
190   The hills, like giants at a hunting, lay,
Chin upon hand, to see the game at bay,—
    "Now stab and end the creature—to the heft!"[12]

---

[12]handle of a dagger.

XXXIII

Not hear? when noise was everywhere! it tolled
    Increasing like a bell. Names in my ears
195   Of all the lost adventurers my peers,—
How such a one was strong, and such was bold,
And such was fortunate, yet each of old
    Lost, lost! one moment knelled the woe of years.

XXXIV

There they stood, ranged along the hill-sides, met
200   To view the last of me, a living frame
    For one more picture! in a sheet of flame
I saw them and I knew them all. And yet
Dauntless the slug-horn[13] to my lips I set,
    And blew. "*Childe Roland to the Dark Tower came.*"

(1855)

Walt Whitman   (1819–1892)

A visionary who helped to shape modern poetry, Walt Whitman was born on Long Island, New York. He worked as a labourer, teacher, printer, journalist, and, during the American Civil War, a nurse. He published *Leaves of Grass*, the first major collection by an American poet, in 1855, but he revised and expanded it several times. Positioning himself as the bard of the new Republic, Whitman celebrated the diversity and greatness of America in poems that were iconoclastic in form and content. He viewed his free verse, which flowed over long, passionate lines, as something organically developing from his subject. That subject was the dignity of the common man and the ideals of democracy and individualism. Eschewing the poetic figures of conventional poetry, he drew his images from his experience of Americans as they actually were. As a consequence, critics sometimes complained that his poems contained obscene passages. They also complained that his poems, which he organized associatively by developing thematic motifs, were massive and formless. The shorter poems below, however, are tightly controlled. They reveal a craftsman who was passionate about the common person, who loved his country and mourned its slain president, and who was an heir of the transcendental idealism of Emerson and Thoreau.

When I Heard the Learn'd Astronomer

When I heard the learn'd astronomer,
When the proofs, the figures, were ranged in columns before me,
When I was shown the charts and diagrams, to add, divide, and measure them,

➡️

[13]trumpet.

When I sitting heard the astronomer where he lectured with much applause in the lecture-room,

5   How soon unaccountable I became tired and sick,
    Till rising and gliding out I wander'd off by myself,
    In the mystical moist night-air, and from time to time,
    Look'd up in perfect silence at the stars.

(1865)

O Captain! My Captain![1]

O Captain! my Captain! our fearful trip is done,
The ship has weather'd every rack, the prize we sought is won,
The port is near, the bells I hear, the people all exulting,
While follow eyes the steady keel, the vessel grim and daring;
5   But O heart! heart! heart!
            O the bleeding drops of red,
                Where on the deck my Captain lies,
                    Fallen cold and dead.

O Captain! my Captain! rise up and hear the bells;
10 Rise up—for you the flag is flung—for you the bugle trills,
    For you bouquets and ribbon'd wreaths—for you the shores a-crowding,
    For you they call, the swaying mass, their eager faces turning;
        Here Captain! dear father!
            This arm beneath your head!
15   It is some dream that on the deck,
                    You've fallen cold and dead.

My Captain does not answer, his lips are pale and still,
My father does not feel my arm, he has no pulse nor will,
The ship is anchor'd safe and sound, its voyage closed and done,
20 From fearful trip the victor ship comes in with object won;
        Exult O shores, and ring O bells!
            But I with mournful tread,
                Walk the deck my Captain lies,
                    Fallen cold and dead.

(1865)   (1871)

---

[1]written in memory of Abraham Lincoln (1809–1865), president of the United States during the American Civil War, who was assassinated by John Wilkes Booth.

One's-Self I Sing

One's-Self I sing, a simple separate person,
Yet utter the word Democratic, the word En-Masse.[1]

Of physiology from top to toe I sing,
Not physiognomy[2] alone nor brain alone is worthy for the Muse, I say the
    Form complete is worthier far,
5   The Female equally with the Male I sing.

Of Life immense in passion, pulse, and power,
Cheerful, for freest action form'd under the laws divine,
The Modern Man I sing.

(1867)   (1871)

A Noiseless Patient Spider

A noiseless patient spider,
I mark'd where on a little promontory it stood isolated,
Mark'd how to explore the vacant vast surrounding,
It launch'd forth filament, filament, filament, out of itself,
5   Ever unreeling them, ever tirelessly speeding them.

And you O my soul where you stand,
Surrounded, detached, in measureless oceans of space,
Ceaselessly musing, venturing, throwing, seeking the spheres to connect them,
Till the bridge you will need be form'd, till the ductile anchor hold,
10 Till the gossamer thread you fling catch somewhere, O my soul.

(1868)   (1881)

Matthew Arnold   (1822–1888)

Arnold, the eldest son of Thomas Arnold, headmaster of Rugby, was educated at Oxford, stayed on as professor of poetry for ten years, and was subsequently appointed an inspector of schools in 1851. He became one of the leading social and literary critics of the age, and such critical works as *Culture and Anarchy* (1869), an investigation into the question of whether the anarchy of individualism should be checked by the authority of culture, are now often considered to be of greater significance than his poetical works. The two genres of poetry and criticism come together in his

---

[1]in a group. [2]facial features.

once-influential theory of critical "touchstones" in "The Study of Poetry" (1888), an attempt to establish standards for distinguishing poetry of "high seriousness." Frequently referred to as the poet of alienation, Arnold is preoccupied with the isolation of the individual and the difficulty of knowing the self. His work is suffused with a sense of frustration, a sharp awareness of the failings of his age, and a poignant nostalgia for a basically illusory earlier age when questions of faith and moral integrity were more easily answered. At the same time, Arnold reveals an unfailing optimistic belief in the efficacy of cultural institutions in bringing about change. The resulting self-division is aptly captured in the haunting lyricism of "Dover Beach." In looking back to a better time and yet still believing in human progress, Arnold is quintessentially Victorian, a man, as he so memorably says in "Stanzas from the Grande Chartreuse" (1855), "Wandering between two worlds, one dead, / The other powerless to be born."

Dover Beach

The sea is calm to-night.
The tide is full, the moon lies fair,
Upon the straits;—on the French coast the light
Gleams and is gone; the cliffs of England stand,
5 Glimmering and vast, out in the tranquil bay.
Come to the window, sweet is the night-air!
Only, from the long line of spray
Where the sea meets the moon-blanch'd land,
Listen! you hear the grating roar
10 Of pebbles which the waves draw back, and fling,
At their return, up the high strand,
Begin, and cease, and then again begin,
With tremulous cadence slow, and bring
The eternal note of sadness in.

15 Sophocles long ago
Heard it on the Ægæan, and it brought
Into his mind the turbid ebb and flow
Of human misery;[1] we
Find also in the sound a thought,
20 Hearing it by this distant northern sea.
The Sea of Faith
Was once, too, at the full, and round earth's shore
Lay like the folds of a bright girdle furl'd.
But now I only hear

➡

[1] see Sophocles, *Antigone* 2.583ff.

25 Its melancholy, long, withdrawing roar,
Retreating, to the breath
Of the night-wind, down the vast edges drear
And naked shingles² of the world.

Ah, love, let us be true
30 To one another! for the world, which seems
To lie before us like a land of dreams,
So various, so beautiful, so new,
Hath really neither joy, nor love, nor light,
Nor certitude, nor peace, nor help for pain;
35 And we are here as on a darkling plain
Swept with confused alarms of struggle and flight,
Where ignorant armies clash by night.

(1867)

Christina Rossetti (1830–1894)

Rossetti, younger sister of the poet-painter Dante Gabriel Rossetti, was educated at home and lived with her family in London for most of her life. Like her mother and sister, she was a devout High Anglican with a great interest in the Oxford Movement, which attempted to merge Catholic doctrine and ritual with the Anglican faith. In 1862 she established her reputation as a poet with the publication of her most famous work, "Goblin Market." Rossetti was the only woman in the Pre-Raphaelite circle to achieve recognition for her own work, to be the creative rather than simply the inspirational force, and she is also the only British woman poet of the nineteenth century to have consistently drawn critical acclaim right up to the present day. She wrote much religious poetry and many children's rhymes, as well as numerous ballads and lyrics that reveal a deep ambivalence toward romantic love and the conventional roles of women; they have a strong critical subtext rejecting the limitations imposed upon women by society. Unhappy or frustrated love between men and the women they betray is often the focus of her frequently melancholy works, and the women she depicts find their only consolation in resignation, postponement, and the love of God.

Song

When I am dead, my dearest,
Sing no sad songs for me;

→

²pebbled beaches.

Plant thou no roses at my head,
    Nor shady cypress tree:
5   Be the green grass above me
    With showers and dewdrops wet;
And if thou wilt, remember,
    And if thou wilt, forget.

I shall not see the shadows,
10   I shall not feel the rain;
I shall not hear the nightingale
    Sing on as if in pain:
And dreaming through the twilight
    That doth not rise nor set,
15 Haply I may remember,
    And haply may forget.

(1848)   (1862)

The World

By day she woos me, soft, exceeding fair:
    But all night as the moon so changeth she;
    Loathsome and foul with hideous leprosy,
And subtle serpents gliding in her hair.
5 By day she woos me to the outer air,
    Ripe fruits, sweet flowers, and full satiety:
    But thro' the night a beast she grins at me,
A very monster void of love and prayer.
By day she stands a lie: by night she stands
10   In all the naked horror of the truth,
With pushing horns and clawed and clutching hands.
Is this a friend indeed, that I should sell
    My soul to her, give her my life and youth,
Till my feet, cloven too, take hold on hell?

(1854)   (1862)

Emily Dickinson (1830–1886)

Born in Amherst, Massachusetts, where she lived all her life, Emily Dickinson spent her last twenty-five years, those of her greatest poetic creativity, a relative recluse. For several decades after her death she was regarded as a timid hermit. However, recent studies reveal that, while she seldom ventured outside the family home, she read widely in the classics, contemporary philosophy, and particularly the works of major nineteenth-century women poets and novelists. At a time when intellectual activity was considered detrimental to the emotional and physical health of women and their greatest fulfillment was believed to be found in domestic life, Emily Dickinson was a truly radical woman in her attitudes about religion, society, and art. Although she thought, as she said, "New Englandly," her ideas anticipate by nearly a century those of many modern feminists. During her lifetime, only a handful of her more than seventeen hundred poems were published. Today, she is one of the most widely read and studied American writers. None of her poems is long; most are written within a pattern resembling the four-line stanza characteristic of New England hymns, with alternating lines containing 4, 3, 4, and 3 strong beats. Yet within this limitation, Dickinson achieved tremendous variety of poetic effect and complexity of theme. Using dashes to indicate breath pauses, incomplete and inverted syntax, startling images of nature, and homely domestic images, she depicted the individual consciousness questioning itself in relation to other people, society at large, nature, and death.

288

I'm Nobody! Who are you?
Are you—Nobody—Too?
Then there's a pair of us?
Don't tell! they'd advertise—you know!
5 How dreary—to be—Somebody!
How public—like a Frog—
To tell one's name—the livelong June—
To an admiring Bog!

(c. 1861)   (1891)

303

The Soul selects her own Society—
Then—shuts the Door—
To her divine Majority—
Present no more—

5 Unmoved—she notes the Chariots—pausing—
At her low Gate—
Unmoved—an Emperor be kneeling
Upon her Mat—

I've known her—from an ample nation—
10 Choose One—   ➜

Then—close the Valves of her attention—
Like Stone—

(c. 1862)   (1890)

328

A Bird came down the Walk—
He did not know I saw—
He bit an Angleworm in halves
And ate the fellow, raw,

5 And then he drank a Dew
From a convenient Grass—
And then hopped sidewise to the Wall
To let a Beetle pass—

He glanced with rapid eyes
10 That hurried all around—
They looked like frightened Beads, I thought—
He stirred his Velvet Head

Like one in danger, Cautious,
I offered him a Crumb
15 And he unrolled his feathers
And rowed him softer home—

Than Oars divide the Ocean,
Too silver for a seam—
Or Butterflies, off Banks of Noon
20 Leap, plashless as they swim.

(c. 1862)   (1891)

465

I heard a Fly buzz—when I died—
The Stillness in the Room
Was like the Stillness in the Air—
Between the Heaves of Storm—

5 The Eyes around—had wrung them dry—
And Breaths were gathering firm
For that last Onset—when the King
Be witnessed—in the Room—

I willed my Keepsakes—Signed away
10 What portion of me be
Assignable—and then it was
There interposed a Fly—

With Blue—uncertain stumbling Buzz—
Between the light—and me—
15 And then the Windows failed—and then
I could not see to see—

(c. 1862)   (1896)

712

Because I could not stop for Death—
He kindly stopped for me—
The Carriage held but just Ourselves—
And Immortality.

5 We slowly drove—He knew no haste
And I had put away
My labor and my leisure too,
For His Civility—

We passed the School, where Children strove
10 At Recess—in the Ring—
We passed the Fields of Gazing Grain—
We passed the Setting Sun—

Or rather—He passed Us—
The Dews drew quivering and chill—
15 For only Gossamer, my Gown—
My Tippet[1]—only Tulle[2]—

We paused before a House that seemed
A Swelling of the Ground—
The Roof was scarcely visible—
20 The Cornice—in the Ground—

Since then—'tis Centuries—and yet
Feels shorter than the Day
I first surmised the Horses' Heads
Were toward Eternity—

(c. 1863)   (1890)

[1]a covering for the shoulders, like a stole. [2]a fine netting.

Gerard Manley Hopkins   (1844–1889)

Hopkins was born near London and educated at Oxford during a time of violent religious controversy. He converted to Catholicism in 1866, became a Jesuit priest, and spent the remainder of his life serving the order. Hopkins is generally considered one of the most powerful of the religious poets and one of the most daring innovators in poetic technique. Two notions central to his work are what he calls "inscape," the unique quality that distinguishes one thing from every other, and "instress," the response evoked by the perception of inscape. The attempt to capture these elements in his work can be seen in the lyrically powerful "The Windhover."

Pied Beauty[1]

Glory be to God for dappled things—
　　　For skies of couple-colour as a brinded[2] cow;
　　　　　For rose-moles all in stipple[3] upon trout that swim;
Fresh-firecoal chestnut-falls;[4] finches' wings;
5　　　Landscape plotted and pieced—fold, fallow, and plough;
　　　　　And áll trádes, their gear and tackle and trim.

All things counter, original, spare, strange;
　　　Whatever is fickle, freckled (who knows how?)
　　　　　With swift, slow; sweet, sour; adazzle, dim;
10　He fathers-forth whose beauty is past change:
　　　　　　　　　　Praise him.

(1877)　　　　　　　　　　　　　　　　　　　　　　　　　　　　　(1918)

God's Grandeur

The world is charged with the grandeur of God.
　　　It will flame out, like shining from shook foil;[1]
　　　It gathers to a greatness, like the ooze of oil
Crushed.[2] Why do men then now not reck his rod?
5　Generations have trod, have trod, have trod;
　　　And all is seared with trade; bleared, smeared with toil;
　　　And wears man's smudge and shares man's smell: the soil
Is bare now, nor can foot feel, being shod.

And for all this, nature is never spent;

---

[1]having two or more colours; in patches or blotches. [2]streaked. [3]method in painting of applying colour in dots. [4]chestnuts dappling the dark ground like bright coals. [1]foil leaf or tinsel. [2]like oil crushed out of olives or seeds.

10
There lives the dearest freshness deep down things;
And though the last lights off the black West wen
   Oh, morning, at the brown brink eastward, springs—
Because the Holy Ghost over the bent
   World broods with warm breast and with ah! bright wings.

(1877)   (1917)

The Windhover[1]

TO CHRIST OUR LORD

I caught this morning morning's minion,[2] king-
   dom of daylight's dauphin,[3] dapple-dawn-drawn Falcon, in his riding
   Of the rolling level underneath him steady air, and striding
High there, how he rung upon the rein of a wimpling wing[4]
5
In his ecstasy! then off, off forth on swing,
   As a skate's heel sweeps smooth on a bow-bend: the hurl and gliding
   Rebuffed the big wind. My heart in hiding
Stirred for a bird,—the achieve of, the mastery of the thing!

Brute beauty and valour and act, oh, air, pride, plume, here
10
Buckle![5] AND the fire that breaks from thee then, a billion
Times told lovelier, more dangerous, O my chevalier![6]

   No wonder of it: shéer plód makes plough down sillion[7]
Shine, and blue-bleak embers, ah my dear,
   Fall, gall themselves, and gash gold-vermilion.

(1877)   (1918)

A. E. Housman   (1859–1936)

Born in Worcestershire and educated at Oxford, Housman failed his final examinations and subsequently worked for ten years as a civil servant before becoming professor of Latin at University College, London. *A Shropshire Lad* (1896), from which the following selections are taken, initially met with little interest, but became immensely popular during World War I, probably because of the recurrent intermingled themes of mutability, pessimism, and patriotism, and the recurrent theme of doomed youth. Housman's output was limited: he published only two small volumes during his lifetime, *A Shropshire Lad* and *Last Poems* (1922); a third, *More Poems* (1936), appeared after his death. Housman is

[1]small hawk. [2]favourite. [3]name given to the heir to the French throne. [4]in falconry, to ring means to rise in the air spirally. [5]*buckle* has many possible meanings: fasten, join, enclose, grapple, submit, bend, and crumple. [6]knight, nobleman, champion. [7]the ridge between two furrows.

important as a link between the Victorian and the modern world, and he is at his best when he avoids the rather artificial, decadent style that influenced him in his youth and produces the finely crafted, concentrated poems marked by a vigorous, deceptive simplicity for which he is best known. Revealing the influence of the classical lyric and the popular ballad, these works skillfully exploit balance and opposition and frequently close with a pervasive gentle melancholy undercut by the sudden introduction of irony or bathos.

Lovelist of trees, the cherry now

Loveliest of trees, the cherry now
Is hung with bloom along the bough,
And stands about the woodland ride
Wearing white for Eastertide.

5   Now, of my threescore years and ten,
Twenty will not come again,
And take from seventy springs a score,
It only leaves me fifty more.

And since to look at things in bloom
10   Fifty springs are little room
About the woodlands I will go
To see the cherry hung with snow.

(1896)

To an Athlete Dying Young

The time you won your town the race
We chaired you through the market-place;
Man and boy stood cheering by,
And home we brought you shoulder-high.

5   To-day, the road all runners come,
Shoulder-high we bring you home,
And set you at your threshold down,
Townsman of a stiller town.

Smart lad, to slip betimes away
10   From fields where glory does not stay
And early though the laurel[1] grows
It withers quicker than the rose.[2]

[1]symbol of victory, traditionally awarded by the Greeks to the victor in the Pythian Games. [2]symbol of beauty.

Eyes the shady night has shut
Cannot see the record cut,
15   And silence sounds no worse than cheers
After earth has stopped the ears:

Now you will not swell the rout
Of lads that wore their honours out,
Runners whom renown outran
20   And the name died before the man.

So set, before its echoes fade,
The fleet foot on the sill of shade,
And hold to the low lintel up
The still-defended challenge-cup.

25   And round that early-laurelled head
Will flock to gaze the strengthless dead
And find unwithered on its curls
The garland briefer than a girl's.

(1896)

Sir Charles G. D. Roberts   (1860–1943)

Credited with creating the first truly Canadian literary form, the realistic animal tale, Charles George Douglas Roberts also played a significant role in the development of Canadian poetry. His first volume, *Orion and Other Poems* (1880), inspired both his cousin, Bliss Carman, and Archibald Lampman, who, together with Duncan Campbell Scott and Roberts, formed the Confederation Poets, a group that consciously sought to create a distinctive Canadian poetry. Born in Douglas, New Brunswick, Roberts worked as an editor and then an English professor, but after 1897 he earned his living by writing prose, living in New York, London, and Europe until his return to Canada in 1925. Paradoxically, his most enduring and universal poems are not the obtrusively moralizing ones in which he deliberately tried to be universal, but the early ones in which he was most regional in subject. These poems show three major influences: his classical training, in the highly organized form and choice of allusions; the English Romantics, especially Wordsworth, in the presentation of sharply detailed landscapes in language that avoids consciously poetic diction; and the Victorian intellectual poets, particularly Matthew Arnold, in the probing for spiritual or philosophical significance. These poems support his claim in "The Poetry of Nature" that "nature-poetry is not mere description of landscape in metrical form, but the expression of one or another of many vital relationships between external nature and 'the deep heart of man.'"

Tantramar[1] Revisited

Summers and summers have come, and gone with the flight of the swallow;
Sunshine and thunder have been, storm, and winter, and frost;
Many and many a sorrow has all but died from remembrance,
Many a dream of joy fall'n in the shadow of pain.
5   Hands of chance and change have marred, or moulded, or broken,
Busy with spirit or flesh, all I most have adored;
Even the bosom of Earth is strewn with heavier shadows,—
Only in these green hills, aslant to the sea, no change!
Here where the road that has climbed from the inland valleys and woodlands,
10 Dips from the hill-tops down, straight to the base of the hills,—
Here, from my vantage-ground, I can see the scattering houses,
Stained with time, set warm in orchards, meadows, and wheat,
Dotting the broad bright slopes outspread to southward and eastward,
Wind-swept all day long, blown by the south-east wind.
15 Skirting the sunbright uplands stretches a riband[2] of meadow,
Shorn of the labouring grass, bulwarked well from the sea,
Fenced on its seaward border with long clay dikes from the turbid
Surge and flow of the tides vexing the Westmoreland shores.
Yonder, toward the left, lie broad the Westmoreland marshes,—
20 Miles on miles they extend, level, and grassy, and dim,
Clear from the long red sweep of flats to the sky in the distance,
Save for the outlying heights, green-rampired[3] Cumberland Point;
Miles on miles outrolled, and the river-channels divide them,—
Miles on miles of green, barred by the hurtling gusts.

25 Miles on miles beyond the tawny bay is Minudie.
There are the low blue hills; villages gleam at their feet.
Nearer a white sail shines across the water, and nearer
Still are the slim, grey masts of fishing boats dry on the flats.
Ah, how well I remember those wide red flats, above tide-mark
30 Pale with scurf[4] of the salt, seamed and baked in the sun!
Well I remember the piles of blocks and ropes, and the net-reels
Wound with the beaded nets, dripping and dark from the sea!
Now at this season the nets are unwound; they hang from the rafters
Over the fresh-stowed hay in upland barns, and the wind
35 Blows all day through the chinks, with the streaks of sunlight, and sways them
Softly at will; or they lie heaped in the gloom of a loft.

[1]saltwater tidal marshes along the New Brunswick coast of the Bay of Fundy, where Roberts spent his childhood. Minudie (line 25) is across the bay in Nova Scotia, [2]ribbon. [3]containing ramparts (protective embankments). [4]scales.

Now at this season the reels are empty and idle; I see them
Over the lines of the dikes, over the gossiping grass,
Now at this season they swing in the long strong wind, thro' the lonesome
40   Golden afternoon, shunned by the foraging gulls.
Near about sunset the crane will journey homeward above them;
Round them, under the moon, all the calm night long,
Winnowing soft grey wings of marsh-owls wander and wander,
Now to the broad, lit marsh, now to the dusk of the dike.
45   Soon, thro' their dew-wet frames, in the live keen freshness of morning,
Out of the teeth of the dawn blows back the awakening wind.
Then, as the blue day mounts, and the low-shot shafts of the sunlight
Glance from the tide to the shore, gossamers jewelled with dew
Sparkle and wave, where late sea-spoiling fathoms of drift-net
50   Myriad-meshed, uploomed sombrely over the land.

Well I remember it all. The salt, raw scent of the margin;
While, with men at the windlass, groaned each reel, and the net,
Surging in ponderous lengths, uprose and coiled in its station;
Then each man to his home,—well I remember it all!

55   Yet, as I sit and watch, this present peace of the landscape,—
Stranded boats, these reels empty and idle, the hush,
One grey hawk slow-wheeling above yon cluster of haystacks,—
More than the old-time stir this stillness welcomes me home.
Ah, the old-time stir, how once it stung me with rapture,—
60   Old-time sweetness, the winds freighted with honey and salt!
Yet will I stay my steps and not go down to the marshland,—
Muse and recall far off, rather remember than see,—
Lest on too close sight I miss the darling illusion,
Spy at their task even here the hands of chance and change.

(1883)

The Potato Harvest

A high bare field, brown from the plough, and borne
        Aslant from sunset; amber wastes of sky
        Washing the ridge; a clamour of crows that fly
In from the wide flats where the spent tides mourn
5   To yon their rocking roosts in pines wind-torn;
        A line of grey snake-fence that zigzags by
        A pond and cattle; from the homestead nigh
The long deep summonings of the supper horn.

Black on the ridge, against that lonely flush,
10   A cart, and stoop-necked oxen; ranged beside
          Some barrels; and the day-worn harvest-folk,
Here emptying their baskets, jar the hush
      With hollow thunders. Down the dusk hillside
          Lumbers the wain;[1] and day fades out like smoke.

(1886)

The Winter Fields

Winds here, and sleet, and frost that bites like steel.
      The low bleak hill rounds under the low sky.
      Naked of flock and fold the fallows lie,
Thin streaked with meagre drift. The gusts reveal
5   By fits the dim grey snakes of fence, that steal
      Through the white dusk. The hill-foot poplars sigh,
      While storm and death with winter trample by,
And the iron fields ring sharp, and blind lights reel.
Yet in the lonely ridges, wrenched with pain,
10   Harsh solitary hillocks, bound and dumb,
Grave glebes[1] close-lipped beneath the scourge and chain,
      Lurks hid the germ of ecstasy—the sum
Of life that waits on summer, till the rain
      Whisper in April and the crocus come.

(1890)

Archibald Lampman   (1861–1899)

Born in 1861 in Morpeth, Canada West (Ontario), Lampman graduated from the University of Toronto in 1882 and spent his working life as a clerk with the Post Office Department, Ottawa. The most accomplished of the Confederation Poets—a group of literary nationalists intent on developing a distinctive Canadian literature—he had a talent for precise observation of nature. Lampman refined his knowledge of nature with walking tours in the countryside and canoe trips into the wilderness with his friend and fellow poet, Duncan Campbell Scott. Not surprisingly, perhaps, his poetry was heavily influenced by the English Romantics, who recorded in poetry their responses to similar excursions. The influence of Keats is especially prominent in Lampman's characteristic device: a detailed description of nature leads to the focus on a solitary observer who begins to "dream," to experience a state of transcendent harmony. It is also evident in his concern for exploiting the

[1]wagon. [1]field

musical possibilities of language. Romantic reverie represents only one side of Lampman's poetry, however. He sometimes shows an ambivalence about Canadian nature, presenting it as both beautiful and frightening.

Heat

From plains that reel to southward, dim,
    The road runs by me white and bare;
Up the steep hill it seems to swim
    Beyond, and melt into the glare.
Upward half-way, or it may be
    Nearer the summit, slowly steals
A hay-cart, moving dustily
    With idly clacking wheels.

By his cart's side the wagoner
    Is slouching slowly at his ease,
Half-hidden in the windless blur
    Of white dust puffing to his knees.
This wagon on the height above,
    From sky to sky on either hand,
Is the sole thing that seems to move
    In all the heat-held land.

Beyond me in the fields the sun
    Soaks in the grass and hath his will;
I count the marguerites one by one;
    Even the buttercups are still.
On the brook yonder not a breath
    Disturbs the spider or the midge.
The water-bugs draw close beneath
    The cool gloom of the bridge.

Where the far elm-tree shadows flood
    Dark patches in the burning grass,
The cows, each with her peaceful cud,
    Lie waiting for the heat to pass.
From somewhere on the slope near by
    Into the pale depth of the noon
A wandering thrush slides leisurely
    His thin revolving tune.

In intervals of dreams I hear
    The cricket from the droughty ground;

→

35 The grasshoppers spin into mine ear
    A small innumerable sound.
I lift mine eyes sometimes to gaze:
    The burning sky-line blinds my sight:
The woods far off are blue with haze:
40   The hills are drenched in light.

And yet to me not this or that
    Is always sharp or always sweet;
In the sloped shadow of my hat
    I lean at rest, and drain the heat;
45 Nay more, I think some blessèd power
    Hath brought me wandering idly here:
In the full furnace of this hour
    My thoughts grow keen and clear.

(1888)

In November

With loitering step and quiet eye,
Beneath the low November sky,
I wandered in the woods, and found
A clearing, where the broken ground
5 Was scattered with black stumps and briers,
And the old wreck of forest fires.
It was a bleak and sandy spot,
And, all about, the vacant plot,
Was peopled and inhabited
10 By scores of mulleins[1] long since dead.
A silent and forsaken brood
In that mute opening of the wood,
So shrivelled and so thin they were,
So gray, so haggard, and austere,
15 Not plants at all they seemed to me,
But rather some spare company
Of hermit folk, who long ago,
Wandering in bodies to and fro,
Had chanced upon this lonely way,
20 And rested thus, till death one day
Surprised them at their compline[2] prayer,
And left them standing lifeless there.

[1] tall plants with coarse, woolly leaves and dense spikes of flowers. [2] the last of seven canonical hours; the last service of the day.

There was no sound about the wood
Save the wind's secret stir. I stood
25   Among the mullein-stalks as still
As if myself had grown to be
One of their sombre company,
A body without wish or will.
And as I stood, quite suddenly,
30   Down from a furrow in the sky
The sun shone out a little space
Across that silent sober place,
Over the sand heaps and brown sod,
The mulleins and dead goldenrod,
35   And passed beyond the thickets gray,
And lit the fallen leaves that lay,
Level and deep within the wood,
A rustling yellow multitude.

All around me the thin light,
40   So sere, so melancholy bright,
Fell like the half-reflected gleam
Or shadow of some former dream;
A moment's golden reverie
Poured out on every plant and tree
45   A semblance of weird joy, or less,
A sort of spectral happiness;
And I, too, standing idly there,
With muffled hands in the chill air,
Felt the warm glow about my feet,
50   And shuddering betwixt cold and heat,
Drew my thoughts closer, like a cloak,
While something in my blood awoke,
A nameless and unnatural cheer,
A pleasure secret and austere.

(1895)

Winter Evening

To-night the very horses springing by
Toss gold from whitened nostrils. In a dream
The streets that narrow to the westward gleam
Like rows of golden palaces; and high
5   From all the crowded chimneys tower and die

→

A thousand aureoles. Down in the west
The brimming plains beneath the sunset rest,
One burning sea of gold. Soon, soon shall fly
The glorious vision, and the hours shall feel
10   A mightier master; soon from height to height,
With silence and the sharp unpitying stars,
Stern creeping frosts, and winds that touch like steel,
Out of the depth beyond the eastern bars,
Glittering and still shall come the awful night.

(1899)

Duncan Campbell Scott   (1862–1947)

One of the Confederation Poets, a group inspired by the success of
Charles G. D. Roberts to work toward a distinctly Canadian poetry,
Duncan Campbell Scott often substituted for the pastoral subjects that
characterized the work of his colleagues portraits of the indigenous
peoples and of wilderness landscapes. Born in Ottawa, Scott was a life-
long civil servant who rose to be deputy superintendent general in the
Department of Indian Affairs. As a consequence of his duties, which
enabled him to travel throughout the Canadian North and West, he came
to believe that the Native peoples were doomed to extinction as separate
peoples, a belief evident in a number of his poems. His experiences also
developed in him a deep feeling for the wilderness, which he described
as a replacement for the church of his youth. Scott was both lyrical and
intellectual. He declared in "An Autobiographical Note" that "Everything
I write starts with its rhythmical life ..." and that "I value brain power at
the bottom of everything." As a lyric poet, he organized this "rhythmical
life" through carefully developed metres, rhymes, and repetition; as an
intellectual poet, he characteristically exercised "brain power" by
organizing poems according to dialectic oppositions or paired terms.

The Onondaga[1] Madonna

She stands full-throated and with careless pose,
This woman of a weird and waning race,
The tragic savage lurking in her face,
Where all her pagan passion burns and glows;
Her blood is mingled with her ancient foes,

[1]one of the five groups forming what became known as the League of Five Nations, or the
Iroquois Confederacy, the Onondaga originated in upper New York State; many moved to
Canada after the American Revolution and now form part of the Six Nations of the Grand
River First Nation near Brantford, Ontario.

And thrills with war and wildness in her veins;
Her rebel lips are dabbled with the stains
Of feuds and forays and her father's woes.

And closer in the shawl about her breast,
The latest promise of her nation's doom,
Paler than she her baby clings and lies,
The primal warrior gleaming from his eyes;
He sulks, and burdened with his infant gloom,
He draws his heavy brows and will not rest.

(1898)

The Forsaken

I

Once in the winter
Out on a lake
In the heart of the north-land,
Far from the Fort
5   And far from the hunters,
A Chippewa woman
With her sick baby,
Crouched in the last hours
Of a great storm.
10 Frozen and hungry,
She fished through the ice
With a line of the twisted
Bark of the cedar,
And a rabbit-bone hook
15 Polished and barbed;
Fished with the bare hook
All through the wild day,
Fished and caught nothing;
While the young chieftain
20 Tugged at her breasts,
Or slept in the lacings
Of the warm *tikanagan*.[1]
All the lake-surface
Streamed with the hissing
25 Of millions of iceflakes

→

[1]cradle-board to which is fastened a moss-bag for carrying an infant.

Hurled by the wind;
Behind her the round
Of a lonely island
Roared like a fire
30 With the voice of the storm
In the deeps of the cedars.
Valiant, unshaken,
She took of her own flesh,
Baited the fish-hook,
35 Drew in a gray-trout,
Drew in his fellows,
Heaped them beside her,
Dead in the snow.
Valiant, unshaken,
40 She faced the long distance,
Wolf-haunted and lonely,
Sure of her goal
And the life of her dear one:
Tramped for two days,
45 On the third in the morning,
Saw the strong bulk
Of the Fort by the river,
Saw the wood-smoke
Hang soft in the spruces,
50 Heard the keen yelp
Of the ravenous huskies
Fighting for whitefish:
Then she had rest.

II

Years and years after,
55 When she was old and withered,
When her son was an old man
And his children filled with vigour,
They came in their northern tour on the verge of winter,
To an island in a lonely lake.
60 There one night they camped, and on the morrow
Gathered their kettles and birch-bark
Their rabbit-skin robes and their mink-traps,
Launched their canoes and slunk away through the islands,

→

Left her alone forever,
65 Without a word of farewell,
Because she was old and useless,
Like a paddle broken and warped,
Or a pole that was splintered.
Then, without a sigh,
70 Valiant, unshaken,
She smoothed her dark locks under her kerchief,
Composed her shawl in state,
Then folded her hands rigid with sinews and corded with veins,
Folded them across her breasts spent with the nourishing of children,
75 Gazed at the sky past the tops of the cedars,
Saw two spangled nights arise out of the twilight,
Saw two days go by filled with the tranquil sunshine,
Saw, without pain, or dread, or even a moment of longing:
Then on the third great night there came thronging and thronging
80 Millions of snowflakes out of a windless cloud;
They covered her close with a beautiful crystal shroud,
Covered her deep and silent.
But in the frost of the dawn,
Up from the life below,
85 Rose a column of breath
Through a tiny cleft in the snow,
Fragile, delicately drawn,
Wavering with its own weakness,
In the wilderness a sign of the spirit,
90 Persisting still in the sight of the sun
Till day was done.
Then all light was gathered up by the hand of God and hid in His breast,
Then there was born a silence deeper than silence,
Then she had rest.

(1905)

William Butler Yeats (1865–1939)

Born and raised in Dublin, Ireland, William Butler Yeats became one of the leaders in the Irish nationalist movement in the late nineteenth and early twentieth centuries, and was influential in the formation of the Irish Literary Society and the Irish National Theatre Company. Many of his poems and plays are based on Irish legends and folklore. Yeats rejected conventional religious beliefs and studied a variety of religious and philo-sophical systems, out of which he developed his own poetic mythology, published in *A Vision* (1925, revised in 1937). He believed that history was divided into 2000-year cycles. As he implied in "Leda and the Swan," the classical age had begun with the union of the god Zeus (who assumed the form of a swan) and a human being, Leda. The Christian age, which ended the classical, commenced with the union of the Holy Spirit (in the form of a dove) and the Virgin Mary. The period of the Byzantine Empire, between the fifth and fifteenth centuries, represented the Christian age's era of greatest artistic achievement, while the twentieth century marked the final phase of its destruction. Many of the ideas in his system are complex and obscure. Some dismiss his system as muddle-headed and foolish, but it provided him with a number of symbols that, in "The Second Coming," "Sailing to Byzantium," and "Among School Children," present the individual's quest for meaning in the chaotic modern world. In such poems as "Easter 1916," Yeats commented on the tumultuous and often tragic conflicts between the Irish and the British.

Easter 1916[1]

I have met them at close of day
Coming with vivid faces
From counter or desk among grey
Eighteenth-century houses.
5 I have passed with a nod of the head
Or polite meaningless words,
Or have lingered awhile and said
Polite meaningless words,
And thought before I had done
10 Of a mocking tale or a gibe
To please a companion
Around the fire at the club,
Being certain that they and I
But lived where motley[2] is worn:
15 All changed, changed utterly:
A terrible beauty is born.

That woman's days were spent
In ignorant good-will,
Her nights in argument
20 Until her voice grew shrill.
What voice more sweet than hers
When, young and beautiful,
She rode to harriers?[3]

→

[1]at Easter 1916, Irish nationalists unsuccessfully rebelled against the British government. Many nationalists were executed. [2]many-coloured cloth often used in the clothing of court jesters. [3]i.e., on a hunt with hounds.

This man had kept a school
25 And rode our wingèd horse;[4]
This other his helper and friend
Was coming into his force;
He might have won fame in the end,
So sensitive his nature seemed,
30 So daring and sweet his thought.
This other man I had dreamed
A drunken, vainglorious lout.
He had done most bitter wrong
To some who are near my heart,
35 Yet I number him in the song;
He, too, has resigned his part
In the casual comedy;
He, too, has been changed in his turn,
Transformed utterly:
40 A terrible beauty is born.

Hearts with one purpose alone
Through summer and winter seem
Enchanted to a stone
To trouble the living stream.
45 The horse that comes from the road,
The rider, the birds that range
From cloud to tumbling cloud,
Minute by minute they change;
A shadow of cloud on the stream
50 Changes minute by minute;
A horse-hoof slides on the brim,
And a horse plashes within it;
The long-legged moor-hens dive,
And hens to moor-cocks call;
55 Minute by minute they live:
The stone's in the midst of all.
Too long a sacrifice
Can make a stone of the heart.
O when may it suffice?
60 That is Heaven's part, our part
To murmur name upon name,
As a mother names her child

→

4Pegasus, the winged horse associated with poetry in Greek mythology.

When sleep at last has come
On limbs that had run wild.
65 What is it but nightfall?
No, no, not night but death;
Was it needless death after all?
For England may keep faith
For all that is done and said.
70 We know their dream; enough
To know they dreamed and are dead;
And what if excess of love
Bewildered them till they died?
I write it out in a verse—
75 MacDonagh and MacBride
And Connolly and Pearse[5]
Now and in time to be,
Wherever green is worn,
Are changed, changed utterly:
80 A terrible beauty is born.

(1916)   (1921)

The Second Coming[1]

Turning and turning in the widening gyre[2]
The falcon cannot hear the falconer;
Things fall apart; the centre cannot hold;
Mere anarchy is loosed upon the world,
5 The blood-dimmed tide is loosed, and everywhere
The ceremony of innocence is drowned;
The best lack all conviction, while the worst
Are full of passionate intensity.

Surely some revelation is at hand;
10 Surely the Second Coming is at hand.
The Second Coming! Hardly are those words out
When a vast image out of *Spiritus Mundi*[3]
Troubles my sight; somewhere in sands of the desert
A shape with lion body and the head of a man,
15 A gaze blank and pitiless as the sun,

[5]four Irish patriots who were executed by the British after the Easter uprising. [1]traditionally, the coming of Jesus Christ on the Day of Judgment. [2]spiral. [3]the Spirit of the Universe.

Is moving its slow thighs, while all about it
Reel shadows of the indignant desert birds.
The darkness drops again; but now I know
That twenty centuries of stony sleep
20   Were vexed to nightmare by a rocking cradle,
And what rough beast, its hour come round at last,
Slouches towards Bethlehem[4] to be born?

(1919)   (1920)

Leda and the Swan[1]

A sudden blow: the great wings beating still
Above the staggering girl, her thighs caressed
By the dark webs, her nape caught in his bill,
He holds her helpless breast upon his breast.

5   How can those terrified vague fingers push
The feathered glory from her loosening thighs?
And how can body, laid in that white rush,
But feel the strange heart beating where it lies?

A shudder in the loins engenders there
10   The broken wall, the burning roof and tower[2]
And Agamemnon dead.[3]
              Being so caught up,
So mastered by the brute blood of the air,
Did she put on his knowledge with his power
Before the indifferent beak could let her drop?

(1923)   (1924)

Sailing to Byzantium[1]

I

That is no country for old men. The young
In one another's arms, birds in the trees

[4]birthplace of Jesus Christ. [1]Zeus, in the form of a swan, raped Leda, a Spartan Queen, who subsequently gave birth to Helen and Clytemnestra. [2]Helen, the most beautiful woman in the world, married Menelaus, but Paris abducted her, thus causing the war that ended in the destruction of Troy. [3]Agamemnon, the leader of the Greek forces attacking Troy, was murdered by Clytemnestra, his wife, when he returned from the Trojan War. [1]Greek city on whose site was built the city of Constantinople (now known as Istanbul), noted for its exceptional art.

—Those dying generations—at their song,
The salmon-falls, the mackerel-crowded seas,
5   Fish, flesh, or fowl, commend all summer long
Whatever is begotten, born, and dies.
Caught in that sensual music all neglect
Monuments of unageing intellect.

II

An aged man is but a paltry thing,
10   A tattered coat upon a stick, unless
Soul clap its hands and sing, and louder sing
For every tatter in its mortal dress,
Nor is there singing school but studying
Monuments of its own magnificence;
15   And therefore I have sailed the seas and come
To the holy city of Byzantium.

III

O sages standing in God's holy fire
As in the gold mosaic of a wall,
Come from the holy fire, perne in a gyre,[2]
20   And be the singing-masters of my soul.
Consume my heart away; sick with desire
And fastened to a dying animal
It knows not what it is; and gather me
Into the artifice of eternity.

IV

25   Once out of nature I shall never take
My bodily form from any natural thing,
But such a form as Grecian goldsmiths make
Of hammered gold and gold enamelling
To keep a drowsy Emperor awake;
30   Or set upon a golden bough to sing
To lords and ladies of Byzantium
Of what is past, or passing, or to come.

(1926)   (1927)

---

[2]spin in a spiral motion.

Among School Children

I

I walk through the long schoolroom questioning;
A kind old nun in a white hood replies;
The children learn to cipher and to sing,
To study reading-books and histories,
To cut and sew, be neat in everything
In the best modern way—the children's eyes
In momentary wonder stare upon
A sixty-year-old smiling public man.

II

I dream of a Ledaean[1] body, bent
Above a sinking fire, a tale that she
Told of a harsh reproof, or trivial event
That changed some childish day to tragedy—
Told, and it seemed that our two natures blent
Into a sphere from youthful sympathy,
Or else, to alter Plato's parable,[2]
Into the yolk and white of the one shell.

III

And thinking of that fit of grief or rage
I look upon one child or t'other there
And wonder if she stood so at that age—
For even daughters of the swan can share
Something of every paddler's heritage—
And had that colour upon cheek or hair,
And thereupon my heart is driven wild:
She stands before me as a living child.

IV

Her present image floats into the mind—
Did Quattrocento[3] finger fashion it
Hollow of cheek as though it drank the wind

---

[1]like Leda, a beautiful woman in Greek mythology. [2]in this legend, human beings originally
had four legs, four arms, and two faces. This body later split into two. The embrace of love
was an attempt to become reunified. [3]fifteenth century. The term usually refers to Italian
painting of the period.

And took a mess of shadows for its meat?
And I though never of Ledaean kind
30   Had pretty plumage once—enough of that,
Better to smile on all that smile, and show
There is a comfortable kind of old scarecrow.

V

What youthful mother, a shape upon her lap
Honey of generation had betrayed,
35   And that must sleep, shriek, struggle to escape
As recollection or the drug decide,
Would think her son, did she but see that shape
With sixty or more winters on its head,
A compensation for the pang of his birth,
40   Or the uncertainty of his setting forth?

VI

Plato thought nature but a spume that plays
Upon a ghostly paradigm of things;
Solider Aristotle played the taws
Upon the bottom of a king of kings;
45   World-famous golden-thighed Pythagoras[4]
Fingered upon a fiddle-stick or strings
What a star sang and careless Muses heard:
Old clothes upon old sticks to scare a bird.

VII

Both nuns and mothers worship images,
50   But those the candles light are not as those
That animate a mother's reveries,
But keep a marble or a bronze repose.
And yet they too break hearts—O Presences
That passion, piety or affection knows,
55   And that all heavenly glory symbolise—
O self-born mockers of man's enterprise;

VIII

Labour is blossoming or dancing where
The body is not bruised to pleasure soul,

[4]Plato, Aristotle, and Pythagoras were ancient Greek philosophers.

Nor beauty born out of its own despair,
60   Nor blear-eyed wisdom out of midnight oil.
O chestnut-tree, great-rooted blossomer,
Are you the leaf, the blossom or the bole?
O body swayed to music, O brightening glance,
How can we know the dancer from the dance?

(1926)   (1927)

Robert Frost   (1874–1963)

Though born in California, Robert Frost wrote most of his poetry about life in New England, where his family originated and where he moved at age eleven with his widowed mother. Frost had the ability, rare in modern times, to appeal to both sophisticated and unsophisticated audiences with the same poems, and he eventually became the most popular serious poet of his country. But success did not come easily. He wrote in obscurity until middle age, supporting his family mainly by farming and teaching, and received recognition in his own country only after his first two books, *A Boy's Will* (1913) and *North of Boston* (1914), had been published and praised in England.

Although Frost was learned and intellectual, and taught in various universities after 1915, he preferred to present himself as a rustic sage whose wisdom was derived from common sense and the everyday experiences he explored in his poetry. Despite its wide appeal, this public persona, together with Frost's reliance on traditional forms and his treatment of homely subjects, gives many of his best-known poems the deceptive appearance of slightness, but Frost confronts the darkness and philosophical uncertainty of modern life as honestly as any of his contemporaries, and his work is highly innovative in its use of vernacular speech and conversational rhythms.

After Apple-Picking

My long two-pointed ladder's sticking through a tree
Toward heaven still,
And there's a barrel that I didn't fill
Beside it, and there may be two or three
5   Apples I didn't pick upon some bough.
But I am done with apple-picking now.
Essence of winter sleep is on the night,
The scent of apples: I am drowsing off.
I cannot rub the strangeness from my sight
10   I got from looking through a pane of glass
I skimmed this morning from the drinking trough

→

And held against the world of hoary grass.
It melted, and I let it fall and break.
But I was well
15 Upon my way to sleep before it fell,
And I could tell
What form my dreaming was about to take.
Magnified apples appear and disappear,
Stem end and blossom end,
20 And every fleck of russet showing clear.
My instep arch not only keeps the ache,
It keeps the pressure of a ladder-round.
I feel the ladder sway as the boughs bend.
And I keep hearing from the cellar bin
25 The rumbling sound
Of load on load of apples coming in.
For I have had too much
Of apple-picking: I am overtired
Of the great harvest I myself desired.
30 There were ten thousand thousand fruit to touch,
Cherish in hand, lift down, and not let fall.
For all
That struck the earth,
No matter if not bruised or spiked with stubble,
35 Went surely to the cider-apple heap
As of no worth.
One can see what will trouble
This sleep of mine, whatever sleep it is.
Were he not gone,
40 The woodchuck could say whether it's like his
Long sleep, as I describe its coming on,
Or just some human sleep.

(1914)

Mending Wall

Something there is that doesn't love a wall,
That sends the frozen-ground-swell under it
And spills the upper boulders in the sun,
And makes gaps even two can pass abreast.
5 The work of hunters is another thing:

→

I have come after them and made repair
Where they have left not one stone on a stone,
But they would have the rabbit out of hiding,
To please the yelping dogs. The gaps I mean,
10   No one has seen them made or heard them made,
But at spring mending-time we find them there.
I let my neighbor know beyond the hill;
And on a day we meet to walk the line
And set the wall between us once again.
15   We keep the wall between us as we go.
To each the boulders that have fallen to each.
And some are loaves and some so nearly balls
We have to use a spell to make them balance:
"Stay where you are until our backs are turned!"
20   We wear our fingers rough with handling them.
Oh, just another kind of outdoor game,
One on a side. It comes to little more:
There where it is we do not need the wall:
He is all pine and I am apple orchard.
25   My apple trees will never get across
And eat the cones under his pines, I tell him.
He only says, "Good fences make good neighbors."
Spring is the mischief in me, and I wonder
If I could put a notion in his head:
30   "Why do they make good neighbors? Isn't it
Where there are cows? But here there are no cows.
Before I built a wall I'd ask to know
What I was walling in or walling out,
And to whom I was like to give offense.
35   Something there is that doesn't love a wall,
That wants it down." I could say "Elves" to him,
But it's not elves exactly, and I'd rather
He said it for himself. I see him there,
Bringing a stone grasped firmly by the top
40   In each hand, like an old-stone savage armed.
He moves in darkness as it seems to me,
Not of woods only and the shade of trees.
He will not go behind his father's saying,
And he likes having thought of it so well
45   He says again, "Good fences make good neighbors."

(1914)

The Road Not Taken

Two roads diverged in a yellow wood,
And sorry I could not travel both
And be one traveler, long I stood
And looked down one as far as I could
5 To where it bent in the undergrowth;

Then took the other, as just as fair,
And having perhaps the better claim,
Because it was grassy and wanted wear;
Though as for that, the passing there
10 Had worn them really about the same,

And both that morning equally lay
In leaves no step had trodden black.
Oh, I kept the first for another day!
Yet knowing how way leads on way,
15 I doubted if I should ever come back.

I shall be telling this with a sigh
Somewhere ages and ages hence:
Two roads diverged in a wood, and I—
I took the one less traveled by,
20 And that has made all the difference.

(1916)

Stopping by Woods on a Snowy Evening

Whose woods these are I think I know.
His house is in the village though;
He will not see me stopping here
To watch his woods fill up with snow.

5 My little horse must think it queer
To stop without a farmhouse near
Between the woods and frozen lake
The darkest evening of the year.

He gives his harness bells a shake
10 To ask if there is some mistake.
The only other sound's the sweep
Of easy wind and downy flake.

The woods are lovely, dark and deep,
But I have promises to keep,
And miles to go before I sleep,
And miles to go before I sleep.

(1923)

Design

I found a dimpled spider, fat and white,
On a white heal-all,[1] holding up a moth
Like a white piece of rigid satin cloth—
Assorted characters of death and blight
Mixed ready to begin the morning right,
Like the ingredients of a witches' broth—
A snow-drop spider, a flower like a froth,
And dead wings carried like a paper kite.

What had that flower to do with being white,
The wayside blue and innocent heal-all?
What brought the kindred spider to that height,
Then steered the white moth thither in the night?
What but design of darkness to appall?—
If design govern in a thing so small.

(1936)

Wallace Stevens   (1879–1955)

Born in Pennsylvania and educated at Harvard and the New York Law School, Wallace Stevens lived most of his adult life in Hartford, Connecticut, where he advanced to the rank of vice-president with the Hartford Accident and Indemnity Company. Although Stevens began writing poetry seriously when at university, he devoted much of his energy to law and business in the years that followed and was forty-four when his first collection of poems, *Harmonium* (1923), was published. From late middle age on, having become financially secure, Stevens devoted himself increasingly to his poetry. Although he is a philosophical poet, much concerned with ideas of order and the relationship between imagination and reality, Stevens is also a master at evoking complex sensuous experience; his poems are distinguished by the originality of their opulent, intricate images and their subtle, deftly controlled rhythms.

---

[1]plant (*Prunella vulgaris*, also called woundwort), normally with blue flowers, thought to have healing power.

The Emperor of Ice-Cream

Call the roller of big cigars,
The muscular one, and bid him whip
In kitchen cups concupiscent[1] curds.
Let the wenches dawdle in such dress
5   As they are used to wear, and let the boys
Bring flowers in last month's newspapers.
Let be be finale of seem.
The only emperor is the emperor of ice-cream.

Take from the dresser of deal.[2]
10   Lacking the three glass knobs, that sheet
On which she embroidered fantails[3] once
And spread it so as to cover her face.
If her horny feet protrude, they come
To show how cold she is, and dumb.
15   Let the lamp affix its beam.
The only emperor is the emperor of ice-cream.

(1923)

The Snow Man

One must have a mind of winter
To regard the frost and the boughs
Of the pine-trees crusted with snow;

And have been cold a long time
5   To behold the junipers shagged with ice,
The spruces rough in the distant glitter

Of the January sun; and not to think
Of any misery in the sound of the wind,
In the sound of a few leaves,

10   Which is the sound of the land
Full of the same wind
That is blowing in the same bare place

For the listener, who listens in the snow,
And, nothing himself, beholds
15   Nothing that is not there and the nothing that is.

(1923)

[1]filled with strong desire; lustful. [2]made of fir or pine; hence, cheap. [3]a breed of fancy pigeon.

E. J. Pratt   (1882–1964)

Edwin John Pratt, son of a Methodist minister, was born in Western Bay, Newfoundland. After graduating from St. John's Methodist College and serving as both a teacher and a preacher in several outport villages, he attended Victoria College, University of Toronto, receiving a B.A. (1911), M.A. (1912), B.D. (1913), and Ph.D. (1917). Although ordained in 1913, Pratt never served as a minister. Instead, he became a member of the Victoria College English Department in 1920. He is best known for his lengthy narratives, such as *The Titanic* (1935), *Brébeuf and His Brethren* (1940), and *Towards the Last Spike* (1952), the latter two of which won Governor General's Awards. Pratt's concern for scientific and technological matters, ranging from evolution to communication, is evident throughout his work. His religious background and ethical ideas are embodied in biblical references and images of individuals sacrificing themselves for the common good or enduring inevitable suffering.

The Shark

He seemed to know the harbour,
So leisurely he swam;
His fin,
Like a piece of sheet-iron,
5   Three-cornered,
And with knife-edge,
Stirred not a bubble
As it moved
With its base-line on the water.

10   His body was tubular
And tapered
And smoke-blue,
And as he passed the wharf
He turned,
15   And snapped at a flat-fish
That was dead and floating.
And I saw the flash of a white throat,
And a double row of white teeth,
And eyes of metallic grey,
20   Hard and narrow and slit.

Then out of the harbour,
With that three-cornered fin
Shearing without a bubble the water
Lithely,

→

25 Leisurely,
    He swam—
    That strange fish,
    Tubular, tapered, smoke-blue,
    Part vulture, part wolf,
30 Part neither—for his blood was cold.

(1923)

From Stone to Steel

From stone to bronze, from bronze to steel
Along the road-dust of the sun,
Two revolutions of the wheel
From Java[1] to Geneva[2] run.

5   The snarl Neanderthal[3] is worn
Close to the smiling Aryan[4] lips,
The civil polish of the horn
Gleams from our praying finger tips.

The evolution of desire
10 Has but matured a toxic wine,
Drunk long before its heady fire
Reddened Euphrates or the Rhine.[5]

Between the temple and the cave
The boundary lies tissue-thin:
15 The yearlings still the altars crave
As satisfaction for a sin.

The road goes up, the road goes down—
Let Java or Geneva be—
But whether to the cross or crown,
20 The path lies through Gethsemane.[6]

(1932)

[1]the site of the discovery in 1891 of the fossil remains of an early type of human, Pithecanthropus, or, as he was popularly called, "Java Ape Man." [2]a city long identified with advocating humane and reasonable conduct—the Geneva Convention of 1864 codified rules of war, for example—it was chosen as headquarters for the League of Nations in 1919. [3]cave-dwelling early human of the Upper Pleistocene Age, whose remains were first located in sites in Europe. [4]even before Hitler assumed power in 1933, the term, originally describing a prehistoric group of peoples whose language was presumed to be the basis of most Indo-European languages, was being used to refer to non-Jews of European, especially Nordic, descent. [5]the Euphrates, a major river in southwest Asia, and the Rhine, the principal waterway of Europe, were influential in developing civilizations and were sites of numerous wars. [6]a garden outside the walls of Jerusalem, it was the site of what is known as the agony of Christ: the sorrowing Christ prayed that his coming trials might be removed, yet also resigned himself, saying that God's will, not his own, should prevail. Shortly afterward, Judas betrayed Christ in this garden.

William Carlos Williams   (1883–1963)

A medical doctor as well as a writer, William Carlos Williams spent most of his life in Rutherford, New Jersey, where he maintained a busy practice as a pediatrician. Williams worked in various genres, producing more than two dozen volumes of poetry, fiction, essays, plays, and autobiography, but he was most influential as a poet. While studying at the University of Pennsylvania, he developed a lasting friendship with Ezra Pound, and through Pound was influenced by imagism, an Anglo-American poetic movement stressing concentration, freedom in form and subject matter, and especially precise, concrete images. Working from imagism, Williams developed a distinctive style of free verse, characterized by careful observation, vivid images, and a reliance on the rhythms and diction of common American speech. Although he was initially overshadowed by other modernist poets, Williams's influence on American poets since World War II has equalled that of any of his contemporaries.

Spring and All

By the road to the contagious hospital
under the surge of the blue
mottled clouds driven from the
northeast—a cold wind. Beyond, the
5   waste of broad, muddy fields
brown with dried weeds, standing and fallen

patches of standing water
the scattering of tall trees

All along the road the reddish
10   purplish, forked, upstanding, twiggy
stuff of bushes and small trees
with dead, brown leaves under them
leafless vines—

Lifeless in appearance, sluggish
15   dazed spring approaches—

They enter the new world naked,
cold, uncertain of all
save that they enter. All about them
the cold, familiar wind—

20   Now the grass, tomorrow
the stiff curl of wildcarrot leaf

One by one objects are defined—
It quickens: clarity, outline of leaf

But now the stark dignity of
25   entrance—Still, the profound change
has come upon them: rooted, they
grip down and begin to awaken

(1923)

The Red Wheelbarrow

so much depends
upon

a red wheel
barrow

5   glazed with rain
water

beside the white
chickens.

(1923)

Ezra Pound   (1885–1972)

Ezra Pound was born in Idaho but grew up in Pennsylvania. He specialized in Romance languages and literature at the University of Pennsylvania and received an M.A. in 1906. Considering his native country intellectually oppressive, Pound lived most of the rest of his life in Europe. A leader in the modernist revolution in literature, Pound influenced and assisted dozens of modern writers, including James Joyce, W. B. Yeats, Ernest Hemingway, and T. S. Eliot, whose famous poem "The Waste Land" he edited. Early in his poetic career, he advocated the concentration, free forms, and precise, concrete images of the imagist movement, and while he soon moved away from imagism to write erudite, esoterically allusive poems that all but specialists find daunting, his early insistence on unforced rhythms and clear detail had a pervasive, lasting effect on twentieth-century poetry.

Critical opinion of Pound's own work is divided, partly because it varies in quality and is sometimes extremely difficult, and partly because it reflects his unpopular social and political views. Living in Italy between the world wars and increasingly convinced that art prospered in stable societies with strong leaders, Pound actively supported Italian dictator Benito Mussolini. He became stridently anti-Semitic and attacked the American political and economic system in both writing and radio broadcasts. Charged with treason at the end of World War II, he was confined at Pisa and brought to the United States only after his mental condition had deteriorated to the point where he was judged unfit to stand trial. He was confined at St. Elizabeth's Hospital for the criminally insane in Washington until efforts by American writers led to his release in 1958, after which he lived the remainder of his life in Italy.

The River-Merchant's Wife: A Letter[1]

While my hair was still cut straight across my forehead
I played about the front gate, pulling flowers.
You came by on bamboo stilts, playing horse,
You walked about my seat, playing with blue plums.
5   And we went on living in the village of Chokan:[2]
Two small people, without dislike or suspicion.
At fourteen I married My Lord you.
I never laughed, being bashful.
Lowering my head, I looked at the wall.
10   Called to, a thousand times, I never looked back.

At fifteen I stopped scowling,
I desired my dust to be mingled with yours
Forever and forever and forever.
Why should I climb the look out?

15   At sixteen you departed,
You went into far Ku-to-yen,[3] by the river of swirling eddies,
And you have been gone five months.
The monkeys make sorrowful noise overhead.

You dragged your feet when you went out.
20   By the gate now, the moss is grown, the different mosses,
Too deep to clear them away!
The leaves fall early this autumn, in wind
The paired butterflies are already yellow with August
Over the grass in the West garden;
25   They hurt me. I grow older.
If you are coming down through the narrows of the river Kiang,
Please let me know beforehand,
And I will come out to meet you
          As far as Cho-fu-Sa.[4]

(1915)

---

[1]adapted from a translation of the Chinese poet Li Po (701?–762), called Rihaku in Japanese.
[2]suburb of Nanjing, China. [3]island hundreds of miles up the Kiang River from Nanjing.
[4]beach on the Kiang River not far from Ku-to-yen.

In a Station of the Metro

The apparition of these faces in the crowd;
Petals on a wet, black bough.

(1916)

Ancient Music[1]

Winter is icummen in,
Lhude sing Goddamm,
Raineth drop and staineth slop,
And how the wind doth ramm!
5   Sing: Goddamm.
Skiddeth bus and sloppeth us,
An ague hath my ham.
Freezeth river, turneth liver,
         Damn you, sing: Goddamm.
10 Goddamm, Goddamm, 'tis why I am, Goddamm.
        So 'gainst the winter's balm.
Sing goddamm, damm, sing Goddamm,
Sing goddamm, sing goddamm, DAMM.

(1917)

T. S. Eliot   (1888–1965)

Thomas Stearns Eliot grew up in St. Louis, Missouri, where his grandfather had founded Washington University. His parents were well-to-do; his mother wrote poetry and supported cultural activities. Eliot attended Harvard, from which he received an M.A., the Sorbonne in Paris, and Oxford. After 1914, he lived mainly in England and became a British subject in 1927. While he first made his living as a teacher, then from 1917 to 1925 as a banker, and later as an editor with the British publisher Faber and Faber, Eliot also devoted himself to writing criticism. In his essays, no less than in his poetry, he had an immense influence on the literature of his time.

The development of Eliot's poetry reflects his personal struggle to find meaning and order in an age that seemed to many to deny them. Such early poems as "The Love Song of J. Alfred Prufrock" and "The Waste Land" captured the mood of doubt, the loss of confidence in Western traditions and religion, that followed World War I. *The Four*

[1]parody of the medieval lyric "The Cuckoo Song" (see page 24).

Quartets and his verse plays, written after his conversion to Anglo-Catholicism in the late 1920s, reflect his personal solutions to this earlier doubt. Despite its changing perspective, however, most of Eliot's poetry, early and late, shows his concern with literary and religious tradition, which is reflected in a wealth of allusions; his interest in symbols, not only as literary devices but as manifestations of culture as well; and his facility for capturing speaking voices. Eliot's achievements were recognized with the Nobel Prize for literature in 1948.

The Love Song of J. Alfred Prufrock

S'io credesse che mia risposta fosse
A persona che mai tornasse al mondo,
Questa fiamma staria senza piu scosse.
Ma perciocche giammai di questo fondo
Non torno vivo alcun, s'i' odo il vero,
Senza tema d'infamia ti rispondo.[1]

Let us go then, you and I,
When the evening is spread out against the sky
Like a patient etherised upon a table;
Let us go, through certain half-deserted streets,
5   The muttering retreats
Of restless nights in one-night cheap hotels
And sawdust restaurants with oyster-shells:
Streets that follow like a tedious argument
Of insidious intent
10   To lead you to an overwhelming question . . .
Oh, do not ask, "What is it?"
Let us go and make our visit.

In the room the women come and go
Talking of Michelangelo.

15   The yellow fog that rubs its back upon the window-panes,
The yellow smoke that rubs its muzzle on the window-panes
Licked its tongue into the corners of the evening,
Lingered upon the pools that stand in drains,

[1] in Dante's *Inferno* XXXVII.61–66, Guido da Montefeltro answers Dante through the tongue of flame that imprisons him: "If I thought I were answering someone who could ever return to the world, this flame would be still; but since no one has returned alive from this depth, if what I hear is true, I respond without fear of ill repute".

Let fall upon its back the soot that falls from chimneys,
20   Slipped by the terrace, made a sudden leap,
And seeing that it was a soft October night,
Curled once about the house, and fell asleep.

And indeed there will be time
For the yellow smoke that slides along the street,
25   Rubbing its back upon the window-panes;
There will be time, there will be time
To prepare a face to meet the faces that you meet;
There will be time to murder and create,
And time for all the works and days of hands
30   That lift and drop a question on your plate;
Time for you and time for me,
And time yet for a hundred indecisions,
And for a hundred visions and revisions,
Before the taking of a toast and tea.

35   In the room the women come and go
Talking of Michelangelo.

And indeed there will be time
To wonder, "Do I dare?" and, "Do I dare?"
Time to turn back and descend the stair,
40   With a bald spot in the middle of my hair—
[They will say: "How his hair is growing thin!"]
My morning coat, my collar mounting firmly to the chin,
My necktie rich and modest, but asserted by a simple pin—
[They will say: "But how his arms and legs are thin!"]
45   Do I dare
Disturb the universe?
In a minute there is time
For decisions and revisions which a minute will reverse.

For I have known them all already, known them all—
50   Have known the evenings, mornings, afternoons,
I have measured out my life with coffee spoons;
I know the voices dying with a dying fall
Beneath the music from a farther room.
        So how should I presume?

55   And I have known the eyes already, known them all—
The eyes that fix you in a formulated phrase,

→

And when I am formulated, sprawling on a pin,
When I am pinned and wriggling on the wall,
Then how should I begin
60 To spit out all the butt-ends of my days and ways?
    And how should I presume?

And I have known the arms already, known them all—
Arms that are braceleted and white and bare
[But in the lamplight, downed with light brown hair!]
65 Is it perfume from a dress
That makes me so digress?
Arms that lie along a table, or wrap about a shawl.
    And should I then presume?
    And how should I begin?

     . . . . .

70 Shall I say, I have gone at dusk through narrow streets
And watched the smoke that rises from the pipes
Of lonely men in shirt-sleeves, leaning out of windows? . . .

I should have been a pair of ragged claws
Scuttling across the floors of silent seas.

     . . . . .

75 And the afternoon, the evening, sleeps so peacefully!
Smoothed by long fingers,
Asleep—tired—or it malingers,
Stretched on the floor, here beside you and me.
Should I, after tea and cakes and ices,
80 Have the strength to force the moment to its crisis?
But though I have wept and fasted, wept and prayed,
Though I have seen my head [grown slightly bald] brought in upon a platter,[2]
I am no prophet—and here's no great matter;
I have seen the moment of my greatness flicker,
85 And I have seen the eternal Footman hold my coat, and snicker,
And in short, I was afraid.

And would it have been worth it, after all,
After the cups, the marmalade, the tea,
Among the porcelain, among some talk of you and me,
90 Would it have been worth while,

→

[2]the head of John the Baptist was presented on a platter to Queen Herodias (see Matthew 14; Mark 6).

To have bitten off the matter with a smile,
To have squeezed the universe into a ball
To roll it toward some overwhelming question,
To say: "I am Lazarus, come from the dead,[3]
95 Come back to tell you all, I shall tell you all"—
If one, settling a pillow by her head,
    Should say: "That is not what I meant at all.
    That is not it, at all."
And would it have been worth it, after all,
100 Would it have been worth while,
After the sunsets and the dooryards and the sprinkled streets,
After the novels, after the teacups, after the skirts that trail along the floor—
And this, and so much more?—
It is impossible to say just what I mean!
105 But as if a magic lantern threw the nerves in patterns on a screen:
Would it have been worth while
If one, settling a pillow or throwing off a shawl,
And turning toward the window, should say:
    "That is not it at all,
110   That is not what I meant, at all."

       . . . . .

No! I am not Prince Hamlet, nor was meant to be;
Am an attendant lord, one that will do
To swell a progress, start a scene or two,
Advise the prince; no doubt, an easy tool,
115 Deferential, glad to be of use,
Politic, cautious, and meticulous;
Full of high sentence, but a bit obtuse;
At times, indeed, almost ridiculous—
Almost, at times, the Fool.

120 I grow old ... I grow old ...
I shall wear the bottoms of my trousers rolled.

Shall I part my hair behind? Do I dare to eat a peach?
I shall wear white flannel trousers, and walk upon the beach.
I have heard the mermaids singing, each to each.

125 I do not think that they will sing to me.

[3]Christ raised Lazarus from the dead. See John 11.

I have seen them riding seaward on the waves
Combing the white hair of the waves blown back
When the wind blows the water white and black.

130   We have lingered in the chambers of the sea
By sea-girls wreathed with seaweed red and brown
Till human voices wake us, and we drown.

(1915)

The Hollow Men

Mistah Kurtz—he dead.[1]
        A penny for the Old Guy[2]

I

We are the hollow men
We are the stuffed men
Leaning together
5   Headpiece filled with straw. Alas!
Our dried voices, when
We whisper together
Are quiet and meaningless
As wind in dry grass
10   Or rats' feet over broken glass
In our dry cellar

Shape without form, shade without colour,
Paralysed force, gesture without motion;

Those who have crossed
15   With direct eyes, to death's other Kingdom
Remember us—if at all—not as lost
Violent souls, but only
As the hollow men
The stuffed men.

[1]in Joseph Conrad's *Heart of Darkness*, Kurtz's European cultural values fail him in the African jungle and he dies insane. [2]refers to an English children's custom of begging on Guy Fawkes Day (November 5), the anniversary of the execution of the leading conspirator in the plot to blow up the Houses of Parliament in 1605.

II

Eyes I dare not meet in dreams
20   In death's dream kingdom
These do not appear:
There, the eyes are
Sunlight on a broken column
There, is a tree swinging
25   And voices are
In the wind's singing
More distant and more solemn
Than a fading star.

Let me be no nearer
30   In death's dream kingdom
Let me also wear
Such deliberate disguises
Rat's coat, crowskin, crossed staves
In a field
35   Behaving as the wind behaves
No nearer—

Not that final meeting
In the twilight kingdom

III

This is the dead land
40   This is cactus land
Here the stone images
Are raised, here they receive
The supplication of a dead man's hand
Under the twinkle of a fading star.

45   Is it like this
In death's other kingdom
Waking alone
At the hour when we are
Trembling with tenderness
50   Lips that would kiss
Form prayers to broken stone.

IV

The eyes are not here
There are no eyes here
In this valley of dying stars
55   In this hollow valley
This broken jaw of our lost kingdoms
In this last of meeting places
We grope together
And avoid speech
60   Gathered on this beach of the tumid river

Sightless, unless
The eyes reappear
As the perpetual star
Multifoliate rose
65   Of death's twilight kingdom
The hope only
Of empty men.

V

Here we go round the prickly pear
Prickly pear prickly pear
70   *Here we go round the prickly pear*
At five o'clock in the morning.

Between the idea
And the reality
Between the motion
75   And the act
Falls the Shadow
             For Thine is the Kingdom

Between the conception
And the creation
80   Between the emotion
And the response
Falls the Shadow
             Life is very long

Between the desire
85   And the spasm
Between the potency

→

And the existence
Between the essence
And the descent
90 Falls the Shadow
        For Thine is the Kingdom

For Thine is
Life is
For Thine is the

95 *This is the way the world ends*
    This is the way the world ends
    This is the way the world ends
    Not with a bang but a whimper.

(1925)

Journey of the Magi[1]

"A cold coming we had of it,
Just the worst time of the year
For a journey, and such a long journey:
The ways deep and the weather sharp,
5 The very dead of winter."[2]
And the camels galled, sore-footed, refractory,
Lying down in the melting snow.
There were times we regretted
The summer palaces on slopes, the terraces,
10 And the silken girls bringing sherbet.
Then the camel men cursing and grumbling
And running away, and wanting their liquor and women,
And the night-fires going out, and the lack of shelters,
And the cities hostile and the towns unfriendly
15 And the villages dirty and charging high prices:
A hard time we had of it.
At the end we preferred to travel all night,
Sleeping in snatches,

[1]the wise men who brought gifts to the infant Jesus (see Matthew 2). [2]adapted from a
Christmas sermon by Bishop Lancelot Andrewes (1555–1626), who helped prepare the 1611
King James version of the Bible.

With the voices singing in our ears, saying
That this was all folly.

20   Then at dawn we came down to a temperate valley,
Wet, below the snow line, smelling of vegetation;
With a running stream and a water-mill beating the darkness,
And three trees on the low sky,
And an old white horse galloped away in the meadow.
25 Then we came to a tavern with vine-leaves over the lintel,
Six hands at an open door dicing for pieces of silver,
And feet kicking the empty wine-skins.
But there was no information, and so we continued
And arrived at evening, not a moment too soon
30 Finding the place; it was (you may say) satisfactory.

      All this was a long time ago, I remember,
And I would do it again, but set down
This set down
This: were we led all that way for
35 Birth or Death? There was a Birth, certainly,
We had evidence and no doubt. I had seen birth and death,
But had thought they were different; this Birth was
Hard and bitter agony for us, like Death, our death.
We returned to our places, these Kingdoms,
40 But no longer at ease here, in the old dispensation,
With an alien people clutching their gods.
I should be glad of another death.

(1927)

Edna St. Vincent Millay   (1892–1950)

Born in Rockland, Maine, and educated at Vassar College, Edna St. Vincent
Millay became famous in the 1920s as a free-spirited jazz-age poet and playwright. Millay first achieved recognition in 1912 when she won fourth prize
in a contest—a number of notable critics contended that she should have
been the winner—and publication of her poem "Renascence" in *The Lyric
Year*. She published her first volume, *Renascence and Other Poems* (1917),
the same year that she graduated from Vassar. She then moved to
Greenwich Village, where she enthusiastically entered into the unconventional and hedonistic life of a Bohemian writer while still working diligently
to sell her work. A position as a European correspondent for *Vanity Fair*
allowed her to go abroad for two years. Returning in 1923, she married a
widower, Eugene Jan Boissevai, with whom she had an unconventional
"open" marriage. That same year *The Harp-Weaver and Other Poems* won

her a singular honour: she became the first woman to win the Pulitzer Prize for poetry. Millay, who acted with the Provincetown Players, also wrote poetic dramas, one of which was staged as an opera by the Metropolitan Opera Company in 1927. Her sense of social justice was offended by the conviction of Sacco and Vanzetti, so in 1927 she joined protests against their impending execution. Arrested for her part in the demonstrations, she later commemorated them in five poems. At the height of her career, Millay was the voice of the New Woman, a lyric poet who called for love free from the old social and legal constraints, for honest self-examination of one's feelings, and for a woman's right to develop her own identity.

I, Being Born a Woman and Distressed

I, being born a woman and distressed
By all the needs and notions of my kind,
Am urged by your propinquity to find
Your person fair, and feel a certain zest
5   To bear your body's weight upon my breast:
So subtly is the fume of life designed,
To clarify the pulse and cloud the mind,
And leave me once again undone, possessed.
Think not for this, however, the poor treason
10   Of my stout blood against my staggering brain,
I shall remember you with love, or season
My scorn with pity,—let me make it plain:
I find this frenzy insufficient reason
For conversation when we meet again.

(1923)

An Ancient Gesture

I thought, as I wiped my eyes on the corner of my apron:
Penelope[1] did this too.
And more than once: you can't keep weaving all day
And undoing it all through the night;
5   Your arms get tired, and the back of your neck gets tight;
And along towards morning, when you think it will never be light,
And your husband has been gone, and you don't know where, for years,
Suddenly you burst into tears;

[1] in Homer's *Odyssey*, Penelope, the wife of Ulysses, is importuned by suitors when her husband does not return from the Trojan Wars. She suggests to them that she will choose a suitor once she has completed a tapestry, but each evening she undoes the work that she performed during the day. After a twenty-year absence, Ulysses returns to drive away the suitors.

There is simply nothing else to do.

10 And I thought, as I wiped my eyes on the corner of my apron:
This is an ancient gesture, authentic, antique,
In the very best tradition, classic, Greek;
Ulysses did this too.
But only as a gesture,—a gesture which implied
15 To the assembled throng that he was much too moved to speak.
He learned it from Penelope ...
Penelope, who really cried.

(1954)

Archibald MacLeish (1892–1982)

A distinguished poet and playwright who won three Pulitzer prizes, Archibald MacLeish was also, among other things, a soldier, lawyer, journalist analyzing both American society and international developments, speech writer for Franklin D. Roosevelt, librarian of Congress, director of a war-time propaganda agency, presidential envoy, chairman of the American delegation to UNESCO, and university professor. Born in Glencoe, Illinois, MacLeish majored in English at Yale University (1911–15) and then entered Harvard Law School. Service in France during World War I interrupted his studies, but he resumed them, graduating at the head of his class in 1919. In 1923, after a brief law career, he moved his family to Paris, where he spent five years among the American expatriate writers. "Ars Poetica," one of his most famous poems, expresses the ideals of modernism that generally guided this group of writers and, more particularly, imagist poets. Those ideals rejected the ornate and, to a generation that had witnessed death and destruction in the trenches of Europe, false rhetoric of earlier poetry in favour of poems constructed from specific images. After his return to America, MacLeish himself moved away from modernism, especially as it favoured a poetic voice detached from society, because, for him, poetry was necessarily implicated in social conditions. "Ars Poetica" remains, however, as a significant literary monument, a terse expression of some of the tenets of one of the central literary movements of the twentieth century.

Ars Poetica[1]

A poem should be palpable and mute
As a globed fruit,

---

[1]"The Art of Poetry," title of a treatise by the Roman poet Quintus Horatius Flaccus (65 B.C.–8 B.C.), who is known in English as Horace.

Dumb
As old medallions to the thumb,

5   Silent as the sleeve-worn stone
Of casement ledges where the moss has grown—

A poem should be wordless
As the flight of birds.
*

A poem should be motionless in time
10   As the moon climbs,

Leaving, as the moon releases
Twig by twig the night-entangled trees,

Leaving, as the moon behind the winter leaves,
Memory by memory the mind—

15   A poem should be motionless in time
As the moon climbs.
*

A poem should be equal to:
Not true.

For all the history of grief
20   An empty doorway and a maple leaf.

For love
The leaning grasses and two lights above the sea—

A poem should not mean
But be.

(1926)

Wilfred Owen   (1893–1918)

Although his best poems were written in the year before his death in action during World War I, Wilfred Owen had decided to become a poet while a boy in Shropshire, England. He was critical of conventional religious beliefs before the war and had written many war poems before his 1917 meeting with Siegfried Sassoon; however, the meeting was the catalyst for the creation of the works for which he is now remembered, many of which were included in the libretto of composer Benjamin Britten's *War Requiem* (1962). In the Preface to his *Collected Poems*, Owen stated: "My subject is War, and the pity of War. The Poetry is in the pity." He achieves his startling, moving effects through the sharp contrasts of his language and the careful modulation of rhythms, rhyme schemes, and sound patterns. In *"Dulce et Decorum Est,"* the Latin motto, with its conventional notions of glorious, patriotic death, is set against vivid, realistic details of a gas attack. "Anthem for Doomed Youth" juxtaposes the noises of war with the quietness of mourning.

Anthem[1] for Doomed Youth

What passing-bells[2] for these who die as cattle?
   —Only the monstrous anger of the guns.
   Only the stuttering rifles' rapid rattle
Can patter out their hasty orisons.[3]
No mockeries now for them; no prayers nor bells;
   Nor any voice of mourning save the choirs,—
The shrill, demented choirs of wailing shells;
   And bugles calling for them from sad shires.[4]

What candles may be held to speed them all?
   Not in the hands of boys but in their eyes
Shall shine the holy glimmers of goodbyes.
   The pallor of girls' brows shall be their pall;
Their flowers the tenderness of patient minds,
And each slow dusk a drawing-down of blinds.

(1917)   (1920)

Dulce et Decorum Est[1]

Bent double, like old beggars under sacks,
Knock-kneed, coughing like hags, we cursed through sludge,
Till on the haunting flares we turned our backs
And towards our distant rest began to trudge.
Men marched asleep. Many had lost their boots
But limped on, blood-shod. All went lame; all blind;
Drunk with fatigue; deaf even to the hoots
Of tired, outstripped Five-Nines[2] that dropped behind.

Gas! GAS! Quick, boys!—An ecstasy of fumbling,
Fitting the clumsy helmets just in time;
But someone still was yelling out and stumbling,

[1]song of praise. [2]church bells rung to announce a death. [3]prayers. [4]districts, counties. [1]"It is sweet and fitting [to die for one's country]" (Horace *Odes* III.2.13). [2]shells that are 5.9 inches (or 150 mm) in diameter.

And flound'ring like a man in fire or lime ...
Dim, through the misty panes and thick green light,
As under a green sea, I saw him drowning.

15 In all my dreams, before my helpless sight,
He plunges at me, guttering, choking, drowning.

If in some smothering dreams you too could pace
Behind the wagon that we flung him in,
And watch the white eyes writhing in his face,
20 His hanging face, like a devil's sick of sin;
If you could hear, at every jolt, the blood
Come gargling from the froth-corrupted lungs,
Obscene as cancer, bitter as the cud
Of vile, incurable sores on innocent tongues,—
25 My friend, you would not tell with such high zest
To children ardent for some desperate glory,
The old Lie: Dulce et decorum est
Pro patria mori.

(1917)   (1920)

e. e. cummings   (1894–1962)

Born in Cambridge, Massachusetts, and educated at Harvard, Edward
Estlin Cummings became one of the most unconventional of modern
American poets. He was a successful painter, and he wrote both fiction
and drama, but his greatest artistic achievement was his poetry.
Sometimes lyric, sometimes satirical, cummings's poetry celebrates spontaneous feeling, individualism, the love of nature, and erotic love; it attacks
institutions, formality, and stuffiness generally. He has sometimes been
criticized for being exhibitionist and overly playful in his manipulations of
diction, syntax, stanzaic forms, and typography, but, notwithstanding his
eccentricities, cummings was always a careful craftsman and serious artist.
His ardent rebellion against both poetic conventions and what he considered the complacent, middle-class narrowness of his country gave him
considerable influence with poets after World War II.

it may not always be so; and i say

it may not always be so; and i say
that if your lips, which i have loved, should touch
another's, and your dear strong fingers clutch
his heart, as mine in time not far away;
5 if on another's face your sweet hair lay

→

in such a silence as i know, or such
great writhing words as, uttering overmuch,
stand helplessly before the spirit at bay;

if this should be, i say if this should be—
10   you of my heart, send me a little word;
that i may go unto him, and take his hands,
saying, Accept all happiness from me.
Then shall i turn my face, and hear one bird
sing terribly afar in the lost lands.

(1923)

in Just- spring

in Just-
spring   when the world is mud-
luscious the little
lame balloonman

5   whistles   far   and wee

and eddieandbill come
running from marbles and
piracies and it's
spring

10   when the world is puddle-wonderful

the queer
old balloonman whistles
far   and   wee
and bettyandisbel come dancing

15   from hop-scotch and jump-rope and

it's
spring
and
      the

20   goat-footed

balloonMan   whistles
far
and
wee

(1923)

next to of course god america i

"next to of course god america i
love you land of the pilgrims' and so forth oh
say can you see by the dawn's early my
country 'tis of centuries come and go
5 and are no more what of it we should worry
in every language even deafanddumb
thy sons acclaim your glorious name by gorry
by jingo by gee by gosh by gum
why talk of beauty what could be more beaut-
10 iful than these heroic happy dead
who rushed like lions to the roaring slaughter
they did not stop to think they died instead
then shall the voice of liberty be mute?"

He spoke. And drank rapidly a glass of water

(1926)

anyone lived in a pretty how town

anyone lived in a pretty how town
(with up so floating many bells down)
spring summer autumn winter
he sang his didn't he danced his did.

5 Women and men (both little and small)
cared for anyone not at all
they sowed their isn't they reaped their same
sun moon stars rain

children guessed(but only a few
10 and down they forgot as up they grew
autumn winter spring summer)
that noone loved him more by more

when by now and tree by leaf
she laughed his joy she cried his grief
15 bird by snow and stir by still
anyone's any was all to her

someones married their everyones
laughed their cryings and did their dance
(sleep wake hope and then)they
20 said their nevers they slept their dream

stars rain sun moon
(and only the snow can begin to explain
how children are apt to forget to remember
with up so floating many bells down)

25 one day anyone died i guess
(and noone stooped to kiss his face)
busy folk buried them side by side
little by little and was by was

all by all and deep by deep
30 and more by more they dream their sleep
noone and anyone earth by april
wish by spirit and if by yes.

Women and men(both dong and ding)
summer autumn winter spring
35 reaped their sowing and went their came
sun moon stars rain

(1940)

l(a

l(a

le
af
fa

5 ll

s)
one
l

iness

(1958)

F. R. Scott   (1899–1985)

The son of Frederick George Scott (1861–1944), an Anglican clergyman
and minor poet of the Confederation group, Francis Reginald Scott made
remarkable contributions to Canadian life in several areas. Born in
Quebec City, he was educated at Bishop's College, Oxford University,
where he was a Rhodes Scholar, and McGill University, where he

eventually became dean of the law school. As a social reformer, he was active in founding the Co-operative Commonwealth Federation, the fore-runner of the New Democratic Party. As a lawyer, he defended civil liber-ties in several important court cases. As a professor of constitutional law, he promoted the cause of social justice and served as a member of the Royal Commission on Bilingualism and Biculturalism. As a poet and anthologist, he was a leader in the fight against romantic and traditional poetry as outmoded and insincere forms of verse. He began writing while still a student, but his first collection was not published until 1945. His *Collected Poems* (1981) won the Governor General's Award. Often sharply satirical, his poetry is notable for its precision and grace of expres-sion, its unpretentious allusions, and its wit.

The Canadian Authors Meet[1]

Expansive puppets percolate self-unction
Beneath a portrait of the Prince of Wales.[2]
Miss Crotchet's muse has somehow failed to function,
Yet she's a poetess. Beaming, she sails

5   From group to chattering group, with such a dear
Victorian saintliness, as is her fashion,
Greeting the other unknowns with a cheer—
Virgins of sixty who still write of passion.

The air is heavy with Canadian topics,
10 And Carman, Lampman, Roberts, Campbell, Scott,
Are measured for their faith and philanthropics,
Their zeal for God and King, their earnest thought.

The cakes are sweet, but sweeter is the feeling
That one is mixing with the *literati*;[3]
15 It warms the old, and melts the most congealing.
Really, it is a most delightful party.

Shall we go round the mulberry bush, or shall
We gather at the river, or shall we
Appoint a Poet Laureate this fall,
20 Or shall we have another cup of tea?

[1]an earlier version of this poem appeared in the *McGill Fortnightly Review* in April 1927, shortly after Scott had attended a meeting of the Canadian Authors' Association. Scott viewed the CAA as a group smugly content with the clichés and forms of the past and inca-pable of appreciating or promoting meaningful writing of the present. [2]Edward, Prince of Wales when the poem was written, became King Edward VIII on January 21, 1936, and abdi-cated on December 11, 1936, in order to marry an American divorcée, Wallis Warfield Simpson. [3]people of letters; the learned.

O Canada, O Canada, Oh can
A day go by without new authors springing
To paint the native maple, and to plan
More ways to set the selfsame welkin[4] ringing?

(1927)   (1945)

Trans Canada

Pulled from our ruts by the made-to-order gale
We sprang upward into a wider prairie
And dropped Regina below like a pile of bones.[1]

Sky tumbled upon us in waterfalls,
5   But we were smarter than a Skeena[2] salmon
And shot our silver body over the lip of air
To rest in a pool of space
On the top storey of our adventure.

A solar peace
10   And a six-way choice.

Clouds, now, are the solid substance,
A floor of wool roughed by the wind
Standing in waves that halt in their fall.
A still of troughs.

15   The plane, our planet,
Travels on roads that are not seen or laid
But sound in instruments on pilots' ears,
While underneath
The sure wings
20   Are the everlasting arms of science.

Man, the lofty worm, tunnels his latest clay,
And bores his new career.

This frontier, too, is ours.
This everywhere whose life can only be led
25   At the pace of a rocket

→

---

[4]sky, or vault of heaven; a poetic archaism. [1]because of a huge pile of bones left after buffalo hunts, Regina was originally known as Pile of Bones Creek. [2]the Skeena River, which empties into the Pacific Ocean near Prince Rupert, British Columbia, has been an important salmon fishery for well over a hundred years.

Is common to man and man,
And every country below is an I land.

The sun sets on its top shelf,
And stars seem farther from our nearer grasp.

30 I have sat by night beside a cold lake
And touched things smoother than moonlight on still water,
But the moon on this cloud sea is not human,
And here is no shore, no intimacy,
Only the start of space, the road to suns.

(1945)

Laurentian Shield

Hidden in wonder and snow, or sudden with summer,
This land stares at the sun in a huge silence
Endlessly repeating something we cannot hear.
Inarticulate, arctic,
5 Not written on by history, empty as paper,
It leans away from the world with songs in its lakes
Older than love, and lost in the miles.

This waiting is wanting.
It will choose its language
10 When it has chosen its technic,
A tongue to shape the vowels of its productivity.
A *language of flesh and of roses*.[1]

Now there are pre-words,
Cabin syllables,
15 Nouns of settlement
Slowly forming, with steel syntax,
The long sentence of its exploitation.

The first cry was the hunter, hungry for fur,
And the digger for gold, nomad, no-man, a particle;
20 Then the bold commands of monopoly, big with machines,
Carving its kingdoms out of the public wealth;

---

[1] line from Stephen Spender's "The Making of a Poem," an essay in which Spender discusses the landscape of an English mining region as a kind of language expressing human thoughts and wishes; Spender argues that humans aspire to "a language of flesh and roses."

And now the drone of the plane, scouting the ice,
Fills all the emptiness with neighbourhood
And links our future over the vanished pole.

25

But a deeper note is sounding, heard in the mines,
The scattered camps and the mills, a language of life,
And what will be written in the full culture of occupation
Will come, presently, tomorrow,
From millions whose hands can turn this rock into children.

(1954)

Langston Hughes   (1902–1967)

Born in Joplin, Missouri, but raised in a number of mid-western states, Langston Hughes attended Columbia University for a year before travelling to Africa and Europe as a seaman. After returning to America, he studied at Lincoln University, Pennsylvania, receiving his B.A. in 1929. He then moved to New York, where he became a leading figure in the Harlem Renaissance, a period of high productivity and acclaim for African-American writers. In addition to poetry, Hughes wrote fiction, screenplays, an autobiography, and articles. His poetry is notable for capturing a sense of the life of ordinary people in Harlem and for its use of jazz and blues rhythms.

The Weary Blues

Droning a drowsy syncopated tune,
Rocking back and forth to a mellow croon,
    I heard a Negro play.
Down on Lenox Avenue[1] the other night

5

By the pale dull pallor of an old gas light
        He did a lazy sway . . . .
        He did a lazy sway . . . .
To the tune o'those Weary Blues.
With his ebony hands on each ivory key

10

He made that poor piano moan with melody.
        O Blues!

→

[1]a main thoroughfare in Harlem, New York City.

Swaying to and fro on his rickety stool
He played that sad raggy tune like a musical fool.
      Sweet Blues!
Coming from a black man's soul.
      O Blues!
In a deep song voice with a melancholy tone
I heard that Negro sing, that old piano moan —
      "Ain't got nobody in all this world,
            Ain't got nobody but ma self.
            I's gwine to quit ma frownin'
            And put ma troubles on the shelf."

Thump, thump, thump, went his foot on the floor.
He played a few chords then he sang some more —
      "I got the Weary Blues
            And I can't be satisfied.
            Got the Weary Blues
            And can't be satisfied —
            I ain't happy no mo'
            And I wish that I had died."
And far into the night he crooned that tune.
The stars went out and so did the moon.
The singer stopped playing and went to bed
While the Weary Blues echoed through his head.
He slept like a rock or a man that's dead.

(1926)

Theme for English B

The instructor said,

      Go home and write
      a page tonight.
      And let that page come out of you—
      Then, it will be true.

I wonder if it's that simple?
I am twenty-two, colored, born in Winston-Salem.
I went to school there, then Durham, then here
to this college on the hill above Harlem.
I am the only colored student in my class.

The steps from the hill lead down into Harlem,
through a park, then I cross St. Nicholas,
Eighth Avenue, Seventh, and I come to the Y,
the Harlem Branch Y, where I take the elevator
15 up to my room, sit down, and write this page:

It's not easy to know what is true for you or me
at twenty-two, my age. But I guess I'm what
I feel and see and hear, Harlem, I hear you:
hear you, hear me—we two—you, me, talk on this page.
20 (I hear New York, too.) Me—who?
Well, I like to eat, sleep, drink, and be in love.
I like to work, read, learn, and understand life.
I like a pipe for a Christmas present,
or records—Bessie[1], bop, or Bach.
25 I guess being colored doesn't make me *not* like
the same things other folks like who are other races.
So will my page be colored that I write?
Being me, it will not be white.
But it will be
30 a part of you, instructor.
You are white—
yet a part of me, as I am a part of you.
That's American.
Sometimes perhaps you don't want to be a part of me.
35 Nor do I often want to be a part of you.
But we are, that's true!
As I learn from you,
I guess you learn from me—
although you're older—and white—
40 and somewhat more free.

This is my page for English B.

(1951)

Earle Birney (1904–1995)

Born in Calgary, Birney grew up on a farm in the British Columbia
interior and in Banff. He studied at British Columbia and Toronto before

[1]Bessie Smith (1894?–1937), popular American singer often called "The Empress of the Blues."

completing a Ph.D. on Chaucer's irony at the University of Toronto in 1938. He spent most of his academic career at the University of British Columbia. Twice winner of the Governor General's Award, for his first volume, *David and Other Poems* (1942), and for *Now Is Time* (1945), he also wrote two novels, the first of which, *Turvey* (1949), won the Leacock Medal for humour.

Literally and figuratively, Birney was a peripatetic poet. For much of his life he travelled throughout the world, writing poems about his observations. He also journeyed widely through poetic forms, producing everything from poems based on Anglo-Saxon metrics (see "Anglosaxon Street") to concrete poetry mobiles. Not surprisingly, journeys of various kinds are prominent thematic elements in much of his poetry. In fact, Birney saw life itself as a journey, and his poems are "signals out of the loneliness into which all of us are born and in which we die, affirmations of kinship with other wayfarers...."

Vancouver Lights

About me the night   moonless   wimples[1] the mountains
wraps ocean   land   air   and mounting
sucks at the stars   The city   throbbing below
webs the sable peninsula   The golden
5   strands overleap the seajet   by bridge and buoy
vault the shears of the inlet   climb the woods
toward me   falter   and halt   Across to the firefly
haze of a ship on the gulf's erased horizon
roll the lambent spokes of a lighthouse

10   Through the feckless years we have come to the time
when to look on this quilt of lamps is a troubling delight
Welling from Europe's bog   through Africa flowing
and Asia   drowning the lonely lumes[2] on the oceans
tiding up over Halifax   now to this winking
15   outpost comes flooding the primal ink[3]

On this mountain's brutish forehead with terror of space
I stir   of the changeless night and the stark ranges
of nothing   pulsing down from beyond and between
the fragile planets   We are a spark beleaguered
20   by darkness   this twinkle we make in a corner of emptiness
how shall we utter our fear that the black Experimentress

[1]veils. [2]lights. [3]in *The Cow Jumped Over the Moon* (1972), Birney explains that this stanza describes the spreading of blackouts during World War II.

will never in the range of her microscope find it?   Our Phoebus[4]
himself is a bubble that dries on Her slide   while the Nubian[5]
wears for an evening's whim a necklace of nebulae

25 Yet we must speak   we the unique glowworms
Out of the waters and rocks of our little world
we conjured these flames   hooped these sparks
by our will   From blankness and cold we fashioned stars
to our size   and signalled Aldebaran[6]
30 This must we say   whoever may be to hear us
if murk devour   and none weave again in gossamer:

These rays were ours
we made and unmade them   Not the shudder of continents
doused us   the moon's passion   nor crash of comets
35 In the fathomless heat of our dwarfdom   our dream's combustion
we contrived the power   the blast that snuffed us
No one bound Prometheus   Himself he chained
and consumed his own bright liver[7]   O stranger
Plutonian[8]   descendant   or beast in the stretching night—
40 there was light

(1941)   (1942)

Anglosaxon Street

Dawndrizzle ended   dampness steams from
blotching brick and   blank plasterwaste
Faded housepatterns   hoary and finicky
unfold stuttering   stick like a phonograph

5 Here is a ghetto   gotten for goyim[1]
O with care denuded   of nigger and kike

No coonsmell rankles   reeks only cellarrot
attar of carexhaust   catcorpse and cookinggrease
Imperial hearts   heave in this haven
10 Cracks across windows   are welded with slogans
There'll Always Be An England   enhances geraniums
and V's for Victory   vanquish the housefly

[4]Phoebus Apollo, the sun. [5]black native from Nubia, in northeastern Africa. [6]the brightest
star in the constellation Taurus. [7]Prometheus stole fire for mankind, and Zeus punished him
by chaining him to a rock, where every day an eagle ate his liver, which was renewed each
night. [8]pertaining to Pluto, god of the dead, or to the dark lower world where the souls of the
dead lived. [1]Gentiles; non-Jews.

Ho! with climbing sun   march the bleached beldames
festooned with shopping bags   farded[2] flatarched
15   bigthewed Saxonwives[3]   stepping over buttrivers
waddling back wienerladen   to suckle smallfry

Hoy! with sunslope   shrieking over hydrants
flood from learninghall   the lean fingerlings
Nordic nobblecheeked[4]   not all clean of nose
20   leaping Commandowise   into leprous lanes

What! after whistleblow!   spewed from wheelboat
after daylong doughtiness   dire handplay
in sewertrench or sandpit   come Saxonthegns[5]
Junebrown Jutekings   jawslack for meat

25   Sit after supper   on smeared doorsteps
not humbly swearing   hatedeeds on Huns[6]
profiteers politicians   pacifists Jews
Then by twobit magic   to muse in movie
unlock picturehoard   or lope to alehall
30   soaking bleakly   in beer skittleless

Home again to hotbox   and humid husbandhood
in slumbertrough adding   sleepily to Anglekin
Alongside the lanenooks   carling[7] and leman[8]
caterwaul and clip   careless of Saxonry
35   with moonglow and haste   and a higher heartbeat

Slumbers now slumtrack   unstinks cooling
waiting brief for milkmaid   mornstar and worldrise

(*Toronto 1942*)   (1966)

Bushed

He invented a rainbow but lightning struck it
shattered it into the lake-lap of a mountain
so big his mind slowed when he looked at it

Yet he built a shack on the shore
5   learned to roast porcupine belly and
wore the quills on his hatband

---

[2]painted, here with cosmetics. [3]the Saxons were one of three Germanic tribes, the others—mentioned later in the poem—being the Jutes and the Angles, who conquered Britain in the fifth century. [4]ulcerous or pimpled. [5]a thegn was a freeman who held land by virtue of military service. [6]fierce Asiatic tribe of nomads who conquered much of eastern and central Europe; a derogatory appellation for Germans during the two world wars. [7]woman. [8]lover.

At first he was out with the dawn
whether it yellowed bright as wood-columbine
or was only a fuzzed moth in a flannel of storm
10   But he found the mountain was clearly alive
sent messages whizzing down every hot morning
boomed proclamations at noon and spread out
a white guard of goat
before falling asleep on its feet at sundown

15   When he tried his eyes on the lake   ospreys
would fall like valkyries[1]
choosing the cut-throat[2]
He took then to waiting
till the night smoke rose from the boil of the sunset

20   But the moon carved unknown totems
out of the lakeshore
owls in the beardusky woods derided him
moosehorned cedars circled his swamps and tossed
their antlers up to the stars
25   then he knew   though the mountain slept   the winds
were shaping its peak to an arrowhead
poised

And now he could only
bar himself in and wait
30   for the great flint to come singing into his heart

(*Wreck Beach 1951*)   (1952)

The Bear on the Delhi Road

Unreal   tall as a myth
by the road the Himalayan bear
is beating the brilliant air
with his crooked arms
5   About him two men   bare
spindly as locusts   leap

One pulls on a ring
in the great soft nose   His mate

➡️

[1]in Norse mythology, the Valkyries (Choosers of the Slain) were handmaidens of Odin who hovered over battlefields in order to choose the heroes killed in battle and escort them to Valhalla. [2]this pun points to both the slain warriors awaiting the Valkyries and a kind of large trout found in the Rocky Mountain region.

10   flicks   flicks with a stick
up at the rolling eyes

They have not led him here
down from the fabulous hills
to this bald alien plain
and the clamorous world   to kill
15   but simply to teach him to dance

They are peaceful both   these spare
men of Kashmir   and the bear
alive is their living   too
If   far on the Delhi way

20   around him galvanic they dance
it is merely to wear   wear
from his shaggy body the tranced
wish forever to stay
only an ambling bear
25   four-footed in berries

It is no more joyous for them
in this hot dust to prance
out of reach of the praying claws
sharpened to paw for ants
30   in the shadows of deodars[1]
It is not easy to free
myth from reality
or rear this fellow up
to lurch   lurch with them
35   in the tranced dancing of men

(*Srinagar* 1958/*Île des Porquerolles* 1959)   (1962)

W. H. Auden   (1907–1973)

Though born in Britain and educated at Oxford, Wystan Hugh Auden lived in the United States much of the time after 1939 and became an American citizen in 1946. He began writing poetry in school, revealed a remarkable talent for handling various styles, and established himself as a leader among the younger poets in Britain while he was still in his twenties. Early in his career, Auden was influenced by Marxism and was much concerned with satirizing the British middle class. Later, however,

---

[1]the deodar, or "tree of the gods," is a cedar native to the Western Himalayas.

while still showing an ironic bent, his work became more generally philosophical as it explored the need for meaning in modern life. Typically less personal and more analytical than most modern poets, Auden demonstrated an unsurpassed gift for capturing the political and intellectual temper of the times in which he lived.

The Unknown Citizen

(To JS/07/M/378
This Marble Monument
Is Erected by the State)

He was found by the Bureau of Statistics to be
One against whom there was no official complaint,
And all the reports on his conduct agree
That, in the modern sense of an old-fashioned word, he was a saint,
5   For in everything he did he served the Greater Community.
Except for the War till the day he retired
He worked in a factory and never got fired,
But satisfied his employers, Fudge Motors Inc.
Yet he wasn't a scab or odd in his views,
10   For his Union reports that he paid his dues,
(Our report on his Union shows it was sound)
And our Social Psychology workers found
That he was popular with his mates and liked a drink.
The Press are convinced that he bought a paper every day
15   And that his reactions to advertisements were normal in every way.
Policies taken out in his name prove that he was fully insured,
And his Health-card shows he was once in hospital but left it cured.
Both Producers Research and High-Grade Living declare
He was fully sensible to the advantages of the Instalment Plan
20   And had everything necessary to the Modern Man,
A phonograph, a radio, a car and a frigidaire.
Our researchers into Public Opinion are content
That he held the proper opinions for the time of year;
When there was peace, he was for peace; when there was war, he went.
25   He was married and added five children to the population,
Which our Eugenist says was the right number for a parent of his generation,
And our teachers report that he never interfered with their education.
Was he free? Was he happy? The question is absurd:
Had anything been wrong, we should certainly have heard.

(1939)

In Memory of W. B. Yeats

(*D. Jan.* 1939)

I

He disappeared in the dead of winter:
The brooks were frozen, the airports almost deserted,
And snow disfigured the public statues;
The mercury sank in the mouth of the dying day.
5   What instruments we have agree
The day of his death was a dark cold day.

Far from his illness
The wolves ran on through the evergreen forests,
The peasant river was untempted by the fashionable quays;
10   By mourning tongues
The death of the poet was kept from his poems.

But for him it was his last afternoon as himself,
An afternoon of nurses and rumours;
The provinces of his body revolted,
15   The squares of his mind were empty,
Silence invaded the suburbs,
The current of his feeling failed; he became his admirers.

Now he is scattered among a hundred cities
And wholly given over to unfamiliar affections,
20   To find his happiness in another kind of wood
And be punished under a foreign code of conscience.
The words of a dead man
Are modified in the guts of the living.

But in the importance and noise of to-morrow
25   When the brokers are roaring like beasts on the floor of the Bourse,[1]
And the poor have the sufferings to which they are fairly accustomed,
And each in the cell of himself is almost convinced of his freedom,
A few thousand will think of this day
As one thinks of a day when one did something slightly unusual.
30   What instruments we have agree
The day of his death was a dark cold day.

[1]French Stock Exchange.

II

You were silly like us; your gift survived it all:
The parish of rich women, physical decay,
Yourself. Mad Ireland hurt you into poetry.
Now Ireland has her madness and her weather still,
For poetry makes nothing happen: it survives
In the valley of its making where executives
Would never want to tamper, flows on south
From ranches of isolation and the busy griefs,
Raw towns that we believe and die in; it survives,
A way of happening, a mouth.

III

Earth, receive an honoured guest:
William Yeats is laid to rest.
Let the Irish vessel lie
Emptied of its poetry.[2]

In the nightmare of the dark
All the dogs of Europe bark,
And the living nations wait,
Each sequestered in its hate;

Intellectual disgrace
Stares from every human face,
And the seas of pity lie
Locked and frozen in each eye.

Follow, poet, follow right
To the bottom of the night,
With your unconstraining voice
Still persuade us to rejoice;

With the farming of a verse
Make a vineyard of the curse,
Sing of human unsuccess
In a rapture of distress;

In the deserts of the heart
Let the healing fountain start,
In the prison of his days
Teach the free man how to praise.

(1939)   (1966)

[2]in the original version written in 1939, Auden included three more stanzas here in which
Time, while indifferent to other gifts and virtues, is said to pardon the failings of those who
write well.

Musée des Beaux Arts[1]

About suffering they were never wrong,
The Old Masters: how well they understood
Its human position; how it takes place
While someone else is eating or opening a window or just walking dully along;
5 How, when the aged are reverently, passionately waiting
For the miraculous birth, there always must be
Children who did not specially want it to happen, skating
On a pond at the edge of the wood:

They never forgot
10 That even the dreadful martyrdom must run its course
Anyhow in a corner, some untidy spot
Where the dogs go on with their doggy life and the torturer's horse
Scratches its innocent behind on a tree.

In Brueghel's *Icarus*,[2] for instance: how everything turns away
15 Quite leisurely from the disaster; the ploughman may
Have heard the splash, the forsaken cry,
But for him it was not an important failure; the sun shone
As it had to on the white legs disappearing into the green
Water; and the expensive delicate ship that must have seen
20 Something amazing, a boy falling out of the sky,
Had somewhere to get to and sailed calmly on.

(1940)

A. D. Hope   (1907–2000)

The son of a Presbyterian minister, Alec Derwent Hope became a poet whose works were suppressed under Australian censorship laws because of their blunt treatment of sexuality. Born in Cooma, New South Wales, Hope grew up in Tasmania, where his mother home-educated him. He graduated from England's Oxford University and eventually established a teaching career at the University of Melbourne and Canberra University College (now the Australian National University). Although he began writing when he was a child, Hope did not publish his first volume of poetry, *The Wandering Islands*, until 1955. Nevertheless, he managed to produce a dozen more volumes of poetry and criticism, and he received numerous

---

[1]refers to the Museum of Fine Arts in Brussels, Belgium, where *The Fall of Icarus*, a painting by Flemish painter Pieter Brueghel the Elder (c. 1525–1569), still hangs. [2]in Greek myth, the skilled craftsman Daedalus made wings of wax and feathers in order to escape with Icarus, his son, from the Cretan labyrinth, which he himself had designed. When Icarus flew too near the sun, the wax melted and he fell into the sea.

awards. He once said, "I don't think of myself as a contemporary poet, although I know I occupy contemporary time-space." One sign of this alienation is his commitment to formalism. In fact, in his essay "Free Verse: A Post-Mortem" (1965), he labelled free verse "a very common cheap and popular substitute for poetry." Although he could engage in metaphysical meditation and could produce moving lyrics about love, his most notorious poetry is overtly—some say crudely—sexual. The combination of earthy subject matter and traditional, polished poetic form, however, produces extraordinarily witty entertainments.

The Elegy

VARIATIONS ON A THEME OF THE SEVENTEENTH CENTURY[1]

Madam, no more! The time has come to eat.
The spirit of man is nourished, too, with meat.
Those heroes and the warriors of old—
Feasting between their battles made them bold.
5 When Venus in the west hung out her lamp,[2]
The rattling sons of Mars[3] marched home to camp;

And while around the fires their wounds were dressed,
And tale was matched with tale, and jest with jest,
Flagons of wine and oxen roasted whole
10 Refreshed their bodies and restored the soul.

Come, leave the bed; put on your dress; efface
Awhile this dazzling armoury of grace!
Flushed and rejoicing from the well-fought fight
Now day lies panting in the arms of night;
15 The first dews tremble on the darkening field;
Put up your naked weapons, the bright shield
Of triumph glinting to the early stars;
Call our troops home with trumpets from their wars;
And, as wise generals, let them rest and dine
20 And celebrate our truce with meat and wine.
See, the meek table on our service waits;
The devil in crystal winks beside our plates;
These veterans of love's war we shall repay
And crown with feasts the glories of the day.
25 Think no disgrace, if now they play a part

➡️

[1]although the term "elegy" is now used almost exclusively to describe a poem of mourning, it was used also, until the end of the seventeenth century, to denote poems about love, particularly witty, erotic ones. See, for example, John Donne's "Elegy XIX: To His Mistress Going to Bed." [2]in this case, the evening star; Venus is the Roman goddess of love. [3]soldiers; Mars is the Roman god of war.

Less worthy of the soldiers of the heart.
Though these we led were granted, even as we,
Their moment's draught of immortality,
We do but snatch our instant on the height
30 And in the valleys still live out the night.
Yet they surrender nothing which is theirs.
Nature is frugal in her ministers;
Each to some humbler office must return,
And so must we. Then grudge it not, but learn
35 In this the noble irony of kind:[4]
These fierce, quick hands that rove and clasp must find
Other employment now with knife and fork;
Our mouths that groaned with joy, now eat and talk;
These chief commanders, too, without debate,
40 Sink to the lowliest service of the state.
Only our eyes observe no armistice;
Sparkling with love's perpetual surprise,
Their bright vedettes[5] keep watch from hill to hill
And, when they meet, renew the combat still.
45 And yet to view you would I linger on:
This is the rarest moment, soonest gone.
While now the marching stars invest the sky
And the wide lands beneath surrendered lie,
Their streams and forests, parks and fields and farms,
50 Like this rich empire tranquil in my arms,
Seem lovelier in the last withdrawing light
And, as they vanish, most enchant the sight.
Still let me watch those countries as they fade
And all their lucid contours sink in shade;
55 The mounting thighs, the line of flank and breast,
Yet harbour a clear splendour from the west;
Though twilight draws into its shadowy reign
This breathing valley and that glimmering plain,
Still let my warrior heart with fresh delight
60 Rove and reflect: "Here, here began the fight;
Between those gentle hills I paused to rest,
And on this vale the kiss of triumph pressed;
There, full encircled by the frantic foe,
I rode between the lilies and the snow;
65 And, in this copse that parts the dark and shine,
Plundered the treasures of the hidden mine;

→

---

[4]sexual intercourse. [5]mounted sentinels stationed away from the main camp.

Down those long slopes in slow retreat I drew;
And here renewed the charge; and here, anew
Met stroke with stroke and touched, at the last breath,
70   The unimagined ecstasy of death."

Full darkness! Time enough the lamps were lit.
Let us to dinner, Madam; wine and wit
Must have their hour, even as love and war,
And what's to come revives what went before.
75   Come now, for see the Captain of my lust,
He that so stoutly fought and stiffly thrust,
Fallen, diminished on the field he lies;
Cover his face, he dreams in paradise.
We, while he sleeps, shall dine; and, when that's done,
80   Drink to his resurrection later on.

(1955)

Theodore Roethke   (1908–1963)

Theodore Roethke's family operated greenhouses in Saginaw, Michigan, and, growing up surrounded by plants, he developed the almost mystical sympathy with primitive life that characterized his early nature lyrics. He received an M.A. from the University of Michigan, did graduate work at Harvard, and devoted his working life to college teaching as well as writing poetry.

During much of his adult life, Roethke suffered from alcoholism and mental illness, which caused him to experience alternating bouts of manic energy and depression. He managed to turn these problems to poetic advantage, however, by exploring his changing mental states as poetic journeys through interior psychic landscapes.

My Papa's Waltz

The whiskey on your breath
Could make a small boy dizzy;
But I hung on like death:
Such waltzing was not easy.

5   We romped until the pans
Slid from the kitchen shelf;
My mother's countenance
Could not unfrown itself.

The hand that held my wrist
10   Was battered on one knuckle;

→

At every step you missed
My right ear scraped a buckle.

You beat time on my head
With a palm caked hard by dirt,
15   Then waltzed me off to bed
Still clinging to your shirt.

(1948)

I Knew a Woman

I knew a woman, lovely in her bones,
When small birds sighed, she would sigh back at them;
Ah, when she moved, she moved more ways than one:
The shapes a bright container can contain!
5   Of her choice virtues only gods should speak,
Or English poets who grew up on Greek
(I'd have them sing in chorus, cheek to cheek).

How well her wishes went! She stroked my chin,
She taught me Turn, and Counter-turn, and Stand;[1]
10   She taught me Touch, that undulant white skin;
I nibbled meekly from her proffered hand;
She was the sickle; I, poor I, the rake,
Coming behind her for her pretty sake
(But what prodigious mowing we did make.)

15   Love likes a gander, and adores a goose:
Her full lips pursed, the errant note to seize;
She played it quick, she played it light and loose;
My eyes, they dazzled at her flowing knees;
Her several parts could keep a pure repose,
20   Or one hip quiver with a mobile nose
(She moved in circles, and those circles moved).

Let seed be grass, and grass turn into hay:
I'm martyr to a motion not my own;
What's freedom for? To know eternity.
25   I swear she cast a shadow white as stone.
But who would count eternity in days?
These old bones live to learn her wanton ways:
(I measure time by how a body sways).

(1958)

[1] a Pindaric ode is divided into three movements called the strophe, or turn; the antistrophe, or counter-turn; and the epode, or stand.

A. M. Klein   (1909–1972)

Abraham Moses Klein was born in Ratno, Ukraine, and came to Montreal with his parents in 1910. After receiving a B.A. from McGill University in 1930, he studied law at the Université de Montréal and was admitted to the bar in 1933. A mental breakdown and several suicide attempts forced his retirement in 1956. Klein became reclusive and completely abandoned all writing, but he had already made a permanent literary contribution as one of the leading figures in the development of modern poetry in Canada.

Jewish themes dominate Klein's writing: his first book, *Hath Not a Jew* ... (1940), celebrates the rich heritage and customs of the Jewish people, and much of his later work treats Jewish suffering. *The Rocking Chair* (1948), winner of the Governor General's Award for poetry, contained poems about Quebec, as well as his finest work, "Portrait of the Poet as Landscape." He returned to Jewish themes in his complex visionary novel, *The Second Scroll* (1951). Klein's poetry is both intellectual and witty; it is characterized by learned allusions, metaphors, puns, archaisms, and words derived from several languages.

Heirloom

My father bequeathed me no wide estates;
No keys and ledgers were my heritage;
Only some holy books with *yahrzeit* dates[1]
Writ mournfully upon a blank front page—

5 Books of the Baal Shem Tov,[2] and of his wonders;
Pamphlets upon the devil and his crew;
Prayers against road demons, witches, thunders;
And sundry other tomes for a good Jew.

Beautiful: though no pictures on them, save
10 The scorpion crawling on a printed track;
The Virgin floating on a scriptural wave,
Square letters twinkling in the Zodiac.[3]

The snuff left on this page, now brown and old,
The tallow stains of midnight liturgy—

[1]anniversary dates of the death of ancestors. [2]the eighteenth-century rabbi who founded Hasidism, a Jewish movement that emphasizes communion with God through joyful prayer, encourages religious expression in song and dance, and values the experience of the natural world and a simple delight in service to God more than the legal dialectic of traditional study of the Torah. [3]in a letter to A.J. M. Smith dated January 21, 1943, Klein explained that "Hebrew prayer books are never illustrated. The only drawings that appear in the liturgy are the signs of the Zodiac illustrating the prayers for rain and fertility."

15 These are my coat of arms, and these unfold
My noble lineage, my proud ancestry!

And my tears, too, have stained this heirloomed ground,
When reading in these treatises some weird
Miracle, I turned a leaf and found
20 A white hair fallen from my father's beard.

(1940)

Portrait of the Poet as Landscape

i

Not an editorial-writer, bereaved with bartlett,[1]
mourns him, the shelved Lycidas.[2]
No actress squeezes a glycerine[3] tear for him.
The radio broadcast lets his passing pass.
5 And with the police, no record. Nobody, it appears,
either under his real name or his alias,
missed him enough to report.

It is possible that he is dead, and not discovered.
It is possible that he can be found some place
10 in a narrow closet, like the corpse in a detective story,
standing, his eyes staring, and ready to fall on his face.
It is also possible that he is alive
and amnesiac, or mad, or in retired disgrace,
or beyond recognition lost in love.

15 We are sure only that from our real society
he has disappeared; he simply does not count,
except in the pullulation[4] of vital statistics—
somebody's vote, perhaps, an anonymous taunt
of the Gallup poll, a dot in a government table—
20 but not felt, and certainly far from eminent—
in a shouting mob, somebody's sigh.

O, he who unrolled our culture from his scroll—
the prince's quote, the rostrum-rounding roar—
who under one name made articulate

---

[1]*Familiar Quotations*, first published in 1855 by John Bartlett and frequently updated. [2]"Lycidas" (1638), a pastoral elegy by John Milton, mourns the drowning of Edward King, a young poet, (See Page 53). [3]used to simulate tears on stage. [4]teeming; rapid sprouting or breeding.

25 heaven, and under another the seven-circled air,[5]
is, if he is at all, a number, an x,
a Mr. Smith in a hotel register,—
incognito, lost, lacunal.[6]

ii

The truth is he's not dead, but only ignored—
30 like the mirroring lenses forgotten on a brow
that shine with the guilt of their unnoticed world.
The truth is he lives among neighbours, who, though they will allow
him a passable fellow, think him eccentric, not solid,
a type that one can forgive, and for that matter, forgo.

35 Himself he has his moods, just like a poet.
Sometimes, depressed to nadir,[7] he will think all lost,
will see himself as throwback, relict,[8] freak,
his mother's miscarriage, his great-grandfather's ghost,
and he will curse his quintuplet senses, and their tutors
40 in whom he put, as he should not have put, his trust.

Then he will remember his travels over that body—
the torso verb, the beautiful face of the noun,
and all those shaped and warm auxiliaries!
A first love it was, the recognition of his own.
45 Dear limbs adverbial, complexion of adjective,
dimple and dip of conjugation!

And then remember how this made a change in him
affecting for always the glow and growth of his being;
how suddenly was aware of the air, like shaken tinfoil,[9]
50 of the patents of nature, the shock of belated seeing,
the loneliness peering from the eyes of crowds;
the integers of thought; the cube-roots of feeling.

Thus, zoomed to zenith, sometimes he hopes again,
and sees himself as a character, with a rehearsed role:

---

[5]before Nicolaus Copernicus (1473–1543), people believed that the earth was the fixed
centre of the universe and that it was surrounded by seven concentric circles. [6]a lacuna is a
blank space or missing portion. [7]the lowest point; the point opposite the zenith.
[8]plant or animal surviving from a previous age. [9]see line 2 of "God's Grandeur," by Gerard
Manley Hopkins.

55 the Count of Monte Cristo,[10] come for his revenges;
the unsuspecting heir, with papers; the risen soul;
or the chloroformed prince awakening from his flowers;
or—deflated again—the convict on parole.

iii

He is alone; yet not completely alone.
60 Pins on a map of a colour similar to his,
each city has one, sometimes more than one;
here, caretakers of art, in colleges;
in offices, there, with arm-bands, and green-shaded;
and there, pounding their catalogued beats in libraries,—

65 everywhere menial, a shadow's shadow.
And always for their egos—their outmoded art.
Thus, having lost the bevel[11] in the ear,
they know neither up nor down, mistake the part
for the whole, curl themselves in a comma,
70 talk technics, make a colon their eyes. They distort—
such is the pain of their frustration—truth
to something convolute and cerebral.
How they do fear the slap of the flat of the platitude!
Now Pavlov's victims[12] their mouths water at bell,
75 the platter empty.
                    See they set twenty-one jewels
into their watches; the time they do not tell!

Some, patagonian[13] in their own esteem,
and longing for the multiplying word,
join party and wear pins, now have a message,
80 an ear, and the convention-hall's regard.
Upon the knees of ventriloquists, they own,
of their dandled[14] brightness, only the paint and board.

And some go mystical, and some go mad.

[10]in *The Count of Monte Cristo* (1844–45), by Alexandre Dumas *père* (1802–1870), Edmond Dantes elaborately plots the ruin of those whose false accusations led to his prolonged imprisonment. [11]instrument for determining angles, thus, the sense of balance. [12]Ivan Petrovich Pavlov (1849–1936), a Russian physiologist, studied conditioned reflexes by ringing a bell when he provided food to dogs. Later, even if he did not serve them food, the dogs salivated when he rang the bell. [13]the natives of Patagonia, at the extreme southern tip of South America, were reputed to be the tallest people in the world; figuratively, patagonian means gigantic. [14]to be moved up and down on one's knee, as with a child.

One stares at a mirror all day long, as if
to recognize himself; another courts
angels,—for here he does not fear rebuff;
and a third, alone, and sick with sex, and rapt,
doodles him symbols convex and concave.

O schizoid solitudes! O purities
curdling upon themselves! Who live for themselves,
or for each other, but for nobody else;
desire affection, private and public loves;
are friendly, and then quarrel and surmise
the secret perversions of each other's lives.

iv

He suspects that something has happened, a law
been passed, a nightmare ordered. Set apart,
he finds himself, with special haircut and dress,
as on a reservation. Introvert.
He does not understand this; sad conjecture
muscles and palls thrombotic on his heart.

He thinks an impostor, having studied his personal biography,
his gestures, his moods, now has come forward to pose
in the shivering vacuums his absence leaves.
Wigged with his laurel, that other, and faked with his face,
he pats the heads of his children, pecks his wife,
and is at home, and slippered, in his house.

So he guesses at the impertinent silhouette
that talks to his phone-piece and slits open his mail.
Is it the local tycoon who for a hobby
plays poet, he so epical in steel?
The orator, making a pause? Or is that man
he who blows his flash of brass in the jittering hall?

Or is he cuckolded by the troubadour
rich and successful out of celluloid?
Or by the don who unrhymes atoms? Or
the chemist death built up? Pride, lost impostor'd pride,
it is another, another, whoever he is,
who rides where he should ride.

v

Fame, the adrenalin:[15] to be talked about;
120   to be a verb; to be introduced as *The*:
to smile with endorsement from slick paper; make
caprices anecdotal; to nod to the world; to see
one's name like a song upon the marquees played;
to be forgotten with embarrassment; to be—
125   to be.

It has its attractions, but is not the thing;
nor is it the ape mimesis[16] who speaks from the tree
ancestral; nor the merkin[17] joy ...
Rather it is stark infelicity
130   which stirs him from his sleep, undressed, asleep
to walk upon roofs and window-sills and defy
the gape of gravity.

vi

Therefore he seeds illusions. Look, he is
the nth Adam taking a green inventory
135   in world[18] but scarcely uttered, naming, praising,
the flowering fiats in the meadow, the
syllabled fur, stars aspirate, the pollen
whose sweet collusion sounds eternally.
For to praise

140   the world—he, solitary man—is breath
to him. Until it has been praised, that part
has not been. Item by exciting item—
air to his lungs, and pressured blood to his heart—
they are pulsated, and breathed, until they map,
145   not the world's, but his own body's chart!

And now in imagination he has climbed
another planet, the better to look
with single camera view upon this earth—
its total scope, and each afflated[19] tick,
150   its talk, its trick, its tracklessness—and this,
this, he would like to write down in a book!

---

[15]Milton's "Lycidas" also argues about a poet's motivation, first declaring that "Fame is the spur" (line 70) and then rejecting this notion. [16]imitation. [17]false hairpiece for the female genitalia. [18]in Genesis 2:19–20, Adam names the animals. [19]inspired.

To find a new function for the *déclassé*[20] craft
archaic like the fletcher's;[21] to make a new thing;
to say the word that will become sixth sense;
155   perhaps by necessity and indirection bring
new forms to life, anonymously, new creeds—
O, somehow pay back the daily larcenies of the lung!

These are not mean ambitions. It is already something
merely to entertain them. Meanwhile, he
160   makes of his status as zero a rich garland,
a halo of his anonymity,
and lives alone, and in his secret shines
like phosphorus. At the bottom of the sea.

(1948)

Dorothy Livesay   (1909–1996)

Dorothy Livesay's poetry developed through a number of distinct phases. Born in Winnipeg, Livesay began her career while an undergraduate at the University of Toronto. Thematically, her first book, *Green Pitcher* (1928), displayed her sensitivity to nature and its relationship to people; technically, it showed the influence of the imagists. After studying at the Sorbonne and returning to Toronto for a degree in social work, she joined the Communist Party and was active as an organizer. Her poetry during the Depression and war years was dominated by political issues and her concern for workers' rights. Two collections of her leftist poetry won the Governor General's Award—*Day and Night* (1944) and *Poems for People* (1947). Livesay served as a teacher in Zambia (1960–63) and earned her M.Ed. at the University of British Columbia in 1964. After this, her career entered a new phase. With the publication of *The Unquiet Bed* (1967), she established herself as a lyric poet capable of giving fresh, sensitive, and forceful expression to issues of female identity and sexuality.

Bartok[1] and the Geranium

She lifts her green umbrellas
Towards the pane
Seeking her fill of sunlight
Or of rain;

---

[20]outmoded. [21]arrow-maker's. [1]Béla Bartók (1881–1945), a Hungarian composer of intense, passionate music, exerted a profound influence on modern music through his efforts to free himself from strict tonality and the bar-measure system.

5　　Whatever falls
　　　She has no commentary
　　　Accepts, extends,
　　　Blows out her furbelows,[2]
　　　Her bustling boughs;

10　　And all the while he whirls
　　　Explodes in space,
　　　Never content with this small room:
　　　Not even can he be
　　　Confined to sky
15　　But must speed high and higher still
　　　From galaxy to galaxy,
　　　Wrench from the stars their momentary notes
　　　Steal music from the moon.

　　　She's daylight
20　　He is dark
　　　She's heaven-held breath
　　　He storms and crackles
　　　Spits with hell's own spark.

　　　Yet in this room, this moment now
25　　These together breathe and be:
　　　She, essence of serenity,
　　　He in a mad intensity
　　　Soars beyond sight
　　　Then hurls, lost Lucifer,
30　　From heaven's height.

　　　And when he's done, he's out:
　　　She leans a lip against the glass
　　　And preens herself in light.

(1955)

The Three Emilys[1]

These women crying in my head
Walk alone, uncomforted:
The Emilys, these three

[2]ornamental pleats or flounces. [1]a note identifying the three as Emily Brontë, Emily Dickinson, and Emily Carr appeared with first publication of this poem in *The Canadian Forum* (September 1953). Emily Brontë (1818–1848) was a British poet and author of the novel *Wuthering Heights* (1848); Emily Dickinson (1830–1886) was an American poet (see pages 182–186); Emily Carr (1871–1945) was a Canadian painter and author.

Cry to be set free—
5   And others whom I will not name
Each different, each the same.

Yet they had liberty!
Their kingdom was the sky:
They batted clouds with easy hand,
10 Found a mountain for their stand;
From wandering lonely they could catch
The inner magic of a heath—
A lake their palette, any tree
Their brush could be.

15 And still they cry to me
As in reproach—
I, born to hear their inner storm
Of separate man in woman's form,
I yet possess another kingdom, barred
20 To them, these three, this Emily.[2]
I move as mother in a frame,
My arteries
Flow the immemorial way
Towards the child, the man;
25 And only for brief span
Am I an Emily on mountain snows
And one of these.

And so the whole that I possess
Is still much less—
30 They move triumphant through my head:
I am the one
Uncomforted.

(1953)   (1972)

Irving Layton   (1912–2006)

Born in Romania, Layton (originally Lazarovitch) came to Montreal as an infant. He was educated at Macdonald College and McGill University, taught parochial school in Montreal, and eventually became an English professor at York University. A prolific writer, he published his first book in

[2]none of the three Emilys married or gave birth, whereas Livesay married and raised two children.

1945. *A Red Carpet for the Sun* (1959) won the Governor General's Award. Layton is probably as well known for his controversial attacks on those who disagreed with him or criticized him as he is for his poetry. The guardians of official morality, intellectuals, women resistant to his charms, and Christians—all of whom he grouped among the forces of repression—felt his deliberately outrageous assaults. In spite of the provocations and bombast in his public statements, his poetry is not always acerbic: it can express tenderness, pathos, humour, and complex ideas, often in elegantly memorable language. Furthermore, Layton had a lofty vision of his calling, which he expressed in terms of his Jewish heritage. He believed that the true poet is, like the Hebrew prophets, one who knows truth, one whose work is of extreme importance: "Poetry, by giving dignity and utterance to our distress, enables us to hope, makes compassion reasonable."

The Birth of Tragedy[1]

And me happiest when I compose poems.
            Love, power, the huzza of battle
            are something, are much;
yet a poem includes them like a pool
5   water and reflection.
In me, nature's divided things—
            tree, mould on tree—
            have their fruition;
I am their core. Let them swap,
10 bandy, like a flame swerve
I am their mouth; as a mouth I serve.

And I observe how the sensual moths
            big with odour and sunshine
            dart into the perilous shrubbery;
15 or drop their visiting shadows
            upon the garden I one year made
of flowering stone to be a footstool
            for the perfect gods:
            who, friends to the ascending orders,
20 sustain all passionate meditations
and call down pardons
for the insurgent blood.

---

[1] in *The Birth of Tragedy* (1872), the German philosopher Friedrich Nietzsche (1844–1900) sought to explain the origins of Greek tragedy in a fusion of opposite tendencies. One, the Apollonian, stood for order and idealism; the other, the Dionysian, represented energy and actual experience.

A quiet madman, never far from tears,
        I lie like a slain thing
            under the green air the trees
inhabit, or rest upon a chair
        towards which the inflammable air
tumbles on many robins' wings;
            noting how seasonably
            leaf and blossom uncurl
and living things arrange their death,
while someone from afar off
blows birthday candles for the world.

(1954)

The Fertile Muck

There are brightest apples on those trees
        but until I, fabulist, have spoken
they do not know their significance
or what other legends are hung like garlands
        on their black boughs twisting
like a rumour. The wind's noise is empty.

Nor are the winged insects better off
        though they wear my crafty eyes
wherever they alight. Stay here, my love;
you will see how delicately they deposit
            me on the leaves of elms
or fold me in the orient dust of summer.

And if in August joiners and bricklayers
        are thick as flies around us
building expensive bungalows for those
who do not need them, unless they release
            me roaring from their moth-proofed cupboards
their buyers will have no joy, no ease.

I could extend their rooms for them without cost
        and give them crazy sundials
to tell the time with, but I have noticed
how my irregular footprint horrifies them
            evenings and Sunday afternoons:
they spray for hours to erase its shadow.

25 How to dominate reality? Love is one way;
   imagination another. Sit here
beside me, sweet; take my hard hand in yours.
We'll mark the butterflies disappearing over the hedge
   with tiny wristwatches on their wings,
30 our fingers touching the earth, like two Buddhas.

(1956)

Douglas LePan (1914–1998)

Winner of the Governor General's Award for both poetry and fiction, Douglas LePan was a professor and a member of the diplomatic service. Born in Toronto, he was educated at the University of Toronto and Oxford. His first published volume, *The Wounded Prince* (1948), contains some of his best-known and most important work, including "A Country without a Mythology." A significant contribution to the tradition that stretches at least as far back as Charles G. D. Roberts and the Confederation Poets—the attempt to create a distinctly Canadian poetry through treatment of the Canadian landscape—this poem contains sharply rendered scenes of external nature. It is not, however, simply another romantic landscape poem: its concern with myth transforms it into a compelling mental landscape and gives it an ironic edge as a comment on the traditions and possibilities of Canadian poetry.

A Country without a Mythology

No monuments or landmarks guide the stranger
Going among this savage people, masks
Taciturn or babbling out an alien jargon
And moody as barbaric skies are moody.

5 Berries must be his food. Hurriedly
He shakes the bushes, plucks pickerel from the river,
Forgetting every grace and ceremony,
Feeds like an Indian, and is on his way.

And yet, for all his haste, time is worth nothing.
10 The abbey clock, the dial in the garden,
Fade like saint's days and festivals.
Months, years, are here unbroken virgin forests.

There is no law—even no atmosphere
To smooth the anger of the flagrant sun.
15   November skies sting sting like icicles.
The land is open to all violent weathers.

Passion is not more quick. Lightnings in August
Stagger, rocks split, tongues in the forest hiss,
As fire drinks up the lovely sea-dream coolness.
20   This is the land the passionate man must travel.

Sometimes—perhaps at the tentative fall of twilight—
A belief will settle that waiting around the bend
Are sanctities of childhood, that melting birds
Will sing him into a limpid gracious Presence.

25   The hills will fall in folds, the wilderness
Will he a garment innocent and lustrous
To wear upon a birthday, under a light
That curls and smiles, a golden-haired Archangel.

And now the channel opens. But nothing alters.
30   Mile after mile of tangled struggling roots,
Wild-rice, stumps, weeds, that clutch at the canoe,
Wild birds hysterical in tangled trees.

And not a sign, no emblem in the sky
Or boughs to friend him as he goes; for who
35   Will stop where, clumsily constructed, daubed
With war-paint, teeters some lust-red manitou?[1]

(1948)

Dylan Thomas   (1914–1953)

Gifted with a richly expressive voice, Dylan Thomas attracted many who had never previously felt the beauty and emotional power of poetry. At the same time, he often repelled those who met him because of his excessive drinking and blunt, irreverent wit. Born in Swansea, Wales, Thomas earned fame with his first collection, *Eighteen Poems* (1934). Later collections, such as *The Map of Love* (1939) and *Deaths and Entrances* (1946), consolidated his reputation as the leading lyric poet of his generation. Thomas, who worked at the beginning of his career as a scriptwriter and

[1]the spirit worshipped as a force of nature by Algonquin Indians.

broadcaster for the BBC, was also an accomplished prose writer, his best-known works being the novel *Portrait of the Artist as a Young Dog* (1940), the radio drama *Under Milk Wood* (1954), and his reminiscence, *A Child's Christmas in Wales* (1954). Much of his popularity, however, came because of performances—readings of poems by himself and others, phonograph recordings, and three American tours. His readings stressed the musical and oral qualities of the poetry. His own poems are distinctive in employing a profusion of sonorous images, for, as he once said, "A poem by myself *needs* a host of images, because its centre is a host of images." Although his sequences of images can sometimes seem an incoherent, surrealistic jumble, his best work unifies the abundant imagery through theme. His major themes are childhood experience, the cycle of nature, religious sensibility, sex, and death.

And Death Shall Have No Dominion[1]

And death shall have no dominion.
Dead men naked they shall be one
With the man in the wind and the west moon;
When their bones are picked clean and the clean bones gone,
5   They shall have stars at elbow and foot;
Though they go mad they shall be sane,
Though they sink through the sea they shall rise again;
Though lovers be lost love shall not;
And death shall have no dominion.

10   And death shall have no dominion.
Under the windings of the sea
They lying long shall not die windily;
Twisting on racks when sinews give way,
Strapped to a wheel, yet they shall not break;
15   Faith in their hands shall snap in two,
And the unicorn evils run them through;
Split all ends up they shan't crack;
And death shall have no dominion.

And death shall have no dominion.
20   No more may gulls cry at their ears
Or waves break loud on the seashores;
Where blew a flower may a flower no more
Lift its head to the blows of the rain;

---

[1]an echo of Romans 6:9: "Knowing that Christ being raised from the dead dieth no more; death hath no more dominion over him."

Though they be mad and dead as nails,
25 Heads of the characters hammer through daisies;
Break in the sun till the sun breaks down,
And death shall have no dominion.

(1934)

The Force That Through the Green Fuse Drives the Flower

The force that through the green fuse drives the flower
Drives my green age; that blasts the roots of trees
Is my destroyer.
And I am dumb to tell the crooked rose
5 My youth is bent by the same wintry fever.
The force that drives the water through the rocks
Drives my red blood; that dries the mouthing streams
Turns mine to wax.
And I am dumb to mouth unto my veins
10 How at the mountain spring the same mouth sucks.

The hand that whirls the water in the pool
Stirs the quicksand; that ropes the blowing wind
Hauls my shroud sail.
And I am dumb to tell the hanging man
15 How of my clay is made the hangman's lime.

The lips of time leech to the fountain head;
Love drips and gathers, but the fallen blood
Shall calm her sores.
And I am dumb to tell a weather's wind
20 How time has ticked a heaven round the stars.

And I am dumb to tell the lover's tomb
How at my sheet goes the same crooked worm.

(1934)

Fern Hill[1]

Now as I was young and easy under the apple boughs
About the lilting house and happy as the grass was green,

[1]the Welsh farm of Ann Jones, the aunt with whom Thomas spent holidays away from Swansea.

The night above the dingle[2] starry,
    Time let me hail and climb
5   Golden in the heydays of his eyes,
And honoured among wagons I was prince of the apple towns
And once below a time I lordly had the trees and leaves
        Trail with daisies and barley
    Down the rivers of the windfall[3] light.

10 And as I was green and carefree, famous among the barns
About the happy yard and singing as the farm was home,
        In the sun that is young once only,
           Time let me play and be
    Golden in the mercy of his means,
15 And green and golden I was huntsman and herdsman, the calves
Sang to my horn, the foxes on the hills barked clear and cold,
        And the sabbath rang slowly
    In the pebbles of the holy streams.

All the sun long it was running, it was lovely, the hay
20 Fields high as the house, the tunes from the chimneys, it was air
        And playing, lovely and watery
           And fire green as grass.
        And nightly under the simple stars
As I rode to sleep the owls were bearing the farm away,
25 All the moon long I heard, blessed among stables, the nightjars[4]
        Flying with the ricks,[5] and the horses
           Flashing into the dark.

And then to awake, and the farm, like a wanderer white
With the dew, come back, the cock on his shoulder: it was all
30   Shining, it was Adam and maiden,
           The sky gathered again
        And the sun grew round that very day.
So it must have been after the birth of the simple light
In the first, spinning place, the spellbound horses walking warm
35   Out of the whinnying green stable
           On to the fields of praise.

And honoured among foxes and pheasants by the gay house
Under the new made clouds and happy as the heart was long,

---

[2]deep dell or hollow, usually wooded. [3]a transferred epithet: windfall apples are those blown down by the wind. [4]common nocturnal bird. [5]stacks of hay.

In the sun born over and over,
        I ran my heedless ways,
    My wishes raced through the house high hay
And nothing I cared, at my sky blue trades, that time allows
In all his tuneful turning so few and such morning songs
        Before the children green and golden
            Follow him out of grace,

Nothing I cared, in the lamb white days, that time would take me
Up to the swallow thronged loft by the shadow of my hand,
        In the moon that is always rising,
            Nor that riding to sleep
        I should hear him fly with the high fields
And wake to the farm forever fled from the childless land.
Oh as I was young and easy in the mercy of his means,
        Time held me green and dying
        Though I sang in my chains like the sea.

                                                        (1946)

Do Not Go Gentle into That Good Night[1]

Do not go gentle into that good night,
Old age should burn and rave at close of day;
Rage, rage against the dying of the light.

Though wise men at their end know dark is right,
Because their words had forked no lightning they
Do not go gentle into that good night.

Good men, the last wave by, crying how bright
Their frail deeds might have danced in a green bay,
Rage, rage against the dying of the light.

Wild men who caught and sang the sun in flight,
And learn, too late, they grieved it on its way,
Do not go gentle into that good night.

Grave men, near death, who see with blinding sight
Blind eyes could blaze like meteors and be gay,
Rage, rage against the dying of the light.

And you, my father, there on the sad height,
Curse, bless, me now with your fierce tears, I pray.

[1]written in 1951 and addressed to his dying father.

Do not go gentle into that good night.
Rage, rage against the dying of the light.

(1952)

P. K. Page (1916–2010)

Patricia Kathleen Page was born in Swanage, England, and came to Red Deer, Alberta, when she was two. She began her career as a poet in Montreal, where she was associated with the founders of *Preview*, a literary journal that championed formally sophisticated and intellectually demanding poetry. Her first collection, published in 1946, showed concern with both social issues and psychology. Page was also a graphic artist, and the abundant imagery and profusion of metaphors in her poetry are signs of her intensely visual sensibility. Nevertheless, Page tried to present more than surface appearance. In doing so, especially in her later work, she was influenced by Sufism. Thus in her poetry, Page was a mystic, seeking, with what she calls her "two-dimensional consciousness," a glimpse of the three-dimensional unity beyond mundane appearances.

Stories of Snow

Those in the vegetable rain retain
an area behind their sprouting eyes
held soft and rounded with the dream of snow
precious and reminiscent as those globes—
5   souvenir of some never-nether land—
which hold their snow-storms circular, complete,
high in a tall and teakwood cabinet.

In countries where the leaves are large as hands
where flowers protrude their fleshy chins
10   and call their colours,
an imaginary snow-storm sometimes falls
among the lilies.
And in the early morning one will waken
to think the glowing linen of his pillow
15   a northern drift, will find himself mistaken
and lie back weeping.
And there the story shifts from head to head,
of how in Holland, from their feather beds

hunters arise and part the flakes and go
20   forth to the frozen lakes in search of swans—
the snow-light falling white along their guns,
their breath in plumes.
While tethered in the wind like sleeping gulls
ice-boats wait the raising of their wings
25   to skim the electric ice at such a speed
they leap jet strips of naked water,
and how these flying, sailing hunters feel
air in their mouths as terrible as ether.
And on the story runs that even drinks
30   in that white landscape dare to be no colour;
how flasked and water clear, the liquor slips
silver against the hunters' moving hips.
And of the swan in death these dreamers tell
of its last flight and how it falls, a plummet,
35   pierced by the freezing bullet
and how three feathers, loosened by the shot,
descend like snow upon it.
While hunters plunge their fingers in its down
deep as a drift, and dive their hands
40   up to the neck of the wrist
in that warm metamorphosis of snow
as gentle as the sort that woodsmen know
who, lost in the white circle, fall at last
and dream their way to death.

45   And stories of this kind are often told
in countries where great flowers bar the roads
with reds and blues which seal the route to snow—
as if, in telling, raconteurs unlock
the colour with its complement and go
50   through to the area behind the eyes
where silent, unrefractive whiteness lies.

(1946)

The Landlady

Through sepia air the boarders come and go,
impersonal as trains. Pass silently
the craving silence swallowing her speech;
click doors like shutters on her camera eye.

5   Because of her their lives become exact:
their entrances and exits are designed;
phone calls are cryptic. Oh, her ticklish ears
advance and fall back stunned.

Nothing is unprepared. They hold the walls
10   about them as they weep or laugh. Each face
is dialled to zero publicly. She peers
stippled with curious flesh;

pads on the patient landing like a pulse,
unlocks their keyholes with the wire of sight,
15   searches their rooms for clues when they are out,
pricks when they come home late.

Wonders when they are quiet, jumps when they move,
dreams that they dope or drink, trembles to know
the traffic of their brains, jaywalks their street
20   in clumsy shoes.

Yet knows them better than their closest friends:
their cupboards and the secrets of their drawers,
their books, their private mail, their photographs
are theirs and hers.

25   Knows when they wash, how frequently their clothes
go to the cleaners, what they like to eat,
their curvature of health, but even so
is not content.

And like a lover must know all, all, all.
30   Prays she may catch them unprepared at last
and palm the dreadful riddle of their skulls—
hoping the worst.

(1974)

Robert Lowell   (1917–1977)

A descendent of distinguished Boston families, Robert Lowell was critical of much of his heritage. His rebellion against his family's expectations expressed itself in his declaration of conscientious objector status in World War II, for which he was imprisoned, and his temporary conversion to Roman Catholicism. Educated at Harvard and Kenyon College, he began his poetic career with somewhat academic, richly allusive, heavily rhetorical, rhymed, and metrically formal poems. In the mid-1950s, however, Lowell began to write a more relaxed kind of poetry that drew directly on his relationships with his family and his personal problems with alcoholism and depression. Because it documented highly personal matters, this new work was commonly labelled as "confessional poetry," and it was highly influential with such younger writers as Anne Sexton and Sylvia Plath.

Skunk Hour

(For Elizabeth Bishop[1])

Nautilus Island's[2] hermit
heiress still lives through winter in her Spartan cottage;
her sheep still graze above the sea.
Her son's a bishop. Her farmer
5   is first selectman[3] in our village;
she's in her dotage.

Thirsting for
the hierarchic privacy
of Queen Victoria's century,
10   she buys up all
the eyesores facing her shore,
and lets them fall.

The season's ill—
we've lost our summer millionaire,
15   who seemed to leap from an L. L. Bean[4]
catalogue. His nine-knot yawl
was auctioned off to lobstermen.
A red fox stain covers Blue Hill.

And now our fairy
20   decorator brightens his shop for fall;
his fishnet's filled with orange cork,
orange, his cobbler's bench and awl;
there is no money in his work,
he'd rather marry.

---

[1]American poet (1911–1971). [2]a private island in Penobscot Bay, Maine. [3]an elected town official. [4]a famous Maine mail-order business specializing in sporting goods and clothing.

25 One dark night,
    my Tudor Ford climbed the hill's skull;
    I watched for love-cars. Lights turned down,
    they lay together, hull to hull,
    where the graveyard shelves on the town....
30 My mind's not right.

    A car radio bleats,
    "Love, O careless Love..."[5] I hear
    my ill-spirit sob in each blood cell,
    as if my hand were at its throat....
35 I myself am hell;
    nobody's here—

    only skunks, that search
    in the moonlight for a bite to eat.
    They march on their soles up Main Street:
40 white stripes, moonstruck eyes' red fire
    under the chalk-dry and spar spire
    of the Trinitarian Church.

    I stand on top
    of our back steps and breathe the rich air—
45 a mother skunk with her column of kittens swills the garbage
        pail.
    She jabs her wedge-head in a cup
    of sour cream, drops her ostrich tail,
    and will not scare.

(1959)

Al Purdy   (1918–2000)

Born in Wooler, Ontario, Alfred Purdy left school after Grade 10, riding freight trains to Vancouver, where he worked in a mattress factory and at other manual labour. Purdy published his first book in 1944 and won the Governor General's Award for *The Cariboo Horses* (1965). Much of his early poetry relies upon his experiences as a labourer and uses the voice of a "common person." Combining colloquial expressions, vulgarity, and poetic sentimentality, this conversational voice is frequently an effective vehicle for philosophic thought and social criticism because

---

[5]a traditional song often recorded, especially in blues and jazz versions.

it casts ideas into unexpected forms. Purdy travelled widely and wrote about his travels throughout Canada, including the Arctic, and such places as Cuba, Mexico, South America, Greece, and Japan. Nevertheless, he was quintessentially the poet of a single place, the area around his home of Ameliasburg, Ontario. Purdy conveys his love of Canada, of ordinary working people, and of tradition in these poems, which mingle past and present and thereby transform the area into a mythic landscape.

The Country North of Belleville

Bush land scrub land—
    Cashel Township and Wollaston
Elzevir McClure and Dungannon
green lands of Weslemkoon Lake
5 where a man might have some
        opinion of what beauty
is and none deny him
           for miles—

Yet this is the country of defeat
10 where Sisyphus[1] rolls a big stone
year after year up the ancient hills
picnicking glaciers have left strewn
with centuries' rubble
          backbreaking days
15   in the sun and rain
when realization seeps slow in the mind
without grandeur or self deception in
        noble struggle
of being a fool—

20 A country of quiescence and still distance
lean land
      not like the fat south
with inches of black soil on
      earth's round belly—
25 And where the farms are
      it's as if a man stuck
both thumbs in the stony earth and pulled

---

[1]king of Corinth whose punishment in Hades was to roll a heavy stone up a hill, only to have it roll down again when it neared the top.

it apart
to make room

30   enough between the trees
for a wife
            and maybe some cows and
            room for some
of the more easily kept illusions—
35   And where the farms have gone back
to forest
            are only soft outlines
            shadowy differences—

Old fences drift vaguely among the trees
40   a pile of moss-covered stones
gathered for some ghost purpose
has lost meaning under the meaningless sky
            —they are like cities under water
and the undulating green waves of time
45   are laid on them—

This is the country of our defeat
            and yet
during the fall plowing a man
might stop and stand in a brown valley of the furrows
50   and shade his eyes to watch for the same
            red patch mixed with gold
            that appears on the same
            spot in the hills
            year after year
55   and grow old
plowing and plowing a ten-acre field until
the convolutions run parallel with his own brain—

And this is a country where the young
            leave quickly
60   unwilling to know what their fathers know
or think the words their mothers do not say—

Herschel Monteagle and Faraday
lakeland rockland and hill country
a little adjacent to where the world is
65   a little north of where the cities are and
sometime

➙

we may go back there
                    to the country of our defeat
Wollaston Elzevir and Dungannon
70   and Weslemkoon lake land
where the high townships of Cashel
                    McClure and Marmora once were—
But it's been a long time since
and we must enquire the way
75   of strangers—

(1965)   (1972)

Lament for the Dorsets

(*Eskimos extinct in the 14th century A.D.*)[1]

Animal bones and some mossy tent rings
scrapers and spearheads   carved ivory swans
all that remains of the Dorset giants
who drove the Vikings back to their long ships
5   talked to spirits of earth and water
—a picture of terrifying old men
so large they broke the backs of bears
so small they lurk behind bone rafters
in the brain of modern hunters
10   among good thoughts and warm things
and come out at night
to spit on the stars

The big men with clever fingers
who had no dogs and hauled their sleds
15   over the frozen northern oceans
awkward giants
                    killers of seal
they couldn't compete with little men
who came from the west with dogs
20   Or else in a warm climatic cycle
the seals went back to cold waters
and the puzzled Dorsets scratched their heads

[1] in about A.D. 1000, the Dorset people were displaced from most of the Arctic regions by Thule Inuit from Alaska, but they continued to live in northern Quebec and Labrador until about A.D. 1500, when they disappeared.

with hairy thumbs around 1350 A.D.
—couldn't figure it out
25 went around saying to each other
plaintively
            "What's wrong? What happened?
            Where are the seals gone?"
And died

30 Twentieth-century people
apartment dwellers
executives of neon death
warmakers with things that explode
—they have never imagined us in their future
35 how could we imagine them in the past
squatting among the moving glaciers
six hundred years ago
with glowing lamps?
As remote or nearly
40 as the trilobites and swamps
when coal became
or the last great reptile hissed
at a mammal the size of a mouse
that squeaked and fled

45 Did they ever realize at all
what was happening to them?
Some old hunter with one lame leg
a bear had chewed
sitting in a caribou-skin tent
50 —the last Dorset?
Let's say his name was Kudluk
and watch him sitting there
carving 2-inch ivory swans
for a dead grand-daughter
55 taking them out of his mind
the places in his mind
where pictures are
He selects a sharp stone tool
to gouge a parallel pattern of lines
60 on both sides of the swan
holding it with his left hand

→

bearing down and transmitting
his body's weight
from brain to arm and right hand
65　and one of his thoughts
turns to ivory
The carving is laid aside
in beginning darkness
at the end of hunger
70　and after a while wind
blows down the tent and snow
begins to cover him

After 600 years
the ivory thought
75　is still warm

(1968)

Wilderness Gothic

Across Roblin Lake, two shores away,
they are sheathing the church spire
with new metal. Someone hangs in the sky
over there from a piece of rope,
5　hammering and fitting God's belly-scratcher,
working his way up along the spire
until there's nothing left to nail on—
Perhaps the workman's faith reaches beyond:
touches intangibles, wrestles with Jacob,[1]
10　replacing rotten timber with pine thews,
pounds hard in the blue cave of the sky,
contends heroically with difficult problems of
gravity, sky navigation and mythopeia,
his volunteer time and labour donated to God,
15　minus sick benefits of course on a non-union job—

Fields around are yellowing into harvest,
nestling and fingerling are sky and water borne,
death is yodelling quiet in green woodlots,

[1]Jacob wrestled with an angel, refusing to release him until the angel gave him a blessing; see
Genesis 32:24–29.

and bodies of three young birds have disappeared
20 in the sub-surface of the new county highway—
That picture is incomplete, part left out
that might alter the whole Dürer[2] landscape:
gothic ancestors peer from medieval sky,
dour faces trapped in photograph albums escaping
25 to clop down iron roads with matched greys:
work-sodden wives groping inside their flesh
for what keeps moving and changing and flashing
beyond and past the long frozen Victorian day.
A sign of fire and brimstone? A two-headed calf
30 born in the barn last night? A sharp female agony?
An age and a faith moving into transition,
the dinner cold and new-baked bread a failure,
deep woods shiver and water drops hang pendant,
double yolked eggs and the house creaks a little—
35 Something is about to happen. Leaves are still.
Two shores away, a man hammering in the sky.
Perhaps he will fall.

(1968)

Lawrence Ferlinghetti (1919)

Born in Yonkers, New York, Lawrence Ferlinghetti survived a precarious childhood: his father died before he was born, his mother was committed to an asylum shortly after his birth, he was sent to France in the care of a French aunt for five years, and then, following a stint in an American orphanage, he was eventually given over to the care of a wealthy couple. After serving in the navy during World War II, Ferlinghetti received an M.A. from Columbia University and a doctorate from the Sorbonne in Paris. Following his return to America and his marriage, he moved to San Francisco, where he was co-founder in 1952 of City Lights Books, the first all-paperback bookstore in the United States. Ferlinghetti soon expanded the business into an influential press publishing avant-garde poets. He became an important figure in the beat movement, which rejected conventional American society as corrupt, materialistic, and shallow, prizing, instead, states of personal beatitude. Although he has a learned background, Ferlinghetti is far from a bookish poet; he aims his poems, which are designed to be read aloud, at a broad audience.

[2]landscapes in many paintings and engravings by German artist Albrecht Dürer (1471–1528) are elaborate, often gloomy combinations of realistic details and visionary symbolism.

Constantly risking absurdity

Constantly risking absurdity
               and death
       whenever he performs
             above the heads
                    of his audience
   the poet like an acrobat
          climbs on rime
             to a high wire of his own making
and balancing on eyebeams
               above a sea of faces
       paces his way
           to the other side of day
   performing entrechats[1]
          and sleight-of-foot tricks
and other high theatrics
         and all without mistaking
     any thing
       for what it may not be

   For he's the super realist
            who must perforce perceive
    taut truth
        before the taking of each stance or step
  in his supposed advance
        toward that still higher perch
where Beauty stands and waits
       with gravity
         to start her death-defying leap

   And he
     a little charleychaplin[2] man
        who may or may not catch
     her fair eternal form
        spreadeagled in the empty air
    of existence

                    (1958)

---

[1] ballet leaps during which the legs are rapidly crossed before and behind each other.
[2] Charlie Chaplin (1889–1977) wrote, starred in, and directed numerous silent films; his most famous character, the kind-hearted Little Tramp, allowed Chaplin to display his considerable talents for acrobatic physical comedy.

Oodgeroo Noonuccal (Kath Walker)   (1920–1993)

The first prominent Aboriginal poet and protest writer in Australia, Kath Walker, who used her Aboriginal name, Oodgeroo Noonuccal, was born on Stradbroke Island, off the Queensland coast near Brisbane. At the age of thirteen, she began work as a domestic servant. When she was sixteen, she encountered a powerful example of official discrimination: because she was part Aboriginal, she was denied admission to nursing studies. A leading advocate of Aboriginal rights, she was involved in the campaign that led to the 1967 repeal of constitutional discrimination against Aborigines. The title of her first volume of poetry, *We Are Going* (1964), she has said, was "a warning to the white people: we can go out of existence, or with proper help we could also go on and live in this world in peace and harmony..." She has also said that her poems are "sloganistic, civil rightish, plain and simple." At their best, however, they are powerfully emotional presentations of the culture and history of the Aborigines; they clearly portray the abuses whites have inflicted, the dignity of Aborigines, and the value of an ancient way of life lived close to the land.

We Are Going

For Grannie Coolwell

They came in to the little town
A semi-naked band subdued and silent,
All that remained of their tribe.
They came here to the place of their old bora ground[1]
5   Where now the many white men hurry about like ants.
Notice of estate agent reads: "Rubbish May Be Tipped Here."
Now it half covers the traces of the old bora ring.
They sit and are confused, they cannot say their thoughts:
"We are as strangers here now, but the white tribe are the strangers.
10 We belong here, we are of the old ways.
We are the corroboree[2] and the bora ground,
We are the old sacred ceremonies, the laws of the elders.
We are the wonder tales of Dream Time,[3] the tribal legends told.

[1] the term *bora* is applied both to the most solemn of Aboriginal rites, in which a young boy is admitted to the rights of manhood, and to the site of the ceremony. The bora ground is usually called a bora ring because it is most often a circular earthen bank or an area marked off by a ring of stones. [2] Aboriginal dance ceremony, sometimes sacred and sometimes secular, involving singing and rhythmical musical accompaniment. [3] the time of mythic events; the time of the first ancestors or the time, beyond living memory, in which the physical, spiritual, and moral world was developed.

We are the past, the hunts and the laughing games, the wandering camp fires.
15 We are the lightning-bolt over Gaphembah Hill[4]
Quick and terrible,
And the Thunderer[5] after him, that loud fellow.
We are the quiet daybreak paling the dark lagoon.
We are the shadow-ghosts creeping back as the camp fires burn low.
We are nature and the past, all the old ways
20 Gone now and scattered.
The scrubs are gone, the hunting and the laughter.
The eagle is gone, the emu[6] and the kangaroo are gone from this place.
The bora ring is gone.
The corroboree is gone.
And we are going."

(1964)

Hone Tuwhare (1922–2008)

The most celebrated Maori poet writing in English, Hone Tuwhare spoke Maori for the first nine years of his life. Born into the Nga Puhi tribe in the northern New Zealand town of Kaikoke, he moved with his father to Aukland after the death of his mother. Although he did well in school, he lacked the money for more than a basic education and was apprenticed at the Otahuhu Railway Workshops. He became active in trade union movements and was a member of the Communist Party until the Soviet Union invaded Hungary in 1956. His first book of poems, *No Ordinary Sun* (1964), now considered to be one of the most important books in New Zealand's literary history, received wide acclaim. Following his success, Tuwhare became a prominent figure in the promotion of Maori political and cultural causes. In 1999 he was named the second Te Mata Poet Laureate. Although allusions to local geography and customs make some of his poems, especially later ones, difficult for those unfamiliar with the geography, history, and culture of New Zealand, many others are quite accessible: they reveal a sharp satirical edge, a deep passion for nature, a

[4]on Stradbroke Island, behind Myora Springs and near Moongalba, where the author, also known as Oodgeroo Noonuccal Moongalba, lived. [5]thunder; Aboriginal beliefs tend to be localized, rather than universal among the various tribes, and mythic figures, such as Thunderer, are often attached to specific sites or regions. [6]large, flightless bird that can run at a speed of approximately 50 kilometres per hour.

tendency to mix Maori words and colloquial English, and a commitment to the oral qualities of poetry.

To a Maori Figure Cast in Bronze Outside the Chief Post Office, Auckland

I hate being stuck up here, glaciated, hard all over
and with my guts removed: my old lady is not going
to like it

I've seen more efficient scarecrows in seedbed
5   nurseries. Hell, I can't even shoo the pigeons off

Me: all hollow inside with longing for the marae[1] on
the cliff at Kohimarama,[2] where you can watch the ships
come in curling their white moustaches

Why didn't they stick me next to Mickey Savage?[3]
10   'Now then,' he was a good bloke
Maybe it was a Tory City Council that put me here

They never consulted me about naming the square
It's a wonder they never called it: Hori-in-gorge-at-
bottom-of-hill. Because it is like that: a gorge,
15   with the sun blocked out, the wind whistling around
your balls (your balls mate) And at night, how I
feel for the beatle-girls with their long-haired
boyfriends licking their frozen finger-chippy lips
hopefully. And me again beetling

20   my tent eyebrows forever, like a brass monkey with
real worries: I mean, how the hell can you welcome
the Overseas Dollar, if you can't open your mouth
to poke your tongue out, eh?

If I could only move from this bloody pedestal I'd
25   show the long-hairs how to knock out a tune on the

[1]a cleared and clearly demarcated sacred area used for both religious and social purposes.
[2]a residential area of Aukland overlooking the harbour. [3]Michael Joseph Savage
(1872–1940), New Zealand's first Labour Prime Minister, is buried in a clifftop mausoleum at
Bastion Point, Aukland, overlooking the Waitemata Harbour.

souped-up guitar, my mere quivering, my taiaha[4] held
at the high port. And I'd fix the ripe kotiro[5] too
with their mini-piupiu-ed[6] bums twinkling: yeah!

Somebody give me a drink: I can't stand it

(1972)

Deep River Talk

It's cold: it's golden; a magnificent
orange disc playing peek-a-boo
from the far-side of straggly
strings of leafless rastafarian willows
growing on the other side of the river.
The river's wide here: it's

undecided: it's steeling itself
never to turn and go back uphill.
Steam's rising from it and it's
not the early morning sun that's
doin' it; I can't raise heat
from the sun yet.

The veins of the river are swollen.
They're bending to the tide's
up-swing: tempers are like sails
shredding in a gale.

There's talk of a merger. A know-all
insect on stilts has just walked out
on top of the waters to supervise
the talks; I suppose pretending
to be Jesus.
In the sunlight mullet are jumpin'
and making lovin' archways of silver
for the migratory ocean-seeking eels
eeling their way down down; down
to the river-mouth and away.

[4]a traditional long wooden weapon used in close combat to stab or strike an opponent. [5]girls.
[6]flax skirt; traditionally, Maori women wore long ones, whereas men wore shorter ones.

The river's pushy, 'Back off! Thus far
and NO further –'

30 'I'll see YOU outside, mate,' says
the sea, turning. A swish, a tiny
whip and swirl of water –

Snap!

Daddy-long-legs has joined his
ancestors by way of a hungry trout's
35 stomach & stomach-ejector.

Happens to people too, nowadays–with
sharks hangin' around a lot.

(1993)

Anthony Hecht   (1923–2004)

Anthony Hecht was born in New York City, and although he produced a relatively small body of work, he earned numerous awards. Hecht studied at Bard College, receiving his degree in 1944 in absentia because he was serving overseas with the military during World War II. When he returned to the United States, he studied at Kenyon College (working with the poet John Crowe Ransom) and Columbia University, from which he received an M.A. in 1950. During his career, Hecht taught at Bard College, the University of Rochester, and Georgetown University. His first poetry collection, *A Summoning of Stones* (1950), set the tone for his later works by establishing him as a traditionalist in his use of language and form, but also by revealing him to be an erudite and frequently witty poet. His stinging wit is evident in his most popular poem, "The Dover Bitch," an accomplished parody of Matthew Arnold's "Dover Beach."

The Dover Bitch

A Criticism of Life
for Andrews Wanning

So there stood Matthew Arnold and this girl
With the cliffs of England crumbling away behind them,
And he said to her, "Try to be true to me,
And I'll do the same for you, for things are bad

→

5   All over, etc., etc."
     Well now, I knew this girl. It's true she had read
     Sophocles in a fairly good translation
     And caught that bitter allusion to the sea,
     But all the time he was talking she had in mind
10   The notion of what his whiskers would feel like
     On the back of her neck. She told me later on
     That after a while she got to looking out
     At the lights across the channel, and really felt sad,
     Thinking of all the wine and enormous beds
15   And blandishments in French and the perfumes.
     And then she got really angry. To have been brought
     All the way down from London, and then be addressed
     As a sort of mournful cosmic last resort
     Is really tough on a girl, and she was pretty.
20   Anyway, she watched him pace the room
     And finger his watch-chain and seem to sweat a bit,
     And then she said one or two unprintable things.
     But you mustn't judge her by that. What I mean to say is,
     She's really all right. I still see her once in a while
25   And she always treats me right. We have a drink
     And I give her a good time, and perhaps it's a year
     Before I see her again, but there she is,
     Running to fat, but dependable as they come.
     And sometimes I bring her a bottle of *Nuit d' Amour.*

                                                        (1968)

Dennis Brutus   (1924–2009)

Born in Salisbury, Rhodesia (now Harare, Zimbabwe), Brutus was raised in
Port Elizabeth, South Africa. He earned degrees from the University of
Fort Hare and the University of the Witwatersrand. Brutus first came to
prominence for leading a campaign against apartheid in sports that
eventually saw South Africa suspended from the 1964 and 1968 Olympic
Games and expelled from the Olympic movement in 1970. Because of his
activism, Brutus was banned from meeting more than two non-family
members at any time. Arrested for breaking the ban, he fled to
Mozambique, but was returned to South Africa, where he was shot while
trying to escape custody. He was then sentenced to sixteen months
imprisonment on Robben Island, where he occupied a cell next to Nelson

Mandela. Upon his release, Brutus left South Africa, going to Britain and then the United States, where he taught at several universities. When the ban against him was removed in 1990, he returned to teach in South Africa. A champion of racial rights throughout his life, Brutus wrote poetry that movingly revealed the plight of the victims of South Africa's notorious apartheid regime.

Nightsong: City

Sleep well, my love, sleep well:
the harbour lights glaze over restless docks,
police cars cockroach through the tunnel streets;

from the shanties creaking iron-sheets
5   violence like a bug-infested rag is tossed
and fear is immanent as sound in the wind-swung
        bell;

the long day's anger pants from sand and rocks;
but for this breathing night at least,
10 my land, my love, sleep well.

(1963)

Letters to Martha 18

I remember rising one night
after midnight
and moving
through an impulse of loneliness
5   to try and find the stars.

And through the haze
the battens of fluorescents made
I saw pinpricks of white
I thought were stars.

10 Greatly daring
I thrust my arm through the bars
and easing the switch in the corridor
plunged my cell in darkness

I scampered to the window
15 and saw the splashes of light
where the stars flowered.

But through my delight
thudded the anxious boots
and a warning barked
20 from the machine-gun post
on the catwalk.

And it is the brusque inquiry
and threat
that I remember of that night
25 rather than the stars.
            [20 December 1965]

                                                (1968)

Robert Creeley   (1926–2005)

Born in Massachusetts, Robert Creeley lived in various regions of the
United States, as well as Central America, East Asia, and Europe. Creeley
taught briefly at Black Mountain College and became a leader of the
poetic movement associated with that school. Influenced by William
Carlos Williams and the Black Mountain poets, he concentrated on
recording the actual details of experience, rather than supplying organized analyses of experience. Creeley accepted Charles Olson's dictum that
"form is never more than an extension of content," but his own poetry is
generally more formal than that of the other leading poets of the Black
Mountain group.

The Rhythm

It is all a rhythm,
from the shutting
door, to the window
opening,

5   the seasons, the sun's
light, the moon,
the oceans, the
growing of things,

the mind in men
10 personal, recurring
in them again,
thinking the end

is not the end, the
time returning,
15 themselves dead but
someone else coming.

If in death I am dead,
then in life also
dying, dying ...
20 And the women cry and die.

The little children
grow only to old men.
The grass dries,
the force goes.

25 But is met by another
returning, oh not mine,
not mine, and
in turn dies.

The rhythm which projects
30 from itself continuity
bending all to its force
from window to door,
from ceiling to floor,
light at the opening,
35 dark at the closing.

(1967)

James K. Baxter (1926–1972)

James K. Baxter was born in Dunedin, New Zealand, and had a varied career. Educated at the University of Otago, Wellington Teacher's College, and the University of Victoria, he was employed at various times as a labourer, postman, teacher, drug counsellor, journalist, and editor. Waging a life-long battle with alcoholism, Baxter found spiritual solace in his conversion to Roman Catholicism. In 1968, he had a dream that told him to "Go to Jerusalem," so he moved to a small Maori village by that name. The rigorous conditions under which he lived there eventually affected his health, and he died at the age of 46. Baxter was a prolific writer, publishing his first collection of poems when he was only eighteen and producing more than thirty books before his death. Always a craftsman, he gradually moved away from the regular rhythm and rhyme of his early lyrics to concentrate on compact two-line structures. He was also a poet of ideas, criticizing social abuses and political duplicity, celebrating traditional Maori culture, attacking the modern materialism that threatened that traditional life, and offering fervent testimonies to the power of religious faith.

Wild Bees

Often in summer, on a tarred bridge plank standing,
Or downstream between willows, a safe Ophelia[1] drifting
In a rented boat—I had seen them come and go,
Those wild bees swift as tigers, their gauze wings a-glitter
5   In passionless industry, clustering black at the crevice
Of a rotten cabbage tree, where their hive was hidden low.

But never strolled too near. Till one half-cloudy evening
Of ripe January, my friends and I
Came, gloved and masked to the eyes like plundering
          desperadoes,
10   To smoke them out. Quiet beside the stagnant river
We trod wet grasses down, hearing the crickets chitter
And waiting for light to drain from the wounded sky.

Before we reached the hive their sentries saw us
And sprang invisible through the darkening air,
15   Stabbed, and died in stinging. The hive woke. Poisonous fuming
Of sulphur filled the hollow trunk, and crawling
Blue flame sputtered—yet still their suicidal
Live raiders dived and clung to our hands and hair.

O it was Carthage under the Roman torches,
20   Or loud with flames and falling timber, Troy![2]
A job well botched. Half of the honey melted
And half the rest young grubs. Through earth-black
          smouldering ashes
And maimed bees groaning, we drew out our plunder.

[1]in Shakespeare's *Hamlet*, Ophelia, having gone mad, drowns while drifting down a river.
[2]the Romans destroyed Carthage by fire in 146 B.C.; the Greeks burned Troy at the conclusion of the Trojan War.

Little enough their gold, and slight our joy.

25 Fallen then the city of instinctive wisdom.
Tragedy is written distinct and small:
A hive burned on a cool night in summer.
But loss is a precious stone to me, a nectar
Distilled in time, preaching the truth of winter
30 To the fallen heart that does not cease to fall.

(1953)

The Ikons

Hard, heavy, slow, dark,
Or so I find them, the hands of Te Whaea[1]

Teaching me to die. Some lightness will come later
When the heart has lost its unjust hope

5 For special treatment. Today I go with a bucket
Over the paddocks of young grass,

So delicate like fronds of maidenhair,
Looking for mushrooms. I find twelve of them,

Most of them little, and some eaten by maggots,
10 But they'll do to add to the soup. It's a long time now

Since the great ikons fell down,
God, Mary, home, sex, poetry,

Whatever one uses as a bridge
To cross the river that only has one beach,

15 And even one's name is a way of saying—
'This gap inside a coat'—the darkness I call God,

The darkness I call Te Whaea, how can they translate
The blue calm evening sky that a plane tunnels through

Like a little wasp, or the bucket in my hand,
20 Into something else? I go on looking

For mushrooms in the field, and the fist of longing
Punches my heart, until it is too dark to see.

(1971)

[1]Maori words meaning "The Mother."

Allen Ginsberg   (1926–1997)

Part of the beat movement of the 1950s, Allen Ginsberg became a controversial figure at the forefront of various protest movements in the 1960s. Ginsberg grew up in Paterson, New Jersey, and received a B.A. from Columbia University, where he wrote poems based on traditional models. He soon rebelled against both poetic convention and the staid norms of post-war America. His long poem "Howl," published by Lawrence Ferlinghetti, survived charges of obscenity to become the best-selling poem of the decade. Ginsberg's poetry is characterized by long declamatory lines of free verse, rhetorically charged diction, and a blend of social commentary and self-revelation.

A Supermarket in California

What thoughts I have of you tonight, Walt Whitman,[1] for I walked down the sidestreets under the trees with a headache self-conscious looking at the full moon.

In my hungry fatigue, and shopping for images, I went into the neon fruit supermarket, dreaming of your enumerations!

What peaches and what penumbras! Whole families shopping at night! Aisles full of husbands! Wives in the avocados, babies in the tomatoes!— and you, García Lorca,[2] what were you doing down by the watermelons?

I saw you, Walt Whitman, childless, lonely old grubber, poking among the meats in the refrigerator and eyeing the grocery boys.

I heard you asking questions of each: Who killed the pork chops? What price bananas? Are you my Angel?

I wandered in and out of the brilliant stacks of cans following you, and followed in my imagination by the store detective.

We strode down the open corridors together in our solitary fancy tasting artichokes, possessing every frozen delicacy, and never passing the cashier.

Where are we going, Walt Whitman? The doors close in an hour. Which way does your beard point tonight?

(I touch your book and dream of our odyssey in the supermarket and feel absurd.)

Will we walk all night through solitary streets? The trees add shade to shade, lights out in the houses, we'll both be lonely.

[1]American poet Walt Whitman (1819–1892) experimented with free verse, influencing many twentieth-century poets, including Ginsberg, who in this poem also identifies with Whitman's homosexuality. [2]Spanish poet and dramatist (1899–1936) who wrote an "Ode to Walt Whitman."

Will we stroll dreaming of the lost America of love past blue automo-
biles in driveways, home to our silent cottage?

Ah, dear father, graybeard, lonely old courage-teacher, what America
did you have when Charon quit poling his ferry and you got out on a
smoking bank and stood watching the boat disappear on the black waters
of Lethe?[3]

(Berkeley, 1955) (1956)

Phyllis Webb (b. 1927)

Born in Victoria, B.C., Phyllis Webb received her B.A. from the University
of British Columbia and studied briefly at McGill. She has taught at UBC
and the University of Victoria and was writer in residence at the
University of Alberta. She has also been a producer for the Canadian
Broadcasting Corporation. Her first book of poetry was *Trio* (1954), which
also featured the work of two other poets. *The Vision Tree: Selected
Poems* (1982) won the Governor General's Award. An intellectual with an
often bleak vision of the world, Webb develops ideas carefully through
complex structures and careful arrangements of sounds, creating what
she calls "the dance of the intellect in the syllables."

Marvell's Garden[1]

Marvell's garden, that place of solitude,
is not where I'd choose to live
yet is the fixed sundial
that turns me round
unwillingly
in a hot glade
as closer, closer I come to contradiction
to the shade green within the green shade.[2]

The garden where Marvell scorned love's solicitude—
that dream—and played instead an arcane solitaire,

---

[3]in Greek mythology, the dead drank the waters of Lethe, the river of forgetfulness, before
Charon ferried them across the river Styx to the underworld. [1]see Andrew Marvell's "The
Garden" (page 63), in which a garden symbolizes the solitary contemplative life. [2]in "The
Garden," Marvell speaks of "a green thought in a green shade" (line 48). Green symbolizes a
cool detachment from human concerns.

shuffling his thoughts like shadowy chance
across the shrubs of ecstasy,
and cast the myths away to flowering hours[3]
as yes, his mind, that sea,[4] caught at green
thoughts shadowing a green infinity.

And yet Marvell's garden was not Plato's[5]
garden—and yet—he did care more for the form
of things than for the thing itself—
ideas and visions,
resemblances and echoes,
things seeming and being
not quite what they were.

That was his garden, a kind of attitude
struck out of an earth too carefully attended,
wanting to be left alone.
And I don't blame him for that.
God knows, too many fences fence us out
and his garden closed in on Paradise.[6]

On Paradise! When I think of his hymning
Puritans in the Bermudas, the bright oranges
lighting up that night![7] When I recall
his rustling tinsel hopes
beneath the cold decree of steel,
Oh, I have wept for some new convulsion
to tear together this world and his.[8]
But then I saw his luminous plumèd Wings
prepared for flight,

---

[3]the fourth stanza of "The Garden" recounts the stories of Daphne and Syrinx, maidens
who escaped seduction when they were transformed into, respectively, a laurel and a reed.
[4]Marvell's poem (lines 43–44) refers to the mind as an ocean because, like the ocean, which
was thought to contain a form of everything on land, the mind contains a resemblance of
everything on earth. [5]Plato argued that any earthly thing was but a pale reflection or shadow
of the ideal form or idea of that thing. [6]Marvell compared his garden, a solitary place—and
thus free from sexual passion—to Eden before the creation of Eve: "Two paradises 'twere in one,
To live in paradise alone" (lines 63–64). [7]in "Bermudas" (1681), Marvell wrote of Puritans
seeking refuge from English bishops in a land "far kinder than our own." In praising God, who
gave the Puritans such a beautiful refuge, he says God "hangs in shades the orange bright, / Like
golden lamps in a green night." [8]in "The Definition of Love" (1681), a poem about a lover's
despair because he can never consummate his love, Marvell speaks of "feeble hope," which
"vainly flapped its tinsel wing." Fate's "decrees of steel" separate the lovers as if they were the
poles of the earth. He declares that they will remain apart "Unless the giddy heaven fall, / And
earth some new convulsion tear," joining the lovers by flattening the globe.

and then I heard him singing glory
in a green tree,
40   and then I caught the vest he'd laid aside
all blest with fire.[9]

And I have gone walking slowly in
his garden of necessity
leaving brothers, lovers, Christ
45   outside my walls
where they have wept without
and I within.

(1956)

Treblinka[1] Gas Chamber

Klostermayer ordered another count of the children.
Then their stars were snipped off and thrown into
the center of the courtyard. It looked like a field of
buttercups.
　　　　　—Joseph Hyams, *A Field of Buttercups*

fallingstars
　　　　　　"a field of
　　　　　　　　　buttercups"

　　　　　　yellow stars
5　　　　　　　　　　of David
　　　　　　　　　　　　falling

the prisoners
　　　　　　　the children
　　　　　　　　　　falling

10　　　　　　　in heaps
　　　　　　　　　on one another
　　　　　　　　　　　　they go down

Thanatos[2]
　　　　　showers
15　　　　　　　his dirty breath
　　　　　　　　　they must breathe
　　　　　　　　　　　　him in

➡

[9]in the seventh stanza of "The Garden," Marvell speaks of his soul casting off "the body's vest" to fly like a bird into the trees. [1]extermination camp in Poland where the Nazis gassed thousands of Jews during World War II. [2]the ancient Greek personification of Death.

they see stars

behind their

eyes

20

David's

"a field of

buttercups"

a metaphor

25

where all that's

left lies down

(1980)

Jayanta Mahapatra   (b. 1928)

Born in Cuttack, in the eastern Indian state of Orissa, Jayanta Mahapatra
came to writing poetry relatively late in life, but he became an influential figure in English poetry in India. For most of his life, he taught physics
at various schools in Orissa state, retiring from Ravenshaw College in
1986. He began writing poetry when he was nearly forty, publishing his
first book in 1971. He is often cited as one of the three main figures in
the development of English poetry in India, and in 1981 he became the
first Indian English poet to receive the Sahitya Akademi Award. In 2009,
the government of India presented him with its highest civilian award,
the Padmashree Award, for his contributions to literature. In an interview, he said of his poems, "Main source of inspiration: my land, my
people, my place, what I see, what social injustice I see, and political injustice." Living in one of the poorest areas of India, Mahapatra expresses his
vision in poems that are often bleak and sometimes bitter.

The Abandoned British Cemetery
at Balasore[1]

This is history.
I would not disturb it: the ruins of stone and marble,
the crumbling wall of brick, the coma of alienated decay.
How exactly should the archaic dead make me behave?

---

[1]Balasore, known also as Baleshwar, is a city in the state of Orissa that was a strategic military
base during colonial times.

5   A hundred and fifty years ago
I might have lived. Now nothing offends my ways.
A quietness of bramble and grass holds me to a weed.
Will it matter if I know who the victims were, who survived?

And yet, awed by the forgotten dead,
10   I walk around them: thirty-nine graves, their legends
floating in a twilight of baleful littoral,
the flaking history my intrusion does not animate.

Awkward in the silence, a scrawny lizard
watches the drama with its shrewd, hooded gaze.
15   And a scorpion, its sting drooping,
two eerie arms spread upon the marble, over an alien name.

In the circle the epitaphs run: Forence R . . . , darling wife
of Captain R . . . R . . . , aged nineteen, of cholera. . .
Helen, beloved daughter of Mr. & Mrs. . . . , of cholera,
20   aged seventeen, in the year of our Lord, eighteen hundred. . .

Of what concern to me is a vanished empire?
Or the conquest of my ancestors' timeless ennui?
It is the dying young who have the power to show
what the heart will hide, the grass shows no more.

25   Who watches now in the dark near the dead wall?
The tribe of grass in the cracks of my eyes?
It is the cholera still, death's sickly trickle,
that plagues the sleepy shacks beyond this hump of earth,

moving easily, swiftly, with quick power
30   through both past and present, the increasing young,
into the final bone, wearying all truth with ruin.
This is the iron

rusting in the vanquished country, the blood's unease,
the useless rain upon my familiar window;
35   the tired triumphant smile left behind by the dead
on a discarded anchor half-sunk in mud beside the graves:

out there on the earth's unwavering gravity
where it waits like a deity perhaps
for the elaborate ceremonial of a coming generation
40   to keep history awake, stifle the survivor's issuing cry.

(1980)

Total Solar Eclipse
(*Puri*[1], *February 16, 1980*)

It was the drawn-out cry of day
that left behind no echo,
day that became meek as a frightened child.
A banner of pale human skin
5   fluttered on top of the temple of Jagannath.

From the maze of alleys
that lead down to the giant temple street
the souls of simple men
groaned in the harsh voices of ash,
10 afraid to reveal their bodies,
peering here and there like hunted dogs.

Above was the pallid face of a corpse,
the wretched bowel of time:
emerging from the dark caves of space
15 the wind, the obsession, the nightmare,
to affirm what only these men would let come
through precious paschal fast, dire superstition.

Quietly the moon's dark well moves on,
against the stone pillars, the disturbed blood,
20 the dust, the pigments and embers, the clear ash,
against the lonely foetus of Puri.

The cobra slides along the waiting hill
with its unveiled peril,
the hyena sniffs at the sudden cool air
25 and lets out a despairing wail,
bewildered by this new image of night.

Slowly the vultures turn away
from the still-warm belly of the sky,
recognising the silence of the black wind
30 whose throat drips horizons of fire.
Sparrows converge upon the palpitating gulmohar,[2]
leaves already seamed for sleep.

---

[1]a coastal city in the state of Orissa, and site of the Jagannath Temple, which was built in the eleventh century and is dedicated to worship of Lord Jagannath, a Hindu deity who is a form of Vishnu. [2]a flowering plant with bright-green fern-like leaves and vividly coloured flowers.

And cautiously the crocodile
pushes its long snout from the deep water
35   like the fearsome Brahmin[3] priest in the temple,
secure by shadowy layers of sleep,
so out of date, in alleviative belief,
using darkness to be a portent of the gods
who had just revealed a last occasion
40   to hide the disrobing of human values
by a rabid civilization.

(1983)

Adrienne Rich   (b. 1929)

Born in Baltimore, Adrienne Rich achieved recognition with her first book of poetry, *A Change of World* (1951). Published in the same year that she graduated Phi Beta Kappa from Radcliffe College, this winner of the prestigious Yale Younger Poets Award is impressive in its formal control and development of contextual symbols. After marrying in 1953, Rich had what she has described as "a radicalizing experience," giving birth to three children within four years. With the publication of her third book, *Snapshots of a Daughter-in-Law* (1963), this new radicalism manifested itself in intensive meditations on the divisions between the traditional representations of women's lives and their actual experiences. Change, and controlling that change, then became one of her central concerns. Poetically, she began to move away from closed forms to open structures that allow for the varied rhythms of an individual voice and the more overt expression of emotions. In the public sphere, she became actively involved in promoting change, supporting such causes as the protest against the Vietnam War and various feminist movements. Because she explored what it means to write "directly and overtly as a woman, out of a woman's body and experience," she has had a particularly profound influence on lesbian and feminist movements. One of the most distinguished poets of the last half century, Rich continues to explore and reinterpret the linkages between language, sexuality, and the politics of power, making her poetry both a chronicle of her personal changes and a compelling invitation to direct our own psychological, social, and political changes.

Aunt Jennifer's Tigers

Aunt Jennifer's tigers prance across a screen,
Bright topaz denizens of a world of green.

---

[3]a member of the highest caste, the caste of scholars and priests.

They do not fear the men beneath the tree;
They pace in sleek chivalric certainty.

5 Aunt Jennifer's fingers fluttering through her wool
Find even the ivory needle hard to pull.
The massive weight of Uncle's wedding band
Sits heavily upon Aunt Jennifer's hand.

When Aunt is dead, her terrified hands will lie
10 Still ringed with ordeals she was mastered by.
The tigers in the panel that she made
Will go on prancing, proud and unafraid.

(1951)

A Woman Mourned by Daughters

Now, not a tear begun,
we sit here in your kitchen,
spent, you see, already.
You are swollen till you strain
5 this house and the whole sky.
You, whom we so often
succeeded in ignoring!
You are puffed up in death
like a corpse pulled from the sea;
10 we groan beneath your weight.
And yet you were a leaf,
a straw blown on the bed,
you had long since become
crisp as a dead insect.
15 What is it, if not you,
that settles on us now
like satin you pulled down
over our bridal heads?
What rises in our throats
20 like food you prodded in?
Nothing could be enough.
You breathe upon us now
through solid assertions
of yourself: teaspoons, goblets,
25 seas of carpet, a forest
of old plants to be watered,

→

an old man in an adjoining
room to be touched and fed.
And all this universe
30   dares us to lay a finger
anywhere, save exactly
as you would wish it done.

(1963)

Diving into the Wreck

First having read the book of myths,
and loaded the camera,
and checked the edge of the knife-blade,
I put on
5   the body-armor of black rubber
the absurd flippers
the grave and awkward mask.
I am having to do this
not like Cousteau[1] with his
10   assiduous team
aboard the sun-flooded schooner
but here alone.
There is a ladder.
The ladder is always there
15   hanging innocently
close to the side of the schooner.
We know what it is for,
we who have used it.
Otherwise
20   it's a piece of maritime floss
some sundry equipment.

I go down.
Rung after rung and still
the oxygen immerses me
25   the blue light
the clear atoms
of our human air.
I go down.
My flippers cripple me,

➡

[1]Jacques Cousteau (1910–1997), French author, filmmaker, and underwater explorer.

30 I crawl like an insect down the ladder
and there is no one
to tell me when the ocean
will begin.

First the air is blue and then
35 it is bluer and then green and then
black I am blacking out and yet
my mask is powerful
it pumps my blood with power
the sea is another story
40 the sea is not a question of power
I have to learn alone
to turn my body without force
in the deep element.

And now: it is easy to forget
45 what I came for
among so many who have always
lived here
swaying their crenellated fans
between the reefs
50 and besides
you breathe differently down here.

I came to explore the wreck.
The words are purposes.
The words are maps.
55 I came to see the damage that was done
and the treasures that prevail.
I stroke the beam of my lamp
slowly along the flank
of something more permanent
60 than fish or weed.

the thing I came for:
the wreck and not the story of the wreck
the thing itself and not the myth
the drowned face always staring
65 toward the sun
the evidence of damage
worn by salt and sway into this threadbare beauty
the ribs of the disaster
curving their assertion
70 among the tentative haunters.

This is the place.
And I am here, the mermaid whose dark hair
streams black, the merman in his armored body
We circle silently
75   about the wreck
we dive into the hold.
I am she: I am he

whose drowned face sleeps with open eyes
whose breasts still bear the stress
80   whose silver, copper, vermeil cargo lies
obscurely inside barrels
half-wedged and left to rot
we are the half-destroyed instruments
that once held to a course
85   the water-eaten log
the fouled compass

We are, I am, you are
by cowardice or courage
the one who find our way
90   back to this scene
carrying a knife, a camera
a book of myths
in which
our names do not appear.

(1973)

Derek Walcott   (b. 1930)

Recipient of the Nobel Prize for literature in 1992, Derek Walcott was born in Castries on the Caribbean island of St. Lucia. He proved to be a precocious writer, publishing his first collection of poems when he was only eighteen and seeing his first play produced when he was just twenty. After he graduated from the University College of the West Indies, Jamaica, in 1953, Walcott moved to Trinidad, where he worked full-time as a writer, art critic, and theatre director. He took up a position as a professor of creative writing at Boston University in 1981. In poems characterized by wit, passion, and learning, Walcott presents the Caribbean as a region in which the landscape and the memories it triggers keep alive a history of oppression. At the same time, as a person whose education has taught him to value European culture and whose own ancestry is racially mixed (see the final note to "A Far Cry from Africa"), he expresses deeply divided feelings about the conflicts between colonialists and native populations.

A Far Cry from Africa

A wind is ruffling the tawny pelt
Of Africa. Kikuyu,[1] quick as flies,
Batten upon the bloodstreams of the veldt.[2]
Corpses are scattered through a paradise.
5 Only the worm, colonel of carrion, cries:
"Waste no compassion on these separate dead!"
Statistics justify and scholars seize
The salients of colonial policy.
What is that to the white child hacked in bed?
10 To savages, expendable as Jews?

Threshed out by beaters,[3] the long rushes break
In a white dust of ibises[4] whose cries
Have wheeled since civilization's dawn
From the parched river or beast-teeming plain.
15 The violence of beast on beast is read
As natural law, but upright man
Seeks his divinity by inflicting pain.
Delirious as these worried beasts, his wars
Dance to the tightened carcass of a drum,
20 While he calls courage still that native dread
Of the white peace contracted by the dead.
Again brutish necessity wipes its hands
Upon the napkin of a dirty cause, again
A waste of our compassion, as with Spain,[5]
25 The gorilla wrestles with the superman.
I who am poisoned with the blood of both,[6]
Where shall I turn, divided to the vein?

I who have cursed
The drunken officer of British rule, how choose
30 Between this Africa and the English tongue I love
Betray them both, or give back what they give?

[1]tribe from the highlands of south-central Kenya whose members formed the Mau Mau, a secret
revolutionary organization that employed terrorist activities in order to drive out British colonialists. [2]open country covered with grass and bushes, but having few trees. [3]natives hired to drive
game birds and animals from cover. [4]wading birds notable for their long, downward-curving
bills. [5]in the Spanish Civil War (1936–39), the Loyalists, supported by liberal intellectuals and
Soviet Communists, were defeated by the insurgents of Generalissimo Francisco Franco
(1892–1975), who were supported by Nazi Germany and Fascist Italy. [6]Walcott is of mixed
ancestry: both of his grandfathers were white, and both of his grandmothers were black.

How can I face such slaughter and be cool?
How can I turn from Africa and live?

(1962)

Ruins of a Great House[1]

though our longest sun sets at right declensions and
makes but winter arches, it cannot be long before we
lie down in darkness, and have our light in ashes …
                    —Browne, Urn Burial[2]

Stones only, the disjecta membra[3] of this Great House,
Whose moth-like girls are mixed with candledust,
Remain to file the lizard's dragonish claws.
The mouths of those gate cherubs shriek with stain;
5   Axle and coach wheel silted under the muck
Of cattle droppings.
                    Three crows flap for the trees
And settle, creaking the eucalyptus boughs.
A smell of dead limes quickens in the nose
The leprosy of empire.
10   "Farewell, green fields,
                    Farewell, ye happy groves!"
Marble like Greece, like Faulkner's[4] South in stone,

Deciduous beauty prospered and is gone,
But where the lawn breaks in a rash of trees
15   A spade below dead leaves will ring the bone
Of some dead animal or human thing
Fallen from evil days, from evil times.

It seems that the original crops were limes
Grown in the silt that clogs the river's skirt;
20   The imperious rakes are gone, their bright girls gone,
The river flows, obliterating hurt.

[1]the main house on a plantation, usually the residence of the owner or manager.
[2]*Hydriotaphia, Urne-Buriall* (1658) is a meditation on death and burial practices that
Sir Thomas Browne (1605–1682), an English physician, wrote after viewing old funeral
urns excavated in Norwich. [3]scattered limbs or parts; from "disjecti membra poetae,"
"the scattered limbs of the poet"(*Satires* of Horace). [4]William Faulkner (1897–1962), an
American novelist and winner of the Nobel Prize for literature (1949), wrote about the
collapse of the aristocratic South and the guilt its slave-holding culture bequeathed to
future generations.

I climbed a wall with the grille ironwork
Of exiled craftsmen protecting that great house
From guilt, perhaps, but not from the worm's rent
25   Nor from the padded cavalry of the mouse.
And when a wind shook in the limes I heard
What Kipling[5] heard, the death of a great empire, the abuse
Of ignorance by Bible and by sword.

A green lawn, broken by low walls of stone,
30   Dipped to the rivulet, and pacing, I thought next
Of men like Hawkins, Walter Raleigh, Drake,[6]
Ancestral murderers and poets, more perplexed
In memory now by every ulcerous crime.
The world's green age then was a rotting lime
35   Whose stench became the charnel galleon's text.
The rot remains with us, the men are gone.
But, as dead ash is lifted in a wind
That fans the blackening ember of the mind,
My eyes burned from the ashen prose of Donne.[7]
40   Ablaze with rage I thought,
Some slave is rotting in this manorial lake,
But still the coal of my compassion fought
That Albion too was once
A colony like ours, "part of the continent, piece of the main,"
45   Nook-shotten, rook o'erblown, deranged
By foaming channels and the vain expense
Of bitter faction.

        All in compassion ends
So differently from what the heart arranged:
"as well as if a manor of thy friend's ..."

                      (1962)

[5]Rudyard Kipling (1865–1936), an Indian-born English author, was famous for the imperialistic sentiments he expressed in many of his works. [6]Sir John Hawkins (1532–1595), Sir Walter Raleigh (1552–1618), and Sir Francis Drake (c. 1540–1596) were English explorers and adventurers, who sailed to the West Indies. [7]John Donne (1572–1631), English metaphysical poet and clergyman; phrases from a famous passage in "Meditation XVII" of his *Devotions upon Emergent Occasions* (1624) are quoted, somewhat incorrectly, in lines 44 and 49: "No man is an island, entire of itself; every man is a piece of the continent, a part of the main. If a clod be washed away by the sea, Europe is the less, as well as if a promontory were, as well as if a manor of thy friend's or thine own were."

Ted Hughes   (1930–1998)

Born in the small Yorkshire town of Mytholmroyd, Hughes received B.A. and M.A. degrees from Cambridge. His first wife was the American poet Sylvia Plath. Hughes, who was appointed England's Poet Laureate in 1984, achieved critical respect with his very first volume of poems, *The Hawk in the Rain* (1957), which introduced one of his dominant subjects, animal life. Although some critics contend that Hughes celebrates raw power and brutality in his animal poems, even accusing him of presenting the figure of a fascist in "Hawk Roosting," Hughes contends that he is presenting "Nature thinking. Simply Nature." Hughes says: "What excites my imagination is the war between vitality and death, and my poems may be said to celebrate the exploits of the warriors of either side." For him, animals combine "the arrogance of blood and bone" with "an energy too strong for death." Hughes compares his poetic technique to that of a composer. He says that he turns each of his combatants "into a bit of music" and then resolves "the whole uproar into as formal and balanced a figure of melody and rhythm as I can."

Pike

Pike, three inches long, perfect
Pike in all parts, green tigering the gold.
Killers from the egg: the malevolent aged grin.
They dance on the surface among the flies.

5   Or move, stunned by their own grandeur,
Over a bed of emerald, silhouette
Of submarine delicacy and horror.
A hundred feet long in their world.

In ponds, under the heat-struck lily pads—
10   Gloom of their stillness:
Logged on last year's black leaves, watching upwards.
Or hung in an amber cavern of weeds

The jaws' hooked clamp and fangs
Not to be changed at this date;
15   A life subdued to its instrument;
The gills kneading quietly, and the pectorals.

Three we kept behind glass,
Jungled in weed: three inches, four,
And four and a half: fed fry to them—
20   Suddenly there were two. Finally one.

With a sag belly and the grin it was born with.
And indeed they spare nobody.

➜

Two, six pounds each, over two feet long,
High and dry and dead in the willow-herb—

25 One jammed past its gills down the other's gullet:
The outside eye stared: as a vice locks—
The same iron in this eye
Though its film shrank in death.

A pond I fished, fifty yards across,
30 Whose lilies and muscular tench[1]
Had outlasted every visible stone
Of the monastery that planted them—

Stilled legendary depth:
It was as deep as England. It held
35 Pike too immense to stir, so immense and old
That past nightfall I dared not cast

But silently cast and fished
With the hair frozen on my head
For what might move, for what eye might move.
40 The still splashes on the dark pond,

Owls hushing the floating woods
Frail on my ear against the dream
Darkness beneath night's darkness had freed,
That rose slowly towards me, watching.

                                                    (1960)

Hawk Roosting

I sit in the top of the wood, my eyes closed.
Inaction, no falsifying dream
Between my hooked head and hooked feet:
Or in sleep rehearse perfect kills and eat.

5 The convenience of the high trees!
The air's buoyancy and the sun's ray
Are of advantage to me;
And the earth's face upward for my inspection.

My feet are locked upon the rough bark.
10 It took the whole of Creation

                    →

---

[1]freshwater fish that inhabits still, deep waters.

To produce my foot, my each feather:
Now I hold Creation in my foot

Or fly up, and revolve it all slowly—
I kill where I please because it is all mine.
15   There is no sophistry in my body:
My manners are tearing off heads—

The allotment of death.
For the one path of my flight is direct
Through the bones of the living.
20   No arguments assert my right:

The sun is behind me.
Nothing has changed since I began.
My eye has permitted no change.
I am going to keep things like this.

(1960)

Sylvia Plath   (1932–1963)

The daughter of German and Austrian parents who taught at Boston University, Sylvia Plath was both precocious and ambitious. She excelled at school and college, began writing as a child, and was publishing in popular magazines while still in her teens. She was also manic-depressive and suffered emotionally from the pressure she felt to succeed at everything. Married to English poet Ted Hughes and living in England with her two young children, she committed suicide at age thirty.

Plath's early poems are deftly controlled but fairly conventional, and it is mainly to her later work, most of which appeared in book form only after her death, that she owes her reputation. In her later poems, Plath turned inward to confront the darker side of her psyche—her anger at her parents, her resentment at the cost to her art of motherhood, her sense of evil in modern society, and her obsession with self-destruction as a means of escape—in powerful, highly original, intensely disturbing poems.

Daddy[1]

You do not do, you do not do
Any more, black shoe

[1]Plath's father was of German descent but came to America from Poland at age fifteen. He was an expert on bees and taught at Boston University until his early death in 1940.

In which I have lived like a foot
For thirty years, poor and white,
5   Barely daring to breathe or Achoo.

Daddy, I have had to kill you.
You died before I had time—
Marble-heavy, a bag full of God,
Ghastly statue with one gray toe[2]
10   Big as a Frisco seal

And a head in the freakish Atlantic
Where it pours bean green over blue
In the waters off beautiful Nauset.
I used to pray to recover you.
15   Ach, du.[3]

In the German tongue, in the Polish town
Scraped flat by the roller
Of wars, wars, wars.
But the name of the town is common.
20   My Polack friend

Says there are a dozen or two.
So I never could tell where you
Put your foot, your root,
I never could talk to you.
25   The tongue stuck in my jaw.

It stuck in a barb wire snare.
Ich, ich, ich, ich,[4]
I could hardly speak.
I thought every German was you.
30   And the language obscene

An engine, an engine
Chuffing me off like a Jew.
A Jew to Dachau, Auschwitz, Belsen.[5]
I began to talk like a Jew.
35   I think I may well be a Jew.

The snows of the Tyrol, the clear beer of Vienna
Are not very pure or true.

---

[2]Plath's father died of blood poisoning when his diabetes led to gangrene in a toe. [3]Ah, you
(German). [4]I, I, I, I (German). [5]Nazi concentration camps.

With my gipsy ancestress and my weird luck
And my Taroc pack and my Taroc pack
40   I may be a bit of a Jew.

I have always been scared of *you*,
With your Luftwaffe, your gobbledygoo.
And your neat mustache
And your Aryan eye, bright blue.
45   Panzer-man, panzer-man, O You—

Not God but a swastika
So black no sky could squeak through.
Every woman adores a Fascist,
The boot in the face, the brute
50   Brute heart of a brute like you.

You stand at the blackboard, daddy,
In the picture I have of you,
A cleft in your chin instead of your foot
But no less a devil for that, no not
55   Any less the black man who

Bit my pretty red heart in two.
I was ten when they buried you.
At twenty I tried to die
And get back, back, back to you.
60   I thought even the bones would do.

But they pulled me out of the sack,
And they stuck me together with glue.
And then I knew what to do.
I made a model of you,
65   A man in black with a Meinkampf[6] look

And a love of the rack and the screw.
And I said I do, I do.
So daddy, I'm finally through.
The black telephone's off at the root,
70   The voices just can't worm through.

If I've killed one man, I've killed two—
The vampire who said he was you

➡️

[6]before coming to power, Adolf Hitler (1889–1945) outlined his plans for world domination in *Mein Kampf*, "my struggle" in German.

And drank my blood for a year,
Seven years, if you want to know.
75 Daddy, you can lie back now.

There's a stake in your fat black heart
And the villagers never liked you.
They are dancing and stamping on you.
They always *knew* it was you.
80 Daddy, daddy, you bastard, I'm through.

(1965)

Mirror

I am silver and exact. I have no preconceptions.
Whatever I see I swallow immediately
Just as it is, unmisted by love or dislike.
I am not cruel, only truthful—
5 The eye of a little god, four-cornered.
Most of the time I meditate on the opposite wall.
It is pink, with speckles. I have looked at it so long
I think it is a part of my heart. But it flickers.
Faces and darkness separate us over and over.
10 Now I am a lake. A woman bonds over me,
Searching my reaches for what she really is.
Then she turns to those liars, the candles or the moon.
I see her back, and reflect it faithfully.
She rewards me with tears and an agitation of hands.
15 I am important to her. She comes and goes.
Each morning it is her face that replaces the darkness.
In me she has drowned a young girl, and in me an old woman
Rises toward her day after day, like a terrible fish.

(1961)   (1971)

Lady Lazarus[1]

I have done it again.
One year in every ten
I manage it—

[1]Lazarus was brought back from death by Jesus (John 11).

A sort of walking miracle, my skin
Bright as a Nazi lampshade,
My right foot

A paperweight,
My face a featureless, fine
Jew linen.

Peel off the napkin
O my enemy.
Do I terrify?—

The nose, the eye pits, the full set of teeth?
The sour breath
Will vanish in a day.

Soon, soon the flesh
The grave cave ate will be
At home on me

And I a smiling woman.
I am only thirty.
And like the cat I have nine times to die.

This is Number Three.
What a trash
To annihilate each decade.

What a million filaments.
The peanut-crunching crowd
Shoves in to see

Them unwrap me hand and foot—
The big strip tease.
Gentlemen, ladies

These are my hands
My knees.
I may be skin and bone,

Nevertheless, I am the same, identical woman.
The first time it happened I was ten.
It was an accident.

The second time I meant
To last it out and not come back at all.
I rocked shut

40 As a seashell.
They had to call and call
And pick the worms off me like sticky pearls.

Dying
Is an art, like everything else.
45 I do it exceptionally well.

I do it so it feels like hell.
I do it so it feels real.
I guess you could say I've a call.

It's easy enough to do it in a cell.
50 It's easy enough to do it and stay put.
It's the theatrical

Comeback in broad day
To the same place, the same face, the same brute
Amused shout:

55 "A miracle!"
That knocks me out.
There is a charge

For the eyeing of my scars, there is a charge
For the hearing of my heart—
60 It really goes.

And there is a charge, a very large charge
For a word or a touch
Or a bit of blood

Or a piece of my hair or my clothes.
65 So, so, Herr Doktor.
So, Herr Enemy.

I am your opus,
I am your valuable,
The pure gold baby

70 That melts to a shriek.
I turn and burn.
Do not think I underestimate your great concern.

Ash, ash—
You poke and stir.
75 Flesh, bone, there is nothing there—

A cake of soap,
A wedding ring,
A gold filling.

Herr God, Herr Lucifer
80 Beware
Beware.

Out of the ash
I rise with my red hair
And I eat men like air.

(1965)

Wole Soyinka   (b. 1934)

A poet, playwright, novelist, essayist, filmmaker, and academic, Wole Soyinka won the Nobel Prize for literature in 1986, becoming the first African to do so. Born in Abeokuta, Nigeria, Soyinka was educated at the University College, Ibadan, and at Leeds University, where he took a degree in English. A passionate defender of human freedom, Soyinka has had several brushes with Nigerian authorities. During the Nigerian Civil War, he was imprisoned by the military government, an experience that produced some of his most powerful prose and poetry. After he protested the cancellation of election results in 1993, the government seized his passport. Soyinka was forced to live in exile, travelling on a U.N. passport. Nevertheless, the Nigerian government charged him with treason in March 1997, claiming that he and other dissidents were instrumental in a series of bombings of army installations. In 1999, the year after the charges were dropped, Soyinka visited Nigeria. He also published *The Burden of Memory, the Muse of Forgiveness,* about African crimes against humanity and the problems of reconciliation.

Although he can write biting satire, such as "Telephone Conversation," Soyinka tends to be a profound and complex writer, drawing on sources as disparate as Yoruba culture, the Bible, and Greek mythology. He can evoke a sense of the African landscape as a physical and psychological setting, but his dominant concerns are universal: a respect for life and a desire for a society in which individuals can live in dignity and freedom.

Telephone Conversation

The price seemed reasonable, location
Indifferent. The landlady swore she lived

→

Off premises. Nothing remained
But self-confession. "Madam," I warned,
"I hate a wasted journey—I am African."
Silence. Silenced transmission of
Pressurized good-breeding. Voice, when it came,
Lipstick coated, long gold-rolled
Cigarette-holder pipped. Caught I was, foully.
"HOW DARK?" ... I had not misheard ... "ARE YOU LIGHT
OR VERY DARK?" Button B. Button A.[1] Stench
Of rancid breath of public hide-and-speak.
Red booth. Red pillar-box.[2] Red double-tiered
Omnibus squelching tar. It *was* real! Shamed
By ill-mannered silence, surrender
Pushed dumbfoundment to beg simplification.
Considerate she was, varying the emphasis—
"ARE YOU DARK? OR VERY LIGHT?" Revelation came.
"You mean—like plain or milk chocolate?"
Her assent was clinical, crushing in its light
Impersonality. Rapidly, wave-length adjusted,
I chose. "West African sepia"—and as afterthought,
"Down in my passport." Silence for spectroscopic[3]
Flight of fancy, till truthfulness clanged her accent
Hard on the mouthpiece. "WHAT'S THAT?" conceding
"DON'T KNOW WHAT THAT IS." "Like brunette."
"THAT'S DARK, ISN'T IT?" "Not altogether.
Facially, I am brunette, but madam, you should see
The rest of me. Palm of my hand, soles of my feet
Are a peroxide blonde. Friction, caused—
Foolishly madam—by sitting down, has turned
My bottom raven black—One moment madam!"—sensing
Her receiver rearing on the thunderclap
About my ears—"Madam," I pleaded, "wouldn't you rather
See for yourself?"

(1960)

[1] at the time the poem was written, on coin-operated telephones in England the caller pressed Button A to make a connection and Button B to cancel the call and to retrieve coins if the number was busy or if no one answered. [2] cylindrical postal box. [3] a spectroscope is an instrument that enables analysis of a range of colours.

Lost Tribe

Ants disturbed by every passing tread,
The wandering tribe still scurries round
In search of lost community. Love by rote,
Care by inscription. Incantations without magic.
5   Straws outstretched to suck at every passing broth,
Incessant tongues pretend to a way of thought—
Where language mints are private franchise,
The coins prove counterfeit on open markets.

Hard-sell pharmacies dispense all social pills:
10   "Have a nice day now." "Touch someone."
There's premium on the verb imperative—some
Instant fame psychologist pronounced it on TV—
He's now forgotten like tomorrow's guru,
Instant cult, disposable as paper diaper—
15   Firm commands denote sincerity;
The wish is wishy-washy, lacks "contact
Positive." The waiter barks: "Enjoy your meal,"
Or crisper still: *"Enjoy!"* You feel you'd better!
Buses, subway, park seats push the gospel,
20   Slogans like tickertapes emblazon foreheads—
"Talk it over with someone—now, not later!"
"Take down fences, not mend them."
"Give a nice smile to someone." But, a tear-duct
Variant: "Have you hugged your child today?"

(1988)

Alden Nowlan   (1933–1983)

Although he had a limited formal education—he left school after Grade 5—Nowlan became one of the leading literary figures in Atlantic Canada. Born in Windsor, Nova Scotia, he held various jobs as a manual labourer until he moved to New Brunswick to work as a journalist. He began his literary career as a poet, publishing his first collection in 1958. *Bread, Wine and Salt* (1967) won the Governor General's Award. Later, he turned his hand to other genres, producing plays, stories, and a novel. Although he is a regionalist, painting relatively realistic pictures of nature and society in Atlantic Canada, Nowlan infuses his poems with universal significance. He can also, like a backwoods storyteller, be by turns sentimental and ironic. "The Bull Moose," his most famous poem, shows his

characteristic attitudes; he evokes sympathy for victims and imbues even
mundane events with religious or spiritual importance.

The Bull Moose

Down from the purple mist of trees on the mountain,
lurching through forests of white spruce and cedar,
stumbling through tamarack swamps,
came the bull moose
5   to be stopped at last by a pole-fenced pasture.

Too tired to turn or, perhaps, aware
there was no place left to go, he stood with the cattle.
They, scenting the musk of death, seeing his great head
like the ritual mask of a blood god, moved to the other end
10   of the field, and waited.

The neighbours heard of it, and by afternoon
cars lined the road. The children teased him
with alder switches and he gazed at them
like an old, tolerant collie. The women asked
15   if he could have escaped from a Fair.

The oldest man in the parish remembered seeing
a gelded moose yoked with an ox for plowing.
The young men snickered and tried to pour beer
down his throat, while their girlfriends took their pictures.

20   And the bull moose let them stroke his tick-ravaged flanks,
let them pry open his jaws with bottles, let a giggling girl
plant a little purple cap
of thistles on his head.

When the wardens came, everyone agreed it was a shame
25   to shoot anything so shaggy and cuddlesome.
He looked like the kind of pet
women put to bed with their sons.

So they held their fire. But just as the sun dropped in the river
the bull moose gathered his strength
30   like a scaffolded king, straightened and lifted his horns
so that even the wardens backed away as they raised their rifles.
When he roared, people ran to their cars. All the young men
leaned on their automobile horns as he toppled.

(1962)

Leonard Cohen (b. 1934)

Born into a wealthy Montreal family, Cohen received a B.A. from McGill University in 1955. Since then, he has moved freely between literature and popular culture, becoming an internationally successful poet and singer, and a controversial experimental novelist. He is also an ordained Buddhist monk. He won, but refused to accept, the Governor General's Award for *Selected Poems* (1968). Cohen has received several Juno Awards for his recordings. In 1993 he was honoured for his lifetime achievement with a Governor General's Performing Arts Award, and in 2003 was made a Companion of the Order of Canada.

In much of Cohen's work, traditional poetic elements contrast with the contemporary subject matter. That is to say, their lush imagery and abundant musical qualities mark his poems as conventionally romantic and deliberately "poetic" works. However, their bleakness and shocking assaults on conventional moral assumptions make them thoroughly modern. Cohen frequently combines images from classical mythology or religion (drawing on both his own Jewish heritage and that of the dominant Catholic culture of Quebec) with images of sex, suffering, violence, and death. In this way he attempts to create an informal mythology to replace what he considers the worn-out myths of the past. The exact meaning of Cohen's poems is often elusive, but one figure is central. The "saint" renounces the ordinary world, enduring consequent suffering and even destruction of the self in order to achieve the purity necessary to attain a higher state. In Cohen's mythic world, the only winners are beautiful losers.

A Kite Is a Victim

A kite is a victim you are sure of.
You love it because it pulls
gentle enough to call you master,
strong enough to call you fool;
5   because it lives
like a trained falcon
in the high sweet air,
and you can always haul it down
to tame it in your drawer.

10   A kite is a fish you have already caught
in a pool where no fish come,
so you play him carefully and long,
and hope he won't give up,
or the wind die down.

15   A kite is the last poem you've written,
so you give it to the wind,
but you don't let it go

until someone finds you
something else to do.

20 A kite is a contract of glory
that must be made with the sun,
so you make friends with the field
the river and the wind,
then you pray the whole cold night before,
25 under the travelling cordless moon,
to make you worthy and lyric and pure.

(1961)

Suzanne Takes You Down

Suzanne takes you down
to her place near the river,
you can hear the boats go by
you can stay the night beside her.
5 And you know that she's half crazy
but that's why you want to be there
and she feeds you tea and oranges
that come all the way from China.
Just when you mean to tell her
10 that you have no gifts to give her,
she gets you on her wave-length
and she lets the river answer
that you've always been her lover.
        And you want to travel with her,
15   you want to travel blind
        and you know that she can trust you
        because you've touched her perfect body
        with your mind.

Jesus was a sailor
20 when he walked upon the water
and he spent a long time watching
from a lonely wooden tower
and when he knew for certain
only drowning men could see him
25 he said All men will be sailors then

→

until the sea shall free them,
but he himself was broken
long before the sky would open,
forsaken, almost human,
30 he sank beneath your wisdom like a stone.
    And you want to travel with him,
    you want to travel blind
    and you think maybe you'll trust him
    because he touched your perfect body
35   with his mind.

Suzanne takes your hand
and she leads you to the river,
she is wearing rags and feathers
from Salvation Army counters.
40 The sun pours down like honey
on our lady of the harbour
as she shows you where to look
among the garbage and the flowers,
there are heroes in the seaweed
45 there are children in the morning,
they are leaning out for love
they will lean that way forever
while Suzanne she holds the mirror.
    And you want to travel with her
50   and you want to travel blind
    and you're sure that she can find you
    because she's touched her perfect body
    with her mind.

(1966)

Les Murray (b. 1938)

Born in Nabiac, New South Wales, Australia, Les Murray grew up on his grandfather's dairy farm. He attended the University of Sydney, but left before completing his degree. He worked as a translator and public servant before devoting himself full time to writing. Murray eventually repurchased part of his family farm in Bunyah and moved there. Many of his poems are autobiographical, describing his reactions to personal experiences, but they also express his deep connection to Australian landscape and history. Firmly convinced that rural life is superior to urban life and that the "Bush" is the source of Australians' finest qualities, he has expressed admiration for both Aborigines and Australia's pioneers. He also expresses religious and spiritual values—he converted to Roman Catholicism—and an awareness of the suffering and injustice that those lacking power can suffer. An opponent of what he considered to be the elitist post-modernist style that began to develop in Australian poetry, Murray writes in a loose, colloquial style designed to convey to a wide audience both personal and public themes.

The Tin Wash Dish

Lank poverty, dank poverty,
its pants wear through at fork and knee.
It warms its hands over burning shames,
refers to its fate as Them and He
5 and delights in things by their hard names:
rag and toejam, feed and paw –
don't guts that down, there ain't no more!
Dank poverty, rank poverty,
it hums with a grim fidelity
10 like wood-rot with a hint of orifice,
wet newspaper jammed in the gaps of artifice,
and disgusts us into fierce loyalty.
It's never the fault of those you love:
poverty comes down from above.
15 Let it dance chairs and smash the door,
it arises from all that went before
and every outsider's the enemy –
Jesus Christ turned this over with his stick
and knights and philosophers turned it back.
20 Rank poverty, lank poverty,
chafe in its crotch and sores in its hair,
still a window's clean if it's made of air,
not webby silver like a sleeve.
Watch out if this does well at school
25 and has to leave and longs to leave:
someone, sometime, will have to pay.
Shave with toilet soap, run to flesh,
astound the nation, rule the army,
still you wait for the day you'll be sent back
30 where books or toys on the floor are rubbish

→

and no one's allowed to come and play
because home calls itself a shack
and hot water crinkles in the tin wash dish.

(1990)

Dog Fox Field

The test for feeblemindedness was, they had to make up a sentence
using the words dog, fox *and* field.

– Judgement at Nuremberg

These were no leaders, but they were first
into the dark on Dog Fox Field:

Anna who rocked her head, and Paul
who grew big and yet giggled small,

5   Irma who looked Chinese, and Hans
who knew his world as a fox knows a field.

Hunted with needles, exposed, unfed,
this time in their thousands they bore sad cuts

for having gaped, and shuffled, and failed
10   to field the lore of prey and hound

they then had to thump and cry in the vans
that ran while stopped in Dog Fox Field.

Our sentries, whose holocaust does not end,
they show us when we cross into Dog Fox Field.

(1990)

Seamus Heaney (b. 1939)

Winner of the 1995 Nobel Prize for literature, Seamus Heaney has been praised for his evocative language and for the integrity of his treatment of the troubles in Northern Ireland. Born in County Derry in Northern Ireland, he graduated from Queen's University, Belfast, in 1961 and obtained a teacher's diploma the next year. He has held a number of teaching appointments, including positions at his alma mater and at Harvard University. He published his first full-length collection, *Death of* a *Naturalist,* to critical acclaim in 1966. A Roman Catholic increasingly upset by the conflict in Northern Ireland, Heaney moved to the Irish Republic in 1972 in order, he said, "to put the practice of poetry more deliberately at the centre of my life." Ireland—its traditions, its rural landscape, and its political and religious difficulties—is at the centre of Heaney's poetry, but he also explores universal themes, such as the role of the poet and the nature of art. A poet whose unobtrusive craftsmanship produces works that are immediately accessible but also deeply moving and memorable, he has described poetry "as a point of entry into the buried life of the feelings or as a point of exit for it."

Death of a Naturalist

All year the flax-dam festered in the heart
Of the townland; green and heavy headed
Flax had rotted there, weighted down by huge sods.
Daily it sweltered in the punishing sun.
5 Bubbles gargled delicately, bluebottles
Wove a strong gauze of sound around the smell.
There were dragon-flies, spotted butterflies,
But best of all was the warm thick slobber
Of frogspawn that grew like clotted water
10 In the shade of the banks. Here, every spring
I would fill jampotfuls of the jellied
Specks to range on window-sills at home,
On shelves at school, and wait and watch until
The fattening dots burst into nimble-
15 Swimming tadpoles. Miss Walls would tell us how
The daddy frog was called a bullfrog
And how he croaked and how the mammy frog
Laid hundreds of little eggs and this was
Frogspawn. You could tell the weather by frogs too
20 For they were yellow in the sun and brown
In rain.

      Then one hot day when fields were rank
With cowdung in the grass the angry frogs
Invaded the flax-dam; I ducked through hedges
25 To a coarse croaking that I had not heard
Before. The air was thick with a bass chorus.
Right down the dam gross-bellied frogs were cocked
On sods; their loose necks pulsed like sails. Some hopped:
The slap and plop were obscene threats. Some sat

→

30   Poised like mud grenades, their blunt heads farting.
      I sickened, turned, and ran. The great slime kings
      Were gathered there for vengeance and I knew
      That if I dipped my hand the spawn would clutch it.

                                                        (1966)

Digging

      Between my finger and my thumb
      The squat pen rests; snug as a gun.

      Under my window, a clean rasping sound
      When the spade sinks into gravelly ground:
5   My father, digging. I look down

      Till his straining rump among the flowerbeds
      Bends low, comes up twenty years away
      Stooping in rhythm through potato drills
      Where he was digging.

10   The coarse boot nestled on the lug, the shaft
      Against the inside knee was levered firmly.
      He rooted out tall tops, buried the bright edge deep
      To scatter new potatoes that we picked,
      Loving their cool hardness in our hands.

15   By God, the old man could handle a spade.
      Just like his old man.

      My grandfather cut more turf in a day
      Than any other man on Toner's bog.
      Once I carried him milk in a bottle
20   Corked sloppily with paper. He straightened up
      To drink it, then fell to right away
      Nicking and slicing neatly, heaving sods
      Over his shoulder, going down and down
      For the good turf. Digging.

25   The cold smell of potato mould, the squelch and slap
      Of soggy peat, the curt cuts of an edge
      Through living roots awaken in my head.
      But I've no spade to follow men like them.

Between my finger and my thumb
30   The squat pen rests.
I'll dig with it.

(1966)

The Singer's House

When they said *Carrickfergus*[1] I could hear
the frosty echo of saltminers' picks.
I imagined it, chambered and glinting,
a township built of light.

5   What do we say any more
to conjure the salt of our earth?
So much comes and is gone
that should be crystal and kept

and amicable weathers
10   that bring up the grain of things,
their tang of season and store,
are all the packing we'll get.

So I say to myself *Gweebarra*[2]
and its music hits off the place
15   like water hitting off granite.
I see the glittering sound

framed in your window,
knives and forks set on oilcloth,
and the seal's heads, suddenly outlined,
20   scanning everything.

People here used to believe
that drowned souls lived in the seals.
At spring tides they might change shape.
They loved music and swam in for a singer

25   who might stand at the end of summer
in the mouth of a whitewashed turf-shed,
his shoulder to the jamb, his song
a rowboat far out in evening.

[1]Northern Irish salt-mining area and seaport, the subject of a popular Irish folksong. [2]the bay
in County Donegal in the Irish Republic.

When I came here first you were always singing,
30   a hint of the clip of the pick
in your winnowing climb and attack.
Raise it again, man. We still believe what we hear.

(1979)

Margaret Atwood   (b. 1939)

Internationally successful as both a poet and a novelist, Margaret Atwood was born in Ottawa and educated at the University of Toronto and Radcliffe College, Harvard. She has worked as a book editor, has taught English at several universities, and has been a university writer in residence. Her first book was a thin volume of poems, *Double Persephone* (1961). Her second collection, *The Circle Game* (1966), won the Governor General's Award. Her novels include *Surfacing* (1972) and *The Handmaid's Tale* (1985), winner of the Governor General's Award for fiction. *Survival* (1972) is a controversial study of Canadian literature in which she expands upon Northrop Frye's analysis of the "garrison mentality" and argues that Canadian literature is dominated by images of victims. In her own poetry, she often explores victimization and liberation, dissecting the personal, psychological, cultural, political, and sexual ideas or myths confining the individual. This exploration frequently challenges both conventional perceptions of reality and conventional logic. Although she has said that sound and phrasing are important elements in her poetry, Atwood does not indulge in verbal pyrotechnics. Typically, her narrators employ startlingly provocative and often violent images, but they make thematic pronouncements in a flat, unemotional voice. In this way, she conveys both the violence of the modern world and the alienation of its victims.

Progressive Insanities of a Pioneer

i

He stood, a point
on a sheet of green paper
proclaiming himself the centre,

with no walls, no borders
5   anywhere; the sky no height
above him, totally un-
enclosed
and shouted:

Let me out!

ii

10 He dug the soil in rows,
imposed himself with shovels
He asserted
into the furrows, I
am not random.

15 The ground
replied with aphorisms:

a tree-sprout, a nameless
weed, words
he couldn't understand.

iii

20 The house pitched
the plot staked
in the middle of nowhere.

At night the mind
inside, in the middle
25 of nowhere.

The idea of an animal
patters across the roof.

In the darkness the fields
defend themselves with fences
30 in vain:
        everything
        is getting in.

iv

By daylight he resisted.
He said, disgusted
35 with the swamp's clamourings and the outbursts
of rocks,
        This is not order
        but the absence
        of order.

40 He was wrong, the unanswering
forest implied:

It was
an ordered absence

v

For many years
45 he fished for a great vision,
dangling the hooks of sown
roots under the surface
of the shallow earth.

It was like
50 enticing whales with a bent
pin. Besides he thought

in that country
only the worms were biting.

vi

If he had known unstructured
55 space is a deluge
and stocked his log house-
boat with all the animals

even the wolves,

he might have floated.

60 But obstinate he
stated, The land is solid
and stamped,

watching his foot sink
down through stone
65 up to the knee.

vii

Things
refused to name themselves; refused
to let him name them.

The wolves hunted
70 outside.

On his beaches, his clearings,
by the surf of under-
growth breaking

→

at his feet, he foresaw
75   disintegration
        and in the end

through eyes
made ragged by his
effort, the tension
80   between subject and object,

the green
vision, the unnamed
whale invaded.

(1968)

The Animals in That Country

In that country the animals
have the faces of people:

the ceremonial
cats possessing the streets

5   the fox run
politely to earth, the huntsmen
standing around him, fixed
in their tapestry of manners

the bull, embroidered
10   with blood and given
an elegant death, trumpets, his name
stamped on him, heraldic brand
because

(when he rolled
15   on the sand, sword in his heart, the teeth
in his blue mouth were human)

he is really a man

even the wolves, holding resonant
conversations in their
20   forests thickened with legend.

      In this country the animals
      have the faces of
      animals.

Their eyes
25 flash once in car headlights
and are gone.

Their deaths are not elegant.

They have the faces of
no-one.

(1968)

you fit into me

you fit into me
like a hook into an eye

a fish hook
an open eye

(1973)

Siren Song[1]

This is the song everyone
would like to learn: the song
that is irresistible:

the song that forces men
5   to leap overboard in squadrons
even though they see the beached skulls

the song nobody knows
because anyone who has heard it
is dead, and the others can't remember.

10 Shall I tell you the secret
and if I do, will you get me
out of this bird suit?

I don't enjoy it here
squatting on this island
15 looking picturesque and mythical

---

[1] in Greek mythology, the three sirens, who were half woman and half bird, lured sailors to destruction with enchanting songs.

with these two feathery maniacs,
I don't enjoy singing
this trio, fatal and valuable.

I will tell the secret to you,
20 to you, only to you.
Come closer. This song

is a cry for help: Help me!
Only you, only you can,
you are unique

25 at last. Alas
it is a boring song
but it works every time.

(1974)

Variations on the Word *Love*

This is a word we use to plug
holes with. It's the right size for those warm
blanks in speech, for those red heart-
shaped vacancies on the page that look nothing
5   like real hearts. Add lace
and you can sell
it. We insert it also in the one empty
space on the printed form
that comes with no instructions. There are whole
10 magazines with not much in them
but the word *love*, you can
rub it all over your body and you
can cook with it too. How do we know
it isn't what goes on at the cool
15 debaucheries of slugs under damp
pieces of cardboard? As for the weed-
seedlings nosing their tough snouts up
among the lettuces, they shout it.
Love! Love! sing the soldiers, raising
20 their glittering knives in salute.

Then there's the two
of us. This word

→

is far too short for us, it has only
four letters, too sparse
25   to fill those deep bare
vacuums between the stars
that press on us with their deafness.
It's not love we don't wish
to fall into, but that fear.
30   This word is not enough but it will
have to do. It's a single
vowel in this metallic
silence, a mouth that says
O again and again in wonder
35   and pain, a breath, a finger-
grip on a cliffside. You can
hold on or let go.

(1981)

Helen of Troy[1] Does Counter Dancing

The world is full of women
who'd tell me I should be ashamed of myself
if they had the chance. Quit dancing.
Get some self-respect
5   and a day job.
Right. And minimum wage,
and varicose veins, just standing
in one place for eight hours
behind a glass counter
10   bundled up to the neck, instead of
naked as a meat sandwich.
Selling gloves, or something.
Instead of what I do sell.
You have to have talent
15   to peddle a thing so nebulous
and without material form.

[1]according to Greek legend, Helen was the most beautiful woman in the world and the cause
of the Trojan War. Her mother was Leda, and her father was Zeus, who assumed the form of
a swan and raped Leda. Helen, who had many suitors, married Menelaus, but Paris seduced
her and carried her off to Troy. Menelaus and her Greek suitors then waged war on Troy to
recover her. (See also Yeats's "Leda and the Swan," page 198.)

Exploited, they'd say. Yes, any way
you cut it, but I've a choice
of how, and I'll take the money.

20   I do give value.
Like preachers, I sell vision,
like perfume ads, desire
or its facsimile. Like jokes
or war, it's all in the timing.
25   I sell men back their worst suspicions:
that everything's for sale,
and piecemeal. They gaze at me and see
a chain-saw murder just before it happens,
when thigh, ass, inkblot, crevice, tit, and nipple
30   are still connected.
Such hatred leaps in them,
my beery worshippers! That, or a bleary
hopeless love. Seeing the rows of heads
and upturned eyes, imploring
35   but ready to snap at my ankles,
I understand floods and earthquakes, and the urge
to step on ants. I keep the beat,
and dance for them because
they can't. The music smells like foxes,
40   crisp as heated metal
searing the nostrils
or humid as August, hazy and languorous
as a looted city the day after,
when all the rape's been done
45   already, and the killing,
and the survivors wander around
looking for garbage
to eat, and there's only a bleak exhaustion.

Speaking of which, it's the smiling
50   tires me out the most.
This, and the pretence
that I can't hear them.
And I can't, because I'm after all
a foreigner to them.
55   The speech here is all warty gutturals

→

obvious as a slab of ham,
but I come from the province of the gods
where meanings are lilting and oblique.
I don't let on to everyone,
60 but lean close, and I'll whisper:
My mother was raped by a holy swan.
You believe that? You can take me out to dinner.
That's what we tell all the husbands.
There sure are a lot of dangerous birds around.

65 Not that anyone here
but you would understand.
The rest of them would like to watch me
and feel nothing. Reduce me to components
as in a clock factory or abattoir.
70 Crush out the mystery.
Wall me up alive
in my own body.
They'd like to see through me,
but nothing is more opaque
75 than absolute transparency.
Look—my feet don't hit the marble!
Like breath or a balloon, I'm rising,
I hover six inches in the air
in my blazing swan-egg of light.
80 You think I'm not a goddess?
Try me.
This is a torch song.[2]
Touch me and you'll burn.

(1995)

Fred Wah   (b. 1939)

Fred Wah was born in Swift Current, Saskatchewan. While majoring in music at the University of British Columbia, he played in a musical group that solidified for him the connection between poetry and jazz. Deeply influenced by the Black Mountain poets (he studied with both Robert Creeley at the University of New Mexico and Charles Olson at the University of New York at Buffalo), Wah developed his own theories about breath and poetry, constantly experimenting with sound,

[2]song concerned with failure in love.

especially that of his own name. Another major concern in his poems has been personal identity. Of mixed racial background, Wah has repeatedly explored the idea of race and his own connections to it.

my father hurt-

my father hurt-
ing at the table
sitting hurting
at suppertime
5   deep inside very
far down inside
because I can't stand the ginger
in the beef and greens
he cooked for us tonight
10   and years later tonight
that look on his face
appears now on mine
my children
my food
15   their food
my father
their father
me mine
the father
20   very far
very very far
inside

(1981)

Gwendolyn MacEwen   (1941–1987)

Born in Toronto, Gwendolyn MacEwen grew up there and in Winnipeg. She discovered her calling as a writer early: at the age of seventeen she published her first poem, and she left school the next year to pursue her career. In addition to poetry, MacEwen wrote two novels, a collection of short stories, two children's books, and a number of radio plays and documentaries. Her books of poetry include *A Breakfast for Barbarians* (1966), *The Shadow-Maker* (1969), winner of the Governor General's Award, and *The T. E. Lawrence Poems* (1982). MacEwen said of her work: "I write basically to communicate joy, mystery, passion . . . not the joy that naively exists without knowledge of pain, but that joy which arises out of and conquers pain. I want to construct a myth." MacEwen constructs her myth, which celebrates the triumph of the human spirit, with materials borrowed from a variety of traditions. Lush, even exotic, imagery establishes the dualities that are central to her mythic vision. Throughout her poetry, she explores meaningful relationships between spiritual and physical worlds, archetypal and mundane experience, waking and dreaming consciousness, past and present times, painful and joyful events, and male and female lives.

A Breakfast for Barbarians

my friends, my sweet barbarians,
there is that hunger which is not for food—
but an eye at the navel turns the appetite
round
5   with visions of some fabulous sandwich,
the brain's golden breakfast
eaten with beasts
with books on plates

let us make an anthology of recipes,
10   let us edit for breakfast
our most unspeakable appetites—
let us pool spoons, knives
and all cutlery in a cosmic cuisine,
let us answer hunger
15   with boiled chimera[1]
and apocalyptic tea,
an arcane salad of spiced bibles,
tossed dictionaries—
(O my barbarians
20   we will consume our mysteries)

and can we, can we slake the gaping eye of our desires?
we will sit around our hewn wood table
until our hair is long and our eyes are feeble,
eating, my people, O my insatiates,
25   eating until we are no more able
to jack up the jaws any longer—

to no more complain of the soul's vulgar cavities,
to gaze at each other over the rust-heap of cutlery,
drinking a coffee that takes an eternity—
30   till, bursting, bleary,

➡

[1]in Greek mythology, a fire-breathing monster with a lion's head, a goat's body, and a serpent's tail; also used figuratively to indicate an absurdly fanciful or impossible idea.

we laugh, barbarians, and rock the universe—
and exclaim to each other over the table
over the table of bones and scrap metal
over the gigantic junk-heaped table:

35   by God that was a meal

(1966)

Dark Pines under Water

This land like a mirror turns you inward
And you become a forest in a furtive lake;
The dark pines of your mind reach downward,
You dream in the green of you time,
5   You memory is a row of sinking pines.

Explorer, you tell yourself this is not what you came for
Although it is good here, and green;
You had meant to move with a kind of largeness,
You had planned a heavy grace, an anguished dream.

10   But the dark pines of your mind dip deeper
And you are sinking, sinking, sleeper
In an elementary world;
There is something down there and you want it told.

(1969)

Michael Ondaatje   (b. 1943)

Born in Colombo, Ceylon (now Sri Lanka), Ondaatje moved to England when he was eleven and came to Canada in 1962. He received a B.A. from the University of Toronto and an M.A. from Queen's University. He currently teaches at York University. Ondaatje began his career as a poet, publishing his first book in 1967. He has also produced novels, films, criticism, and anthologies. Two of his poetry collections have won the Governor General's Award: *The Collected Works of Billy the Kid* (1970), in which he combined poetry and prose, and *There's a Trick with a Knife I'm Learning to Do: Poems 1973–1978* (1979). He also received the Governor General's Award and the Booker Prize for his novel *The English Patient* (1992). His complex novel about civil unrest in Sri Lanka, *Anil's Ghost* (2000), was co-winner of the Giller Prize. Ondaatje most frequently explores the tensions between the subjective inner vision and the supposedly objective and logical realm of outward reality. Dissatisfied with traditional classifications and methods, he challenges both conventional perceptions and literary forms by mixing prose and poetry, fact and fiction, realism and surrealism, lyricism and violence.

Elizabeth[1]

Catch, my Uncle Jack[2] said
and oh I caught this huge apple
red as Mrs Kelly's[3] bum.
It's red as Mrs Kelly's bum, I said
5 and Daddy[4] roared
and swung me on his stomach with a heave.
Then I hid the apple in my room
till it shrunk like a face
growing eyes and teeth ribs.

10 Then Daddy took me to the zoo
he knew the man there
they put a snake around my neck
and it crawled down the front of my dress.
I felt its flicking tongue
15 dripping onto me like a shower.
Daddy laughed and said Smart Snake
and Mrs Kelly with us scowled.

In the pond where they kept the goldfish
Philip[5] and I broke the ice with spades
20 and tried to spear the fishes;
we killed one and Philip ate it,
then he kissed me
with raw saltless fish in his mouth.

My sister Mary's got bad teeth
25 and said I was lucky, then she said
I had big teeth, but Philip said I was pretty.
He had big hands that smelled.

I would speak of Tom,[6] soft laughing,
who danced in the mornings round the sundial
30 teaching me the steps from France, turning
with the rhythm of the sun on the warped branches,

[1] the speaker is Elizabeth I (1533–1603). [2] fictitious character, probably not an actual uncle but a man given that title because of familiarity with the child. [3] fictitious character, probably a nurse. [4] Elizabeth's father, Henry VIII (1491–1547). [5] Philip II of Spain (1527–1598) married Elizabeth's sister, Mary Tudor (1515–1558), in 1554. After Mary's death, he unsuccessfully sought to marry Elizabeth. [6] Lord Thomas Seymour of Sudeley (c. 1508–1549) was executed for intriguing against his brother, Edward, Duke of Somerset, Lord Protector of the Realm. He vainly sought the hand of Elizabeth, having treated her with marked indelicacy when she stayed at his house.

who'd hold my breast and watch it move like a snail
leaving his quick urgent love in my palm.
And I kept his love in my palm till it blistered.

35 When they axed his shoulders and neck
the blood moved like a branch into the crowd.
And he staggered with his hanging shoulder
cursing their thrilled cry, wheeling,
waltzing in the French style to his knees
40 holding his head with the ground,
blood settling on his clothes like a blush;
this way
when they aimed the thud into his back.

And I find cool entertainment now
45 with white young Essex,[7] and my nimble rhymes.[8]

(1967)

Letters & Other Worlds

"for there was no more darkness for him and, no doubt
like Adam before the fall, he could see in the dark"[1]

My father's body was a globe of fear
His body was a town we never knew
He hid that he had been where we were going
His letters were a room he seldom lived in
5 In them the logic of his love could grow

My father's body was a town of fear
He was the only witness to its fear dance
He hid where he had been that we might lose him
His letters were a room his body scared

10 He came to death with his mind drowning.
On the last day he enclosed himself
in a room with two bottles of gin, later
fell the length of his body
so that brain blood moved

→

[7]Robert Devereux (1566–1601), the second Earl of Essex and one of Elizabeth's confidants, was executed for attempting to raise a rebellion. [8]Elizabeth wrote lyric poetry. [1]from "*Descendit ad infernos*" (He Descends to the Underworld), a chapter from Alfred Jarry's *La dragonne* (1943), quoted in Roger Shattuck's *The Banquet Years: The Arts in France, 1885–1918* (1955). The clause immediately preceding the section Ondaatje quotes is "But soon he could drink no more."

10   to new compartments
that never knew the wash of fluid
and he died in minutes of a new equilibrium.

His early life was a terrifying comedy
and my mother divorced him again and again.
20   He would rush into tunnels magnetized
by the white eye of trains
and once, gaining instant fame,
managed to stop a Perahara[2] in Ceylon
—the whole procession of elephants dancers
25   local dignitaries—by falling
dead drunk onto the street.

As a semi-official, and semi-white at that,
the act was seen as a crucial
turning point in the Home Rule Movement
30   and led to Ceylon's independence in 1948.

(My mother had done her share too—
her driving so bad
she was stoned by villagers
whenever her car was recognized)

35   For 14 years of marriage
each of them claimed he or she
was the injured party.
Once on the Colombo docks
saying goodbye to a recently married couple
40   my father, jealous
at my mother's articulate emotion,
dove into the waters of the harbour
and swam after the ship waving farewell.
My mother pretending no affiliation
45   mingled with the crowd back to the hotel.

Once again he made the papers
though this time my mother
with a note to the editor
corrected the report—saying he was drunk
50   rather than broken hearted at the parting of friends.
The married couple received both editions
of *The Ceylon Times* when their ship reached Aden.[3]

[2]Sinhalese for *procession*; a *perahara* was most frequently associated with a religious celebration or marriage. [3]the capital of the British colony of Aden and later the capital of the People's Democratic Republic of Yemen; port of call on voyages through the Suez Canal.

And then in his last years
he was the silent drinker,
55   the man who once a week
disappeared into his room with bottles
and stayed there until he was drunk
and until he was sober.

There speeches, head dreams, apologies,
60   the gentle letters, were composed.
With the clarity of architects
he would write of the row of blue flowers
his new wife had planted,
the plans for electricity in the house,
65   how my half-sister fell near a snake
and it had awakened and not touched her.
Letters in a clear hand of the most complete empathy
his heart widening and widening and widening
to all manner of change in his children and friends
70   while he himself edged
into the terrible acute hatred
of his own privacy
till he balanced and fell
the length of his body
75   the blood screaming in
the empty reservoir of bones
the blood searching in his head without metaphor

(1973)

The Cinnamon Peeler[1]

If I were a cinnamon peeler
I would ride your bed
and leave the yellow bark dust
on your pillow.

5   Your breasts and shoulders would reek
you could never walk through markets
without the profession of my fingers
floating over you. The blind would
stumble certain of whom they approached

[1]one who peels from the cinnamon tree the bark whose inner layer provides the aromatic spice.

10   though you might bathe
      under rain gutters, monsoon.

      Here on the upper thigh
      at this smooth pasture
      neighbour to your hair
15   or the crease
      that cuts your back. This ankle.
      You will be known among strangers
      as the cinnamon peeler's wife.

      I could hardly glance at you
20   before marriage
      never touch you
      —your keen nosed mother, your rough brothers.
      I buried my hands
      in saffron, disguised them
25   over smoking tar,
      helped the honey gatherers ...

               . . . . .

      When we swam once
      I touched you in water
      and our bodies remained free,
30   you could hold me and be blind of smell.
      You climbed the bank and said

                     this is how you touch other women
      the grass cutter's wife, the lime burner's daughter.
      And you searched your arms
35   for the missing perfume

               and knew

               what good is it
      to be the lime burner's daughter
      left with no trace
40   as if not spoken to in the act of love
      as if wounded without the pleasure of a scar.
      You touched
      your belly to my hands
      in the dry air and said
45   I am the cinnamon
      peeler's wife. Smell me.

                                    (1982)

Bert Almon   (b. 1943)

Although he tags his e-mail messages with the phrase "recovering ironist," Bert Almon frequently relapses into insightful irony in his poetry. Born in Port Arthur, Texas, Almon received his B.A. from the University of Texas at El Paso in 1965. In 1968, three years before completing his Ph.D. at the University of New Mexico, he took a position teaching modern literature and creative writing at the University of Alberta in Edmonton. Almon published his first poetry collection, *The Return and Other Poems,* in 1968. He has since published seven more collections, with an eighth scheduled for publication, and three academic monographs. Almon has said, "I often write about my own experiences, but I've never been interested in confessional poetry." Instead, he turns a wry gaze at the events of ordinary life, catching with gentle humour or unsentimental emotion insights lost on those without his oblique vision.

The Feast of St. Valentine

Edmonton/Stettler/Edmonton[1]

Imagine—
spending Valentine's Day
fetching a side of beef from the country:
that's what our son called out as we drove away.
5   Romance is where you find it, I thought.

While the butcher's boy fetched the hand truck
full of rock-hard packages from the freezer,
I looked over the paper on the wall,
the Licence to Operate an Abattoir.
10   When I first saw abattoir in a book
I thought it was the most beautiful word
in the world. Romance is how you hear it.
Once I was sure that venison
must be the best meat in the world,
15   just from the sound of it. It meant
hunting in Sherwood Forest with Maid Marian[2]
and the feasting and music afterward.
You and I can make a feast with hamburger.

[1]Stettler is 182 km southeast of Edmonton. [2]the lover of the legendary Robin Hood and a member of his band of outlaws, who made their home in Sherwood Forest.

Romance is how you taste it.

20 We had lunch with your relatives
in the White Goose Restaurant,
where Valentine's meant paper hearts on the walls,
a rose on each table. Your brother,
who raised that frozen critter,
25 kidded me, saying we men had better have oysters[3]
if it's Valentine's day. I did, and all the way
to the city I thought of roses:
the antique shop called The White Rose
made me remember the old brands,
30 Five Roses Flour and Four Roses Whisky,
the little miracles of yeast.
Romance is where you see it.
Just before the city, we drove by
The Lucky Horseshoe Ranch,
35 a most auspicious name,
and my heart raced in a delirium
brought on by the oysters,
or Cupid nudging me in the ribs with an arrow.[4]
Romance is how you feel it.

(1998)

Jessica Williams[1] at the Yardbird Suite[2]

William Blake saw the soul of his brother Robert
ascend into heaven clapping its hands.[3]

At the jazz club, Jessica Williams played a song
in memory of her cat. At the break,
5 you told her about our own cat, Hercules,
shuddering and collapsing with a saddle thrombosis.
Williams held your hands with her own,
that famous wide span, and described

[3]popularly believed to be an aphrodisiac. [4]the arrows of Cupid, Roman god of love, caused
a person to fall in love. [1]American pianist and composer (b. 1948). [2]a jazz club in
Edmonton, Alberta. [3]Blake, who attended his brother's deathbed in 1787, later said that,
at the moment of death, he saw his brother's spirit "ascend heavenward clapping its hands
for joy."

how she felt her cat's energy leave its body,
10   rising through the ceiling.

Holding Hercules at the vet,
I felt him twitch once,
very slightly, as the needle entered.

In the second set, Williams played a number
15   with notes so glassy they might have broken,
then kicked it into stride piano.[4] After, we were the ones
who ascended into heaven, clapping our hands.

(2009)

Eavan Boland   (b. 1944)

Eavan Boland was born in Dublin, but she was raised in London and New York, where her father held diplomatic posts. Boland graduated from Trinity College, Dublin, in 1966 and has taught there and at other institutions in both Ireland and the United States. In 1996, she took up a position as a professor at Stanford University, dividing her time between California and Ireland. Boland's poetry often focuses on the history, legends, and social conditions in Ireland. Her poems also frequently treat the position of ordinary women in Irish life, in the male-dominated world of poetry, and in the domestic sphere. In most cases, she tends to use specific and sometimes seemingly ordinary incidents in either history or domestic life to frame her concern for larger issues, thereby giving concreteness and a sense of immediacy to those issues.

That the Science of Cartography[1] is Limited

– and not simply by the fact that this shading of
forest cannot show the fragrance of balsam,
the gloom of cypresses
is what I wish to prove.

5   When you and I were first in love we drove
to the borders of Connacht[2]
and entered a wood there.

Look down you said: this was once a famine road.

---

[4]a rhythmic jazz style in which the left hand "strides" up and down the keyboard. [1]mapmaking.
[2]western province of Ireland.

I looked down at ivy and the scutch grass
10   rough-cast stone had
disappeared into as you told me
in the second winter of their ordeal, in

1847, when the crop had failed twice,[3]
Relief Committees gave
15   the starving Irish such roads to build.

Where they died, there the road ended

and ends still and when I take down
the map of this island, it is never so
I can say here is
20   the masterful, the apt rendering of

the spherical as flat, nor
an ingenious design which persuades a curve
into a plane,
but to tell myself again that

25   the line which says woodland and cries hunger
and gives out among sweet pine and cypress,
and finds no horizon

will not be there.

(1994)

The Pomegranate

The only legend I have ever loved is
the story of a daughter lost in hell.
And found and rescued there.
Love and blackmail are the gist of it.
5   Ceres and Persephone the names.[1]

[3]in 1845, the potato blight began destroying the potato crops upon which most of the
Irish depended for food; in 1846, the second year of the ensuing Great Famine, more than
three-quarters of the potato crop was destroyed. [1]the Roman goddess Ceres (Greek,
Demeter) used blackmail, the withholding of crops from the earth, until she should get back
her daughter, Persephone, whom the lord of the underworld, Pluto (Greek, Hades), had
abducted and taken to his home; Ceres finally succeeded in getting her daughter released,
but Persephone ate six pomegranate seeds before leaving Hades, thus condemning herself to
spending six months of every year in the underworld, during which nothing grows, and six
months in the world above, during which the earth celebrates with renewed fertility.

10 And the best thing about the legend is
I can enter it anywhere. And have.
As a child in exile in
a city of fogs and strange consonants,
I read it first and at first I was
15 an exiled child in the crackling dusk of
the underworld, the stars blighted. Later
I walked out in a summer twilight
searching for my daughter at bed-time.
When she came running I was ready
20 to make any bargain to keep her.
I carried her back past whitebeams
and wasps and honey-scented buddleias.
But I was Ceres then and I knew
winter was in store for every leaf
25 on every tree on that road.
Was inescapable for each one we passed.
And for me.
      It is winter
and the stars are hidden.
30 I climb the stairs and stand where I can see
my child asleep beside her teen magazines,
her can of Coke, her plate of uncut fruit.
The pomegranate! How did I forget it?
She could have come home and been safe
35 and ended the story and all
our heart-broken searching but she reached
out a hand and plucked a pomegranate.
She put out her hand and pulled down
the French sound for apple and
40 the noise of stone and the proof
that even in the place of death,
at the heart of legend, in the midst
of rocks full of unshed tears
ready to be diamonds by the time
45 the story was told, a child can be
hungry. I could warn her. There is still a chance.
The rain is cold. The road is flint-coloured.
The suburb has cars and cable television.
The veiled stars are above ground.

→

50   It is another world. But what else
      can a mother give her daughter but such
      beautiful rifts in time?
      If I defer the grief I will diminish the gift.
      The legend will be hers as well as mine.
55   She will enter it. As I have.
      She will wake up. She will hold
      the papery flushed skin in her hand.
      And to her lips. I will say nothing.

(1994)

Marlene NourbeSe Philip (b. 1947)

Born in Moriah, Tobago, Philip spent much of her youth in Trinidad. After a residence in Jamaica, she received her B.Sc. in economics from the University of the West Indies. Moving to Canada, she earned both an M.A. in political science and an LL.B. at the University of Western Ontario. Philip then practised law for seven years, writing the entire time. Since 1982, she has devoted herself to writing professionally, and has also been a part-time academic. Philip published her first collection of poetry, *Thorns*, in 1980, and her second, *Salmon Courage,* in 1983. In 1988, she won the Casa del las Americas prize for the manuscript version of *She Tries Her Tongue; Her Silence Softly Breaks* (1989). Exploring the same cultural grounds as her previous collections, Philip's third book comprises grouped series of poetic utterances, grammar lessons, multiple choice questions, aphorisms, fictional excerpts, biblical allusions, and linguistic violence. In her essay, "Managing the Unmanagable" (1990), Philip suggests that such formal and linguistic experimentation is necessary for a historically colonized voice to emerge authentically from within the confines of the colonizer's language. By juxtaposing Western and African mythology, standard and demotic English, and male and female sexuality, Philip repeatedly attempts to subvert the hegemonic, white, male construction of history and to give voice to the "mother-tongue," the racial consciousness connecting the diasporic poet to her African ancestors. A relentlessly political artist, Philip is a founding member of Vision 21, a collective dedicated to fighting racism in the arts.

Sprung Rhythm[1]

It was there I learnt to walk
in sprung rhythm,
talk in syncopated bursts of music,
moulding, kneading, distorting, enhancing
5   a foreign language.
There, family was the whole village, if not island,
and came in all shades of black;
there, I first heard the soporific roar
of the ocean, before I grew ears to hear.
10 Where fear was wind and wind was fear,
and terror had branches that moved,
swayed, cracked, moaned, hissed . . . bent low with the trees
There, the swollen heavy bellied sky pressed
hard against a small hand clutching
15 a mother's skirt, before the rains came;
and the sun was always certain,
as we were of it.
Where every yellow March, the poui[2] mocked
Sir Walter Raleigh's gesture to his queen,[3]
20 and spread its coat of sunshine for me,
and the graceful ole time bouganvilla[4]
stroked and brushed heads of boys and girls.
Colour like life was put on
thick with an artist's knife – not brush.
25 Red was hibiscus[5], cock's combs[6] and pomeracs,[7]
and Jacob's coat[8] was a hedge of croton.[9]
There, where neat days patiently dovetailed

[1]term coined by Gerard Manley Hopkins to indicate a poetic meter in which every foot is a stressed syllable alone or begins with a stressed syllable followed by up to four unstressed syllables; Hopkins claimed that this metric system was closest to "the native and natural rhythm of speech." [2]a tropical flowering tree. [3]Sir Walter Raleigh is supposed to have spread his cloak over a mud puddle so that Elizabeth I would not muddy her feet, but scholars believe that the episode is a fiction designed to represent Raleigh as the ideal of courtesy. [4]a thorny flowering vine that usually has white flowers surrounded by papery bracts, or specialized leaves, of varying colours. [5]a fairly large flowering plant with showy, bright flowers. [6]usually called cockscomb, it is flower that comes in several bright colours and that resembles a rooster's comb or a brain. [7]also known as the Malay apple or mountain apple, this tree bears a red pear-shaped fruit and carpets the ground beneath with its fallen petals. [8]according to Genesis 37, Jacob gave to his son Joseph a coat of many colours, thereby making his other sons so jealous and angry that they sold Joseph into slavery. [9]a flowering tree or shrub whose green leaves change to various colours as the plant matures.

each other, glued with rituals of purgings,
school, washing and braiding of hair,
Sunday mass and blackpudding[10] breakfasts.
Was it there that I found the place
to know from,
to laugh and be from,
to return and weep from?
Was it there, or was it here?

(1983)

Meditations on the Declension of Beauty by the Girl with the Flying Cheek-bones

If not   If not   If
Not
If not in yours
        In whose

5   In whose language
Am I
If not in yours
        In whose

In whose language
10   Am I   I am
        If not in yours

In whose
    Am I
(if not in yours)
15   I am yours
In whose language
        Am I not
Am I not   I am yours
If not in yours
20   If not in yours
        In whose
In whose language
    Am I ...

[10]a sausage made with blood and a filler, such as oatmeal or rice, stuffed into a cleaned intestine, usually that of a pig.

Girl with the flying cheek-bones:
25 She is
I am
Woman with the behind that drives men mad
And if not in yours
Where is the woman with a nose broad
30 As her strength
If not in yours
In whose language
Is the man with the full-moon lips
Carrying the midnight of colour
35 Split by the stars—a smile
If not in yours
                    In whose

In whose language

                    Am I
40   Am I not
                    Am I   I am yours
                    Am I not   I am yours

                    Am I   I am

If not in yours
45   In whose
In whose language
                    Am I
If not in yours
                    Beautiful

(1989)

Don Domanski   (b. 1950)

Winner of the Governor General's Award in Poetry in 2007, Don Domanski was born in Sydney, Nova Scotia, and now lives in Halifax. He has said that the Celtic culture of Cape Breton Island immersed him in a natural sense of linguistic playfulness. He also acquired a deep love of nature, one that permeates almost all of his poetry. Domanski incorporates imagery and ideas from many religions, especially Buddhism and Taoism, and several mythologies, notably the Greek and Celtic, arguing that religions, mythologies, and ancient cultures offer a point of origin that the human heart can grasp, a starting point for spiritual discovery and identification.

In an interview, he said, "I see no difference between poetry and spiritual practice." Consequently, his poems tend to move from physical appearance towards spiritual reality. This quest for a spiritual truth that lies beyond linguistic expression leads him to blur the lines between the animate and inanimate and between the phenomenal and noumenal, requiring of readers not a logical analysis but an intuitive grasp of a poem's meaning.

Pearls

out in the dry grass of a grey day
the flies grow old and centreless
gradually drifting off to living rooms
to the screens of afternoon television

5   the family is packed in tight
against the soap opera
each face beautiful   glowing in the moth-light
each body slack and beyond communion
like the dead in the earth
10   with their symmetry poorly attended
making the gesture of pearls in a drawer.

(2007)

A Trace of Finches
for Margo

standing on a hill overlooking the Minas Basin[1]
the sea calm   hidebound with moonlight
stars and throwaway galaxies swaying east
Minerva's bird[2] gliding west on his mouse-run

5   quiet up here among the colourless wands of spruce
moths tracing thin bracelets in the air
fireflies drifting about with their gnomish-milliwatts
hives sighing in the undergrowth   a streamlet
crawling to Byzantium   its eyes down in the moss

10   below farmhouses have nosed in for the night
a fire behind each dream a   solitude behind each fire

---

[1]an inlet of the Bay of Fundy in Nova Scotia. [2]the owl, sacred to Minerva, the Roman goddess of wisdom.

an angel should appear just about now   to still the stillness
a divine messenger to pat down the hair of the sleepers

instead there's this bit of faith floating out there
15   somewhere above the valley floor   a wild belief
that the earth will sustain us   see us through
that we'll be angeled through with light at the end

I like the comfort in that   the small gods in that
gods small as finches   I think of finches
20   because when those birds all rise together into the air
it's like all the holy places
                  pulling away at once from the earth

I like the comfort of finches   a song's redemption
a feather's nudge into flight at the appropriate moment

25   what better wings to carry the soul away
a trace of finches drifting up Mammon's[3] outline
to be elegy-plated high across the grief of the world

a long grief finally at truce with our senses
a flutter of plumage and an avian resolve

30   the way opened to a lingering darkness
a wayward shine from the receding light
the way small birds arrive and take our breath away.

                                        (2007)

Naomi Shihab Nye   (b. 1952)

Naomi Shihab Nye was born in St. Louis, Missouri, to a Palestinian father
and American mother. Nye gained some understanding of her Arabic
heritage through brief stays abroad. The first time was when her family
moved to Jerusalem in 1966; with the outbreak of war in the following
year, they returned to the United States. While she was in high school,
she again returned to live in the Old City in Jerusalem. In the United
States, Nye made her home in San Antonio, where she graduated from
Trinity University. Connections to family and to community, as well as a
sense of place, are dominant themes in many of her poems. Her poetry is
political, but not in a declamatory way. Instead, Nye seizes on small things

---

[3]a negative personification of wealth and materialism as a god.

and events to suggest the importance of the ordinary in shaping lives and values.

Arabic

The man with laughing eyes stopped smiling
to say, "Until you speak Arabic,
you will not understand pain."

Something to do with the back of the head,
5   an Arab carries sorrow in the back of the head
that only language cracks, the thrum of stones

weeping, grating hinge on an old metal gate.
"Once you know," he whispered, "you can
        enter the room
10   whenever you need to. Music you heard
        from a distance,

the slapped drum of a stranger's wedding,
wells up inside your skin, inside rain, a thousand
pulsing tongues. You are changed."

15   Outside, the snow had finally stopped.
In a land where snow rarely falls,
we had felt our days grow white and still.

I thought pain had no tongue. Or every tongue
at once, supreme translator, sieve. I admit my
20   shame. To live on the brink of Arabic, tugging

its rich threads without understanding
how to weave the rug . . . I have no gift.
The sound, but not the sense.

I kept looking over his shoulder for someone else
25   to talk to, recalling my dying friend
        who only scrawled
I can't write. What good would any grammar
        have been

to her then? I touched his arm, held it hard,
30   which sometimes you don't do in the Middle East,
and said, *I'll work on it,* feeling sad

for his good strict heart, but later in the slick street
hailed a taxi by shouting *Pain!* And it stopped
in every language and opened its doors.

(1994)

Brushing Lives

In Alexandria a waitress skimmed between tables
in a black sheath skirt, her jaw precise and elegant,
hair waving out from a definite scalp like 1942—
I saw the most beautiful woman of my life that day.
5   She held herself brilliantly, one gracious arm
balancing a stumpy Coke bottle on a tray.
Said "yes" and "thank you" in a deep, dazed voice.
And the men went on talking. And the cars outside
were not headed toward her door.

10   Later my father appeared with a husky voice.
In a shop so dark he had to blink twice
an ancient man sunk low on a stool said,
"You talk like the men who lived in the world
when I was young." Wouldn't say more,
15   till my father mentioned Palestine
and the gentleman rose, both arms out, streaming
cheeks. "I have stopped saying it. So many years."
My father held him there, held Palestine, in the dark,
at the corner of two honking streets.
20   He got lost coming back to our hotel.

Who else? They're out there.
The ones who could save or break us,
the ones we're lonely for,
the ones with an answer the size of a
25   pocket handkerchief or a shovel,
the ones who know the story before
our own story starts,
the ones who suffered what we most fear
and survived.

30   Sometimes we stand side-by-side
on the platform waiting for the train

→

and the miracle is not the meeting
but the miss—
we feel full already, we have enough friends.

(1994)

Di Brandt   (b. 1952)

Anger and regret, rejection and longing colour the poems of Di Brandt. Born Diana Janzen in Winkler, Manitoba, and raised in the Mennonite community of Reinland, she left that restrictive and patriarchal community at the age of 17. She received a B.A. from the University of Manitoba, during which time she was profoundly influenced by feminist ideas. Marriage, motherhood, and divorce continued to shape her ideas about relationships while she completed an M.A. at the University of Toronto and then a Ph.D. at Manitoba. Her anger and rejection of her strict Mennonite upbringing are evident in her first book, *questions i asked my mother* (1987), in which some of the poems convey a breathless stream-of-consciousness inquisition of her upbringing. At the same time as she rejected what she considered to be a primitive dismissal of females, she recognized that her strict community had given her an appreciation of nature and a sense of something beyond the narcissism that characterizes so much of the culture of the contemporary world she adopted. Combined with her sense of the importance of maternity, these values find expression in poems about the value of nature, which the modern industrial world threatens, and the connections between mother and child. She also has said that the long lines of the language she learned as a child and the incantatory, prophet language of worship have influenced her writing, but that she often needs to tame such ecstatic lines. Whether espousing the independence and integrity of female life or protesting the destruction of nature for momentary material gain, Brandt's poems flow with an energy attributable to the tension between her embrace of her modern life and her respect for and longing for an older way of life that meaningfully unifies natural and human life.

but what do you think

but what do you think my father says this verse means if it's not
about the end of the world look that's obviously a misreading i say
the verb grammatically speaking doesn't have an object in this
instance so it can't possibly be made to that's exactly what i mean
5   he says waving the book in mid air if my father ever shouted he
would be shouting now you don't really care about the meaning all

you ever think about is grammar & fancy words i never even heard of
where i come from the reason you learn to read is to understand God's
Holy Word i only went to school 7 year & it's done me okay what are
10 you going to do with all this hifalutin education anyway don't you
think it's time you got a job & did some honest work for a change
the meaning i say through clenched teeth is related to the structure
of the sentence for godsake anybody can see that you can't just take
some old crackpot idea & say you found it in these words even the
15 Bible has to make some sense the Bible my father says the veins in
his neck turning a slow purple is revealed to those gathered together
in His name you don't even go to church how can you know anything of
the truth you're no better than the heathen on the street the way
you live around here if i'd aknown my own daughter would end up like
20 this you're the one i say who started this conversation what did you
ask me for if i'm not entitled to an opinion please my mother says
crying as usual why don't we go for a walk or something you think
i'll weep i'll not weep we glare at each other with bright fierce
eyes my father & i she still tries after all these years to end this
25 argument between us arrest deflect its bitter motion does she know
this is all there is for us these words dancing painfully across the
sharp etched lines of his God ridden book & does she does he do we
really want this crazy cakewalk to stop

(1992)

Here at the Heart of the Ravaged Heart

Here at the heart of the ravaged heart
of the Dead Land, lilacs mixing with
the dead rain, we like to kill our gods
and eat them too, like all good christians
5   do, no mystery moths or beetles for us,
or locusts shining in the grass, nosiree,
all our trillion little winged deities, bees,
mosquitoes, houseflies, butterflies,
fruitflies, fishflies, horseflies, Junebugs,
10 cicadas now in radical chemical jeopardy,
and our lettuce and raspberries, and yet,
and yet, deer graze in the forest along
the ravine, grasshoppers and crickets
miraculously sing in forgotten ditches
15 along the fields, wasps stray through
chlorpyrifos clouds to out of the way

→

sweet milkweed, thistle, goldenrod
clumps, just then for a moment, above
around below the shadow of the shadow
20 of these endless depleted uranium driven
grey grey grey grey grey apocalyptic
streets, these lurking cancer cells, hawks
and goldfinches, bright coloured, let's
turn it all around, asphalt splitting
25 volcanic magic, blue butterflies, sweet
grass, adrenalin, circling darting
fluttering kicking bursting in

(2003)

Roo Borson   (b. 1952)

Ruth Elizabeth Borson, who is known by a childhood abbreviation of her first name, was born in Berkeley, California. She enrolled at the University of California at Santa Barbara in 1969, and after two years, transferred to Goddard College in Vermont, from which she graduated with a B.A. in 1973. The following year, she moved to Canada, attending the University of British Columbia, where she completed an M.F.A. in Creative Writing in 1977. Borson now resides in Toronto with Kim Maltman, a poet and physicist. Along with Andy Paterson, Borson and Maltman perform as the collaborative poetry group Pain Not Bread, which has published one collection, *Introduction to the Introduction to Wang Wei* (2000). Borson's first published book was *Landfall* (1977), a revised version of her M.F.A. project. Subsequent collections include *The Whole Night Coming Home* (1984), *Night Walk: Selected Poems* (1994), *Water Memory* (1996), and *Short Journey Upriver Toward Oishida* (2004), winner of the Governor General's Award for Poetry. Borson is noted for poems that take sharp looks at both nature and the activities of daily life, finding in them meanings and moods that would escape a casual glance. Her poems make intellectual and emotional connections between the things that she sees in a given moment and past experiences, both her own and those that she has encountered in literature, particularly the works of the classical Japanese poets Saigyo (1118–1190) and Basho (1644–1694). Her major concern, however, is not so much with communicating ideas as it is with transforming her vision of the world into musical speech that makes a direct, aesthetic connection with listeners and readers.

The Ways We're Taught

So he takes her to a place in the hills where he
thinks she'll give in to him.
That's what he's been taught:
girls can't resist pretty things.

5 So he shows her how the lights
shine through the trees
and then undoes his pants.
That's what they've been taught,
the girl to let herself be taken
10 so far and then say no, the boy
to try for anything.
The hills just lie there like rumpled velvet,
and the skull of the moon floats out of them.
This is what it is to be fifteen
15 and not know what to make of being alive.
The party was loud. If you drink a little
the music takes care of everything,
it lifts you off the floor, dancing forward
at unknown miles an hour until somebody
20 falls down and has to be dragged outside.
It's easy to drink too much,
to let it all get away with you.
There's always somebody who never learns
what a bottle and a couple of pills can do.
25 Still, they've always woken up, telling the story
of how beautiful the tall cool trees look
when you're falling backwards.
So nobody's too shaken up,
somebody thinks to put on another record
30 and keep dancing. Feelings,
they run so much smoother
when they're riding on the notes
of somebody else's song.
It's easier to feel anything
35 once it's been said before.
The girls, they're all looking around
for a boy who'll give them anything,
and the boys know it, they've been taught
to take what they can get.
40 So he offers her a ride home.
He says he'll show her something along the way.

(1984)

Spring Cherries

All night, bending
over my back fence: spring.

➡

My neighbour's cherry tree.

No need to go far today.
Just these dandelions
staring down the sky.

Like Saigyō[1] then.
Wandering cold among the blossoms
after night falls—

The blossoming cherry
so alight outside my window
I can read his poems by it.

A poem about a robin—yes,
but that was long ago,
and I was young and foolish. Saigyō,

now I blush, and so become the colour of that robin,
to have been so
"insufficiently impressed."

Suddenly the depths: the morning fresh,
but overcast. Wild honeysuckle,
colours of dawn, all day.

Easy to forget
how sick I used to feel
each spring—

This morning, wanting to shut myself away
even from blossoms—my father's child, as they used to say.
And then those blossoms (knock at the door)
splashed against my neighbour's fence—

A package. First me, then the delivery man—
spring light
looking out
from our faces.

The man around the corner
who used to come out to bother me
must be ill now. As I pass, he calls out weakly
Hey girl—

[1]Noriyoko Sato (1118–1190) adopted the name Saigyō, which means "Western Journey," when he became a Buddhist priest. He wandered across Japan writing poetry. Saigyō was so moved by the beauty of the cherry blossoms on Mt. Yoshino that he wrote a number of celebrated poems about them, and he continued to write about cherry blossoms until his death.

Soon I'll be fifty.
Around the block, another cherry tree.
Another's cherry tree. Like it I want to begin
40   blossoming first from the very tips.

I think of them again:
all those years tramping the sidewalks—
tramping the sidewalks, sometimes finding just the right present!

Wanting to shut myself away even from blossoms,
45   this year
the date of my father's birthday came round again.

First, snow
milling about the house,
then petals—
50   inside: this great dumb winter fly.
Saigyō, is that you?
In the early-morning dark,
lilac breeze through the window,
summer storm behind that—

(2004)

Louise Bernice Halfe   (b. 1953)

Also known as Sky Dancer, Halfe was born in Two Hills, Alberta, and raised on the Saddle Lake Indian Reserve. Interested in improving the social and psychological conditions of Native Canadians, Halfe earned a bachelor of social work from the University of Regina and a certificate in drugs and alcohol counselling from the Nechi Institute (St. Albert, Alberta). Though she had been keeping a journal since high school, it was during a six-year residency in Saskatchewan that Halfe first collected her journal writings into a book of poetry, *Bear Bones & Feathers* (1994). Shortlisted for both the Spirit of Saskatchewan Award and the Gerald Lampert Award, this collection won the Milton Acorn People's Poetry Award in 1996. Her second collection, *Blue Marrow* (1998), which was nominated for the Governor General's Award for Poetry, combines prose, poetry, and journal entries to express the polyphonic voices of her Native ancestors and their spiritual inheritors. The poem reprinted below shows a distinctive feature of Halfe's talent: her ability to use dialect and humour for pointed social comment.

Body Politics

Mama said,

Real woman
don't steal
from the sky and wear clouds
5   on their eyelids.

Real woman
eat rabbit well-done
not left half-raw
on their mouth.

10   Real woman
have lots of meat
on their bones.
They're not starving,
hobbled horses
15   with bony, grinding hips.

Real woman caress
with featherstone hands
not with falcon fingernails
that have never worked.

20   When she was finished talking
she clicked her teeth
lifted her arse
and farted
at the passing
25   city women.

(1994)

Carol Ann Duffy   (b. 1955)

The first woman to be appointed Poet Laureate of the United Kingdom, Carol Ann Duffy was born in Glasgow, Scotland, but moved to Staffordshire, England, at the age of six. She graduated with a degree in philosophy from the University of Liverpool, has taught at a number of institutions, and is currently creative writing director at Manchester Metropolitan University. In addition to her very popular poetry, she has written plays and a number of books for children. When she was appointed Laureate in 1999, Duffy became the first openly bisexual person to hold the position. Although some of her love poems focus on lesbian relationships, Duffy has denied that she is a lesbian poet: "I define myself as a poet and as a mother – that's all." Conventional elements, such as rhyme, are common in her poems, but she has said that she is not interested in deliberately "poetic" language: "I like to use simple words, but in a complicated way." Duffy has also said that "Poetry, above all, is a series of intense moments...." Colloquial language makes these intensely emotional moments widely accessible. Whether her subject matter is her memories of childhood, the emotions of love and the loss of love, family relationships, history, or the fantasies and feelings of ordinary people, and whether she is writing a dramatic monologue or a lyrical poem, Duffy is a powerful poet: she not only evokes strong emotions, but she also entertains with her humour and her sometimes acerbic wit, surprises with the connections and turns between narrative or descriptive elements, and stimulates thought.

Prayer

Some days, although we cannot pray, a prayer
utters itself. So, a woman will lift
her head from the sieve of her hands and stare
at the minims[1] sung by a tree, a sudden gift.

5   Some nights, although we are faithless, the truth
enters our hearts, that small familiar pain;
then a man will stand stock-still, hearing his youth
in the distant Latin chanting of a train.

Pray for us now. Grade I piano scales
10 console the lodger looking out across
a Midlands town. Then dusk, and someone calls
a child's name as though they named their loss.

Darkness outside. Inside, the radio's prayer–
Rockall. Malin. Dogger. Finisterre.[2]

(1993)

The Love Poem

Till love exhausts itself, longs
for the sleep of words –

        my mistress' eyes[1] –

[1] half notes. [2] sea areas named in the weather forecasts broadcast four times daily on BBC Radio; Finisterre was renamed FitzRoy in 2002. [1] see William Shakespeare's Sonnet 130 ("My mistress' eyes are nothing like the sun").

to lie on a white sheet, at rest
in the language –

5   let me count the ways[2] –
or shrink to a phrase like an epitaph –

                           come live
with me[3] –
or fall from its own high cloud as syllables
10 in a pool of verse –

                   one hour with thee.[4]

Till love gives in and speaks
in the whisper of art –

                dear heart,
15 how like you this?[5] –
love's lips pursed to quotation marks
kissing a line –

              look in thy heart
and write[6] –
20 love's light fading, darkening,
black as ink on a page –

                there is a garden
in her face.[7]

Till love is all in the mind –

25   O my America!
my new-found land[8] –
or all in the pen
in the writer's hand –

              behold, thou art fair[9] –
30 not there, except in a poem,
known by heart like a prayer,
both near and far,
near and far –

            the desire of the moth
35 for the star.[10]

(2005)

[2]see Elizabeth Barrett Browning's *Sonnets from the Portuguese* XLIII ("How do I love thee?").[3]see Christopher Marlow's "The Passionate Shepherd to His Love." [4]see Sir Walter Scott's "An Hour with Thee" (not included in this anthology). [5]see Sir Thomas Wyatt's "They Flee from Me" (not included in this anthology). [6]see Sir Philip Sydney's *Astophel and Stella* sonnet "Loving in Truth." [7]see Campion's lyric "There Is a Garden in Her Face" (not included in this anthology). [8]see John Donne's Elegy XIX: To His Mistress on Going to Bed. [9]see The King James version of *The Song of Solomon* 1:15. [10]see Percy Bysshe Shelley's "To —" ("One word is too often profaned") (not included in this anthology).

Marilyn Dumont   (b. 1955)

Born in Olds, Alberta, Dumont received a B.A. from the University of Alberta and an M.F.A. from the University of British Columbia. A descendent of the legendary Gabriel Dumont, who led Métis military forces during the Northwest Resistance of 1885, Dumont has long been a Native educator and rights activist. Her first collection of poetry, A *Really Good Brown Girl* (1996), winner of the Gerald Lampert Award, examines the manifest ways that western hegemonic society, or "White Noise," distorts and does violence to Native and Métis notions of self and culture. In particular, these poems show the debilitating self-consciousness that develops from the feeling that white society constantly judges those people outside the main culture. By juxtaposing images of her Cree/Métis heritage with images showing the dominant culture debasing or suppressing that heritage, especially its verbal heritage, these poems are also self-conscious in a more positive way. Dumont's poems, that is, do more than protest victimization: they express consciousness of an identity formed both by oppression and by traditions and family relationships of which the oppressors lack understanding; they thus celebrate the vitality and persistence of the outsider.

Letter to Sir John A. Macdonald[1]

Dear John: I'm still here and halfbreed,
after all these years
you're dead, funny thing,
that railway you wanted so badly,
5   there was talk a year ago
of shutting it down
and part of it was shut down,
the dayliner at least,
"from sea to shining sea,"
10   and you know, John,
after all that shuffling us around to suit the settlers,
we're still here and Métis.

We're still here
after Meech Lake[2] and

$$\longrightarrow$$

[1]Sir John Alexander Macdonald (1815–1891), the first prime minister of Canada (1867–73, 1878–91), promoted construction of the transcontinental railway, using it before it was even completed to send troops to suppress Louis Riel's last rebellion (see note 4). [2]a proposed amendment to the Constitution Act, agreed to in principle by Prime Minister Brian Mulroney and ten provincial premiers in meetings at Meech Lake, Quebec, on April 30, 1987. The final proposal was issued in Ottawa on June 3, 1987. Because it would have granted Quebec designation as a "distinct society," objectors, notably Manitoba MLA Elijah Harper, an Ojibway Cree, successfully campaigned against ratification of the Meech Lake Accord.

15   one no-good-for-nothin-Indian
holdin-up-the-train,
stalling the "Cabin syllables/Nouns of settlement,
/ ... steel syntax [and]/The long sentence of its exploitation"[3]
and John, that goddamned railroad never made this a great nation,
20   cause the railway shut down
and this country is still quarreling over unity,
and Riel[4] is dead
but he just keeps coming back
in all the Bill Wilsons[5] yet to speak out of turn or favour
25   because you know as well as I
that we were railroaded
by some steel tracks that didn't last
and some settlers who wouldn't settle
and it's funny we're still here and callin ourselves halfbreed.

(1996)

The Devil's Language

1. I have since reconsidered Eliot[1]
    and the Great White way of writing English
    standard that is
    the great white way
5   has measured, judged and assessed me   all my life
    by its
    lily white words
    its picket fence sentences
    and manicured paragraphs
10   one wrong sound and you're shelved in the Native Literature section

➡

---

[3]F. R. Scott, "Laurentian Shield" [Dumont's note]. [4]Louis Riel (1844–1885), leader of Métis uprisings over land rights in the Red River valley (1869) and in Saskatchewan (1884–85). Despite legends of his madness and his official execution for treason, Riel embodies for many native and other Canadians a national revolutionary ideal. [5]Wilson (Hemas Ka-lee-lee-kla), member of the Cape Mudge Indian Band of Comox, B.C., became an important national representative for Native rights, especially through his involvement in the Assembly of First Nations. [1]T. S. Eliot (1888–1965), influential American-born English poet, dramatist, and critic (see pages 225–234), wrote learned, allusive poetry. He expressed his reverence for tradition in his essay "Tradition and the Individual Talent" (1922), which envisions literary history as shaped by the unique talents of great poets, the examples of whom are white males.

resistance writing
a mad Indian
unpredictable
on the war path
15 native ethnic protest
the Great White way could silence us all
if we let it
it's had its hand over my mouth since my first day of school
since Dick and Jane, ABC's and fingernail checks
20 syntactic laws: use the wrong order or
register and you're a dumb Indian
dumb, drunk or violent
my father doesn't read or write
the King's English says he's
25 dumb but he speaks Cree
how many of you speak Cree?
correct Cree not correct English
grammatically correct Cree
is there one?

30 2. is there a Received Pronunciation of Cree, is there
a Modern Cree Usage?
the Chief's Cree not the King's English

as if violating God the Father and standard English
is like talking back(wards)

35 as if speaking the devil's language is
talking back
back(words)
back to your mother's sound, your mother's tongue, your mother's language
back to that clearing in the bush
40 in the tall black spruce

3. near the sound of horses and wind
where you sat on her knee in a canvas tent
and she fed you bannock and tea
and syllables
45 that echo in your mind now, now
that you can't make the sound
of that voice that rocks you and sings you to sleep
in the devil's language.

(1996)

Armand Garnet Ruffo   (b. 1955)

Born in the northern Ontario town of Chapleau, Armand Garnet Ruffo is of Ojibwa ancestry and belongs to the Biscotasing branch of the Sagamok First Nation. He received an honours degree in English at the University of Ottawa and an M.A. in literature and creative writing from the University of Windsor. He currently teaches Native literature at Carleton University. A prolific author of plays, stories, and essays, in addition to poetry, Ruffo investigates in both historical and contemporary contexts issues of aboriginal identity. His poetry is notable for developing progressively more complex and sustained explorations of these issues. For example, in his second book, *Grey Owl: The Mystery of Archie Belaney* (1997), Ruffo composed a poetic biography of the famous English writer who posed as a Native that raises issues of Native rights, culture, and the environment, and in his third book, *At Geronimo's Grave* (2001), he presented events in Geronimo's life as analogues to the continuing struggles of Natives.

Poem for Duncan Campbell Scott[1]

(Canadian poet who "had a long and distinguished career
in the Department of Indian Affairs, retiring in 1932."
The Penguin Book of Canadian Verse)

Who is this black coat and tie?
Christian severity etched in the lines
he draws from his mouth. Clearly a noble man
who believes in work and mission. See
5   how he rises from the red velvet chair,
rises out of the boat with the two Union Jacks
fluttering like birds of prey
and makes his way towards our tents.
This man looks as if he could walk on water
10   and for our benefit probably would,
if he could.

He says he comes from Ottawa way, Odawa country,
comes to talk treaty and annuity and destiny,
to make the inevitable less painful,
15   bearing gifts that must be had.
Notice how he speaks aloud and forthright:
        This or Nothing.
        Beware! Without title to the land

---

[1]see the entry for Duncan Campbell Scott in this anthology.

under the Crown you have no legal right
    to be here.
Speaks as though what has been long decided wasn't.
As though he wasn't merely carrying out his duty
to God and King. But sincerely felt.

Some whisper this man lives in a house of many rooms,
has a cook and a maid and even a gardener
to cut his grass and water his flowers.
Some don't care, they don't like the look of him.
They say he asks many questions but
doesn't wait to listen. Asks
much about yesterday, little about today
and acts as if he knows tomorrow.
Others don't like the way he's always busy writing
stuff in the notebook he carries. Him,
he calls it poetry
and says it will make us who are doomed
live forever.

(1994)

On The Line

Sign, sign,
on the dotted line
and you will be mine
forever and ever,
like the mountains
and the lakes,
sky, soil,
everything I take.

I will supply you
with all
your needs,
a bible,
a blanket,
rations and beads.

If you can't understand me
don't worry

→

or whine,
heed what I say,
what is yours
20   is mine.

So sign on the line,
what more
can be said,
my word is law,
25   you have nothing
to dread.

You can't resist
so don't
even try,
30   I have cannons

and armies,
cities
and spies.

Oh, yes,
35   I do have a home,
it is far
far away,
but I like what I see,
and I've decided
40   to stay.

(2001)

Jan Zwicky   (b. 1955)

An award-winning poet, professional musician, and philosopher, Jan Zwicky was born and raised in Alberta. She received her B.A. from the University of Calgary and an M.A. and Ph.D. in philosophy from the University of Toronto. She taught at the University of New Brunswick before taking a position in the Philosophy Department of the University of Victoria in 1996. Zwicky began her poetry career with publication of *Wittgenstein Elegies* (1986), a volume that clearly sets out her interest in combining lyric poetry and philosophy. She won the Governor General's Award for *Songs for Relinquishing the Earth* (1998), a book that she originally self-published in hand-sewn volumes, each prepared individually for those requesting one. Given her professional role as a philosopher and her accomplishments as a musician, it is not surprising that the connection between music and philosophy is a major concern in both her poetry and prose works. In accepting the Governor General's Award, she declared that "Lyric art is intimate" and that it is "a struggle to achieve an integrity of spirit, body, and mind." For her, lyric poetry is not simply a musical way of writing but is actually part of a mode of thought, a prelinguistic way that connects us to the rhythms of the natural world from which we have been separated because of our reliance on technological, linguistic, and rational habits of mind.

Border Station

There had been flooding all that summer, I recall,
acres of grey-brown footage from the Midwest—
but with reports confined to property, and human interest,
the reasons for the land's incontinence suppressed, those images
5   had skimmed past, seeming, as usual, not quite real.
The day had been hot, clear,
we'd eaten supper on the porch, and
later, quite late, had turned the radio on upstairs—
some thought of midnight news, perhaps—
10   I don't remember now.
The signal we pulled in—strongly,
because we weren't far from the border then—
was the last half-hour of a Brewers–Red Sox game.
It was coming from Milwaukee,
15   top of the ninth, two out, the Brewers leading,
and we hadn't been listening long when the announcer,
between a line out and Hatcher's[1]
coming to the plate, commented on the weather:
there'd been a rain delay, it had been raining heavily before,
20   but now was easing up, just a light shower falling,
though a lot of lightning was still visible to the east and south.
Raised on the prairies, I
could see it clearly, suddenly
could see the whole scene clearly:
25   the crowd dwindling, several
umbrellas, the glittering aluminum of vacated seats,
the misted loaf of arc-lit light, the night,
deeper by contrast, thick and wet and brown
around it, flickering.

[1]Billy Hatcher played outfield for the Boston Red Sox from 1992 to 1994.

30 And at the same time I was struck, too—like
looking out across a huge relief map—by the hundreds of miles
between our bedroom and Milwaukee, by that continental
distance, and was overtaken inexplicably
by sorrow.
35   It was as though
in that moment of deep focus
I had tasted the idea of America.
As though it really might have had
something to do with baseball, and radio, and the beauty
40 of the storms that can form in the vast light above the plains—or,
no, extremity of some kind—clarity, or tenderness—
as though, that close to the end, levels
already rising on the leveed banks again,
the mistakes might have been human:
45 not justifiable, but as though
some sort of story might be told, simply,
from defeat, without apology, the way you might describe
the fatal accident—not to make sense of it,
but just to say, too late but still to say,
50 something had happened:
there was blood, blood everywhere, we hadn't realized,
by the time we noticed, rivers of it,
nothing could be done.

(1996)   (1998)

Poppies

Some days, the wall that separates us from the future
is too thin. Standing in my mother's garden
by the bed of poppies on the northwest slope, wind
in the trees and the five-mile sky billowing over us,
5 I am caught again by their colour: water-colour,
sheer, like ice or silk, or, we imagine,
freedom. Their petals on the ground
collect in drifts, explosions

→

of arterial light.

Or perhaps it's that we are

that membrane, an instant thick, days
shine right through us as we charge around,
looking for some explanation in what hasn't happened yet
or what will never happen again. Like last night at dinner:
glancing up at the picture, the one that's always hung there,
the sudden clear presentiment that I would live
to walk into that dining room someday, after
the last death, and find it
waiting for me, the entire past
dangling from a finishing nail.

Poppies, what can they teach us?
The windshot light fills them
and they are blind.

(1996)   (1998)

Robert Crawford   (b. 1959)

A scholar, an editor, and a poet, Robert Crawford was born in 1959 at Bellshill, near Glasgow. After receiving an M.A. from Glasgow University, he studied at Oxford University, earning the degree of D.Phil. He is now Professor of Modern Scottish Literature at the University of St Andrews. As an academic, Crawford has explored, in such books as *Devolving English Literature* (1992) and *The Scottish Invention of English Literature* (1998), the attempts of Scottish writers to maintain their distinctive culture in spite of the dominance of English political and cultural institutions. As coeditor of the international poetry magazine *Verses* and of *The Penguin Book of Poetry since 1945 from Britain and Ireland* (1998), he has been instrumental in bringing the work of younger poets to critical attention. Crawford himself has published five collections of poetry: *A Scottish Assembly* (1990), *Talkies* (1992), *Masculinity* (1996), *Spirit Machines* (1999), and *The Tip of My Tongue* (2003). This poetry is regional in the best sense of the term, displaying a profound understanding of the ways in which history, social conditions, and rugged landscape have affected the character of the Scottish people. Although they are always evident, even if it is just in the mention of setting, the regional concerns are not always foremost; Crawford also explores deeply personal issues, such as the emotions that arise in modern relationships. In all of his poems, however, Crawford tends to make his points more through implication, through wit and verbal restraint, than through overt pronouncements of ideas.

Anne of Green Gables[1]

Short moneyless summers at West Kilbride[2] you sat out
On the back steps with a view of the outside toilet
Reading the Anne books, one after the datestamped next,

Anne of Windy Willows, Anne of Avonlea,
5   *Anne of the Island, Anne's House of Dreams.*
No books were ever as good as these

From West Kilbride Public Library
That always had to go back.
When we got married, one by one

10   You bought the whole set, reading them through. At first
I was jealous when you sat not speaking,
Then put the books away on your own shelf.

"'How white the moonlight is tonight,' said Anne
Blythe to herself."[3] At first
15   I was jealous. Not now.

(1992)

George Elliott Clarke   (b. 1960)

Born in Windsor Plains, Nova Scotia, Clarke was raised in Halifax. Clarke, who holds a Ph.D. from Queen's University, taught English and Canadian studies at Duke University and was the third Seagram Visiting Chair of Canadian Studies at McGill (1998–99). Now a professor at the University of Toronto, he has published numerous critical articles in creative and scholarly journals. He has also edited *Fire on the Water: An Anthology of Black Nova Scotian Writing* (1991–92) and *Eyeing the North Star: Directions in African-Canadian Literature* (1997). Clarke's first published collection, *Saltwater Spirituals and Deeper Blues* (1983), nominated for the Bliss Carman Award for poetry, explores the aesthetic and spiritual concerns of Nova Scotia's black citizens. In *Whylah Falls* (1990), winner of the Archibald Lampman Award for poetry, Clarke attempts to "remap" Nova Scotia by tracing the spiritual geography of the black community, one that has often been exiled from Canadian historical and political writing. In *Lush Dreams, Blue Exile: Fugitive Poems, 1978–1993* (1994), Clarke coined

[1]Anne Shirley, the central character of Anne of *Green Gables* (1908), by Lucy Maud Montgomery (1874–1942), is an orphan who displays a romantic love of nature and beauty. She is adopted by an elderly brother and sister, who live on a Prince Edward Island farm called Green Gables. Her story continues in a number of sequels, including Anne of *Windy Poplars* (1936), which was released in the United Kingdom as Anne of *Windy Willows, Anne of Avonlea* (1909), Anne of *the Island* (1915), and Anne's *House of Dreams* (1917). In this last title, she marries her one-time school rival, Gilbert Blythe. [2]coastal town in Ayrshire, southwest of Glasgow. [3]first part of the opening sentence of Anne of *Ingleside* (1939).

the term "Africadian" to describe his community. He won the Governor General's Award for *Execution Poems* (2001). Throughout his poetry and other writing, he has sought to make readers aware of the unique Africadian perspective on aesthetic and political values.

Blank Sonnet

The air smells of rhubarb, occasional
Roses, or first birth of blossoms, a fresh,
Undulant hurt, so body snaps and curls
Like flower. I step through snow as thin as script,
5   Watch white stars spin dizzy as drunks, and yearn
To sleep beneath a patchwork quilt of rum.
I want the slow, sure collapse of language
Washed out by alcohol. Lovely Shelley,[1]
I have no use for measured, cadenced verse
10 If you won't read. Icarus-like,[2] I'll fall
Against this page of snow, tumble blackly
Across vision to drown in the white sea
That closes every poem—the white reverse
That cancels the blackness of each image.

(1990)

Casualties

January 16, 1991[1]
Snow annihilates all beauty
this merciless January.
A white blitzkrieg, Klan—cruel,
arsons and obliterates.

5   Piercing lies numb us to pain.
Nerves and words die so we
can't feel agony or passion,
so we can't flinch or cry,

when we spy blurred children's
10 charred bodies protruding
from the smoking rubble

→

[1]Shelley Clemence, a female resident of the fictional Whylah Falls, is the beloved of the narrator, known as X. [2]in Greek mythology, Icarus, son of Daedalus, escaped from Crete on wings his father had made for him. He flew so close to the sun, however, that the wax holding together the wings melted, and he fell into the Aegean Sea. [1]the United States began the Persian Gulf War on January 16, 1991, by launching air attacks against Iraq, which had defied a United Nations' resolution to withdraw from Kuwait by the previous day.

of statistics or see a man

stumbling in a blizzard
of bullets. Everything is
normal, absurdly normal.
We see, as if through a snow-

storm, darkly. Reporters
rat-a-tat-tat tactics,
stratagems. Missiles bristle
behind newspaper lines.

Our minds chill; we weather
the storm, huddle in dreams.
Exposed, though, a woman,
lashed by lightning, repents

of her flesh, becomes a living
X-ray, "collateral damage."
The first casualty of war
is language.

(1992)

Michael Crummey   (b. 1965)

Born in the mining town of Buchans, Newfoundland, Michael Crummey moved to Labrador with his family when he was fourteen. He earned a B.A. from Memorial University, an M.A. from Queen's University, Kingston, and began studies towards a Ph.D. Deciding that he did not want to pursue an academic life, he dropped out of the program and took a series of odd jobs. A novelist and non-fiction author as well as a poet, Crummey focuses most of his attention on the people and history of Newfoundland. He has said in an interview that he has been most influenced by poets like Al Purdy who use common language to narrate the lives of ordinary people. He also notes that Purdy had a deep sense of the past. In much of his work, Crummey is a chronicler of Newfoundland's ordinary people, celebrating them, their deep connection to the land and sea, and their unflagging spirit in spite of the hard lives they lead. He seeks to show the heroic in the ordinary, and he frequently laments the passing of a way of life that, in spite of its hardships, had moments of nobility and profound tenderness. At the same time, however, he also indicates that the past is still a vital force shaping Newfoundlanders' current identity.

What's Lost

The Labrador coastline is a spill of islands,
salt-shaker tumble of stone,

a cartographer's nightmare–
on the coastal boat 50 years ago
5   the third mate marked his location after dark
by the outline of a headland against the stars,
the sweetly acrid smell of bakeapples blowing off
a stretch of bog to port or starboard,
navigating without map or compass
10 where hidden shoals shadow the islands
like the noise of hammers echoed across a valley.

The largest are home to harbours and coves,
a fringe of clapboard houses
threaded by dirt road,
15 grey-fenced cemeteries sinking
unevenly into mossy grass.
Even those too small to be found on the map
once carried a name in someone's mind,
a splinter of local history–
20 a boat wracked up in a gale of wind,
the roof-wrecked remains of a stage house
hunkered in the lee.

Most of what I want him to remember
lies among those islands, among the maze
25 of granite rippling north a thousand miles,
and what he remembers is all I have a claim to.
My father nods toward the coastline,
to the bald stone shoals almost as old as light–
That was 50 years ago, he says,
30 as a warning, wanting me to understand
that what's forgotten is lost
and most of this he cannot even recall
forgetting

(1998)

Loom

Burnt Woods Cemetery, Western Bay, Newfoundland

The meadow grass hemming
the gravesites is coarse as raw wool,

→

thickets of dry thistle
stand like needles clustered
5   in a pincushion; overhead
a shoddy bolt of cloud
gone ragged at the edges.

Headstones facing the Atlantic,
set in rows like figures being
10   fitted by a tailor;
six feet beneath them
the remains of the cloth I was cut from,
the patterns lifted to cobble
my features together.

15   Such a slow undressing –
bones divested of flesh,
purposeless and absurd,
like a dressmaker's dummy
relegated to the basement;
20   skulls hollow as thimbles,
picked clean of every thread
of memory, design.

They were born into times
when you made do,
25   stitched trousers out of burlap sacking,
salvaged skirts from a wreck
of worn curtains,
when there was no disguising
most of a life comes to us piecemeal,
30   second-hand.

Even the love I bear these strangers
is makeshift, threadbare,
fashioned by necessity.
The bitter cold draws thin gloves
35   of blood to my hands
and I follow the footpath
weaving among their graves
as long as I can stand the keen,
surrender them finally to the wind
40   shearing in off the endless
grey loom of the sea.

(2002)

Karen Solie   (b. 1966)

One of Canada's most celebrated younger poets, Karen Solie was born in Moose Jaw, Saskatchewan, and spent several years in Saskatoon before her family moved to a farm in southwest Saskatchewan. After graduating from high school, she attended Medicine Hat College to qualify for entrance to a veterinarian program, but she soon switched to a journalism course at Lethbridge Community College. She then worked as a journalist before completing a B.A. in English at the University of Lethbridge. Solie held a number of jobs, including playing piano in a country band in Austin, Texas, before she resumed studies at the University of Victoria, where she received an M.A., began doctoral studies, and taught English. During this time, she published her first collection, *Short Haul Engine* (2001), which won the Dorothy Livesay Award. After deciding that she did not want to pursue academic work, Solie moved to Toronto to continue her writing career. Her second collection, *Modern and Normal* (2005), was well received, but her third volume, *Pigeon* (2009), established her as a major force in Canadian poetry: it won the Griffin Poetry Prize, the Pat Lowther Memorial Award, and the Trillium Book Award for Poetry. In an interview, Solie said that poetry persists because "it reminds us of the value of paying attention. Because it makes our lives better." Her own poems, whether treating nature, urban life, or domestic situations, are notable for both the clear recounting of details and for an ability to imbue those details with a significance that touches on the lives and experiences of most readers.

Sturgeon

Jackfish and walleye circle like clouds as he strains
the silt floor of his pool, a lost lure in his lip,
Five of Diamonds, River Runt, Lazy Ike,[1]
or a simple spoon, feeding
5   a slow disease of rust through his body's quiet armour.
Kin to caviar, he's an oily mudfish. Inedible.
Indelible. Ancient grunt of sea
in a warm prairie river, prehistory a third eye in his head.
He rests, and time passes as water and sand
10   through the long throat of him, in a hiss, as thoughts
of food. We take our guilts
to his valley and dump them in,
give him quicksilver to corrode his fins, weed killer,
gas oil mix, wrap him in poison arms.

[1]names of lures.

15   Our bottom feeder,
   sin-eater.

   On an afternoon mean as a hook we hauled him
   up to his nightmare of us and laughed
   at his ugliness, soft sucker mouth opening,
20   closing on air that must have felt like ground glass,
   left him to die with disdain
   for what we could not consume.
   And when he began to heave and thrash over yards of rock
   to the water's edge and, unbelievably, in,
25   we couldn't hold him though we were teenaged
   and bigger than everything. Could not contain
   the old current he had for a mind, its pull,
   and his body a muscle called river, called spawn.

(2001)

The Girls

   They stayed at home. They didn't go far.
   Trends do not move them.
   From picture windows of family homes
   they cast wide gazes of manifest pragmatism:
5   hopeful and competent, boundlessly integrated,
   fearless, enviable, eternal.
   Vegas, Florida, Mexico, Florida, Vegas.
   With children they travel backroads
   in first and last light to ball fields
10   and arenas of the Dominion.
   We have no children. We don't own,
   but rent successively, relentlessly,
   to no real end. The high-school reunion
   was a disaster. Our husbands got wasted
15   and fought one another, then with an equanimity
   we secretly despised, made up over
   anthem rock, rye and water.
   Our grudges are prehistoric and literal.
   It seems they will survive us. The girls
20   share a table, each pitying the others their looks,
   their men, their clothes, their lives.

(2009)

Rita Wong   (b. 1968)

Raised in Calgary, Rita Wong received a B.A. in English from the University of Calgary, an M.A. in English from the University of Alberta, a Masters in Archival Science from the University of British Columbia, and a Ph.D. in English from Simon Fraser University. She worked as an archivist and spent time in China, Japan, and Miami, Florida, before joining the staff of Vancouver's Emily Carr University of Art and Design, where she is currently an Associate Professor in Critical and Cultural Studies. Issues of racial and sexual identity, social justice, and environmental responsibility dominate her books. The poems in her first book, *monkeypuzzle* (1998), were experimental in form. Those in her second volume, *forage* (2007), were less experimental but more impassioned. In fact, Wong has called these poems "impassioned rants against the abuses of power." Such rants are not without a degree of thought, however, because she has also said that she is exploring in her writing ways of learning to live ethically in a global economy. In her third volume, *Sybil Unrest* (2008), a long poem written in collaboration with Larissa Lai, she has returned to the experimental, using puns and fragments to explore a range of issues, from those associated with feminism and sexual identity to those involving corporate abuse and environmental responsibility.

Write around the absence

write around the absence, she said, show

its existence   *this is*

demonstrate   *the sound of*

its contours   *my Chinese tongue*

5   how it   *whispering:* nei tou

tastes   gnaw ma?[1] *no*

where   *tones can*

its edges   *survive this*

fall hard   *alphabet*

10   on my stuttering tongue, how its tones &

                  pictograms get flattened out by the

                        steamroller of the english language,

live   its etymology of

half-submerged   assimilation

15   *in the salty home of*   tramples budding

my mother tongue,   memory into sawdusty

shallows   stereotypes, regimented capitals,

                arrogant nouns & more nouns, punctuated

          by subservient descriptors, grammar is the dust on the streets

20   waiting to be washed off by immigrant cleaners or blown into your eyes

by the wind. grammar is the invisible net in the air, holding your

                          ➞

[1]"Are you hungry?"

words in place. grammar, like wealth, belongs in the hands of
the people who produce it.

(1998)

sort by day, burn by night[1]

circuit boards
                    most profitable & most dangerous
if you live in guiyu village,[2]
one of the hundred thousand people who
5   "liberate recyclable metals"
                                    into canals & rivers,
                          turning them into acid sludge,
                                    swollen with lead,
                          barium leachate, mercury bromide.
10   o keyboard irony: the shiny laptop
          a compilation of lead, aluminum, iron,
plastics, orchestrated mercury, arsenic, antimony...
                          sing me the toxic ditty of silica:
          "Yet utter the word Democratic, the word En-masse."[3]

15   where do metals come from?
      where do they return?
                    bony bodies inhale carcinogenic toner dust,
                              burn copper-laden wires,
                    peer at old cathay, cathode ray tubes.
20   what if you don't live in guiyu village?

            what if your pentium got dumped in guiyu village?
      your garbage, someone else's cancer?
                          economy of scale
                          shrinks us all

25   global whether
      here or there
      collapses cancer
      consumes en-masse

(2007)

[1]upon watching the video *Exporting Harm*, http://www.barn.org (author's note). [2]a town on the South China Sea coast that is the world's largest dumping ground for electronic waste; it has become the focus of concern by environmental groups and of scientific tests of the ill effects of its pollution-producing practices. [3]Walt Whitman, "One's Self I Sing" (author's note).

GLOSSARY OF LITERARY TERMS—POETRY

accent The stress that makes a syllable more emphatic or prominent in pronunciation than neighbouring syllables.

alliteration The repetition of consonant sounds, particularly at the beginning of words close to one another.

allusion A reference to characters, places, events, or objects from history, religion, mythology, or literature, which the reader is supposed to recognize and connect to the subject of the work in which the allusion appears.

ambiguity The presence of multiple meanings in a word or phrase, whether intentional or accidental.

amphibrach (amphibrachic) A poetic foot of three syllables, only the middle one being accented. See FOOT and Table 1, "The Metrical Feet," in the Introduction to Poetry.

amphimacer (amphimacric) A poetic FOOT of three syllables, the first and last being accented; also called a cretic. See foot and Table 1, "The Metrical Feet," in the Introduction to Poetry.

anapest (anapestic) A poetic foot of three syllables, only the last being accented. See FOOT and Table 1, "The Metrical Feet," in the Introduction to Poetry.

apostrophe An address to an absent or dead person, to an object, or to an abstraction.

archetype A character type, SYMBOL, plot, or THEME that appears frequently in works of literature and therefore seems to have universal meaning.

assonance Repetition of similar vowel sounds.

ballad A form of narrative poetry used continuously since medieval times, consisting of four-line STANZAS usually alternating IAMBIC TETRAMETER and iambic TRIMETER and rhyming *abcb*, often characterized by repetition and repeated refrains. Ballads are usually classed as either popular or literary ballads. *Popular ballads* were transmitted orally and were frequently intended to be sung; they originated with anonymous authors among the folk, or common people of rural society. *Literary ballads* are conscious imitations of these popular ballads and are intended to be read or recited, not sung. Because they are often composed by individuals familiar with literary traditions, however, they may employ complex symbolism lacking in the popular ballads.

ballad stanza The form of quatrain most commonly found in the ballad, consisting of alternating lines of four feet and three feet (often IAMBIC, but others metres are frequently employed) with a RHYME scheme of *abcb*. Coleridge employed the ballad stanza in "The Rime of the Ancient Mariner." See BALLAD, FOOT, STANZA, and QUATRAIN.

blank verse Lines of unrhymed IAMBIC PENTAMETER.

burden A refrain that is a stanza of at least a COUPLET in length. The term appears in older critical discussions, but modern critics usually do not distinguish between a refrain and a burden. See also REFRAIN and STANZA.

cacophony A harsh or disagreeable sound effect. The opposite of EUPHONY.

caesura A pause within a poetic line, created by punctuation, by the phrasing of ideas, or by the manipulation of METRE.

carpe diem A Latin phrase, meaning "seize the day," often used to describe poems that urge the enjoyment of the moment because time is fleeting.

classic A work considered to be the best of its class.

classical literature The literature of ancient Greece and Rome.

classicism The application of artistic principles supposedly derived from the classical literatures of Greece and Rome, including formal control, proportion, simplicity, unity, and rationality. Classicism emerged on the Continent and in England among the humanists of the fifteenth and sixteenth centuries. See NEOCLASSICISM.

closed couplet See COUPLET.

conceit An elaborate or extended comparison, whether SIMILE or METAPHOR; known as *Petrarchan conceits* (after Petrarch, the poet who popularized them in his sonnets) when they are conventional, as with the comparison of a lover to a ship, and as *metaphysical conceits* (after the metaphysical poets of the seventeenth century) when they are elaborate or ingenious comparisons of things not traditionally linked, as with the comparison of separated lovers to a compass.

connotation The implications of a word; that is, the feelings, ideas, or associations suggested by a word in addition to its denotation, or dictionary meaning.

consonance Repetition of consonants within or at the end of words.

contextual symbol See SYMBOL.

convention A technique or feature included frequently in specific types of literature or in literature from a particular historical period. The Petrarchan CONCEIT is a conventional feature in some Renaissance poetry; the use of heroic COUPLETS is a conventional technique in eighteenth-century poetry.

conventional symbol See SYMBOL.

couplet Two adjacent lines of poetry that RHYME; called a *closed couplet* when the pair is end-stopped by significant punctuation and contains a complete thought; called a *heroic couplet* when the rhymed lines are in IAMBIC PENTAMETER.

cretic See AMPHIMACER.

dactyl (dactylic) A poetic foot of three syllables, only the first being accented. See FOOT and Table 1, "The Metrical Feet," in the Introduction to Poetry.

dactylic rhyme See RHYME.

denotation The dictionary meaning of a word, which depends significantly on context, without reference to its implications and associations.

diction The choice of types of words, specific words, and levels of language. Levels may be *formal* (lofty language such as that used in epics and in the speeches of nobles in Shakespearean drama), *informal* (the speech and idiom of daily life), or *colloquial* (the speech and idioms of particular social classes or groups, such as the Cockneys in England).

dimeter A term of poetic measurement indicating a line containing two feet. See FOOT, METRE, and Table 2, "Line Lengths," in the Introduction to Poetry.

double rhyme See RHYME.

dramatic monologue A form of poetry in which a character speaks to a definite but silent listener and thereby reveals his or her own character.

elegy In classical Greece, a poem on any serious THEME that was written in a COUPLET form known as elegiac METRE; since the Renaissance, used to refer to a LYRIC that laments a death.

end rhyme See RHYME.

end-stopped line A line terminated with a relatively strong pause, usually indicated by the presence of a comma, semicolon, dash, or period; the opposite of ENJAMBMENT.

English sonnet See SONNET, ENGLISH.

enjambment The running over of meaning from one line to another unhindered by punctuation or syntactical pauses; the opposite of an END-STOPPED LINE.

epic A long narrative poem recounting in elevated language the deeds of heroes; settings are vast, sometimes extending beyond earth, and episodes may involve the gods or other supernatural beings.

euphony A pleasant or agreeable sound effect. The opposite of CACOPHONY.

exact rhyme See RHYME.

expressionism An early-twentieth-century artistic movement that emphasized the inner world of emotions and thought and projected this inner world through distortions of real-world objects; unlike impressionism, expressionist literature and drama distort and abstract the external world, creating works that are symbolic, anti-realistic, and often nightmarish in vision; in prose, stream-of-consciousness NARRATION is one of its major techniques.

eye rhyme See RHYME.

feminine rhyme See RHYME.

figurative language Language that uses figures of speech (such as METAPHORS or SIMILES) so that it means more than the simple denotation of the words and, therefore, must be understood in more than a literal way.

foot The basic metrical unit in poetry, consisting of one or more syllables, usually with one stressed or accented; a basic pattern of stressed and unstressed syllables commonly identified by names derived from Greek poetics, the most common being the IAMB, the TROCHEE, the DACTYL, the ANAPEST, and the SPONDEE. See METRE and Glossary entries for each kind, or see Table 1, "The Metrical Feet," in the Introduction to Poetry for a list.

free verse Poetry that is free of regular RHYTHM, RHYME pattern, and verse form; often called *vers libre*.

genre A classification of literature into separate kinds, such as drama, poetry, and prose fiction; a major literary form that sometimes contains other related forms, which are known as subgenres.

heptameter A term of poetic measurement indicating a line containing seven feet. See FOOT, METRE, and Table 2, "Line Lengths," in the Introduction to Poetry.

heroic couplet See COUPLET.

heroic quatrain See QUATRAIN.

hexameter A term of poetic measurement indicating a line containing six feet. See FOOT, METRE, and Table 2, "Line Lengths," in the Introduction to Poetry.

hyperbole A figure of speech depending on exaggeration, the overstatement of the literal situation, to achieve dramatic or comic effects.

iamb (iambic) A poetic foot of two syllables, the second being accented. See FOOT and Table 1, "The Metrical Feet," in the Introduction to Poetry.

image See IMAGERY.

imagery At its most basic, the verbal creation of images, or pictures, in the imagination; also applied to verbal appeals to any of the senses.

imperfect rhyme See RHYME.

internal rhyme See RHYME.

irony A figure of speech that creates a discrepancy between appearance and reality, expectation and result, or surface meaning and implied meaning; traditionally categorized as *verbal irony* (a reversal of denotative meaning in which the thing stated is not the thing meant), *dramatic irony* (in which the discrepancy is between what a character believes or says and the truth possessed by the reader or audience), and *situational irony* (in which the result of a situation is the reverse of what a character expects).

Italian sonnet See SONNET and SONNET, PETRARCHAN.

leitmotif A recurring word, phrase, situation, or THEME running through a literary work. Also see MOTIF.

line length See Table 2, "Line Lengths," in the Introduction to Poetry for a list; consult this Glossary for descriptions of individual kinds.

lyric A form of poetry that is relatively short and that emphasizes emotions, moods, and thoughts, rather than story.

masculine rhyme See RHYME.

metaphor A figure of speech that makes a comparison by equating things, as in "His heart is a stone."

metaphysical conceit See CONCEIT.

metaphysical poets Seventeenth-century poets who linked physical with metaphysical or spiritual elements in their poetry.

metonymy A figure of speech that substitutes one idea or object for a related one, such as saying "the Crown" when referring to the monarchy or the government.

metre A measure of the feet in a line of poetry, and thus a term expressing the number of feet in a line and the pattern of the predominant feet in that line; the rhythmic pattern of a line. See FOOT and Table 1, "The Metrical Feet," in the Introduction to Poetry.

Miltonic sonnet See SONNET, MILTONIC.

modernism An artistic movement of the early twentieth century that deliberately broke from the reliance on established forms and insisted that individual consciousness, not something objective or external, was the source of truth. Modernist literature may be structurally fragmented; its themes tend to emphasize the philosophy of existentialism, the alienation of the individual, and the despair inherent in modern life.

monometer A term of poetic measurement indicating a line containing one foot. See FOOT, METRE, and Table 2, "Line Lengths," in the Introduction to Poetry.

mood A general emotional atmosphere created by the characters and SETTING and by the language chosen to present these.

motif An image, character, object, SETTING, situation, or THEME recurring in many works. Also see LEITMOTIF.

myth A traditional story embodying ideas or beliefs of a people; also a story setting forth the ideas or beliefs of an individual writer.

narration The recounting, in summarized form, of events and conversations.

narrative poem A poem that tells a story.

naturalism A literary movement based on philosophical determinism, the belief that the lives of ordinary people are determined by biological, economic, and social factors; naturalists tend to use the techniques of REALISM in order to present a tragic vision of the fate of individuals crushed by forces they cannot control.

near rhyme See RHYME.

neoclassicism The principles of those writers who emerged with the restoration of Charles II to the throne of England in 1660 and who sought to restore classical restraint in all areas of life. The literature of the Neoclassical Period, which extends until about the 1798 publication of Wordsworth and Coleridge's *Lyrical Ballads*, was highly formal (frequently being based on the heroic COUPLET), praised reason over emotion, and often used SATIRE and IRONY to criticize deviations from decorum and propriety. See CLASSICISM.

oblique rhyme See RHYME.

octameter A term of poetic measurement indicating a line containing eight feet. See FOOT, METRE, and Table 2, "Line Lengths," in the Introduction to Poetry.

octave An eight-line stanza in any METRE or any RHYME scheme; any eight-line unit of poetry, rhymed or unrhymed; the initial eight lines of a SONNET united by the rhyme scheme.

ode A long, often elaborate, LYRIC poem that uses a dignified TONE and STYLE in treating a lofty or serious THEME. Three relatively fixed forms frequently appear in English. The *Pindaric* (regular) ode is divided into three movements called strophe, antistrophe, and epode, or stand; these movements may sometimes be more than a single stanza each. The strophe and antistrophe are identical in metrical pattern, and the epode differs from them. The *Horatian* (homostrophic) ode can contain any number of stanzas, but each must follow the same pattern. The *English*, or *Keatsian*, ode contains three stanzas, each of which has ten lines of IAMBIC PENTAMETER rhyming *ababcdecde*. Also common is the irregular ode, sometimes called the *Cowleyan* ode after Abraham Cowley, who introduced it; the irregular ode does not repeat metrical patterns in its STANZAS or movements, which may be of differing lengths.

off rhyme See RHYME.

onomatopoeia Words that imitate the sounds that they describe.

oxymoron An ironic figure of speech containing an overt contradiction, as in the word *oxymoron* itself, which means "sharp stupidity" in Greek, or in such phrases as "fearful joy" or "paper coin"; see IRONY and PARADOX.

paradox An apparent contradiction that, upon deeper analysis, contains a degree of truth.

parody A humorous imitation that mocks a given literary work by exaggerating or distorting some of its salient features.

pentameter A term of poetic measurement indicating a line containing five feet. See FOOT, METRE, and Table 2, "Line Lengths," in the Introduction to Poetry.

persona Literally, "the mask"; the speaking personality through which the author delivers the words in a poem or other literary work; the fictional "I" who acts as the actual author's mouthpiece in a literary work.

personification The attribution of human traits to inanimate objects or abstract concepts.

Petrarchan conceit See CONCEIT.

Petrarchan sonnet See SONNET and SONNET, PETRARCHAN.

point of view The angle of vision or perspective from which a story is told. The point of view may be *first person* (in which the NARRATOR is a character within the story), *third person* (a character or an implied author outside the story), or, very rarely, *second person* (in which the narrator, as in "choose your adventure" books, addresses the reader as "you"). Narrative point of view also involves questions of knowledge and reliability. Narrators may be *omniscient*, knowing both external events and internal thoughts and motivations, or they may be *limited* to some degree, knowing only some external details. *Reliable* narrators (a category that includes omniscient narrators) tell the truth completely. *Unreliable* narrators have personal limitations, such as youth or lack of education, that make them misunderstand what they narrate.

postcolonial criticism Explorations of the literature written within and about cultures that have experienced European colonization, such as India or Jamaica after British colonial rule; the focus of postcolonial critical approaches is often differences between the way formerly colonized peoples view their own cultural, social, and narrative practices and the way Europeans interpreted them.

postmodernism A highly contested term that can refer to both literary production in the period since about 1965 (although various critics see it beginning to develop as early as the 1950s) and the analysis of that literature and society in general; as a literary attitude, postmodernism is sometimes described as pushing MODERNISM to extremes because, while sharing its sense of meaninglessness and despair, it rejects the elaborate textual constructions and symbolism that characterize many modernist texts and, instead, playfully manipulates conventions, using random, even absurd, organization and including alternative and discontinuous narrative lines to prevent a text from having fixed meanings and to insist that texts are not representations of reality but metafictional, or self-referential, constructions; applied to critical or theoretical approaches to literature, the term has no precise meaning, but postmodernist literary criticism often focuses on the instability or limitations of language and on the self-consciousness or self-referentiality of art. See MODERNISM.

pyrrhic A poetic foot of two syllables, neither of which is accented. See FOOT and Table 1, "The Metrical Feet," in the Introduction to Poetry.

quatrain A four-line STANZA in any METRE or any RHYME scheme, except the heroic quatrain, which is in IAMBIC PENTAMETER and rhymes *abab*; any four-line unit of poetry, rhymed or unrhymed; four lines of a sonnet united by the rhyme scheme.

quintet A five-line stanza in any metre or any rhyme scheme; any five-line unit of poetry, rhymed or unrhymed.

realism The attempt to represent accurately the actual world; a literary movement that developed in reaction to the artificialities of romantic literature and melodramatic drama and that tended to focus on the lives of ordinary people, to use the language of daily speech, and to develop themes that offered social criticism and explored the problems of mundane life.

refrain A phrase, line, or lines repeated at intervals in a poem, most commonly at the end of a stanza. Critics once classified any refrain that was a stanza of at least a COUPLET in length as a burden, but that distinction seldom appears anymore. See also BURDEN and STANZA.

rhyme (rime) The repetition of identical or similar final sounds in words, particularly at the end of lines of poetry. Single, or masculine, rhymes repeat only the last syllable of the words; double, or feminine, rhymes (also sometimes called trochaic rhymes) repeat identical sounds in both an accented syllable and the following unaccented syllable; triple, or dactylic, rhymes repeat identical sounds in an accented syllable and the two following unaccented syllables. End rhyme occurs when the rhyming words are at the end of their respective lines; internal rhyme occurs when one or both of the rhyming words are within a line. Most rhyme involves the exact repetition of sounds; near rhyme (also known as slant, off, imperfect, or oblique rhyme) depends upon the approximation, rather than duplication, of sounds: it repeats either the final consonant (but not the preceding vowels) or the vowels (but not the following consonants) of the words. Eye, or sight, rhyme depends on the similar spelling of words, not their pronunciation, as in *gone* and *lone*.

rhythm The flow of stressed and unstressed syllables; the patterned repetition of beats.

romanticism A literary movement that began in England sometime around the 1798 publication of Wordsworth and Coleridge's *Lyrical Ballads* and was a reaction to the restraint and order of NEOCLASSICISM. The Romantics praised emotion over reason and celebrated the imagination; their literature used a diction that was less formal and elevated than that of the classicists (see CLASSICISM), employed themes based on the supernatural, nature and nature's influence on human beings, and the power of the liberated imagination. "Romantic" and "romanticism" are applied to works that exhibit emotional and imaginative exuberance or that use such themes, whether or not written during the Romantic period.

satire A literary form that uses wit and humour to ridicule persons, things, and ideas, frequently with the declared purpose of effecting a reformation of vices or follies.

scansion The analysis and marking of the metres and feet in a poem; see METRE and FOOT; see also Table 1, "The Metrical Feet," and Table 2, "Line Lengths," in the Introduction to Poetry.

septet A seven-line STANZA in any METRE or any RHYME scheme; any seven-line unit of poetry, rhymed or unrhymed.

sestet A six-line STANZA in any METRE or any RHYME scheme; any six-line unit of poetry, rhymed or unrhymed; the final six lines of a Petrarchan SONNET, which are united by the rhyme scheme.

setting The emotional, physical, temporal, and cultural context in which the action of the poem takes place.

Shakespearean sonnet See SONNET and SONNET, ENGLISH.

sight rhyme See RHYME.

simile A figure of speech making a direct comparison between things by using *like* or as or similar words, as in "His heart is like a stone."

single rhyme See RHYME.

slant rhyme See RHYME.

sonnet A LYRIC form of fourteen lines, traditionally of IAMBIC PENTAMETER and following one of several established RHYME schemes; see SONNET, ENGLISH; SONNET, MILTONIC; SONNET, PETRARCHAN.

sonnet, English Also called the Shakespearean SONNET; a sonnet consisting of three QUATRAINS and a COUPLET, rhyming *abab cdcd efef gg*; when the quatrains employ linked RHYME (*abab bcbc cdcd ee*), known as the Spenserian sonnet.

sonnet, Italian See SONNET, PETRARCHAN.

sonnet, Miltonic A variation of the Petrarchan SONNET that eliminates the pause at the end of the OCTAVE; thus, the VOLTA, when it occurs, usually appears in the middle of the ninth line.

sonnet, Petrarchan Also called the Italian SONNET: the first eight lines (the OCTAVE) state a problem, and the final six lines (the sestet) frequently begin with a VOLTA, or turn, such as *but, yet,* or *however,* and resolve or comment on the problem; originally limited to five rhymes, with the RHYME scheme of the octave usually being *abba abba* (thus dividing into two QUATRAINS), and the rhyme scheme of the sestet varying, but generally being either *cde cde* (thus dividing into two TERCETS, or three-line units) or *cdcdcd.*

sonnet, Shakespearean See SONNET, ENGLISH.

Spenserian sonnet See SONNET, ENGLISH.

spondee (spondaic) A poetic foot of two syllables, both of which are accented. See FOOT and Table 1, "The Metrical Feet," in the Introduction to Poetry.

stanza A division of a poem into a group of lines; traditionally, a grouping of lines according to RHYME scheme, number of lines, or metrical pattern that frequently is repeated in each stanza; a unit of two or more lines that are grouped visually in any poem by being separated from preceding and following lines. See Table 3, "Names of Stanzas and Line Groupings," and Table 4, "Notable Fixed and Complex Forms," in the Introduction to Poetry.

structure The arrangement of elements within a work; the organization of and relationship between parts of a work; the plan, design, or form of a work.

style A writer's selection and arrangement of words.

symbol A figure of speech that links a person, place, object, or action to a meaning that is not necessarily inherent in it; a word so charged with implication that it means itself and also suggests additional meanings, which are the product of convention (the culture traditionally associates a particular image with a particular meaning) or of context (the placement of the image in a work and the details and emphases within that work add suggestiveness to the image, making it symbolic).

synecdoche A figure of speech in which a part stands for the whole or the whole stands for the part, as when the term "hands" signifies "sailors."

tercet A three-line STANZA in any METRE or any RHYME scheme, but usually called a triplet when all three lines rhyme; any three-line unit of poetry, rhymed or unrhymed; three lines united by the rhyme scheme in the SESTET of a Petrarchan SONNET.

tetrameter A term of poetic measurement indicating a line containing four feet. See FOOT, METRE, and Table 2, "Line Lengths," in the Introduction to Poetry.

theme The central idea or meaning of a work; a generalization, or statement of underlying ideas, suggested by the concrete details of language, character, SETTING, and action in a work.

tone The speaker's attitude toward the subject matter or audience, as revealed by the choice of language and the rhythms of speech.

trimeter A term of poetic measurement indicating a line containing three feet. See FOOT, METRE, and Table 2, "Line Lengths," in the Introduction to Poetry.

triple rhyme See RHYME.

triplet A TERCET; usually applied to one in which all three lines RHYME.

trochaic rhyme See RHYME.

trochee (trochaic) A poetic foot of two syllables, the first being accented. See FOOT and Table 1, "The Metrical Feet," in the Introduction to Poetry.

true rhyme See RHYME.

understatement A figure of speech, the opposite of exaggeration, that intensifies meaning ironically by deliberately minimizing, or underemphasizing, the importance of ideas, emotions, and situations.

unity The cohesiveness of a literary work in which all the parts and elements harmonize.

vers libre See FREE VERSE.

villanelle An elaborate French poetic form consisting of nineteen lines of any length divided into six STANZAS: five TERCETS and a concluding QUATRAIN. The form employs two RHYMES and two REFRAINS. Line one and line three of the first tercet rhyme, and they form the two refrains found in the rest of the poem. The remaining tercets rhyme *aba*, and the quatrain rhymes *abaa*. Line one is repeated as lines six, twelve and eighteen; line three is repeated as lines nine, fifteen, and nineteen. Consequently, the quatrain concludes with a COUPLET formed from lines one and three. For an example of the villanelle, see Dylan Thomas's "Do Not Go Gentle into That Good Night." See also QUATRAIN, REFRAIN, STANZA, and TERCET.

volta The turn of thought in a poem, especially after the OCTAVE of a Petrarchan sonnet.

zeugma A device in which one word is grammatically linked to two words (usually a verb to two objects or two subjects), with the linkage being logically appropriate in a different way for each word, as in Pope's "Or stain her Honour, or her new Brocade."

Credits

Almon, Bert "The Feast of St. Valentine" and "Jessica Williams at the Yardbird Suite." Reprinted by permission of the author.

Arnold, Matthew "Dover Beach" from *Arnold: Poetical Works*, edited by C.B. Tinker and H.F. Lowry (Oxford: Oxford University Press, 1950).

Atwood, Margaret "Progressive Insanities of a Pioneer," "The Animals in That Country," "Siren Song," and "Variations on the Word *Love*" from *Selected Poems 1966-1984* by Margaret Atwood. Copyright © Oxford University Press Canada 1990. Reprinted by permission of the publisher. "you fit into me" © 1971, 1996 by Margaret Atwood. Reprinted by permission of House of Anansi Press: www.anansi.ca. "Helen of Troy Does Counter Dancing" from *Morning in the Burned House* by Margaret Atwood © 1995 by O.W. Toad. Published by McClelland & Stewart Ltd. Used with permission of the publisher.

Auden, W.H. "The Unknown Citizen," "In Memory of W.B. Yeats," and "Musée des Beaux Arts" from *Collected Poems of W.H. Auden*, edited by Edward Mendelson (London: Faber and Faber, 1976). Published in 2007 by Vintage. Reprinted by permission of Random House USA.

Barrett Browning, Elizabeth from "Sonnets from the Portuguese: XLIII (How do I love thee?)," "Hiram Powers's Greek Slave," and "A Musical Instrument" from *The Complete Works of Elizabeth Barrett Browning* (New York: T.Y. Crowell, 1900).

Baxter, James K. "Wild Bees" and "The Ikons" from *Collected Poems: James K. Baxter* © 1979 Oxford University Press. Reprinted by permission of the estate of James K. Baxter.

Birney, Earle "Vancouver Lights," "Anglosaxon Street," "Bushed," and "The Bear on the Delhi Road" from *The Collected Poems of Earle Birney*. Used by permission, McClelland & Stewart, Ltd. The Canadian Publishers.

Blake, William "The Lamb," "The Little Black Boy," The Chimney Sweeper (1789)," "Holy Thursday (1789)," "Nurse's Song (1789)," "The Tyger," "The Chimney Sweeper (1794)," "Holy Thursday (1794)," "Nurse's Song (1794)," "The Sick Rose," and "London" from *The Complete Poetry and Prose of William Blake*, revised edition, edited by David V. Erdman (New York: Doubleday, 1962).

Boland, Eavan "That the Science of Cartography is Limited" and "The Pomegranate" Copyright (c) 2005, 1994 by Eavan Boland, from *New Collected Poems* by Eavan Boland. Used by permission of W.W. Norton & Company, Inc.

Borson, Roo "The Ways We're Taught" from *Night Walk* © 1994 Oxford University Press. Reprinted by permission of the author. "Spring Cherries" from *Short Journey Upriver Toward Oishida* by Roo Borson. Copyright © 2004 by Roo Borson. Published by McClelland & Stewart. Used with permission of the publisher.

Bradstreet, Anne "To My Dear and loving Husband" and "Upon the burning of our house, July 10, 1666" from *Poems of Anne Bradstreet*, edited by Robert Hutchinson (New York: Dover Publications, 1969).

Donne, John "Song (Go, and catch a falling star)," "A Valediction: Forbidding Mourning," "The Canonization," "The Flea," "Holy Sonnet X (Death be not proud)," "Holy Sonnet XIV (Batter my heart)," and "Elegy XIX To His Mistress Going to Bed" from *John Donne: The Complete English Poems*, edited by A.J. Smith (Harmondsworth: Penguin, 1971)

Duffy, Carol Ann "Prayer" is taken from *Mean Time* by Carol Ann Duffy published by Anvil Press Poetry in 1993. "The Love Poem" from *Rapture*. Pan Macmillan, London. Copyright © Carol Ann Duffy, 2005.

Dumont, Marilyn "Letter to Sir John A. Macdonald" and "The Devil's Language" from *A Really Good Brown Girl* (London, ON: Brick Books, 1996).

Eliot, T.S. "The Love Song of J. Alfred Prufrock," "The Hollow Men," and "Journey of the Magi" from *Collected Poems 1909–1962* (London: Faber and Faber, 1964). Reprinted by permission of Faber and Faber Limited.

Ferlinghetti, Lawrence "Constantly risking absurdity" by Lawrence Ferlinghetti, from *A Coney Island of the Mind*, copyright ©1958 by Lawrence Ferlinghetti. Reprinted by permission of New Directions Publishing Corp.

Frost, Robert "After Apple-Picking" from the book *The Poetry of Robert Frost*, edited by Edward Connery Lathem. Copyright 1923, 1930, 1939, 1969 by Henry Holt and Company. Copyright 1936, 1951, 1958 by Robert Frost, copyright 1964, 1967 by Lesley Frost Ballantine. Reprinted by arrangement with Henry Holt and Company, LLC. "Mending Wall" from the book, *The Poetry of Robert Frost*, edited by Edward Connery Lathem. Copyright 1916, 1923, 1930, 1939, 1969 by Henry Holt and Company. Copyright 1958 by Robert Frost, copyright 1967 by Lesley Frost Ballantine. Reprinted by arrangement with Henry Holt and Company, LLC. "Stopping by Woods on a Snowy Evening" from the book *The Poetry of Robert Frost*, edited by Edward Connery Lathem. Copyright 1923, 1930, 1939,1969 by Henry Holt and Company. Copyright 1936, 1951, 1958 by Robert Frost, copyright 1964, 1967 by Lesley Frost Ballantine. Reprinted by arrangement with Henry Holt and Company, LLC. "The Road Not Taken" from the book, *The Poetry of Robert Frost*, edited by Edward Connery Lathem. Copyright 1916, 1923, 1930, 1939, 1969 by Henry Holt and Company. Copyright 1958 by Robert Frost, copyright 1967 by Lesley Frost Ballantine. Reprinted by arrangement with Henry Holt and Company, LLC. "Design" from the book *The Poetry of Robert Frost* edited by Edward Connery Lathem. Copyright 1923, 1930, 1939,1969 by Henry Holt and Company. Copyright 1936, 1951, 1958 by Robert Frost, copyright 1964, 1967 by Lesley Frost Ballantine. Reprinted by arrangement with Henry Holt and Company, LLC.

Ginsberg, Allen "A Supermarket in California." All lines from "A Supermarket in California" from *Collected Poems 1947–1980* by Allen Ginsberg. Copyright © 1955 by Allen Ginsberg. Reprinted by permission of HarperCollins Publishers.

Gray, Thomas "Elegy Written in a Country Church-Yard" from *The Complete Poems of Thomas Gray*, edited by H.W. Starr and J.R. Hendrickson (Oxford: Clarendon Press, 1966).

Halfe, Louise Bernice "Body Politics" from *Bear Bones & Feathers* (Regina: Coteau Books, 1994). Copyright © Louise Bernice Halfe, 1994.

Heaney, Seamus "Death of a Naturalist" from *Death of a Naturalist* (London: Faber and Faber, 1969). Reprinted by permission. "Digging" from *Open Ground* (London: Faber and Faber, 1998). Reprinted by permission. "The Singer's House" from *Field Work* (London: Faber and Faber, 1980). Reprinted by permission.

Lord Byron, George Gordon, "She Walks in Beauty" and "On This Day I Complete My Thirty-Sixth Year" from *The Poetical Works of Byron*, edited by Robert F. Gleckner (Boston: Houghton Mifflin, 1975).

Lowell, Robert "Skunk Hour" from *Collected Poems* by Robert Lowell. Copyright © 2003 by Harriet Lowell and Sheridan Lowell. Reprinted by permission of Farrar, Straus and Giroux, LLC.

MacEwen, Gwendolyn "A Breakfast for Barbarians." *From Magic Animals: Selected Poetry of Gwendolyn MacEwen* (Toronto: Macmillan, 1974). Reprinted by permission of the author's family.

MacLeish, Archibald "Ars Poetica" from *Collected Poems: 1917–1982* by Archibald MacLeish. Copyright © 1985 by The Estate of Archibald MacLeish. Reprinted by permission of Houghton Mifflin Harcourt Publishing Company. All rights reserved.

Mahapatra, Jayanta "The Abandoned British Cemetery at Balasore" and "Total Solar Eclipse" by Jayanta Mahapatra, from *Selected Poems*. Reproduced by permission of Oxford University Press India, New Delhi.

Marvell, Andrew "To His Coy Mistress" and "The Garden" from *The Poetical Works of Milton and Marvell, with a Memoir of Each*, Vol. 4 (Boston: Houghton Mifflin, 1880).

Milton, John "Lycidas," "When I consider how my light is spent," and "On the Late Massacre in Piedmont" from *The Poetical Works of John Milton*, edited by D. Masson (London: Macmillan, 1891).

Murray, Les "The Tin Wash Dish" and "Dog Fox Field" from *Learning Human* by Les Murray. Copyright © 1998 by Les Murray. Reprinted by permission of Farrar, Straus and Giroux, LLC.

Nowlan, Alden "The Bull Moose" from *Alden Nowlan: Selected Poems* by Alden Nowlan © 1967. Reprinted with permission of House of Anansi Press. www.anansi.ca

Nye, Naomi Shihab "Arabic" from *Ten Varieties of Gazelle*. Text copyright © 2002 Naomi Shihab Nye. Used by permission of HarperCollins Publishers. "Brushing Lives" from *Red Suitcase*. Copyright © 1994 by Naomi Shihab Nye. Reprinted with the permission of BOA Editions, Ltd. www.boaeditions.org.

Ondaatje, Michael "Elizabeth," "Letter & Other Worlds," and "The Cinnamon Peeler" from *The Cinnamon Peeler* (Toronto: McClelland & Stewart, 1984). Copyright © 1984 by Michael Ondaatje. Reprinted by permission of the author.

Oodgeroo of the Tribe Noonuccal "We Are Going" by Oodgeroo of the Tribe Noonuccal, *From My People*, 4th edition, John Wiley & Sons Australia, Ltd, 2008. Reproduced by permission of John Wiley & Sons Australia, Ltd.

Owen, Wilfred "Anthem for Doomed Youth" and "*Dulce et Decorum Est*" from *The Complete Poems and Fragments*, edited by Jon Stallworthy (London: The Hogarth Press, 1983).

Page, P.K. "Stories of Snow" and "The Landlady" from *The Hidden Room* (The Porcupine's Quill, 1997). Copyright © P.K. Page. Reprinted by permission of the author's estate.

Philip, Marlene NourbeSe "Sprung Rhythm" from *Salmon Courage* © 1983 Williams-Wallace Publishers. Reprinted by permission of the author. "Meditations of the

Declension of Beauty by the Girl with the Flying Cheek-bones" from *She Tries Her Tongue, Her Silence Softly Breaks* (Charlottetown: Ragweed Press, 1989), pp. 52–53. Reprinted by permission of the author.

Plath, Sylvia "Daddy" and "Lady Lazarus" from *Ariel* (London: Faber and Faber, 1966). Reprinted by permission of Faber and Faber Limited. Republished in *Collected Poems*, edited by Ted Hughes (London and Boston: Faber and Faber, 1981). "Mirror" from *Crossing the Water* (London: Faber and Faber, 1971). Reprinted by permission of Faber and Faber Limited. Republished in *Collected Poems*, edited by Ted Hughes (London and Boston: Faber and Faber, 1981).

Pope, Alexander "The Rape of the Lock; An Heroi-Comical Poem" from *The Rape of the Lock and Other Poems*, edited by Geoffrey Tillotson (London: Methuen, 1962).

Pound, Ezra "The River-Merchant's Wife: A Letter" by Ezra Pound, original by Rihaku, "In a Station of the Metro" and "Ancient Music" from *Personae*, copyright ©1926 by Ezra Pound. Reprinted by permission of New Directions Publishing Corp.

Pratt, E.J. "The Shark" and "From Stone to Steel" from *E.J. Pratt: Complete Poems*, edited by Sandra Djwa and R.G. Moyles. Copyright © 1989 by University of Toronto Press. Reprinted by permission of University of Toronto Press Incorporated.

Purdy, Al "The Country North of Belleville," "Lament for the Dorsets," and "Wilderness Gothic" by Al Purdy, *Beyond Remembering: The Collected Poems of Al Purdy*, Harbour Publishing, 2000.

Rich, Adrienne "Aunt Jennifer's Tigers" and "Diving into the Wreck." Copyright © 2002, 1951 by Adrienne Rich. Copyright © 1973 by W.W. Norton & Company, Inc, from *The Fact of a Doorframe: Selected Poems 1950–2001* by Adrienne Rich. Used by permission of the author and W.W. Norton & Company, Inc. "A Woman Mourned by Daughters." Copyright © 1993, 1967, 1963 by Adrienne Rich from *Collected Early Poems: 1950–1970* by Adrienne Rich. Used by permission of the author and W.W. Norton & Company, Inc.

Roberts, Sir Charles G.D. "Tantramar Revisited," "The Potato Harvest," and "Winter Fields" from *The Collected Poems of Sir Charles G.D. Roberts* (Wolfville, NS: The Wombat Press, 1985).

Roethke, Theodore "My Papa's Waltz," copyright 1942 by Hearst Magazines, Inc., from *Collected Poems of Theodore Roethke* by Theodore Roethke. Used by permission of Doubleday, a division of Random House, Inc.; "I Knew a Woman", copyright 1954 by Theodore Roethke, from *Collected Poems of Theodore Roethke* by Theodore Roethke. Used by permission of Doubleday, a division of Random House, Inc.

Rossetti, Christina "Song (When I am dead)," and "The World" from *The Poetical Works of Christina Georgina Rossetti*, edited by William Michael Rossetti (London: Macmillan, 1908).

Ruffo, Armand Garnet "Poem for Duncan Campbell Scott" from *Opening In The Sky* © 1994 Theytus Books. Reprinted by permission of the author. "On the Line" from *At Geronimo's Grave* (Regina: Coteau Books, 2001).

Scott, Duncan Campbell "The Onondaga Madonna" and "The Forsaken" from *The Poems of Duncan Campbell Scott* (Toronto: McClelland & Stewart, 1926).

Scott, F.R. "The Canadian Authors Meet," "Trans Canada," and "Laurentian Shield" from *The Collected Poems of F.R. Scott*, edited by John Newlove. Reprinted with the permission of William Toye, Literary Executor for the Estate of F.R. Scott.

Shelley, Percy Bysshe "Ozymandias," "Ode to the West Wind," and "To a Skylark" from *The Poetical Works of Percy Bysshe Shelley* (London: Macmillan, 1899) "To —— (Music, when soft voices die)" from *The Poetical Works of Percy Bysshe Shelley*, edited by Edward Dowden (New York: Thomas Y. Crowell).

Solie, Karen "The Girls" from *Pigeon*, copyright 2009 by Karen Solie. Reproduced with permission from House of Anansi Press, Toronto. www.anansi.ca. "Sturgeon" from *Short Haul Engine* by Karen Solie © 2001 Brick Books. Reprinted by permission of the publisher.

Soyinka, Wole "Telephone Conversation." From *A Shuttle in the Crypt: Poems* by Wole Soyinka. Copyright © 1962, 1990 by Wole Soyinka. Reprinted with permission by Melanie Jackson Agency, LLC. "Lost Tribe," from *Mandela's Earth and Other Poems* by Wole Soyinka; copyright © 1988 by Wole Soyinka. Used by permission of Random House, Inc.

Stevens, Wallace "The Emperor of Ice-Cream," and "The Snow Man," from *The Collected Poems of Wallace Stevens* by Wallace Stevens, copyright 1954 by Wallace Stevens and renewed 1982 by Holly Stevens. Used by permission of Alfred A. Knopf, a division of Random House, Inc.

St. Vincent Millay, Edna "I, Being Born a Woman and Distressed" and "An Ancient Gesture" from *Collected Poems*, ed. Norma Millay (New York: Harper and Row, 1956).

Tennyson, Alfred, Lord "The Eagle. Fragment," "The Lady of Shalott," and "Ulysses" from *The Poetic and Dramatic Works of Alfred, Lord Tennyson*, edited by W.J. Rolfe (Boston: Houghton Mifflin, 1898).

Thomas, Dylan "And Death Shall Have No Dominion," "The Force That Through the Green Fuse Drives the Flower," "Fern Hill," and "Do Not Go Gentle into That Good Night" from *Dylan Thomas: The Poems* (London: J. M. Dent, 1971).

Tuwhare, Hone "To a Maori Figure Cast in Bronze Outside the Chief Post Office, Auckland" and "Deep River Talk" from *Deep River Talk* by Hone Twhare. University of Hawai'i Press. Honolulu: 1994. Reprinted by permission.

Wah, Fred "my father hurt" from *Waiting for Saskatchewan* by Fred Wah. © 1985 Turnstone Press. Reprinted by permission of the author.

Walcott, Derek "A Far Cry from Africa" and "Ruins of a Great House" from *Collected Poems 1948–1984* by Derek Walcott © 1986 by Derek Walcott. Reprinted by permission of Farrar, Straus and Giroux, LLC.

Webb, Phyllis "Marvell's Garden" and "Treblinka Gas Chamber" from *Selected Poems: The Vision Tree* by Phyllis Webb, © 1982 Phyllis Webb, Talon Books Ltd., Vancouver B.C. Reprinted by permission of the publisher.

Whitman, Walt "When I Heard the Learn'd Astronomer," "O Captain! My Captain!" "One's-Self I Sing," and "A Noiseless Patient Spider" from *Complete Poems and Prose of Walt Whitman* (Philadelphia: Ferguson Bros.).

Williams, William Carlos "Spring and All" and "The Red Wheelbarrow" by William Carlos Williams, from *The Collected Poems: Volume I, 1909–1939*, copyright ©1938 by New Directions Publishing Corp. Reprinted by permission of New Directions Publishing Corp.

Wong, Rita "write around the absence" from *monkeypuzzle poems* © 1998. Reprinted by permission of the author. "Sort by Day, Burn by Night" from *Forage*, Nightwood Editions, 2007, www.nightwoodeditions.com.

Wordsworth, William "Lines Composed a Few Miles above Tintern Abbey," "She dwelt among the untrodden ways," It is a beauteous evening, calm and free," "London, 1802," "The world is too much with us," and "I wandered lonely as a cloud" from *The Poetical Works of Wordsworth*, new edition, revised, edited by Ernest de Selincourt (Oxford: Oxford University Press, 1953).

Wroth, Lady Mary "Song (Love, a child, is ever crying)" and "In this strange labyrinth how shall I turn?" from "A Crowne of Sonetts dedicated to Love," in *Pamphilia to Amhilanthus* (1621).

Wyatt, Sir Thomas "My galley charged with forgetfulness" from *The Poetical Works of Sir Thomas Wyatt and Henry Howard, Earl of Surrey, with a Memoir of Each* (Boston: Houghton Mifflin, 1880).

Yeats, William Butler "Easter 1916," "The Second Coming," "Leda and the Swan," "Sailing to Byzantium," and "Among School Children" from *The Poems of William Butler Yeats* (London: Macmillan Publishing Company, 1961).

Zwicky, Jan "Border Station" and "Poppies" from *Songs for Relinquishing the Earth* (London ON: Brick Books, 1998).

INDEX OF AUTHORS

INDEX OF TITLES AND FIRST LINES